PROVENCE &
THE FRENCH RIVIERA
2008

Rick Steves & Steve Smith

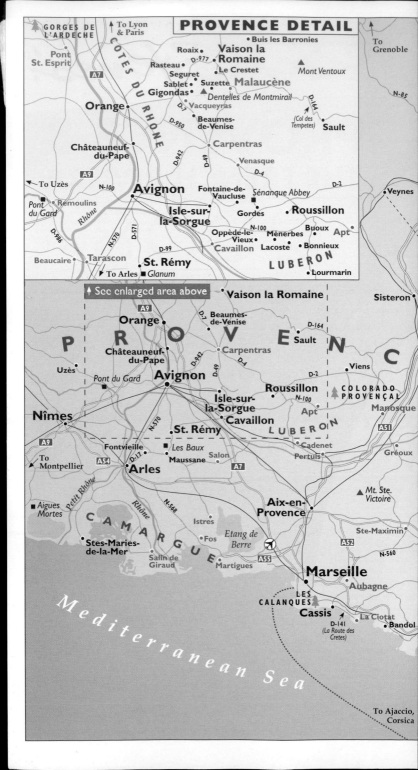

PROVENCE & THE FRENCH RIVIERA

A7 Freeway/Autoroute	
Rail Line	
Bus Line	
Ferry Line	
✈ Airport	
Cassis Recommended location*	
Toulon Just passing through**	
▲ National Park/Natural Wonder	
■ Ruin, Museum, Other Point of Interest	

* Black locations are places of interest to tourists, sized
by importance. Many are covered in this guidebook.

** Gray locations are places of little or no interest to
tourists and are sized by population.

Les Deux-Alpes

Briançon

L'Argentière-la-Bessée

Guillestre

Embrun

Gap · Savines-le-Lac

Le Lauzet-Ubaye · Barcelonnette

F R A N C E

I T A L Y

To Cuneo

Col de Tende
(tunnel)

N-85

Digne-
les-Bains

N-85

Verdon

Var

To
Genoa

Entrevaux

Peillon

Ventimiglia

Castellane

Moustiers-
Ste-Marie

GORGES
DU LOUP

La Turbie

A8 Menton

Eze **MONACO**

Riez

Lac de
St-
Croix

Aiguines

D-71

D-952

Route Napoléon

Tourrettes-
sur-Loup

Gourdon

Le Bar-sur-Loup

Beaulieu

Villefranche

GRAND
CANYON DU
VERDON

Comps

Grasse

St-Paul-
de-Vence

Vence

Nice

Cap Ferrat

Aups

D-956

D-562

Biot

Vallauris

Cagnes-sur-Mer

To Bastia,
Corsica

Draguignan

A8

Antibes

Cannes

Le Luc

Les Arcs

Fréjus

Scenic drive

To l'Isle
Rousse,
Corsica

A8

St-Raphaël

R I V I E R A

A57

Grimaud

Ste.
Maxime

St-Tropez

C Ô T E   D ' A Z U R

N-98

D-559

Hyères

Le Lavandou

Toulon

Iles d'Hyères

0 km	25 km
0 miles	15 miles

Rick Steves'

PROVENCE &
THE FRENCH RIVIERA

2008

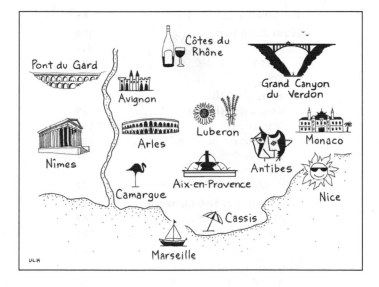

AVALON
TRAVEL

CONTENTS

Top Destinations in Provence & the French Riviera

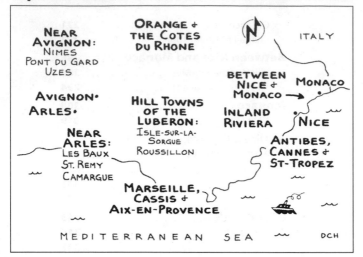

NEAR AVIGNON:
NIMES
PONT DU GARD
UZES

ORANGE & THE COTES DU RHONE

ITALY

BETWEEN NICE & MONACO →

MONACO

AVIGNON•
ARLES•

HILL TOWNS OF THE LUBERON:
ISLE-SUR-LA-SORGUE
ROUSSILLON

INLAND RIVIERA

NICE

NEAR ARLES:
LES BAUX
ST. REMY
CAMARGUE

ANTIBES, CANNES & ST-TROPEZ

MARSEILLE, CASSIS & AIX-EN-PROVENCE

MEDITERRANEAN SEA

DCH

INTRODUCTION

Provence and the French Riviera make an intoxicating bouillabaisse of enjoyable cities, warm stone villages, Roman ruins,
contemporary art, and breathtaking coastlines steaming with sunshine and stirred by the wind. There's something about the play of
light in this region, where natural and man-made beauty mingle
to dazzle the senses and nourish the soul. It all adds up to *une
magnifique* vacation.

Provence and the Riviera stretch along France's southeast
Mediterranean coast from the Camargue (south of Arles) to
Monaco, and they ramble north along the Rhône Valley into the
Alps. The region is about the same size as Massachusetts—you
can take a train or drive from one end to the other in just three
hours—yet it contains more sightseeing opportunities and let's-
retire-here villages than anywhere else in France. Marseille and
Nice, the country's second- and fifth-largest cities, lend good
transportation and an urban perspective to this otherwise relaxed
region, where every day feels like a lazy Sunday.

In Provence, gnarled sycamore-lined roads twist their way
through stone towns and between oceans of vineyards. France's
Riviera is about the sea and money—it's populated by a yacht-
happy crowd wondering where the next "scene" will be. While
Provence feels older and more *español* (with paella on menus and
bullfights on Sundays), the Riviera feels downright Italian—with
fresh-Parmesan-topped pasta and red-orange pastel-colored buildings. For every Roman ruin in Provence, there's a modern-art
museum in the Riviera. Provence is famous for its wines and wind,
while the bikini and ravioli were invented on the Riviera.

This book covers the predictable biggies, but also mixes in
a healthy dose of Back Door intimacy—from jet-setting beach
resorts to remote canyons. Along with the Pont du Gard, Nice,

Provence and the French Riviera

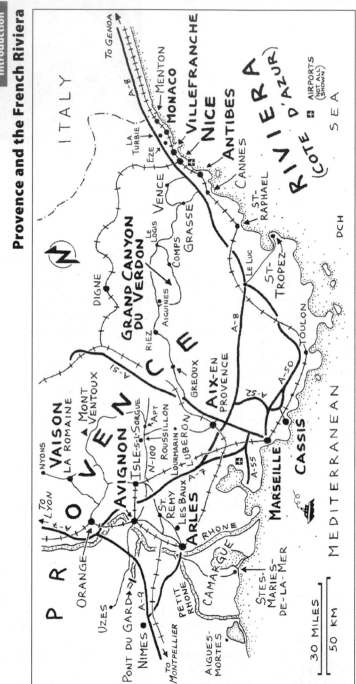

and Avignon, we'll introduce you to our favorite villages. You'll stop by wineries and explore untouristy Roman ruins. You'll marvel at ancient monuments, take a canoe trip down the meandering Sorgue River, and settle into a shaded café on a small square. Discover the ideal beach to call home. At day's end, dive headfirst into a Provençal sunset from a hill-town perch. You'll try tasty-yet-affordable wines while feasting on a healthy cuisine heavy on olives, tomatoes, and spices. Just as important, you'll get on a first-name basis with many of our Provençal friends—hoteliers, restaurateurs, vintners, and lots more.

This book is selective, including only the most exciting sights and romantic villages. There are *beaucoup* Provençal hill towns... but we cover only the most intriguing. And while there are scads of beach towns on the Riviera, we recommend the top three.

The best is, of course, only our opinion. But after spending more than half of our adult lives writing and lecturing about travel, guiding tours, and gaining an appreciation for all things French, we've developed a sixth sense for what touches the traveler's imagination.

About This Book

Rick Steves' Provence & the French Riviera 2008 is a personal tour guide in your pocket. Better yet, it's actually two tour guides in your pocket: The coauthor of this book is Steve Smith. Steve has been traveling to France—as a guide, researcher, home owner, and devout Francophile—every year for the last 20 years. Together, Steve and I keep this book up-to-date and accurate (though for simplicity, from this point "we" will shed our respective egos and become "I").

This book consists of two obvious parts—Provence, and the Riviera (although almost everything covered in this book is officially considered part of the "Provence–Alpes–Côte d'Azur region" by the French government).

The Provence half focuses on Arles and Avignon and their day-trip destinations, the photogenic hill towns of the Côtes du Rhône and Luberon, and the coastal towns of Marseille and Cassis and nearby Aix-en-Provence. On the high-rolling French Riviera, I cover the waterfront destinations of Nice, Villefranche-sur-Mer, Monaco, Antibes, Cannes, and St-Tropez—plus the best of the inland hill towns and the amazing Grand Canyon du Verdon.

In the following chapters, you'll find a host of information:

The introductions to **Provence** and **The French Riviera** acquaint you with the history, cuisine, and wine of the places you'll be visiting, and give practical advice on how to spend your time, how to get around, and lots more. Don't overlook the valuable tips in these chapters.

Planning Your Time offers ideas on how best to use your limited time in each destination. I've also included a day-by-day description of my favorite two-week trip by train and bus (page 398) or by car (page 406).

Orientation material for all key destinations—including tourist information, city transportation, and easy-to-read maps—is designed to make the text clear and your arrival smooth.

Sights, described in detail, are rated:

▲▲▲—Don't miss.

▲▲—Try hard to see.

▲—Worthwhile if you can make it.

No rating—Worth knowing about.

Self-Guided Tours include a stroll along Nice's promenade des Anglais, a walk through Old Nice, and a visit to the Chagall Museum. Smaller **self-guided walks** of various towns (including Avignon, Nîmes, Arles, Aix-en-Provence, Les Baux, Isle-sur-la-Sorgue, Roussillon, Monaco, Antibes, Villefranche-sur-Mer, and Cannes) are in the destination chapters. I also include a few self-guided **driving tours,** allowing you to explore the Côtes du Rhône wine road, the Grand Canyon du Verdon, and inland hill towns of the Riviera with the knowledge of a local.

Sleeping and **Eating,** offering a great range of good-value accommodations and restaurants, covers everything from homey, affordable places to worth-the-splurge experiences. The best trips are a blend of both.

Transportation Connections has specifics on linking destinations by train and bus, plus route tips for drivers.

Traveling with Children offers general tips and destination-specific advice, like kid-friendly hotels and restaurants. Both of this book's authors have kids (from 6 to 20 years old), and we've used our substantial experience traveling with children to improve this book. Our kids have greatly enriched our travels, and we hope the same will be true for you.

Shopping has suggestions for this region's best souvenirs and bargains. Steve's wife, who had a business importing French products to the US, contributed her shopping-savvy advice.

The **appendix** is a traveler's tool kit, with a handy packing checklist, recommended books and films, instructions on how to use the telephone, useful phone numbers, detailed information on trains and driving, a climate chart, French survival phrases, and lots more.

Browse through this book and choose your favorite sights. Then have a *fantastique* trip! Traveling like a temporary local, you'll get the absolute most out of every mile, minute, and euro. As you visit places I know and love, I'm happy you'll be meeting my favorite French people.

PLANNING

Trip Costs

Five components make up your total trip cost: airfare, surface transportation, room and board, sightseeing and entertainment, and shopping and miscellany.

Airfare: Nice is the handiest airport for Provence and the Riviera (though Marseille is attracting more airlines every year). A basic, round-trip United States-to-Nice (or Paris) flight costs $800–1,600, depending on where you fly from and when (cheaper in winter). Smaller budget airlines provide bargain service—often more economical than train travel—from Paris and other European cities to places such as Marseille, Avignon, and Montpellier (see "Cheap Flights" on page 413 for details). Always consider saving time and money in Europe by flying "open jaw"—into one city and out of another. Flying into Nice and out of Paris costs roughly the same as flying round-trip to Paris.

Surface Transportation: Allow $25 per day per person for public transportation (trains, buses, and taxis), or $40 per day for a rental car (based on two people sharing) for rental fees, tolls, gas, and insurance. Car rental is cheapest if arranged from the US. Train passes only make sense if you are traveling to regions beyond Provence and the Riviera, as distances within this region are short, and point-to-point fares are reasonable. Remember that married couples, seniors, students, and families can benefit from discounts (*réduction*, ray-dook-see-own). Railpasses are normally available only outside of Europe (see "Transportation," page 397, for more details on car rental, rail trips, and bus travel).

Room and Board: You can easily manage in Provence and the Riviera on $115 a day per person for room and board. A $115-a-day budget allows an average of $10 for breakfast, $15 for lunch, $35 for dinner with drinks, and $55 for lodging (based on two people splitting the cost of a $110 double room). That's definitely doable. Students and tightwads do it on $40 a day ($20 per bed, $20 for meals and snacks).

Sightseeing and Entertainment: Allow about $5–12 per major sight (Arles' Roman Arena-$7, Nice's Chagall Museum $8, Pont du Gard combo-ticket-$14), $5 for minor ones (climbing church towers), $20 for guided walks, and $30 for splurge experiences (e.g., bullfights or concerts). Arles, Avignon, and Nice each offer a money-saving museum pass (details listed in this book).

Some sights rent audioguides for about $5 (many include them for free). While the information in this book is generally enough (and more interesting), eager students can supplement it with an audioguide and learn even more; bring along extra headphones and a Y-jack for the second person to save money.

An overall average of $15–20 a day for sightseeing and entertainment works for most. Don't skimp here. After all, this category is the driving force behind your trip—you came to sightsee, enjoy, and experience Provence and the French Riviera.

Shopping and Miscellany: Figure $4 per ice cream cone, coffee, or soft drink. Shopping can vary in cost from nearly nothing to a small fortune (to stretch your euro the furthest, see the Shopping chapter, page 365). Good budget travelers find that this category has little to do with assembling a trip full of lifelong and wonderful memories.

Sightseeing Priorities

Depending on the length of your trip, here are my recommended priorities:

5 days:	Arles, Avignon, Les Baux, Pont du Gard, and Nice/Monaco
8 days, add:	Cassis, Orange, and Côtes du Rhône
11 days, add:	Luberon, Grand Canyon du Verdon, and Antibes
14 days, add:	Nîmes, Marseille, Aix-en-Provence, and the Camargue

For details, refer to the appendix for daily itineraries of my favorite two-week trip by public transportation (page 398) or by car (page 406).

When to Go

With more than 300 days of sunshine per year, Provence and the Riviera enjoy France's sunniest weather. Spring and fall are best, with generally comfortable weather—though crowds can be a problem if you're not careful, particularly during holiday weekends (May is worst—see "Major Holidays and Weekends," page 8). April can be damp, and any month can be windy.

Summer means festivals, lavender, steamy weather, long hours at sights, and longer lines of cars along the Riviera. Europeans vacation in July and August, jamming the Riviera, the Gorges du Verdon, and Ardèche (worst from mid-July through mid-Aug), but leaving the rest of this region relatively calm. While many French businesses close in August, the traveler hardly notices.

September brings the grape harvest, when private wineries are off-limits to taste-seeking travelers (for information on wine-tasting, see page 40). Late fall delivers beautiful foliage and a return to tranquility in normally crowded places.

While you can find mild, sunny weather in any season, Provence is famous for its bone-chilling temperatures when the wind blows. Winter travel is OK in Nice and Avignon, but you'll find smaller cities and villages buttoned up tight. Sights and tourist-information offices keep shorter hours, and some tourist

Le Mistral

Provence lives with its vicious mistral winds, which blow 30–60 miles per hour, about 100 days out of the year. Locals say it blows in multiples of threes: three, six, or nine days in a row. The mistral clears people off the streets and turns lively cities into virtual ghost towns. You'll likely spend a few hours or days taking refuge—or searching for cover. The winds are strongest between 12:00 and 15:00.

When the mistral blows, it's everywhere, and you can't escape. Author Peter Mayle said it could blow the ears off a donkey, and I agree. Locals say it ruins crops, shutters, and roofs (look for the stones holding tiles in place on many homes). They'll also tell you that this pernicious wind has driven many people crazy (including young Vincent van Gogh). A weak version of the wind is called a *mistralet.*

The mistral starts above the Alps and Massif Central mountains and gathers steam as it heads south, gaining momentum as it screams over the Rhône Valley (which acts like a funnel between the Alps and Pyrénées) before exhausting itself as it hits the Mediterranean. While this wind rattles shutters throughout the Riviera and Provence, it's strongest over the Rhône Valley...so Avignon, Arles, and the Côtes du Rhône villages bear its brunt. While wiping the dust from your eyes, remember the good news: The mistral brings clear skies.

---

activities (such as English-language castle tours) vanish altogether. To get the latest weather forecast in English, dial 08 99 70 11 11, then press 1. Also see the climate chart in the appendix.

Thanks to Provence's temperate climate, fields of flowers greet the traveler much of the year:

April–May: Wild red poppies *(coquelicots)* start sprouting.

June: Lavender begins to bloom in the lower hills of Provence, generally during the last week of the month.

July: Lavender is in full swing in Provence, and sunflowers are awakening. Cities, towns, and villages everywhere overflow with carefully tended flowers.

August–September: Sunflowers flourish.

October: In the latter half of the month, the countryside glistens with fall colors (since most trees are deciduous). Vineyards go for the gold.

Travel Smart

Your trip to France is like a complex play—easier to follow and really appreciate on a second viewing. While no one does the same

Major Holidays and Weekends

Popular places are even busier on weekends...and inundated on three-day weekends. Holiday weekends can make towns, trains, roads, and hotels more crowded than summer. The French are experts at the long weekend, and you're no match for them when it comes to driving and finding hotels during these peak periods. Book your accommodations well in advance.

In 2008, be ready for unusually big crowds during these holiday periods: Easter weekend and the two weeks following it (March 21–April 6); Labor Day and Ascension weekend (May 1–4); Pentecost weekend (May 9–12); Bastille Day and the week after (July 14–20); Assumption weekend (Aug 15–19); and the winter holidays (Dec 20–Jan 4—note that Christmas week is quieter than the week of New Year's). These two holidays are usually quiet, but holidays nonetheless: All Saints' Day (Nov 1), and Armistice Day weekend (Nov 7–10).

For information on festivals, see page 413 of the appendix.

trip twice to gain that advantage, reading this book in its entirety before your trip accomplishes much the same thing.

Design an itinerary that enables you to visit museums and festivals (see page 414) on the right days. Note the days when sights are closed. Sundays have the same pros and cons as they do for travelers in the US. Special events and weekly markets pop up, sightseeing attractions are generally open, shops and banks are closed, public transportation options are fewer, and there's no rush hour. Saturdays are virtually weekdays (without the rush hours).

If you're using public transportation, read up on the tips for trains and buses (see page 397 of the appendix). If you're driving, peruse my driving tips and study the examples of road signs (see page 411).

Be sure to mix intense and relaxed periods in your itinerary. Every trip (and every traveler) needs at least a few slack days. Pace yourself. Assume you will return.

Reread this book as you travel, and visit local tourist information offices. Upon arrival in a new town, lay the groundwork for a smooth departure; write down the schedule for the train or bus that you'll take when you depart. Use taxis in the big cities, bring along a water bottle, and linger in the shade.

Plan ahead for laundry, picnics, and Internet stops. Get online at Internet cafés or your hotel to research transportation connections, confirm events, check the weather, and get directions to your next hotel. Buy a phone card and use it for reservations, reconfirmations, and double-checking hours.

Know Before You Go

Your trip is more likely to go smoothly if you plan ahead.

Since **airline carry-on restrictions** are always chang-ing, visit the Transportation Security Administration's web-site (www.tsa.gov/travelers) for an up-to-date list of what you can bring on the plane with you...and what you have to check. Remember to arrive with plenty of time to get through security.

Call your **debit- and credit-card companies** to let them know the countries you'll be visiting, so that they'll accept (and not deny) your international charges. Confirm what your daily withdrawal limit is; consider asking to have it raised so that you can take out more cash at each ATM stop.

Be sure that your **passport** is valid at least six months after your ticketed date of return to the US. If you need to get or renew a passport, it can take up to three months (for more on passports, see www.travel.state.gov).

Book your rooms well in advance if you'll be traveling dur-ing any major **holidays** (see "Major Holidays and Weekends," on the previous page).

If you'll be **traveling with children,** read over the list of pre-trip suggestions on page 361.

If you plan to hire a **local guide,** it's smart to reserve ahead by email. Popular guides can get booked up in peak season.

If you're taking an **overnight train** (especially to inter-national destinations), and you need a *couchette* (overnight bunk) or sleeper—and you *must* leave on a certain day—con-sider booking it in advance, even though it may cost more. All high-speed trains in France require a seat reservation, but it's usually possible to make arrangements in France just a few days ahead unless it's a holiday weekend. (For more on train travel, see page 397.)

If you're planning on **renting a car** in France, it's recom-mended—but not required—that you carry an International Driver's Permit (available at your local AAA office for $15 plus the cost of two passport-type photos; see www.aaa.com).

Enjoy the friendliness of the local people. Slow down and ask questions—most locals are eager to point you in their idea of the right direction. Keep a notepad in your pocket for organizing your thoughts. Wear your money belt, and learn the local cur-rency and how to estimate prices in dollars. Those who expect to travel smart, do.

PRACTICALITIES

Red Tape: You need a passport—but no visa or shots—to travel in France. Your passport must be valid for at least six months beyond the time you leave France. Pack a photocopy of your passport in your luggage in case the original is lost or stolen. You are required to have proof of identity on you at all times in France.

Time: In France—and in this book—you'll use the 24-hour clock. It's the same through 12:00 noon, then keep going: 13:00, 14:00, and so on. For anything past 12, subtract 12 and add p.m. (14:00 is 2:00 p.m.)

France, like most of continental Europe, is generally six/nine hours ahead of the East/West Coasts of the US. The exceptions are the beginning and end of Daylight Saving Time: Europe "springs forward" the last Sunday in March (two weeks after most of North America), and "falls back" the last Sunday in October (one week before North America). For a handy online time converter, try www.timeanddate.com/worldclock.

Business Hours: You'll find much of rural France closed weekdays from noon to 14:00 (lunch is sacred). On Sunday, most businesses are closed (family is sacred), though some small stores such as *boulangeries* (bakeries) are open until noon, and museums are open all day. On Monday, some businesses are closed until 14:00 and sometimes all day. Smaller towns are often quiet and downright boring on Sundays and Mondays, unless it's market day.

Shopping: The Shopping chapter, near the end of this book, offers tips on how to enjoy Provence's market days. See the appendix for the nuts-and-bolts details on clothing-size conversions, customs regulations, and VAT refunds (the tax refunded on large purchases made by non-EU residents).

Watt's Up? Europe's electrical system is different from North America's in two ways: the shape of the plug (two round prongs) and the voltage of the current (220 volts instead of 110 volts). For your North American plug to work in Europe, you'll need an adapter, sold inexpensively at travel stores in the US. As for the voltage, most newer electronics or travel appliances (such as hair dryers, laptops, and battery chargers) automatically convert the voltage—if you see a range of voltages printed on the item or its plug (such as "110–220"), it'll work in Europe. Otherwise, you can buy a converter separately in the US (about $20).

News: Americans keep in touch via the *International Herald Tribune* (published almost daily via satellite throughout Europe). Every Tuesday, the European editions of *Time* and *Newsweek* hit the stands with articles of particular interest to European travelers. Sports addicts can get their daily fix online or from *USA Today*.

Trouble in Paradise: Population Growth in Southern France

Amid the breezy, sun-kissed beaches, cities, and villages of Provence and the French Riviera, tension is brewing. The south of France has become a melting pot of people in search of their Provençal paradise. While some say the influx into this region has invigorated the culture, many residents are feeling growing pains. Two major trends are fueling the population boom in the south: rich northern Europeans looking for their place in the sun and North African immigrants looking for a better life in France.

Cheap flights and lightning-fast train service have enabled northern Europeans to experience the south of France as a weekend getaway...and a growing number are choosing to stay. With a sunny climate, relatively inexpensive homes (with pools), and plentiful transportation options, this region is an understandably big draw. Unfortunately, as wealthy northerners pick off local homes and inflate prices, the average Jean is losing out. On every trip to this region, I hear complaints of higher property taxes and less open space—brought on by heat-seeking northern Europeans.

Immigration, particularly from North Africa, is another cause of the population boom. With the historic loss of able-bodied men from World Wars I and II, and native-French birth rates below replacement levels, France looked across the Mediterranean to its old colonies for cheap sources of manual labor. When these workers came, they brought their families, who stayed in France and had large families of their own.

Today, five million North Africans legally reside in France (about 8 percent of the population)—and many more live here illegally. More than 100,000 illegal immigrants arrive in France each year, about half of whom are North African. Most live in the south (a quarter of Marseille's population is North African). This concentration of immigrants among a very Catholic French population, combined with high unemployment (15 percent compared to a national average of 10 percent), has led to the rise of racist politics. This anti-immigrant movement has been spearheaded by the Front National party, which wants to keep "France for the French." Its leader, Jean-Marie Le Pen, has referred to the increasing numbers of North Africans in France as "the silent invasion." The Front National generally receives about 20 percent of this region's vote in national elections.

Just the FAQs, Please

Whom do I call in case of emergency?
Dial 17 for police help. In a medical emergency, call 15.

What if my credit card is stolen?
Act immediately. See "Damage Control for Lost Cards," page 384, for instructions.

How do I make a phone call to, within, or from Europe?
For detailed dialing instructions, refer to page 387.

How can I get tourist information about my destination?
France has a national tourist information office in the US, as well as a network of local offices (see page 379 for specifics on both). Note that Tourist Information is abbreviated **TI** in this book.

What's the best way to pack?
Light. For a recommended packing list, see page 417.

Does Rick have other materials that will help me?
Thanks for asking. For more on Rick's guidebooks, public television series, free audio tours, public radio show, guided tours, travel bags, accessories, and railpasses, see page 380.

Are there any updates to this guidebook?
Check www.ricksteves.com/update for changes to the most recent edition of this book.

Do I need to speak some French?
Many French people—especially those in the tourist trade, and in big cities—speak English. Still, you'll get better treatment if you learn and use the French pleasantries. For background information on the language barrier, see page 394. For a list of survival phrases, see page 419.

Good websites include www.europeantimes.com and http://news.bbc.co.uk.

MONEY

Banking

Throughout Europe, cash machines (ATMs) are the standard way for travelers to get local currency. Bring plastic—credit and/or debit cards—along with several hundred dollars in hard cash as an emergency backup. It's smart to bring two cards, in case one gets demagnetized or eaten by a temperamental machine. Traveler's checks are a waste of time (long waits at slow banks) and a waste of money (in fees).

Can you recommend any good books or movies for my trip?
Sure. For suggestions, see pages 383–384.

Do you recommend any language or cooking schools?
Yes. See page 396 in the appendix for a list.

Do you have information on driving, train travel, and flights?
Absolutely. See "Transportation" on page 397.

How much do I tip?
Relatively little. For tips on tipping, see page 385.

Will I get a student or senior discount?
While discounts aren't listed in this book, seniors (age 60 and over), students with International Student Identification Cards, teachers with proper identification, and youths under 18 or even 26 often get discounts—but you have to ask. If you want a teacher or student ID card, see www.statravel.com or www.isic.org.

How can I get a VAT refund on major purchases?
See the details on page 385.

How do I calculate metric amounts?
Europe uses the metric system. A liter is about a quart, four to a gallon. A kilometer is six-tenths of a mile. I figure kilometers to miles by cutting them in half and adding back 10 percent of the original (120 km: 60 + 12 = 72 miles, 300 km: 150 + 30 = 180 miles). For more metric conversions, see page 415.

Cash from ATMs

To use a bank machine (ATM) to withdraw money from your account, you'll need a debit card (ideally with a Visa or MasterCard logo for maximum usability), plus a PIN code. Know your PIN code in numbers; there are only numbers—no letters—on European keypads.

Before you go, verify with your bank that your card will work overseas, and alert them that you'll be making withdrawals in Europe; otherwise, the bank may not approve transactions if it perceives unusual spending patterns.

French cash machines are labeled *point d'argent* or *distributeur des billets* (the French call them *D.A.B.*—day-ah-bay). You'll find these cash machines all over France—they're always open and

Exchange Rate

1 euro (€) = about $1.30

To convert prices in euros to dollars, add about 30 percent: €20 = about $26, €50 = about $65. Just like the dollar, the euro is broken down into 100 cents. You'll find coins ranging from 1 cent to 2 euros, and bills from 5 euros to 500 euros.

provide quick transactions.

Try to take out large sums of money to reduce your per-transaction bank fees. If the machine refuses your request, try again and select a smaller amount; some cash machines won't let you take out more than about €150 (don't take it personally).

To keep your cash safe, use a money belt—a pouch with a strap that you buckle around your waist like a belt, and wear under your clothes. Thieves target tourists. A money belt provides peace of mind, allowing you to carry lots of cash safely. Don't waste time every few days tracking down a cash machine—change a week's worth of money, stuff it in your money belt, and travel!

Credit and Debit Cards

For purchases, Visa and MasterCard are more commonly accepted than American Express. Just like at home, credit or debit cards work easily at larger hotels, restaurants, and shops, but smaller businesses prefer payment in local currency (in small bills—break large bills at a bank or larger store). Your US credit and debit cards will not work in train-ticket machines or at self-service gas pumps.

Credit and debit cards—whether used for purchases or ATM withdrawals—often come with additional, tacked-on "international transaction" fees of up to 3 percent plus $5 per transaction. To avoid unpleasant surprises, call your bank or credit-card company before your trip to ask about these fees.

If your cards are lost or stolen, see page 384 for advice on what to do.

SIGHTSEEING

Sightseeing can be hard work. Use these tips to make your visits to Provence's and the Riviera's finest sights meaningful, fun, fast, and painless.

Plan Ahead

Set up an itinerary that allows you to fit in all your must-see sights. For a one-stop look at opening hours, see the "At a Glance" sidebars for the bigger cities. Most sights keep stable hours, but you can easily confirm the latest by calling the local TI.

Don't put off visiting a must-see sight—you never know when a place will close unexpectedly for a holiday, strike, or restoration. If you'll be visiting during a holiday, find out if a particular sight will be open by phoning ahead or visiting its website.

When possible, visit key museums first thing (when your energy is best) and save other activities for the afternoon. Hit the highlights first, then go back to other things if you have the stamina and time.

Depending on the sight, there are ways to avoid crowds. This book offers tips on specific sights. Try visiting these sights very early or late: Les Baux, the Pont du Gard, Séguret, Roussillon, Fontaine de Vaucluse, Nice's Chagall and Antibes' Picasso museums, St-Paul-de-Vence, Eze-le-Village, and St-Tropez. The *calanques* near Cassis are best early, but not late.

Read ahead. To get the most out of the self-guided tours and sight descriptions in this book, read them before you visit. Several cities offer sightseeing passes that are worthwhile values for serious sightseers; plan ahead.

At the Sight

All sights have rules, and if you know about these in advance, they're no big deal.

Some important sights have metal detectors or conduct bag searches that will slow your entry.

At churches—which generally offer interesting art (usually free) and a cool, welcome seat—a modest dress code (no bare shoulders or shorts) is encouraged.

Most museums require you to check daypacks and coats. They'll be kept safely. If you have something you can't bear to part with, stash it in a pocket or purse. If you don't want to check a small backpack, carry it (at least as you enter) under your arm like a purse...and hope the guards don't notice.

If you check a bag, the attendant may ask you (in French) if it contains anything of value—camera, phone, money, passport—since these cannot be checked.

Cameras are normally allowed, but not flashes or tripods (without special permission). Flashes damage oil paintings and distract others in the room. Even without a flash, a handheld camera will take a decent picture (or you can buy postcards or posters at the museum bookstore). Video cameras are usually allowed.

Some museums have special exhibits in addition to their permanent collection. Some exhibits are included in the entry price, while others come at an extra cost (which you have to pay even if you don't want to see the exhibit).

Many sights rent audioguides, which offer dry-but-useful recorded descriptions in English (about €5). If you bring along your own pair of headphones and a Y-jack, two people can share one audioguide and save. Guided tours in English (usually €6 and widely ranging in quality) are most likely to occur during peak season.

Expect changes—paintings can be on tour, on loan, out sick, or shifted at the whim of the curator. To adapt, pick up any available free floor plans as you enter, and ask museum staff if you can't find a particular painting. Say the title or artist's name, or point to the photograph in this book, and ask, *"Où est?"* (oo ay; meaning, "Where is?").

Most important sights have an on-site café or cafeteria (usually a good place to rest and have a snack or light meal). The WCs are free and generally clean.

Museums have bookstores selling postcards and souvenirs. Before you leave, scan the postcards and thumb through the biggest guidebook (or skim its index) to be sure you haven't overlooked something that you'd like to see.

Most sights stop admitting people 30–60 minutes before closing time, and some rooms close early (generally about 45 minutes before the actual closing time). Guards usher people out, so don't save the best for last.

Every sight or museum offers more than what is covered in this book. Use this information as an introduction—not the final word.

SLEEPING

Accommodations in Provence and the Riviera are a good value and generally easy to find. Choose from one- to three-star hotels (2 stars is my mainstay), bed-and-breakfasts *(chambres d'hôte)*, hostels, campgrounds, and homes rented on a weekly basis *(gîtes)*. I like places that are clean, small, central, traditional, friendly, and a good value. Most places I list have at least four of these six virtues.

Hotels

In this book, the price for a double room will range from €30 (very simple, toilet and shower down the hall) to €300 (maximum plumbing and more), with most clustering at about €80.

The French have a simple hotel rating system based on amenities (zero through four stars, indicated in this book by * through ****). One star is modest, two has most of the comforts, and three is generally a two-star with a fancier lobby and more elaborately designed rooms. Four stars offer more luxury than you usually have time to appreciate. Two- and three-star hotels are required to have

Types of Rooms

Study the price list on the hotel's website or posted at the desk, so you know your options. Receptionists often don't mention the cheaper rooms—they assume you want a private bathroom or a bigger room. Here are the types of rooms and beds:

une chambre sans douche et WC	room without a private shower or toilet (uncommon these days)
une chambre avec cabinet de toilette	room with a toilet but no shower (some hotels charge for down-the-hall showers)
une chambre avec bain et WC	room with private bathtub and toilet
une chambre avec douche et WC	room with private shower and toilet
chambres communiquantes	connecting rooms (ideal for families)
un grand lit	double bed (55 inches wide)
deux petits lits	twin beds (30–36 inches wide)
deux lits séparés	two beds separated
un lit de cent-soixante	queen-size bed (literally 160 centimeters, or 63 inches wide)
un lit dépliant	folding bed
un bérceau	baby crib
un lit d'enfant	child's bed

an English-speaking staff, though virtually all hotels I recommend have someone who speaks English (unless I note otherwise in the listing). Generally, the number of stars does not reflect room size or guarantee quality. Some two-star hotels are better than many three-star hotels. One- and two-star hotels are inexpensive, but some three-star (and even a few four-star hotels) offer good value, justifying the extra cost. Unclassified hotels (no stars) can be bargains or depressing dumps.

Most hotels have lots of doubles and a few singles, triples, and quads. Traveling alone can be expensive, as singles (except for the rare closet-type rooms that fit only one twin bed) are simply doubles used by one person—so they cost about the same as a double. Room prices vary within each hotel depending on size, and whether the room has a bath or shower, and twin beds or a double bed (tubs and twins cost more than showers and double beds). A triple and a double are often the same room, with a double or queen-size bed plus a sliver-size single. Quad rooms usually have two double beds. Hotels cannot legally allow more in the room than what's shown on their price list. Modern hotels generally have a few family-friendly rooms that open to each other *(chambres communiquantes)*.

You can save as much as €20–25 by finding the rare room without a private shower or toilet. A room with a bathtub costs €10–15 more than a room with a shower (and is generally larger). Hotels often have more rooms with tubs than showers and are inclined to give you a room with a tub (which the French prefer).

A double bed is €5–10 cheaper than twins, though rooms with twin beds tend to be larger, and French double beds are smaller than American double beds. Many hotels have queen-size beds (a bed that's 63 inches wide—most doubles are 55 inches). To find out if a hotel has queen-size beds, ask, *"Avez-vous des lits de cent-soixante?"* (ah-vay-voo day lee duh sahn-swah-sahnt). To make a king-size bed (70 inches wide), some hotels push two twins together under king-size sheets and blankets.

If you prefer a double bed (instead of twins) and a shower (instead of a tub), you need to ask for it—and you can save €10–20. If you'll take either twins or a double, ask generically for *une chambre pour deux* (room for two) to avoid being needlessly turned away.

You'll almost always have the option of breakfast at your hotel, which is pleasant and convenient, but it's more than the price of breakfast at the corner café, and with less ambience (though you get more coffee at your hotel). Some hotels offer only the classic continental breakfast for about €6–8, but others offer buffet breakfasts for about €10–15 (cereal, yogurt, fruit, cheese, croissants, juice, and hard-boiled eggs)—which I usually spring for. (The price of breakfast usually correlates with the price of the room: The more expensive the room, the more expensive the breakfast. This can add up, particularly for families, so beware.) While hotels hope that you'll buy their breakfast, it's optional unless otherwise noted.

Some hotels strongly encourage their peak-season guests to take *demi-pension* (half-pension)—that is, breakfast and either lunch or dinner. By law, they can't require you to take half-pension unless you are staying three or more nights, but, in effect, many do during summer. While the food is usually good, it limits your ability to shop around. I've indicated where I think *demi-pension* is a good value.

Hotels in France must charge a daily tax *(taxe du séjour)* of about €1 per person per day. While some hotels include it in the price list, most add it to your bill.

Rooms are safe. Still, keep cameras and money out of sight. Towels aren't routinely replaced every day; drip-dry and conserve.

If that French Lincoln Log–like pillow isn't your idea of comfort, American-style pillows (and extra blankets) are sometimes in the closet or available on request. To get a pillow, ask for *"Un oreiller, s'il vous plaît"* (un oh-ray-yay, see voo play).

If you're planning to visit southern France in the summer, the extra expense of an air-conditioned room can be money well spent. Most hotel rooms with air-conditioners come with a control stick (like a TV remote) that generally has the same symbols and features: fan icon (click to toggle through wind power, from light to gale); louver icon (choose steady airflow or waves); snowflake and sunshine icons (cold air or heat, depending on season); clock ("O" setting: run X hours before turning off; "I" setting: wait X hours to start); and the temperature control (20 or 21 degrees Celsius is comfortable; also see the thermometer diagram on page 416).

Some hoteliers will ask you to sign their *Livre d'Or* (literally "Golden Book," for client comments). They take this seriously and enjoy reading your remarks.

France is littered with sterile, ultramodern hotels, usually located on cheap land just outside of town, providing drivers with low-stress accommodations. The antiseptically clean and cheap Formule 1 and ETAP chains (about €35–50 per room for up to 3 people), the more attractive Ibis hotels (€80–100 for a double), and the cushier Mercure and Novotel hotels (€110–170 for a double) are all run by the same company, Accor (www.accorhotels.com). While far from quaint, these can be a good value (particularly if you find deals on their website) and some are centrally located. A smaller, up-and-coming chain, Kyriad, has its act together, offering good prices and quality (France tel. 08 25 00 30 03, from overseas tel. 33 1 64 62 46 46—push 1 to make a reservation, www.kyriad.com; these telephone numbers also work for 8 affiliated chains, including Clarine, Climat de France, and Campanile). For a long listing of various hotels throughout France, see www.france.com, and for more personality, check www.charming-french-hotels.com.

Phoning

To call France, you'll need to know its country code: 33. To call France from the US or Canada, dial 011-33-local number (without the initial 0). If calling France from another European country, dial 00-33-local number (without the initial 0).

Making Reservations

It's possible to travel at any time of year without reservations, but given the high stakes and the quality of the gems I've found for this book, I'd book ahead. You can reserve long in advance from home, or book rooms a few days to a week in advance as you travel. (If you have difficulty, ask the fluent receptionist at your current hotel

Sleep Code

(€1 = about $1.30, country code: 33)
To help you sort easily through these listings, I've divided the rooms into three categories based on the price for a standard double room with bath:

$$$ **Higher Priced**
$$ **Moderately Priced**
$ **Lower Priced**

To give maximum information in a minimum of space, I use the following code to describe the accommodations. Prices listed are per room, not per person. Unless otherwise noted, English is spoken and breakfast is not included (but is usually optional). You can assume a hotel takes credit cards unless you see "cash only" in the listing.

S = Single room (or price for one person in a double).
D = Double or twin room.
T = Triple (generally a double bed with a single).
Q = Quad (usually two double beds).
b = Private bathroom with toilet and shower or tub.
s = Private shower or tub only (the toilet is down the hall).
* = French hotel rating system, ranging from zero to four stars.

According to this code, a couple staying at a "Db-€140" hotel would pay a total of €140 (about $180) for a double room with a private bathroom.

to call for you.) If you like more spontaneity (or if you're traveling off-season), you might make a habit of calling between 9:00 and 10:00 on the day you plan to arrive, when the hotel clerk knows who'll be checking out and just which rooms will be available. I've taken great pains to list telephone numbers with long-distance instructions (see page 387 of the appendix). Use a public phone, the convenient prepaid telephone cards, or your mobile phone. Most hotels I list are accustomed to English-only speakers. A hotel receptionist will trust you and hold a room until 16:00 without a deposit, though some will ask for a credit-card number.

If you know where you want to stay each day (and you don't need or want flexibility), reserve your rooms from the US in advance. This is particularly smart for the Riviera—and anywhere during holidays (see "Major Holidays and Weekends," page 8). To reserve from home, email, fax, or call the hotel. Email is preferred. Phone and fax costs are reasonable. To fax, use the form in the appendix (online at www.ricksteves.com/reservation). If you don't get an answer to your fax request, consider that a "no." (Many little places get 20 faxes a day after they're full, and they can't afford to respond.) But if you don't get an email response right away, call to follow up.

When you request a room for a certain time period, use the European style for writing dates: day/month/year. Hoteliers need to know your arrival and departure dates. For example, a two-night stay in July would be "2 nights, 16/07/08 to 18/07/08."

If you receive a response from the hotel stating its rates and room availability, it's not a confirmation. You must confirm that you indeed want a room at the given rate. One night's deposit is generally required. A credit-card number is often accepted as a deposit (though you may need to send a signed traveler's check or, rarely, a bank draft in the local currency). Faxing your card number (rather than emailing it) keeps it private, safer, and out of cyberspace. If you use your credit card for the deposit, you can pay with your card or cash when you arrive. If you don't show up, you'll be billed for one night. To make things easier on yourself and the hotel, be sure you really intend to stay at the hotel on the dates you requested. These small, family-run businesses lose money if they turn away customers while holding a room for someone who doesn't show up. *If you must cancel, give at least two days' notice.*

Reconfirm your reservations a few days in advance for safety, and let them know about what time you'll arrive. Don't needlessly confirm rooms through the tourist office; they'll take a commission of up to 20 percent. On the small chance that a hotel loses track of your reservation, bring along their faxed confirmation or a hard copy of their emailed confirmation.

Bed-and-Breakfasts

B&Bs (*Chambres d'hôte*, abbreviated CH in this book)—a great deal—are generally found in smaller towns and rural areas. They offer double the cultural intimacy for a good deal less than most hotel rooms—and help compensate for the low value of the dollar. While you may lose some hotel conveniences—such as lounges, in-room phones, daily bed-sheet changes, and credit-card payments—I happily make the trade-off for the extra charm. This book and local tourist offices list B&Bs, often by the owner's family name. While some CHs post small *Chambres* or *Chambres d'hôte* signs in their front windows, many are found only through the local tourist office.

I recommend reliable CHs that offer a good value and/or unique experience (such as CHs in renovated mills, châteaux, and wine *domaines*). While *chambres d'hôte* have their own star-rating system, it doesn't quite correspond to the hotels' rating system.

So, to avoid confusion, I haven't listed these stars for CHs. But most of my recommended CHs have private bathrooms in all rooms and some have common rooms with refrigerators. Doubles with breakfast generally cost €50–70 (breakfast may or may not be included—ask). *Tables d'hôte* are CHs that offer an optional, reasonably priced, home-cooked dinner (usually a fine value, must be requested in advance). While your hosts may not speak English, they will almost always be enthusiastic and pleasant.

Hostels

You'll pay about €18 per bed to stay at a hostel *(auberge de jeunesse)*. Travelers of any age are welcome if they don't mind dorm-style accommodations or meeting other travelers. Cheap meals are sometimes available, and kitchen facilities are usually provided for do-it-yourselfers. Expect youth groups in spring, crowds in the summer, snoring, and great variability in quality from one hostel to the next. Family and private rooms are sometimes available on request, but it's basically boys' dorms and girls' dorms. You usually can't check in before 17:00 and must be out by 10:00. There is often a 23:00 curfew. Official hostels are marked with a triangular sign that shows a house and a tree. Some hostels accept reservations only by email. If you'll be staying for several days in an official hostel, consider buying a membership card before you go (www.hihostels.com).

Camping

In Europe, camping is more of a social than an environmental experience. It's a great way for American travelers to make European friends. Camping costs about €15–20 per campsite per night, and almost every destination recommended in this book has a campground within a reasonable walk or bus ride from the town center and train station. A tent and sleeping bag are all you need. Many campgrounds have small grocery stores and washing machines, and some even come with discos and miniature golf. Hot showers are better at campgrounds than at many hotels. Local TIs have camping information. You'll find more detailed information in the annually updated *Michelin Camping France*, available in the United States ($16) and at most French bookstores.

Gîtes and Apartments

Throughout France, you can find reasonably priced rental homes, and nowhere are there more options than in Provence and the Riviera. Because this region is small, and all the sights are within an easy drive, it makes a lot of sense to spend your vacation at one home base.

Gîtes (zheet) are country homes (usually urbanites' second homes) that the government rents out to visitors who want a week in the countryside. The original objective of the *gîte* program was to save characteristic rural homes from abandonment and to make it easy and affordable for families to reacquaint themselves with the French countryside. The government offers subsidies to renovate such homes, then coordinates rentals to make it financially feasible for the owner. Today, France has more than 8,000 *gîtes*. One of your authors restored a farmhouse a few hours north of Provence, and even though he and his wife are 100 percent American, they received the same assistance that French owners get.

Gîtes are best for drivers (they're usually rural, with little public-transport access) and ideal for families and small groups (since they can sleep many for the same price). Homes range in comfort from simple cottages and farmhouses to restored châteaux. Most have at least two bedrooms, a kitchen, a living room, a bathroom or two, and no sheets or linens (though you can usually rent them for extra). Like hotels, all *gîtes* are rated for comfort from one to four (using ears of corn—*épis*—rather than stars). Two or three *épis* are generally sufficient quality, but I'd lean towards three for more comfort. Prices generally range from €300–1200 per week, depending on house size and amenities such as pools. For more information on *gîtes*, visit www.gites-de-france.fr/eng or www.gite .com. My readers also report finding long lists of non-*gîte* homes for rent through TIs and on the Internet, though these are usually more expensive than staying in a *gîte* (try www.villeetvillage.com).

While less common than *gîtes*, **apartments** can be rented in cities and towns along the Riviera (one-week minimum). Tourist offices have lists. Avignon, Aix-en-Provence, Nice, and other Riviera towns have the biggest selection.

EATING

The French eat long and well—nowhere more so than in the south. Relaxed and tree-shaded lunches with a chilled rosé, three-hour dinners, and endless afternoons at outdoor cafés are the norm. The French have a legislated 35-hour workweek...and a self-imposed 36-hour eat-week. Local cafés, cuisine, and wines should become a highlight of any French adventure. It's sightseeing for your palate. Even if the rest of you is sleeping in cheap hotels, let your taste buds travel first class in France. (They can go coach in England.) You can eat well without going broke—but choose carefully: You're just as likely to blow a small fortune on a mediocre meal as you are to dine wonderfully for €20. For specific suggestions on what to order where, see my cuisine suggestions in the introductions to Provence (page 37) and the Riviera (page 234).

Eating out will get even better in 2008 for non-smokers. By law, restaurants and cafés must choose between three options:

going completely smoke-free; allowing smoking throughout (indi-cated by a sign...and clouds of smoke); or having smoking and non-smoking sections that are entirely sealed off from each other. Nearly all restaurants are opting to go smoke-free, though you'll still find a few smoky cafés.

Breakfast

Petit déjeuner (puh-tee day-zhuh-nay) is traditionally café au lait, hot chocolate, or tea; a roll with butter and marmalade; and a croissant—though now many hotels provide breakfast buffets. Breakfast, which costs about €6–15 at your hotel, is cheaper at cor-ner cafés, but you won't get coffee refills (see also "Café Culture," next page). It's fine to buy a croissant or roll at a bakery and eat it with your cup of coffee at a café. Better still, some bakeries offer worthwhile breakfast deals with juice, a croissant, and coffee or tea for about €4–5. If you crave eggs for breakfast, drop into a café and order *une omelette* or *œufs sur le plat* (fried eggs). You could also buy or bring from home plastic bowls and spoons, buy a box of cereal and a small box of milk, and eat in your room before heading out for coffee.

Picnics

For most lunches—*déjeuner* (day-zhuh-nay)—I picnic or munch a take-away sandwich from a *boulangerie* (bakery) or a crêpe from a *crêperie*.

Picnics can be first-class affairs and adventures in high cui-sine. Be daring. Try the smelly cheeses, ugly pâtés, sissy quiches, and miniscule (usually drinkable) yogurts. Local shopkeepers are accustomed to selling small quantities of produce. Try the tasty salads-to-go and ask for a plastic fork *(une fourchette en plastique)*. A small container is *une barquette*.

Gather supplies early for a picnic lunch; you'll probably visit several small stores to assemble a complete meal, and many close at noon for a lunch break. Look for a *boulangerie* (bakery), a *crémerie* or *fromagerie* (cheeses), a *charcuterie* (deli items, meats, salads, and pâtés), an *épicerie* or *magasin d'alimentation* (small grocery with veggies, drinks, and so on), and a *pâtisserie* (delicious pastries). While wine is taboo in public places in the US, it's *pas de problème* in France.

Open-air markets *(marchés)* are fun and photogenic, and they close at about 13:00 (many are listed in this book; local TIs have complete lists). There's much more information about these won-derful Provençal experiences in the Shopping chapter (see "Market Day" on page 366). Local *supermarchés* offer less color and cost, more efficiency, and adequate quality. Department stores often have supermarkets in the basement. On the outskirts of cities, you'll find the monster *hypermarchés*. Drop in for a glimpse of hyper-France in action.

In stores, unrefrigerated soft drinks, bottled water, and beer are one-third the price of cold drinks. Milk, bottled water, and boxed fruit juice are the cheapest drinks. Avoid buying drinks to go at streetside stands; you'll find them far cheaper in a shop. Try to keep a water bottle with you. Water quenches your thirst better and cheaper than anything you'll find in a store or café. I drink tap water throughout France, filling my bottle in hotel rooms as I go.

Sandwiches, Quiche, and Pizza

Everywhere in Provence and the Riviera, you'll find bakeries and small stands selling baguette sandwiches, quiche, and pizza-like items to go for €3–5. Usually filling and tasty, they also streamline the picnic process. (If you don't want your sandwich drenched in mayonnaise, ask for it *sans mayonnaise;* sahn my-oh-nehz). Here are some sandwiches you'll see:

Jambon beurre (zhahn-bohn bur): Ham and butter (boring for most).

Fromage beurre (froh-mahzh bur): Cheese and butter (white on white on beige).

Poulet crudités (poo-lay krew-dee-tay): Chicken with tomatoes, lettuce, carrots, and cucumbers.

Thon crudités (tohn krew-dee-tay): Tuna with tomatoes, lettuce, carrots, and cucumbers.

Jambon crudités (zhahn-bohn krew-dee-tay): Ham with tomatoes, lettuce, carrots, and cucumbers.

Jambon or *Poulet à la provençal* (zhahn-bohn/poo-lay ah lah proh-vehn-sahl): Ham or chicken, usually with marinated peppers, tomatoes, and eggplant. These are great.

Look also for grilled *panini* sandwiches *à la italienne.*

Café Culture

French cafés (or brasseries) provide budget-friendly meals and a refuge from museum and church overload. Feel free to order only a bowl of soup or a salad or *plat* (main course) for lunch or dinner at a café.

Cafés generally open by 7:00, but closing hours vary. Unlike restaurants, which open only for lunch and dinner and close in between, meals are served throughout the day at most cafés—making them the best option for a late lunch or an early dinner.

If you're a novice, it's easier to sit and feel comfortable when you know the system. Check the price list first, which by law must be posted prominently. You'll see two sets of prices: You'll pay more for the same drink if you're seated at a table *(salle)* than if you're seated at the bar or counter *(comptoir).*

Your waiter probably won't overwhelm you with friendliness. Notice how hard they work. They almost never stop. Cozying up to clients (French or foreign) is probably the last thing on their minds.

Standard Menu Items: *Croque monsieur* (grilled ham-and-cheese sandwich) and *croque madame* (*croque monsieur* with a fried egg on top) are generally served day and night. Sandwiches are least expensive but plain—and much better at the *boulangerie* (bakery). To get more than a piece of ham *(jambon)* on a baguette, order a sandwich *jambon crudité*, which means garnished with veggies. Omelets come lonely on a plate with a basket of bread. The daily special—*plat du jour* (plah dew zhoor), or just *plat*—is your fast, hearty, and garnished hot plate for €10–15. At most cafés, feel free to order only entrées (which in French means the first course); many find these lighter and more interesting than a main course. A vegetarian can enjoy a tasty, filling meal by ordering two entrées. Regardless of what you order, bread is free; to get more, just hold up your bread basket and ask, *"Encore, s'il vous plaît."*

Salads: They're typically large—one is perfect for lunch or a light dinner, or split between two people as a first course. Among the classics are *salade niçoise* (nee-swaz), a specialty from Nice that usually includes green salad topped with green beans, boiled potatoes, tomatoes, anchovies, olives, hard-boiled eggs, and lots of tuna; *salade au chèvre chaud,* a mixed green salad topped with warm goat cheese and toasted bread croutons; and *salade composée,* "composed" of any number of ingredients, such as *lardons* (bacon), *comte* (a Swiss-style cheese), Roquefort (bleu cheese), *œuf* (egg), *noix* (walnuts), *jambon* (ham, generally thinly sliced), *saumon fumé* (smoked salmon), and the highly suspect *gesiers* (chicken livers). To get salad dressing on the side, order *la sauce à part* (lah sohs ah par).

For tips on beverages, see next page.

Restaurants

Choose restaurants filled with locals. Consider my suggestions and your hotelier's opinion, but trust your instinct. If a restaurant doesn't post its prices outside, move along. Refer to my restaurant recommendations to get a sense of what a reasonable meal should cost.

Restaurants in the south open for dinner at 19:00 and are typically most crowded about 20:30 (the early bird gets the table). Last seating is usually about 21:00 (22:00 in cities and on the French Riviera, possibly earlier in small villages during the off-season).

If a restaurant serves lunch, it generally begins at 11:30 and goes until 14:00, with last orders taken about 13:30. In contrast, most cafés serve food all day. Go to a café if you're hungry when restaurants are closed (late afternoon), or anytime you want just a soup or salad.

If you ask for the *menu* (muh-noo) at a restaurant, you won't get a list of dishes; you'll get a fixed-price meal. *Menus*, which include three or four courses, are generally a good value if you're hungry: You'll get your choice of soup, appetizer, or salad; your choice of three or four main courses with vegetables; plus a cheese course and/or a choice of desserts. Service is included (*service compris* or *prix net*), but wine and other drinks are generally extra. Restaurants that offer a *menu* for lunch often charge about €5 more for the same *menu* at dinner.

Many restaurants offer cheaper versions of their *menu*, with a choice of two, rather than three or four courses. These pared-down *menus* are commonly called *formules* and feature an *entrée et plat* (first course and main dish), or *plat et dessert* (main dish and dessert). Most restaurants offer a reasonable *menu-enfant* (kids' menu).

Ask for *la carte* (lah kart) if you want to see a menu and order à la carte, like the locals do. Request the waiter's help in deciphering the French. Go with his or her recommendations and anything *de la maison* (of the house), as long as it's not an organ meat *(tripes, rognons, andouillette)*. Galloping gourmets should bring a menu translator; the *Marling Menu-Master* is good. The *Rick Steves' French Phrase Book*, with a menu decoder, works well for most travelers. Wines are often listed in a separate *carte des vins*.

In France, an *entrée* is the first course. *Le plat* or *le plat du jour* (plate of the day) is the main course with vegetables. In the south, I usually order *une entrée* and *un plat* off the menu, then find an ice cream or crêpe stand and take a dessert stroll. If that sounds like too much, just order *un plat* (most places I list don't mind if you order only a main course). Because small dinner salads are usually not offered à la carte, two travelers can split a big salad (usually several salad options), then each get a *plat* (this also works well for other starter courses).

By American standards, the French undercook meats: *bleu* (bluh) is virtually raw (just flame-kissed); *rare* or *saignant* (seh-nyahn) is close to raw; medium or *à point* (ah pwahn) is rare; and well-done or *bien cuit* (bee-yehn kwee) is medium.

To get a waiter's attention, simply say, *"S'il vous plaît"* (see voo play)—"please."

Beverages at Cafés and Restaurants

Water: The French are willing to pay for bottled water with their meal (*eau minérale;* oh mee-nay-rahl) because they prefer the taste over tap water. Badoit is my favorite carbonated water (*l'eau gazeuse;* loh gah-zuhz). If you prefer a free pitcher of tap water, ask for *une carafe d'eau* (oon kah-rahf doh). Otherwise, you may

Coffee and Tea Lingo

By law, the waiter must give you a glass of tap water with your coffee or tea if you request it; ask for *"Un verre d'eau, s'il vous plaît"* (uhn vayr doh, see voo play).

Provence is known for its herbal and fruit teas. Look for *tilleul* (linden), *verveine* (verbena), or interesting blends such as *poire–vanille* (pear–vanilla).

Coffee

French	Pronounced	English
un express	uh nex-press	shot of espresso
une noisette	oon nwah-zeht	espresso with a shot of milk
café au lait	kah-fay oh lay	coffee with lots of steamed milk (closest to an American latte)
un grand crème	uhn grahn krehm	big café au lait
un petit crème	uhn puh-tee	small café au lait
un grand café noir	uhn grahn kah-fay nwahr	cup of black coffee, closest to American-style
un décaffiné	uhn day-kah-fee-nay	decaf—available for any of the above drinks

Tea

French	Pronounced	English
un thé nature	uhn tay nah-tour	plain tea
un thé au lait	uhn tay oh lay	tea with milk
un thé citron	uhn tay see-trohn	tea with lemon
une infusion	oon an-few-see-yohn	herbal tea

unwittingly buy bottled water.

Wine and Beer: House wine at the bar is cheap and good in this region (about €3 per glass at modestly-priced places). At a restaurant, a bottle or carafe of house wine costs €8–14. To get inexpensive wine, order regional table wine (*un vin du pays;* uhn van duh pay) in a pitcher (*un pichet;* uhn pee-shay), rather than a bottle. Note, though, that finer restaurants usually offer only bottles of wine.

If all you want is a glass of wine, ask for *un verre de vin rouge* for red wine or *vin blanc* for white wine (uhn vehr duh van roozh/ blahn). A half-carafe of wine is *un demi-pichet* (uhn duh-mee pee-shay); a quarter-carafe (ideal for one) is *un quart* (uh kar).

The local beer, which costs about €4 at a restaurant, is cheaper on tap (*une pression;* oon pres-yohn) than in the bottle (*bouteille;* boo-teh-ee). France's best beer is Alsatian; try Kronenbourg or the heavier Pelfort. *Une panaché* (oon pah-nah-shay) is a refreshing French shandy (beer and 7-Up).

Regional Specialty Drinks: For a refreshing before-dinner drink, order a *kir* (pronounced keer): a thumb's level of *crème de cassis* (black currant liqueur) topped with white wine. In Provence, try sweet wines such as Muscat de Beaumes de Venise or Rasteau (Vin Doux Naturel). Both should be served chilled (from the fridge, not with ice cubes) and can be enjoyed before dinner or with some desserts, and are terrific with foie gras, melons, peaches, or Roquefort cheese. Look also for sparkling wines, usually inexpensive versions of the pricey Champagne.

If you like brandy, try a *marc* (regional brandy) or an Armagnac, cognac's cheaper twin brother. *Pastis,* the standard southern France aperitif, is a sweet anise (licorice) drink that comes on the rocks with a glass of water. Cut it to taste with lots of water.

Soft Drinks: These cost about €4 in restaurants. Kids love the local lemonade; ask for *citron pressé* (see-trohn preh-say) and add sugar. If you order a *lemonade,* you'll get 7-Up or Sprite. The flavored syrups mixed with bottled water (*sirops à l'eau;* see-roh ah loh) are kid- and adult-friendly. Be adventurous and try *un diablo menthe* (uh dee-ah-bloh mahnt; 7-Up with mint syrup) or *un diablo pêche* (pehsh; 7-Up with peach syrup). The ice cubes have melted since the last Yankee tour group left.

TRAVELING AS A TEMPORARY LOCAL

We travel all the way to Europe to enjoy differences—to become temporary locals. You'll experience frustrations. Certain truths that we find "God-given" or "self-evident," such as cold beer, ice in drinks, bottomless cups of coffee, hot showers, and bigger being better, are suddenly not so true. One of the benefits of travel is the eye-opening realization that there are logical, civil, and even better alternatives.

France is an understandably proud country. To enjoy its people, you need to celebrate the differences. A willingness to go local ensures that you'll enjoy a full dose of French hospitality.

If there is a negative aspect to the image the French have of Americans (apart from our foreign policy), it's that we are big, loud, aggressive, impolite, rich, superficially friendly, and a bit naive.

Given our reluctance to work with the world on climate change issues, Europeans don't respond well to Americans complaining about being too hot or too cold. Bring a sweater in winter, and in summer, be prepared to sweat a little like everyone else.

Americans tend to be noisy in public places, such as restaurants and trains. My French friends place a high value on speaking quietly in these same places. Listen while on the bus or in a restaurant—the place can be packed, but the decibel level is low. Try to remember this nuance, and soften your speaking voice as a way of respecting their culture.

While the French look bemusedly at some of our Yankee excesses—and worriedly at others—they nearly always afford us individual travelers all the warmth we deserve. Judging from all the happy feedback I receive from travelers who have used this book, it's safe to assume you'll enjoy a great, affordable vacation—with the finesse of an independent, experienced traveler.

Thanks, and *bon voyage!*

BACK DOOR TRAVEL PHILOSOPHY
From *Rick Steves' Europe Through the Back Door*

Travel is intensified living—maximum thrills per minute and one of the last great sources of legal adventure. Travel is freedom. It's recess, and we need it.

Experiencing the real Europe requires catching it by surprise, going casual..."Through the Back Door."

Affording travel is a matter of priorities. (Make do with the old car.) You can travel—simply, safely, and comfortably—nearly anywhere in Europe for $100 a day plus transportation costs. In many ways, spending more money only builds a thicker wall between you and what you came to see. Europe is a cultural carnival, and, time after time, you'll find that its best acts are free and the best seats are the cheap ones.

A tight budget forces you to travel close to the ground, meeting and communicating with the people, not relying on service with a purchased smile. Never sacrifice sleep, nutrition, safety, or cleanliness in the name of budget. Simply enjoy the local-style alternatives to expensive hotels and restaurants.

Extroverts have more fun. If your trip is low on magic moments, kick yourself and make things happen. If you don't enjoy a place, maybe you don't know enough about it. Seek the truth. Recognize tourist traps. Give a culture the benefit of your open mind. See things as different, but not better or worse. Any culture has much to share.

Of course, travel, like the world, is a series of hills and valleys. Be fanatically positive and militantly optimistic. If something's not to your liking, change your liking. Travel is addictive. It can make you a happier American as well as a citizen of the world. Our Earth is home to six and a half billion equally important people. It's humbling to travel and find that people don't envy Americans. Europeans like us, but, with all due respect, they wouldn't trade passports.

Globe-trotting destroys ethnocentricity. It helps you understand and appreciate different cultures. Regrettably, there are forces in our society that want you dumbed down for their convenience. Don't let it happen. Thoughtful travel engages you with the world—more important than ever these days. Travel changes people. It broadens perspectives and teaches new ways to measure quality of life. Rather than fear the diversity on this planet, travelers celebrate it. Many travelers toss aside their hometown blinders. Their prized souvenirs are the strands of different cultures they decide to knit into their own character. The world is a cultural yarn shop, and Back Door travelers are weaving the ultimate tapestry. Join in!

PROVENCE

"There are treasures to carry away in this land, which has not found a spokesman worthy of the riches it offers."
—Paul Cézanne

This magnificent region is shaped like a giant wedge of quiche. From its sunburned crust, fanning out along the Mediterranean coast from the Camargue to Marseille, it stretches north along the Rhône Valley to Orange. The Romans were here in force and left many ruins—some of the best anywhere. Seven popes, artists such as Vincent van Gogh and Paul Cézanne, and author Peter Mayle all enjoyed their years in Provence. The region offers a splendid recipe of arid climate, oceans of vineyards, dramatic scenery, captivating cities, and adorable hill towns by the dozen.

Explore the ghost town that is ancient Les Baux and see France's greatest Roman ruins, the Pont du Gard and the theater in Orange. Admire the skill of ball-tossing *boules* players in small squares in every Provençal village and city. Spend a few starry, starry nights where van Gogh did, in Arles. Youthful but classy Avignon bustles in the shadow of its brooding Palace of the Popes. Stylish and self-confident Aix-en-Provence lies 30 minutes from the sea and feels more Mediterranean. It's a short hop from Arles or Avignon into the splendid scenery and villages of the Côtes du Rhône and Luberon regions. Should you need an urban fix—and feel the need to really understand southern France—Marseille is a must. If you prefer a Provençal beach fix, find Cassis, just east of Marseille.

Planning Your Time

With limited time, make Arles or Avignon your sightseeing base—particularly if you have no car (with a car, head for the hill

Provence

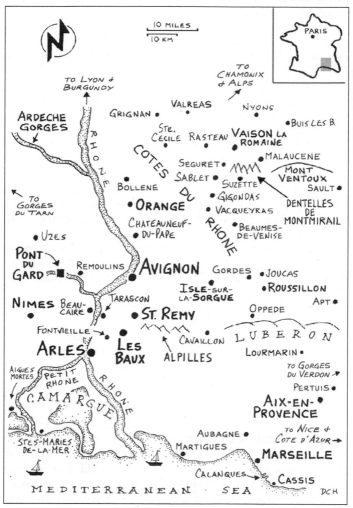

towns). Arles has a blue-collar quality; the entire city feels like van Gogh's bedroom. It also has this region's best-value hotels and is handy to Les Baux, St. Rémy, and the Camargue. Avignon—three times larger than Arles—feels sophisticated, offers more nightlife and shopping, and makes a good base for exploring the Pont du Gard, Nîmes, Uzés, St. Rémy, Isle-sur-la-Sorgue, and Orange. Italophiles prefer smaller Arles, while poodles pick urban Avignon. Many enjoy nights in both cities.

The bare minimum in Provence is three days: one full day for sightseeing in Arles and Les Baux (Arles is best on Wed or Sat, when the morning market rages); a day for the Pont du Gard and Nîmes; and a full day for Avignon and Uzés or St. Rémy. Add two more days to explore the Provençal villages, and allow two days in Cassis, using one of the days for a day trip to Marseille or Aix-en-Provence (or both). Ideally, see the cities—Arles, Nîmes, Avignon, Aix-en-Provence, and Marseille—by train, then rent a car for the countryside.

To measure the pulse of rural Provence, spend at least a few nights in the smaller towns. (They come to life on market days, but can be pretty dead on Mondays, when shops are generally closed.) I've described many towns in the Côtes du Rhône and Luberon. The Côtes du Rhône is ideal for wine connoisseurs and easy to include for those heading to or from the north. The Luberon is for hill-town lovers and works well for travelers heading east, toward Aix-en-Provence or the Riviera. Don't day-trip to these very different areas; nights spent in Provençal villages are what books are written about. Two nights in each area make a terrific start.

The small port town of Cassis is a worthwhile Mediterranean meander between Provence and the Riviera (and more appealing than most Riviera resorts). It has easy day-trip connections to Marseille and Aix-en-Provence.

Depending on the length of your trip, here are my recommended priorities for Provence:

3 days:	Arles and Les Baux; Pont du Gard and Nîmes; and Avignon and either St. Rémy or Uzès
5 days, add:	Orange, Côtes du Rhône villages, and nearby sights
7 days, add:	Cassis, Marseille, Aix-en-Provence
9 days, add:	Luberon hill towns, Camargue

Getting Around Provence

By Bus or Train: Public transit is good between cities and decent to some towns, but marginal at best to the villages. Frequent trains link Avignon, Arles, and Nîmes (about 30 min between each). Avignon has good train connections with Orange. Marseille is well-connected to all cities in Provence, with particularly frequent service to Cassis and Aix-en-Provence (about 30 min to each).

Buses connect many smaller towns. From Arles, you can catch a bus to Stes-Maries-de-la-Mer (in the Camargue) or St. Rémy. From Avignon, you can bus to Pont du Gard, St. Rémy, Uzès, Isle-sur-la-Sorgue (also by train), and less easily to Vaison la Romaine and some Côtes du Rhône villages. St. Rémy, Isle-sur-la-Sorgue, and Uzès are the most accessible small towns.

While a tour of the villages of the Côtes du Rhône or Luberon is best on your own by car, excellent minivan tours and basic bus excursions are available (TIs in Arles and Avignon have

Top 10 Roman Sights in Provence

1. Pont du Gard aqueduct and its museum
2. Roman Theater in Orange
3. Ancient History Museum in Arles
4. Maison Carrée in Nîmes
5. Arena in Nîmes
6. Arena in Arles
7. Ruined aqueduct near Fontvieille
8. Roman city of Glanum (in St. Rémy)
9. Roman city of Vaison la Romaine
10. St. Julien Bridge (near Roussillon)

Top 10 Provençal Towns and Villages

1. Roussillon (beautiful hill town sitting atop a huge ochre deposit giving it a red-rock appeal, popular with American tourists)
2. Uzès (chic town with manicured pedestrian streets, popular with European tourists)
3. Joucas (adorable little village where flowers and stones are lovingly maintained, popular with artists)
4. Brantes (spectacularly situated cliffside village with little tourism)
5. Lourmarin (lovely upscale village, busy in the day but quiet at night)
6. Le Crestet (an overlooked village with a sensational hilltop location and one commercial enterprise)
7. Séguret (a linear hillside village with memorable views and many day-trippers, but few overnighters)
8. Gigondas (world-famous wine village with a nice balance of commercial activity and quiet)
9. Vaison la Romaine (a popular midsize town with Roman ruins and lots of activity, spanning both sides of a river)
10. Nyons (an overlooked midsize town with a few pedestrian streets; famous for its olive oil and ideal climate)

information on bus excursions to regional sights that are hard to reach *sans* car; see "Tours of Provence," later in this chapter).

By Car: The region is made-to-order for a car. The yellow Michelin Local maps #332 and #340 are a godsend. I've described key sights and a variety of full-day drives deep into the countryside. Be wary of thieves: Park only in well-monitored spaces and leave nothing valuable in your car.

Avignon (pop. 100,000) is a headache for drivers; Arles (pop. 35,000) is easier. Les Baux and St. Rémy work well from Arles or Avignon (or vice versa). Nîmes and the Pont du Gard are a short hop west of Avignon and on the way to or from Languedoc for drivers. The town of Orange ties in tidily with a trip to the Côtes du Rhône villages and with destinations farther north. If you're heading north from Provence, consider a three-hour detour through the spectacular Ardèche Gorges (see page 144 of the Orange and the Côtes du Rhône chapter). The Luberon villages are about halfway between Arles or Avignon and Aix-en-Provence (consider basing yourself in little Lourmarin for day trips to Aix-en-Provence), and if you're continuing on to the Riviera, be lured into the Grand Canyon du Verdon detour (see page 354 in the Inland Riviera chapter). Most drivers will prefer exploring congested Marseille by train from Cassis or Aix-en-Provence (both towns have easy parking at their train stations and frequent trains or buses to the center of Marseille).

Tours of Provence

It's possible to take half-day or full-day excursions to most of the sights described in this book (easiest from Avignon, but doable from Arles). Local TIs have brochures on all these excursions and can help you make a reservation. Here are several options (the first two are best):

Wine Safari—Dutchman Mike Rijken runs a one-man show, taking travelers through the region he adopted 20 years ago. Mike came to France to train as a chef, later became a wine steward, and has now found his calling as a driver/guide. His English is fluent, and while his focus is wine and wine villages, Mike knows the region thoroughly and is a good teacher of its history (€45/half-day, €90/day, priced per person; tel. 04 90 35 59 21, mobile 06 19 29 50 81, www.winesafari.net, mikeswinesafari@wanadoo.fr).

Taxi des Oliviers—Friendly Frenchman Roland Vanove offers tours with English commentary. His air-conditioned minivan has room for up to eight people (the same price regardless of the number of passengers). He'll take you wherever you like in his native Provence, or to the Riviera (no preset itineraries). Roland's services are a boon for carless visitors wanting to explore the Luberon and the Côtes du Rhône villages near Vaison la Romaine. He'll happily shuttle bikers to or from their destination, allowing rides to areas farther afield (€280/day, ask about shuttle-trip rates, best to contact by phone, tel. 06 80 75 40 90, taxidesoliviers@wanadoo.fr).

Visit Provence—This tour company, based in Avignon, offers a good variety of guided tours to most destinations covered in this book. They have eight-seat minivans and English commentary (about €50/half-day, €100/day; they'll pick you up at your hotel in Avignon). Their Hop On/Off tour is a clever service, with a bus circulating between Avignon, Pont du Gard, Les Baux, and St. Rémy several times a day, allowing travelers to linger at a sight—

and catch the next bus—if they prefer (€60, valid for two days, June–Sept). Other day-trip destinations vary, but may include Aix-en-Provence, Cassis, and Marseille (last tour of the day allows a drop-off at the TGV station in Marseille, saving money and time if you're headed to the Riviera next). Not all tours include entry fees for sights, but reservations are required for all. Ask about their cheaper big-bus excursions, or consider hiring a van and driver for your own private use (plan on €210/half-day, €400/day, tel. 04 90 14 70 00, check website for current destinations, www.provence-reservation.com).

Lieutaud—This company operates cheap, unguided big-bus excursions from Avignon to many hard-to-reach places at a fraction of the price you'd pay for a taxi (admission fees not included). Different itineraries are available each day, and these can change with the season. Trips often include Pont du Gard (€20/half-day, 3/week) and Les Baux and the Alpilles Mountains (€22/half-day, 2/week, tel. 04 90 86 36 75, www.cars-lieutaud.fr).

Provence's Cuisine Scene

Provence has been called France's "garden market," stressing farm-fresh food (vegetables, fruit, and meats) prepared in a simple way, and meant to be savored with family and friends. Grilled foods are typical, as are dishes derived from lengthy simmering—in part a reflection of long days spent in the fields. Colorful and lively, Provençal cuisine hammers the senses with an extravagant use (by French standards) of garlic, olive oil, and herbs. Order anything *à la provençale,* and you'll be rewarded with aromatic food heightened by rich and pungent sauces. Thanks to the proximity of the Riviera, many seafood dishes show up on Provençal menus (see "The Riviera's Cuisine Scene," page 234).

Unlike other French regional cuisines, the food of Provence is inviting for nibblers. Appetizers (hors d'oeuvres) often consist of

bowls of olives (look for the plump and full-flavored black *tanche* or the green, buttery *picholine*), as well as plates of fresh vegetables served with lusty sauces ready for dipping. These same sauces adorn dishes of hard-boiled eggs, fish, or meat. Look for tapenade, a paste of pureed olives, capers, anchovies, herbs, and sometimes tuna. True anchovy-lovers seek out *anchoïade* (a spread of garlic, anchovy, and parsley) or *bagna caouda* (warm sauce of anchovies and melted butter or olive oil).

Aioli—a rich, garlicky mayonnaise spread over vegetables, potatoes, fish, or whatever—is another Provençal favorite. In the summertime, entire village festivals celebrate this sauce. Look for signs announcing *aioli monstre* (literally "monster aioli"), and for a few euros, dive into a very local eating experience (pass the breath mints, please).

Despite the heat, soup is a favorite in Provence. Look for *soupe au pistou*, a thin yet flavorful vegetable soup with a sauce (called *pistou*) of basil, garlic, and cheese—pesto minus the pine nuts. Or try *soupe à l'ail* (garlic soup). For seafood soups, see "The Riviera's Cuisine Scene," page 234.

Provençal main courses venerate fresh vegetables and meats (eat seafood on the Riviera and meat in Provence). Ratatouille is a mixture of Provençal vegetables (eggplant, zucchini, onions, and peppers are the usual suspects) in a thick, herb-flavored tomato sauce. It's readily found in charcuteries and often served at room temperature, making it the perfect picnic food. Ratatouille veggies also show up on their own, stuffed and served in spicy sauces. Look for *aubergines* (eggplants), *tomates* (tomatoes), *poivrons* (sweet peppers), and *courgettes* (zucchini—especially *fleurs de courgettes*, stuffed and batter-fried zucchini flowers). *Tians* are gratin-like vegetable dishes named for the deep terra-cotta dish in which they are cooked and served. *Artichauts à la barigoule* are stuffed artichokes flavored with garlic, ham, and herbs (*barigoule* is from the Provençal word for thyme, *farigoule*). Also look for *riz de Camargue*—the reddish, chewy, nutty-tasting rice that has taken over the Camargue area, which is otherwise useless for agriculture.

The famous herbs of Provence influence food long before it's cooked. The locally renowned lambs of the *garrigue* (shrub-covered hills), as well as rabbits and other small edible beasts in Provence, dine on wild herbs and spicy shrubs—essentially preseasoning their delicate meat. Look for lamb (*agneau*, most often leg of lamb, *gigot d'agneau*), grilled and served no-frills, or the delicious *lapin à la provençale*—rabbit served with garlic, mustard, tomatoes, and herbs in white wine. Locals have a curious passion for quail *(caille)*. These tiny, bony birds are often grilled and served with any variety of sauces, including sauces sweetened with Provençal cherries or honey and lavender. *Daube*, named for the traditional cooking vessel *daubière*, is generally beef simmered until it is spoon-tender and served with noodles. *Taureau* (bull's meat), usually raised in the marshy Camargue, melts in your mouth.

There are a few dishes to avoid: *Pieds et paquets* is a scary dish of sheep's feet and tripe (no amount of Provençal sauce can hide the flavor here). *Tourte de blettes* is a confused "pie" made with Swiss chard; both savory and sweet, it can't decide whether it should be a first course or dessert (it shows up as both).

Eat goat cheese *(fromage de chèvre)* in Provence. Look for *banon à la feuille* (dipped in *eau-de-vie* to kill bad mold, then wrapped in a chestnut leaf), spicy *picodon* (the name means "spicy" in the old language), or the fresh, creamy *brousse du Rove* (often served mixed with cream and sugar for dessert). On Provençal cheese platters, you'll often find small rounds of bite-size *chèvres*, each flavored with a different herb or spice—and some even rolled in chopped garlic (more breath mints, please).

Desserts tend to be fairly light and fruit-filled, or traditionally French. Look for fresh tarts made with seasonal fruit, Cavaillon melons (served cut in half with a trickle of the sweet Rhône wine Beaumes de Venise), and ice cream or sorbet sweetened with honey and flavored with various herbs such as lavender, thyme, or rosemary.

Wines of Provence

Provence was the first area in France to be planted with grapes, in about 600 B.C., by the Greeks. Romans built on what the Greeks started, realizing even back then that Provence had an ideal climate for growing wine: mild winters and long, warm summers (but not too hot—thanks to the cooling winds). This sun-baked, wine-happy region offers Americans a chance to sample wines blended from several grapes—resulting in flavors unlike anything we get at home (yes, we have good Cabernet Sauvignons, Merlots, and Pinot Noirs, but Rhône wines are new to most of us). Provence's shorts-and-T-shirt climate and abundance of hearty, reasonably priced wines make for an enjoyable experience, particularly if you're willing to learn. See "Provençal Wine-Tasting 101," page 40, for the basics.

In France, wine production is strictly controlled by the government to preserve the overall quality. This obligates vintners to use specified grapes that grow best in that region, and to follow certain wine-growing procedures. The *Appellation d'Origine Controlée* (AOC) label found on many bottles is the government's seal of approval when a wine meets a series of requirements. The type and percentages of grapes used, vinification methods, and taste are all controlled and verified.

Provençal vintners can blend from 13 different grapes—unique in France. (In Burgundy and Alsace, only one grape variety is used for each wine—so Pinot Noir, Chardonnay, Riesling, Tokay, and Pinot Gris are each 100 percent from that grape.) This blending allows Provençal winemakers great range in personalizing their wine. For reds, most vintners blend half a dozen or so different grapes. The most prevalent grapes are Grenache, Mourvèdre, Syrah, Carignan, and Cinsault. For whites, Grenache-Blanc, Roussanne, Marsanne, Bourboulenc, and Clairette grapes are most common.

There are three primary growing areas in Provence: Côtes

du Rhône, Côtes de Provence, and Côteaux d'Aix-en-Provence. A few wines are also grown along the Provençal Mediterranean coast. All regions produce rich, fruity reds and dry, fresh rosés. Only about 5 percent of wine produced here is white (and most Provençal whites are unexceptional).

In Provence, I drink rosé instead of white. Don't confuse these rosés with the insipid blush stuff found in the US; French rosé is often crisp and fruity, a perfect match to the hot days and Mediterranean cuisine. Rosé wines are made from red grapes whose juice is white, until crushed with red grape skins. The white juice is left in contact with the dark-red skins just long enough to produce the pinkish color (usually a few hours). Rosés from Tavel (20 min northeast of Avignon) are the most respected, but you'll find many good producers at affordable prices in other areas as well. Americans unaccustomed to drinking rosés should give them a try here.

Provençal Wine-Tasting 101

The American wine-tasting experience (I'm thinking Napa Valley) is generally informal, chatty, and entrepreneurial (baseball caps and golf shirts with logos). Although Provençal vintners are friendly, welcoming, and more easygoing than in other parts of France, it's a more serious, wine-focused experience—without the distractions of the marketing at US vineyards. Visit several private wineries or stop by a *cave coopérative*—an excellent opportunity to taste wines from a number of local vintners in a single, less intimidating setting.

Provençal winemakers are happy to work with you...*if* they can figure out what you want. When you enter a winery, it helps to know what you like (drier or sweeter, lighter or full-bodied, fruity or more tannic, and so on). The people serving you may know those words in English, but you're better off knowing and using the key words in French (see "French Wine Lingo" sidebar).

For reds, you'll be asked if you want to taste younger wines that still need maturing or older wines, ready to drink now. (Whites and rosés are always ready to drink.) The French like to sample younger wines and determine how they will taste in a few years, allowing them to buy at cheaper prices and stash the bottles in their cellars. Americans want it now—for today's picnic. While many Americans like a big, full-bodied wine, most French tend to prefer more subtle flavors. They judge a wine by virtue of what food it would go well with—and a big, oaky wine would overwhelm most French cuisine.

Remember that the vintner is hoping that you'll buy at least a bottle or two. If you don't buy, you may be asked to pay a minimal fee for the tasting. They know that Americans can't take much

French Wine Lingo

Here are the steps you should follow when entering any wine-tasting:

1. Greetings, Sir/Madam: *Bonjour, Monsieur/Madame.*

2. We would like to taste a few wines: *Nous voudrions déguster quelques vins.* (noo voo-dree-ohn day-goo-stay kehl-kuh van)

3. We want a wine that is _____ and _____: *Nous voudrions un vin _____ et _____.* (noo voo-dree-ohn uhn van _____ ay _____)

Fill in the blanks with your favorites from this list:

English	French	Pronounced
wine	*vin*	van
red	*rouge*	roozh
white	*blanc*	blahn
rosé	*rosé*	roh-zay
light	*léger*	lay-zhay
full-bodied, heavy	*robuste*	roh-boost
fruity	*fruité*	frwee-tay
sweet*	*doux*	doo
tannic	*tannique*	tah-neek
jammy	*confituré*	koh-fee-tuh-ray
fine	*fin, avec finesse*	fan, ah-vehk fee-nehs
ready to drink (mature)	*prêt à boire*	preh ah bwar
not ready to drink	*fermé*	fair-may
oaky	*goût de la chêne*	goo duh lah sheh-nuh
from old vines	*de vieille vignes*	duh vee-yay-ee veen-yah
sparkling	*pétillant*	pay-tee-yahn

*With the exception of the fortified white Beaumes de Venise, few Provençal wines would be considered "sweet."

wine with them, and they don't expect to make a big sale, but they do hope you'll look for their wines in the US. Some of the places I list will ship your purchase home—ask.

Côtes du Rhône Wines

The Côtes du Rhône, which follows the Rhône River from just south of Lyon to near Avignon, is the king of Provence wines. Our focus is on the southern, Provençal section, roughly from Vaison la Romaine to Avignon (though wine-lovers should take note of the big, complex reds found in the northern Rhône wines of St. Joseph, Hermitage, and Cornas, as well as the seductive white of Condrieu). The wines of the southern Rhône are consistently good—and sometimes exceptional. The reds are full-bodied, rosés are dry and fruity, and whites are dry and fragrant, often with hints of flowers. Côtes du Rhône whites aren't nearly as good as

the reds, though the rosés are refreshing and ideal for lunch on the terrace. For more on this wine region, including a self-guided driving tour of local villages and vintners, see the Côtes du Rhône chapter.

Many sub-areas of the southern Côtes du Rhône are recognized as producing distinctly good wines, and have been awarded their own *appellations* (like Châteauneuf-du-Pape, Gigondas, Beaumes de Venise, Côtes de Ventoux, Tavel, and Côtes du Luberon). Wines are often named for the villages that produce them. Those made from grapes coming from several local vintners are called "Côtes du Rhône Villages" and are less expensive because the grapes can come from a larger area.

Here's a summary of what you might find on a Côtes du Rhône *carte des vins* (wine list):

Châteauneuf-du-Pape: Wines from this famous village are almost all reds (often blends; the most dominant grapes are typically Grenache, Mourvèdre, and Syrah). These wines have a velvety quality and can be spicy, with flavors of licorice and prunes. Châteauneuf-du-Pape wines merit lengthy aging. Considered among the best producers are Château de Beaucastel, Le Vieux Télégraphe, and Château la Nerthe.

Gigondas: These wines have many qualities of Châteauneuf-du-Pape, but remain lesser known and therefore cheaper. Gigondas red wines are spicy, meaty, and can be pretty tannic. Again, aging is necessary to bring out the full qualities of the wine. Look for

On the Wine Label

appellation	area in which a wine's grapes are grown
bouchonné	"corked" (spoiled from a bad cork)
bouquet	bouquet (smell when first opened)
cave	cellar
cépage	grape variety (Syrah, Chardonnay, etc.)
côte, côteau	hillside or slope
domaine	wine estate
étiquette	label
fût, tonneau	wine barrel
grand vin	excellent wine
millésimé	wine from a given year
mis en bouteille au château/à la domaine	estate-bottled (bottled where it was made)
vin de table	table wine (can be a blend of several wines)
vin du pays	wine from a given area (a step up from *vin de table*)

Domaine du Terme, Château de Montmirail, or Domaine de Coyeux for good quality.

Beaumes de Venise: While reds from this village are rich and flavorful, Beaumes de Venise is most famous for its Muscat—a sweet, fragrant wine often served as an apéritif or with dessert. It often has flavors of apricots and peaches, and it should be consumed within two years of bottling. Try Domaine de Coyeux, Domaine de Durban, and Château Redortier.

Rasteau: This village sits across the valley from Gigondas and shares many of its qualities at lesser prices. Rasteau makes fine rosés, robust (at times "rough") and fruity reds, and a naturally sweet wine (Vin Doux Naturel). Their Côtes du Rhône Villages can be excellent. The cooperative in Rasteau is good, though you should not miss a visit to Domaine des Girasols (see page 152).

Sablet: This village lies down in the valley below Gigondas and makes decent, fruity, and inexpensive reds and rosés.

Tavel: The queen of French rosés is 15 minutes northwest of Avignon, close to the Pont du Gard. Tavel produces a rosé that is dry, crisp, higher in alcohol, and more full-bodied than other rosés from the region. Look for any rosé from Tavel.

Côtes de Provence Wines

The lesser-known vineyards of the Côtes de Provence run east from Aix-en-Provence almost to St-Tropez. Many wines from this area are sold in an unusual curvy bottle (which makes me feel tipsy before I've had a sip). Typical grapes are Cinsault, Mourvèdre, Grenache, Carignan, and a little Cabernet Sauvignon and Syrah. The wines are commonly full-bodied and fruity, and are meant to be drunk when they're young. It's common to chill reds from this area—and they can be delicious. They cost less than Côtes du Rhônes, and have similar characteristics. But the region is most famous for its "big" rosés that can be served with meat and garlic dishes (rosé accounts for 60 percent of production).

For one-stop shopping, make a point to find the superb **La Maison des Vins Côtes de Provence** on RN-7 in Les Arcs-sur-Argens (a few minutes north of the A-8 autoroute, about half-way between Aix-en-Provence and Nice). This English-speaking wine shop and tasting center represents hundreds of producers and sells their wines at vineyard prices, offering free tastings of up to 16 wines (June–Oct daily 10:00–19:00; Nov–May Mon–Sat 10:00–18:00, closed Sun; tel. 04 94 99 50 20, www.caveaucp.fr).

Côteaux d'Aix-en-Provence Wines

This large wine region, between Les Baux and Aix-en-Provence, produces some interesting reds, whites, and rosés. Commonly used grapes are the same as in Côtes de Provence, though several producers (mainly around Les Baux) use a higher concentration of Cabernet Sauvignon that helps distinguish their wines.

Provençal Mediterranean Wines

Barely east of Marseille, Cassis and Bandol sit side by side, over-looking the Mediterranean. Though very close together, they are technically designated as separate wine-growing areas, given the distinctive nature of their wines. Cassis is one of France's small-est wine regions and is known for its strong, fresh, and very dry whites—arguably the best in Provence. Bandol is known for its luscious, velvety reds, made primarily from the Mourvèdre grape—and is Rick Steves' favorite.

ARLES

By helping Julius Caesar defeat Marseille, Arles (pronounced "arl") earned the imperial nod and was made an important port city. With the first bridge over the Rhône River, Arles was a key stop on the Roman road from Italy to Spain, the Via Domitia. After reigning as the seat of an important archbishop and a trading center for centuries, the city became a sleepy backwater of little importance in the 1700s. Vincent van Gogh settled here a hundred years ago, but left only a chunk of his ear (now gone). American bombers destroyed much of Arles in World War II as the townsfolk hid out in its underground Roman galleries. But today Arles thrives again, with its evocative Roman ruins, an eclectic assortment of museums, made-for-ice-cream pedestrian zones, and squares that play hide-and-seek with visitors.

ORIENTATION

Arles faces the Mediterranean, turning its back on Paris. While the town is built along the Rhône, it completely ignores the river, which was the part of Arles most damaged by Allied bombers in World War II (and is therefore the least appealing today).

Landmarks hide in Arles' medieval tangle of narrow, winding streets. Virtually everything is close—but first-time visitors can walk forever to get there. Hotels have good, free city maps, and Arles provides helpful street-corner signs that point you toward sights and hotels. Racing cars enjoy Arles' medieval lanes, turning sidewalks into tightropes and pedestrians into leaping targets.

Tourist Information

The **main TI** is on the ring road boulevard des Lices, at esplanade Charles de Gaulle (April–Sept daily 9:00–18:45; Oct–March

Mon–Sat 9:00–16:45, Sun 10:00–13:00; tel. 04 90 18 41 20, www .arlestourisme.com). There's also a **train station TI** (Mon–Fri 9:00–13:00 & 14:00–16:45, closed Sat–Sun).

Pick up the city map with current museum prices and hours, note the bus schedules (in books), and get English information on nearby destinations such as the Camargue wildlife area (described in the next chapter). Ask about "bullgames" (Provence's more humane version of bullfights—see "Events in Arles," page 60) and walking tours of Arles. If you're a van Gogh fan, buy the €1 brochure locating his "easels" (explained on page 56). Both TIs charge €1 to reserve hotel rooms (you'll pay a small fraction of the room price here, and the rest at the hotel).

Arrival in Arles

By Train: The train station is on the river, a 10-minute walk from the town center (baggage storage nearby—see "Helpful Hints," below). Before heading into town, get what you need at the train station TI (see above).

To reach the town center, turn left out of the train station, or take bus #3 from the shelter directly across from the station (2/hr, €0.80, buy ticket from driver). Taxis generally wait out front, but if you don't see any, call the posted telephone numbers (rates are fixed, allow about €9 to any of my recommended hotels).

By Bus: The central Centre-Ville bus station is a few blocks below the main TI, located on the ring road at 16–24 boulevard Georges Clemenceau.

By Car: Most hotels have nearby parking—ask for detailed directions. Arles' only parking structure is Parking des Lices, near the TI on boulevard des Lices (€7/24 hours). Otherwise, follow signs to *Centre-Ville*, then *Gare SNCF* (train station). You'll come to a big roundabout (place Lamartine) with a Monoprix department store to the right. You can park along the city wall or in nearby lots; pay attention to *No Parking* signs on Wednesday and Saturday until 13:00 (violators are towed to make way for Arles' huge outdoor produce markets). Theft is a big problem; leave nothing in your car, and trust your hotelier's advice on where to park. From place Lamartine, walk into the city between the two stumpy towers. From here, the hotels I list are no more than a 10-minute walk away.

Helpful Hints

Market Days: The big markets are on Wednesdays and Saturdays. For all the details, see page 60.

Internet Access: Arles has no reliable Internet cafés—ask at the TI.

Baggage Storage and Bike Rental: Helpful Patrick will store your bags for €2 each at **Arles VAE,** located across from the

Arles at a Glance

▲▲▲**Roman Arena** This big amphitheater, once used by gladiators, today hosts summer "bullgames" and occasional bullfights. **Hours:** Daily May–Sept 9:00–18:00, March–April and Oct 9:00–17:30, Nov–Feb 10:00–16:30.

▲▲**Ancient History Museum** Filled with models and sculptures, this is Roman Arles 101. **Hours:** Daily April–Oct 9:00–19:00, Nov–March 10:00–17:00.

▲▲**Forum Square** Lively, café-crammed square that was once the Roman forum. **Hours:** Always open.

▲▲**St. Trophime Church and Cloisters** Church with exquisite Romanesque entrance. **Hours:** Church open daily April–Sept 9:00–12:00 & 14:00–18:30, Oct–March 9:00–12:00 & 14:00–17:00; cloisters open daily May–Sept 9:00–18:00, March–April and Oct 9:00–13:00 & 14:00–17:30, Nov–Feb 10:00–11:30 & 14:00–16:30.

▲▲**Fondation Van Gogh** Small gallery with works by major contemporary artists paying homage to van Gogh (but no Vincent originals). **Hours:** April–June daily 10:00–18:00, July–Sept daily 10:00–19:00, Oct–March Tue–Sun 11:00–17:00, closed Mon.

▲**Arlaten Folk Museum** Shares the treasures and pleasures of Provençal life from the 18th and 19th centuries. **Hours:** June–Aug daily 9:00–13:00 & 14:00–18:30, Sept–May Tue–Sun 9:00–12:00 & 14:00–17:30, closed Mon.

Classical Theater Ruined Roman theater, recently restored and still used for events. **Hours:** Daily May–Sept 9:00–18:00, March–April and Oct 9:00–13:00 & 14:00–17:30, Nov–Feb 10:00–11:30 & 14:00–16:30.

Réattu Museum Decent, mostly modern art collection in a fine 15th-century mansion. **Hours:** Daily July–Aug 10:00–19:00, March–June and Sept–Nov 10:00–12:30 & 14:00–18:30, Dec–Feb 13:00–18:00.

train station (Easter–Oct Mon–Sat 9:00–19:00, closed Sun except July–Aug, Feb–Easter and Nov–Dec Tue–Sat 9:00–18:00, closed Sun–Mon, closed Jan, tel. 04 90 43 33 14, www .arles-vae.com). Patrick also rents bikes for cheap (€5/4 hrs, €10/day). Ask about his electric bikes—handy on windy days. From Arles, you can ride to Les Baux (20 miles round-trip, very steep climb) or into the Camargue (40 miles round-trip, forget it in the wind)—provided you're in great shape.

Laundry: There's a launderette at 12 rue Portagnel (daily 7:00–21:00, you can stay later to finish if you're already inside, English instructions).

Car Rental: Avis is at the train station (tel. 04 90 96 82 42), and **Europcar** and **Hertz** are downtown (2 bis avenue Victor Hugo, Europcar tel. 04 90 93 23 24, Hertz tel. 04 90 96 75 23).

Local Guide: Charming Jacqueline Neujean, an excellent guide, knows Arles and nearby sights intimately and loves her work (€90/2 hrs, tel. 04 90 98 47 51).

Language and Cooking Courses: Food- or language-lovers enjoy classes offered by outgoing American (and Arles resident) Madeleine Vedel and her French husband, Eric. In addition to renting out rooms (see Maison d'Hôtes en Provence under "Sleeping," page 62), they present a wide range of cooking and language-learning experiences: Pick wild asparagus, hunt mushrooms, harvest grapes at an organic winery, or make chocolate. They offer a summer course for teenagers, and have a great variety of adult classes throughout the year (www .cuisineprovencale.com).

Public Pools: Arles has three public pools (indoor and outdoor). Ask at the TI or your hotel.

Boules: The local "*boul*ing alley" is by the river on place Lamartine. After their afternoon naps, the old boys congregate here for a game of *pétanque*—it's fun to watch (see page 174 for details on this popular local pastime).

Getting Around Arles

In this flat city, everything's within walking distance. Only the Ancient History Museum requires a long walk (take a taxi for €9, or a public bus for €0.80—details in "Getting There," page 50). The elevated riverside promenade provides Rhône views and a direct route to the Ancient History Museum (to the southwest) and the train and bus stations (to the northeast). Keep your head up for *Starry Night* memories, but eyes down for decorations by dogs with poorly trained owners.

Arles' **taxis** charge a set fee of about €9, but nothing except the Ancient History Museum is worth a taxi ride. To call a cab, dial 04 90 96 90 03.

Arles

SIGHTS

The worthwhile **Monument Pass** *(le pass monuments)* covers almost all of Arles' sights (adults-€13.50, under 18-€12, sold at each sight except the Arlaten Folk Museum; Fondation Van Gogh discounted, but not fully covered). The less-tempting €9 *Circuit Romain* ticket covers Arles' four Roman sights, but not the Ancient History Museum. With no pass, you'll pay €3–5.50 per sight. While any sight is worth a few minutes, many aren't worth the individual admission.

Start at the Ancient History Museum for a helpful overview (drivers should try to do this museum on their way into Arles), then dive into the city-center sights. Remember, many sights stop selling tickets 30–60 minutes before closing (both before lunch and at the end of the day).

▲▲Ancient History Museum
(Musée de l'Arles et de la Provence Antiques)

Begin your town visit here—it's Roman Arles 101. Located on the site of the Roman chariot racecourse (the arc of which is built

into the parking lot), this air-conditioned, all-on-one-floor museum is just west of central Arles along the river. Models and original sculptures (with almost no English translations) re-create the Roman city, making workaday life and culture easier to imagine.

You're greeted by an impressive row of pagan and early-Christian sarcophagi (from the second to fifth centuries). These would have lined the Via Aurelia outside the town wall. In the early days of the Church, Jesus was often portrayed beardless and as the good shepherd, with a lamb over his shoulder (see relief at end of ramp, #41).

Next, you'll find models of every Roman structure in (and

near) Arles. These are the high-light for me, as they breathe life into buildings as they looked 2,000 years ago. Find the Forum (still the center of town, though only two columns survive today); the pontoon bridge (over the widest, and therefore slowest, part of the river); the Arena (with its movable stadium

Arles

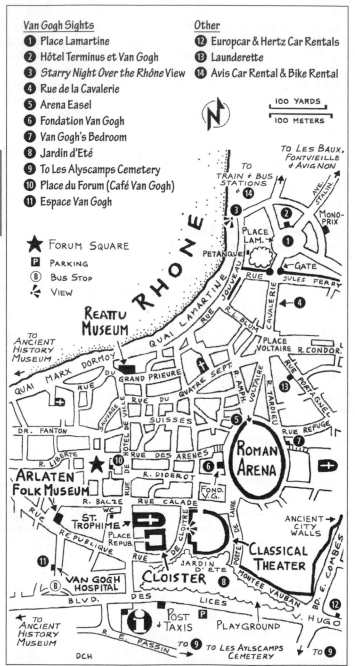

Van Gogh Sights
1. Place Lamartine
2. Hôtel Terminus et Van Gogh
3. *Starry Night Over the Rhône* View
4. Rue de la Cavalerie
5. Arena Easel
6. Fondation Van Gogh
7. Van Gogh's Bedroom
8. Jardin d'Eté
9. To Les Alyscamps Cemetery
10. Place du Forum (Café Van Gogh)
11. Espace Van Gogh

Other
12. Europcar & Hertz Car Rentals
13. Launderette
14. Avis Car Rental & Bike Rental

100 YARDS

100 METERS

★ FORUM SQUARE
P PARKING
B BUS STOP
↙ VIEW

TO LES BAUX, FONTVIEILLE & AVIGNON

TO TRAIN & BUS STATIONS

AVE. STALIN.

MONOPRIX

PLACE LAM.

GATE

PETANQUE

RUE JULES FERRY

RHONE

REATTU MUSEUM

QUAI LAMARTINE

RUE JOUVEAU

RUE R. BLUM

RUE DE LA CAVALERIE

PLACE VOLTAIRE

R. CONDOR.

TO ANCIENT HISTORY MUSEUM

QUAI MARX DORMOY

RUE DU GRAND PRIEURE

RUE DU QUATRE SEPT.

RUE DE L'HOTEL DE VILLE

SUISSES

RUE DES ARENES

R. DIDEROT

RUE AMPH.

VOLTAIRE

RUE TARDIEU

RUE PORTAGNEL

RUE REFUGE

R. SAUVAGE

DR. FANTON

R. LIBERTE

ARLATEN FOLK MUSEUM

ROMAN ARENA

FOND. V.G.

RUE BALZE

RUE CALADE

WC

ST. TROPHIME

PLACE REPUB.

RUE DE CLOITRE

ANCIENT CITY WALLS

PORTE DE LAURE

CLASSICAL THEATER

RUE REPUBLIQUE

VAN GOGH HOSPITAL

CLOISTER

JARDIN D'ETE

MONTEE VAUBAN

BD. E. COMBES

BLVD. DES LICES

PLAYGROUND

V. HUGO

TO ANCIENT HISTORY MUSEUM

R. E. FASSIN

POST & TAXIS

TO 9 TO LES AYLSCAMPS CEMETERY

TO 9

DCH

cover, which sheltered spectators from sun or rain); and the Circus, or chariot racecourse. While long gone, the racecourse must have been like Rome's Circus Maximus in its day—its obelisk is now the centerpiece of Arles' place de la République.

Finally, check out the 3-D model of the aqueduct of Barbegal, with its 16 waterwheels and eight grain mills cascading down a nearby hillside (well worth a side-trip if you have a car—see "Sights Between Les Baux and Arles," page 75).

The model of the Roman city shows that an emphasis on sports—with the Arena and huge stadium—is not unique to modern America. It also illustrates how little Arles seems to have changed over two millennia—with warehouses still on the opposite side of the river and houses clustered around the city center.

All of the museum's statues are original, except for the greatest—the *Venus of Arles*, which Louis XIV took a liking to and had moved to Versailles. It's now in the Louvre—and, as locals say, "When it's in Paris...bye-bye." Jewelry, fine metal and glass artifacts, and well-crafted mosaic floors make it clear that Roman Arles was a city of art and culture.

Cost, Hours, Location: €5.50, covered by Monument Pass, daily April–Oct 9:00–19:00, Nov–March 10:00–17:00, presqu'île du Cirque Romain.

Information: Ask for the English booklet, which provides some background on the collection, as well as whether there are any free English tours (usually daily July–Sept at 17:00, 90 min). Tel. 04 90 18 88 88, www.arles-antique.cg13.fr.

Getting There: To reach the museum by **foot** from the city center (a 25-min walk), turn left at the river and take the riverside path to the big, modern building just past the new bridge. The **taxi** ride costs €9 (museum can call a taxi for your return). **Bus #1** gets you within a five-minute walk (€0.80, 3/hr, daily except Sun). Catch the bus in Arles on boulevard des Lices, then get off at the Musée de l'Arles Antique stop and follow the signs (to your left as you step off the bus).

In Central Arles

Ideally, visit these sights in the order listed below. I've included some walking directions to connect the dots.

▲▲**Forum Square (Place du Forum)**—Named for the Roman forum that once stood here, this square was the political and religious center of Roman Arles. Still lively, this café-crammed square is a local watering hole and popular for a *pastis* (see "Eating," page 64). The bistros on the square, while no place for a fine dinner, can put together a good-enough salad or *plat du jour*—and when you sprinkle on the ambience, that's €10 well spent.

At the corner of Grand Hôtel Nord-Pinus, a plaque shows

how the Romans built a foundation of galleries to make the main square level. The two columns are all that survive of a temple. Steps leading to the entrance are buried (the Roman street level was about 20 feet below you).

The statue on the square is of **Frédéric Mistral** (1830–1914). This popular poet, who wrote in the local dialect rather than in French, was a champion of Provençal culture. After receiving the Nobel Prize in Literature in 1904, Mistral used his prize money to preserve and display the folk identity of Provence. He founded the regional folk museum (see "Arlaten Folk Museum," page 55) at a time when France was rapidly centralizing. (The local mistral wind—literally, "master"—has nothing to do with his name.)

The **bright-yellow café**—called Café Van Gogh today, but previously named Café la Nuit—is famous as the subject of one of Vincent van Gogh's most famous works in Arles. While his painting showed the café in a brilliant yellow from the glow of gas lamps, the facade was bare limestone, just like the other cafés on this square. The café's current owners have painted it to match van Gogh's version...and to cash in on the Vincent-crazed hordes who pay too much to eat or drink here.

• *Walk a block to rue du Hôtel de Ville, turn right, and you'll find the big...*

Republic Square (Place de la République)—This square used to be called "place Royale"...until the French Revolution. The obelisk was the centerpiece of Arles' Roman Circus. The lions at its base are the symbol of the city, whose slogan is (roughly) "the gentle lion." Find a seat and watch the peasants—pilgrims, locals, and street musicians. There's nothing new about this scene.

• *Overlooking this square is...*

▲▲**St. Trophime Church**—Named after a third-century bishop of Arles and located on a large square, this church sports the finest Romanesque main entrance (west portal) I've seen anywhere.

Like a Roman triumphal arch, the church facade trumpets the promise of Judgment Day. The tympanum (the semicircular area above the door) is filled with Christian symbolism. Christ sits in majesty, surrounded by symbols of the four evangelists: Matthew (the winged man), Mark (the winged lion), Luke (the ox), and John (the eagle). The 12 apostles are lined up below Jesus. It's Judgment Day...some are saved and others aren't. Notice the condemned (on the right)—a chain gang doing a sad bunny-hop over the fires of hell. For them, the tune trumpeted by the three angels above

Christ is not a happy one. Below the chain gang, St. Stephen is being stoned to death, with his soul leaving through his mouth and instantly being welcomed by angels. Ride the exquisite detail back to a simpler age. In an illiterate medieval world, long before the vivid images of our Technicolor time, this was a neon billboard over the town square.

There's no charge to enter the church. Just inside the door on the right, a handy chart locates the interior highlights and helps explain the carvings you just saw on the tympanum.

The tall, 12th-century Romanesque nave is decorated by a set of tapestries showing scenes from the life of Mary (17th-century, from French town of Aubusson). Immediately to the left of the entry is a chapel built on an early-Christian sarcophagus from Roman Arles (from about A.D. 300). The heads were lopped off during the French Revolution. On the right side (a dark niche, cut into the wall), the three Magi give gifts to the baby Jesus, and a frieze below shows the flight to Egypt. Amble around the Gothic apse. Just to the left of the high altar, check out the relic chapel—with its fine golden boxes that hold long-venerated bones of obscure saints. This church is a stop on the ancient pilgrimage route to Santiago de Compostela in northwest Spain. For 800 years, pilgrims on their way to Santiago have paused here...and they still do today. As you leave, notice the modern-day pilgrimages advertised on the far right near the church's entry (church open daily April–Sept 9:00–12:00 & 14:00–18:30, Oct–March 9:00–12:00 & 14:00–17:00).

• *Leaving the church, turn left, then left again through a courtyard to enter the cloisters.*

The adjacent **cloisters** are interesting, with many small columns that were scavenged from the ancient Roman theater. Enjoy the sculpted capitals, the rounded 12th-century Romanesque arches, and the pointed 14th-century Gothic ones. On the second floor, you'll walk an angled rooftop designed to catch rainwater—notice the slanted gutter that channeled the water into a cistern (€3.50, daily May–Sept 9:00–18:00, March–April and Oct 9:00–13:00 & 14:00–17:30, Nov–Feb 10:00–11:30 & 14:00–16:30).

• *To get to the next sight (the Classical Theater), face the church, walk left, then take the first right on rue de la Calade.*

Classical Theater (Théâtre Antique)—This first-century B.C. Roman theater once seated 10,000. In the Middle Ages, it served as a convenient town quarry—precious little of the original theater survives (though considerable effort is ongoing to rebuild sections of the seating area).

Walk to a center aisle and pull up a stone seat. To appreciate its original size, look to the upper-left side of the tower and find the protrusion that supported the highest of three seating levels. Today,

3,000 can attend events here. Two lonely Corinthian columns look out from the stage over the audience. The orchestra section is defined by a semicircular pattern in the stone. Stepping up onto the left side of the stage, look down to the slender channel that allowed the curtain to  disappear below, like magic. Go backstage and browse through broken bits of Rome, and loop back to the entry behind the grass (€3, covered by Monument Pass, daily May–Sept 9:00–18:00, March–April and Oct 9:00–13:00 & 14:00–17:30, Nov–Feb 10:00–11:30 & 14:00–16:30). For more on Roman theaters, see page 132 of the Orange chapter. Budget travelers can peek over the fence from rue du Cloître, and see just about everything for free.

• *A block uphill is the...*

▲▲▲**Roman Arena (Amphithéâtre)**—Nearly 2,000 years ago, gladiators fought wild animals here to the delight of 20,000 screaming fans. Today, local daredevils still fight wild animals here—"bullgame" posters around the Arena advertise upcoming spectacles (see "Bullgames," under "Events in Arles," below). A lengthy restoration process is well underway, giving the amphitheater an almost bleached-teeth whiteness.

In Roman times, games were free (sponsored by city bigwigs) and fans were seated by social class. The many exits allowed for  rapid dispersal after the games—fights would break out among frenzied fans if they couldn't leave quickly. Through medieval times and until the early 1800s, the arches were bricked up and the stadium became a fortified town—with 200 humble homes crammed within its circular defenses. Three of the medieval towers survive (the one above the ticket booth is open and rewards those who climb it with a good view). To see two still-sealed arches—complete with cute medieval window frames—turn right as you leave, walk to the Andaluz restaurant, and look back to the second floor (€5.50, covered by Monument Pass, daily May–Sept 9:00–18:00, March–April and Oct 9:00–17:30, Nov–Feb 10:00–16:30, tel. 08 91 70 03 70, www.arenes-arles.com). For more on Roman amphitheaters, see the "Nîmes" section of the Near Avignon chapter (page 114).

• *Turn left out of the Arena and walk uphill to find the...*

▲▲**Fondation Van Gogh**—A refreshing stop for any art-lover and especially interesting to van Gogh fans, this small gallery features works by contemporary artists who pay homage to Vincent through thought-provoking interpretations of his works. Many pieces are explained in English by the artists. The black-and-white photographs (both art and shots of places that Vincent painted) complement the paintings. Unfortunately, this collection is often on the road July through September, when non–van Gogh material is shown (€7, €5 with Monument Pass; great collection of van Gogh souvenirs, prints, and postcards for sale in free entry area; April–June daily 10:00–18:00; July–Sept daily 10:00–19:00; Oct–March Tue–Sun 11:00–17:00, closed Mon; facing Arena at 24 bis rond-point des Arènes, tel. 04 90 49 94 04, www.fondationvangogh-arles.org). For more on Vincent, see "Van Gogh Sights in and near Arles," below.

• *The next two sights are back across town. The Arlaten Folk Museum is close to place du Forum, and the Réattu Museum is near the river.*

▲**Arlaten Folk Museum (Musée Arlaten/Museon Arlaten)**—Built on the remains of the Roman Forum (first century A.D., see the courtyard), this museum houses the treasures of daily Provençal life. It was given to Arles by Nobel Prize winner Frédéric Mistral (see "Forum Square," above). Mistral's vision was to give locals an appreciation of their cultural roots, presented in tableaux that unschooled villagers could understand—"a veritable poem for the ordinary people who cannot read." Even though there are no English descriptions, the museum offers a unique and intimate look at local folk culture from the 18th and 19th centuries.

A one-way route takes you through 30 rooms and past guards in traditional dress. The first few rooms display folk costumes chronologically until about 1900, when traditional garb was replaced by the modern, nondescript norm. Portraits of people are matched with glass cases of artifacts that may have been part of their lives. You'll then see freestanding wedding armoires, which were given to brides by parents and filled with essentials to begin a new home. Finely crafted wooden cages—called *panetières*—hung from walls and kept bread away from mice. *Santons* were popular figurines that gave local nativity scenes a Provençal look.

The second floor covers local history, and a large room shows the lifestyles of residents of the marshy Camargue region. A round thatched hut demonstrates how life was tailored to survive the constant mistral wind. A fascinating case displays antique bullfighting memorabilia, including this region's unique hooks and ribbons used in *courses camarguaises* (see page 60) and a stuffed champion bull named Lion, who died of old age.

The last rooms hold two dioramas, the museum's pride and joy. In one, a wealthy mom is shown with her newborn. Her friends visit with gifts that represent the four physical and moral qualities hoped for in a new baby—good as bread, full as an egg, wise as salt, and straight as a match. The cradle is fully stocked with everything needed to raise an infant in 1888.

The next room shows "the great supper"—a Provençal feast served on Christmas Eve before midnight Mass. It's 1860, and everything on the table is locally produced. Traditionally, 13 sweets—for Jesus and the 12 apostles—were served. Grandma and grandpa warm themselves in front of the fireplace; grandpa pours wine on a log for good luck in the coming year (€4, covered by Monument Pass, free first Sun and last Wed of the month; open June–Aug daily 9:00–13:00 & 14:00–18:30; Sept–May Tue–Sun 9:00–12:00 & 14:00–17:30, closed Mon; last entry 1 hour before closing, enjoyable audioguide-€2, 29 rue de la République, tel. 04 90 96 08 23, www.cg13.fr).

Réattu Museum (Musée Réattu)—Housed in a beautiful 15th-century mansion, this mildly interesting, mostly modern art collection includes 57 Picasso drawings (some two-sided and all done in a flurry of creativity—I liked the bullfights best), a room of Henri Rousseau's Camargue watercolors, and an unfinished painting by the Neoclassical artist Jacques Réattu...but none with English explanations (€4, covered by Monument Pass, €2 extra for special exhibits, daily July–Aug 10:00–19:00, March–June and Sept–Nov 10:00–12:30 & 14:00–18:30, Dec–Feb 13:00–18:00, last entry 30 min before closing for lunch or at end of day, 10 rue du Grand Prieuré, tel. 04 90 96 37 68).

Van Gogh Sights in and near Arles

In the dead of winter in 1888, the 35-year-old Dutch artist Vincent van Gogh left big-city Paris for Provence, hoping to jump-start his floundering career. He was inspired. Coming from the gray skies and flat lands of the north, Vincent was bowled over by everything Provençal—the sun, bright colors, rugged landscape, and unspoiled people. For the next two years he painted furiously, cranking out a masterpiece every few days.

None of the 200-plus paintings that van Gogh did in the south can be found today in the city that so moved him. But you can walk the same streets he knew and see places he painted, marked by about a dozen steel-and-concrete **"easels,"** with photos of the final paintings for then-and-now comparisons. The TI has a €1 brochure that locates all the easels (those described in this book are easily found without the brochure—see the map on page 50). Small stone markers with yellow accents embedded in the pavement lead to the easels.

• *Take a walk in Vincent's footsteps (roughly north to south through Arles' center) and watch his paintings come to life. Start at place Lamartine and find the stone easel located just across from the Hôtel de France, to the left as you face the hotel (this easel was removed in 2007 for cleaning, but should be back in place by the time you read this).*

Vincent arrived in Arles on February 20, 1888, to a foot of snow. He rented a small house on the north side of **place Lamartine.** The house was destroyed in 1944 by an errant, bridge-seeking bomb, but the four-story building behind it—next to the now-defunct Hôtel Terminus et Van Gogh—still stands (find it in the painting). The house had four rooms, including a small studio and the cramped, trapezoid-shaped bedroom made famous in paintings. It was painted yellow inside and out, and Vincent named it..."The Yellow House." You can see a recreation of his bedroom from this house by the Arena (see below).

In late March, spring finally arrived. In those days, a short walk away from place Lamartine led to open fields. Donning his straw hat, Vincent set up his easel outdoors and painted quickly, capturing what he saw and felt—the blossoming fruit trees, gnarled olive trees, peasants sowing and reaping, jagged peaks, and windblown fields, all lit by a brilliant sun that drove him to use ever-brighter paints.

• *Walk to the river and find the easel in the wall where ramps lead down to the river.*

One night, Vincent set up along this river west of place Lamartine and painted the stars boiling above the city skyline— **Starry Night Over the Rhône.** The original bridge in the painting (see the remains on the right), along with many riverfront cafés, were destroyed in World War II. (Note: This painting is not the *Starry Night* you're thinking of—keep reading.)

• *Turn around and walk through the small park, then go into town between the stone towers along* **rue de la Cavalerie.**

Van Gogh walked into town the same way, underneath the arch and along this street. (Note: You'll pass by the Café de la Gare, which was the name of Vincent's favorite restaurant—but the original was along the west side of place Lamartine, also bombed in World War II.) Arles' 19th-century red light district was just east of rue de la Cavalerie, and the far-from-home Dutchman spent many lonely nights in its bars and brothels.

• *Pass through place Voltaire, continue walking up rue Voltaire, and then find the easel at the top of the steps to the Arena, to the right.*

All summer long, fueled by sun and alcohol, Vincent painted the town. He loved the bullfights in the Arena, and sketched the colorful surge of the crowds, spending more time studying the people than watching the bullfights. (Near the Arena, the Fondation Van Gogh—described on page 55—exhibits paintings by artists inspired by van Gogh.) On the opposite side of the Arena, near the Andaluz restaurant, you can visit a recreation of Vincent's humble bedroom during his time in Arles (€3, daily 10:00–18:00).

• *Walk to the upper end of the Arena, out rue de Porte de Laure, and step down into the park. You'll find the easel on the path down to the right.*

Vincent spent many a sunny day painting the leafy **Jardin d'Eté** (south of the classical theater). He never made real friends, though he palled around with (and painted) his mailman and a Foreign Legionnaire. (The fact that locals pronounced his name "vahn-saw van gog" had nothing to do with his psychological struggles here.) Packing his paints and a picnic in a rucksack, he day-tripped to the old Roman cemetery of **Les Alyscamps** (a 10-min detour from here, follow signs leading across the busy ring, then down several blocks).

• *Work your way back to the **place du Forum**, and locate an easel one café down from the yellow Café Van Gogh.*

In October, lonely Vincent—who dreamed of making Arles a magnet for fellow artists—persuaded his friend Paul Gauguin to come. He decorated Gauguin's room with several humble canvases of sunflowers (now some of the world's priciest paintings), knowing that Gauguin had admired a similar painting he'd done in Paris. At first, the two got along well. They spent days side by side, rendering the same subject in their two distinct styles. At night, they hit the bars and brothels. Van Gogh's well-known *Café at Night* captures the glow of an absinthe buzz at Café Van Gogh on place du Forum.

After two months together, the two artists clashed over art and personality differences. The night of December 23, they were drinking absinthe at the café when Vincent suddenly went ballistic. He threw his glass at Gauguin. Gauguin left. Walking through place Victor Hugo, Gauguin heard footsteps behind him and turned to see Vincent coming at him, brandishing a razor. Gauguin quickly fled town. The local paper reported what happened next: "At 11:30 p.m., Vincent Vaugogh [*sic*], painter from Holland, appeared at the brothel at no. 1, asked for Rachel, and gave her his cut-off earlobe, saying, 'Treasure this precious object.' Then he vanished." He woke up the next morning at home with his head wrapped in a bloody towel and his earlobe missing.

*• From here, find the Arlaten Folk Museum, then walk up rue Président Wilson and find **Espace Van Gogh**. There's an easel in the center of the courtyard.*

Vincent was checked into the local hospital, today's **Espace Van Gogh** cultural center. It sur-

rounds a courtyard garden that the artist loved and painted during his month here, as he was being treated for blood loss as well as for hallucinations and severe depression that left him bedridden. The citizens of Arles circulated a petition demanding that the mad Dutchman be kept under medical supervision. (The Espace is free, but only the courtyard is open to the public).

In the spring of 1889, the bipolar genius (a modern diagnosis) transferred to the **St. Paul Hospital in St. Rémy-de-Provence** (see page 78), where he spent a year, thriving in the care of doctors and nuns. Painting was part of his therapy, so they gave him a studio to work in, and he produced more than 100 paintings. Alcohol-free and institutionalized, he did some of his wildest work. With thick, swirling brushstrokes and surreal colors, he made his placid surroundings throb with restless energy.

Today at the hospital, you can see a replica of his bedroom and his studio, plus many scenes he painted—the courtyard, the plane trees, the view out the upstairs window of nearby fields, and the rugged Alpilles mountains. From the hospital grounds, stand among flamelike cypress trees, gaze over the distant skyline of St. Rémy, and realize you're in the midst of van Gogh's most famous work, *The Starry Night*.

In the spring of 1890, Vincent left Provence to be cared for by a doctor in Auvers-sur-Oise, north of Paris. On July 27, he wandered into a field and shot himself. He died two days later.

The next easels are less central, but easily located and worth the effort for van Gogh fans: The **Trinquetaille Bridge** (on the river walkway toward the Ancient History Museum), where the current bridge is a 1951 replacement; the abbey of **Montmajour** (three miles northeast); and—most famously—the **Langlois Drawbridge** (1.5 miles south of town along a Rhône canal; today's bridge is a 1926 duplicate of the original).

EVENTS IN ARLES

▲▲**Wednesday and Saturday Markets**—Twice a week in the morning, Arles' ring road erupts into an open-air market of fish, flowers, produce, and you-name-it. The Wednesday market runs along boulevard Emile Combes, between place Lamartine and bis avenue Victor Hugo; the segment nearest place Lamartine is all about food, and the upper half is about clothing, tablecloths, purses, and so on. On the first Wednesday of the month, it's a flea market, with less produce. The Saturday market is along boulevard des Lices near the TI. Join in, buy flowers, try the olives, sample some wine, and swat a pickpocket. Both markets are open until 12:00.

Much of the market has a North African feel, thanks to the Algerians and Moroccans who live in Arles (see page 11). They came to do the lowly city jobs that locals didn't want, and now mostly they do the region's labor-intensive agricultural jobs (picking olives, harvesting fruit, and working in local greenhouses).

▲▲**Bullgames (Courses Camarguaises)**—Occupy the same seats that fans have used for nearly 2,000 years, and take in Arles' most memorable experience—the *courses camarguaises* in the ancient Arena. These nonviolent "bullgames" are more sporting than bloody Spanish bullfights. The bulls of Arles (who, locals stress, "die of old age") are promoted in posters even more boldly than their human foes. In the bullgame, a ribbon *(cocarde)* is laced between the bull's horns. The *razeteur*, with a special hook, has 15 minutes to snare the ribbon. Local businessmen

encourage a *razeteur* (dressed in white with a red cummerbund) by shouting out how much money they'll pay for the *cocarde*. If the bull pulls a good stunt, the band plays the famous "Toreador" song from *Carmen*. The following day, newspapers report on the games, including how many *Carmens* the bull earned.

Three classes of bullgames—determined by the experience of the *razeteurs*—are advertised in posters: The *course de protection* is for rookies. The *trophée de l'Avenir* comes with more experience. And the *trophée des As* features top professionals. During Easter and the fall rice harvest festival (Féria du Riz), the Arena hosts actual Spanish bullfights (look for *corrida*) with outfits, swords, spikes, and the whole gory shebang. Bullgame tickets run €5–15, while bloody bullfights *(corrida)* are pricier (€12–80). Schedules change every year—ask at the TI or check online at www.arenes-arles.com (in 2007, the bullgames were every Wed at 17:00 July–Aug).

Don't pass on a chance to see *Toro Piscine*, a silly spectacle for warm summer evenings where the bull ends up in a swimming pool (uh-huh...get more details at TI). Nearby villages stage *courses camarguaises* in small wooden bullrings nearly every weekend; the TI has the latest schedule.

SLEEPING

In Arles

Hotels are a great value here; many are air-conditioned, though few have elevators. The Calendal, Musée, and Régence hotels offer exceptional value.

$$$ Hôtel le Calendal*, located between the Arena and Classical Theater, is Provençal chic and does everything right. Its comfortable rooms, in all shapes and sizes, surround a large, palm-shaded courtyard. Enjoy the great €9 buffet breakfast, the €15 salad-and-pasta-bar lunch buffet (daily 12:00–15:00), the children's play area, and the seductive ambience. They even have my Provence video on DVD in the lobby (smallest Db-€51, standard Db-€74–90, Db with balcony-€92–108, price depends on room size, air-con, Wi-Fi and four free laptops for guests, reserve ahead for parking-€10, just above Arena at 5 rue Porte de Laure, tel. 04 90 96 11 89, fax 04 90 96 05 84, www.lecalendal.com, contact @lecalendal.com).

$$$ Hôtel d'Arlatan*, built on the site of a Roman basilica, is classy in every sense of the word. It has sumptuous public spaces, a tranquil terrace, a designer pool, a turtle pond, and antique-filled rooms, most with high, wood-beamed ceilings and stone walls. In the lobby of this 15th-century building, a glass floor looks down into Roman ruins (smallest Db-€90, standard Db-€105–120, bigger Db-€120–155, Db/Qb suites-€180–250, excellent buffet

---

Sleep Code

(€1 = about $1.30, country code: 33)
S = Single, **D** = Double/Twin, **T** = Triple, **Q** = Quad, **b** = bathroom, **s** = shower only, ***** = French hotel rating system (0–4 stars). Unless otherwise noted, credit cards are accepted and English is spoken.

To help you sort easily through these listings, I've divided the rooms into three categories based on the price for a standard double room with bath:

$$$ Higher Priced—Most rooms €80 or more.
$$ Moderately Priced—Most rooms between €55–80.
$ Lower Priced—Most rooms €55 or less.

breakfast-€11, air-con, bathrobes, ice machines, elevator, Wi-Fi, parking-€13–16, 1 block below place du Forum at 26 rue Sauvage, tel. 04 90 93 56 66, fax 04 90 49 68 45, www.hotel-arlatan.fr, contact@hotel-arlatan.fr).

$$ Hôtel du Musée** is a quiet and affordable manor-home hideaway tucked deep in Arles. This delightful refuge comes with 28 air-conditioned rooms, a flowery two-tiered courtyard, and a snazzy art-gallery lounge. The rooms in the new section are worth the few extra euros and steps. Claude and English-speaking Laurence, the gracious owners, are eager to help (Sb-€45–50, Db-€55–70, Tb-€70–80, Qb-€85, higher prices are for new section, Wi-Fi and a laptop available for guests, parking-€8, follow signs to *Réattu Museum* to 11 rue du Grand Prieuré, tel. 04 90 93 88 88, fax 04 90 49 98 15, www.hoteldumusee.com, contact@hoteldumusee .com).

$$ Hôtel de la Muette**, with reserved owners Brigitte and Alain, is a good choice. Located in a quiet corner of Arles, this low-key, traditional hotel is well-kept, with stone walls, wood beams, mini-fridges, and air-conditioning (Db-€48–65, Tb-€65–70, Qb-€80, buffet breakfast with eggs-€8, Internet access and Wi-Fi, parking-€7, 15 rue des Suisses, tel. 04 90 96 15 39, fax 04 90 49 73 16, www.hotel-muette.com, hotel.muette@wanadoo.fr).

$$ Maison d'Hôtes en Provence, run by engaging American Madeleine and her soft-spoken French husband Eric, combines an interesting B&B experience—four spacious and funky-but-comfy rooms—with optional Provençal cooking workshops. Foodies should check out their website for its affordable range of gourmet classes (Db-€65, extra person-€15; good family room, across from launderette at 11 rue Portagnel, tel. & fax 04 90 49 69 20, www .cuisineprovencale.com, actvedel@wanadoo.fr).

$$ Hôtel le Cloître** was originally the cloister provost's resi-dence. Caring owners Jean-François and Agnes run a warm, ram-shackle place with 30 simple but character-filled rooms (so-so beds plus no air-conditioning or elevator). The best rooms are on the first floor. Cheaper rooms are on the second floor (Ss or Ds-€44, Sb or Db-€49, bigger Db-€60–65, Tb-€70, Qb-€80, parking-€5, closed Nov–mid-March, 16 rue du Cloître, tel. 04 90 96 29 50, fax 04 90 96 02 88, www.hotelcloitre.com, hotel_cloitre@hotmail .com).

$ Hôtel Régence**, about the best deal in Arles, has a river-front location, immaculate, comfortable Provençal rooms, good beds, safe parking, and easy access to the train station (Db-€40–50, Tb-€50–60, Qb-€60–70, good buffet breakfast-€6, choose river view or quieter courtyard rooms, most rooms have show-ers, air-con, no elevator but only two floors, Internet access and Wi-Fi; from place Lamartine, turn right immediately after passing

Arles Hotels and Restaurants

1. Hôtel le Calendal
2. Hôtel d'Arlatan
3. Hôtel du Musée
4. Hôtel de la Muette
5. Maison d'Hôtes en Provence
6. Hôtel le Cloître
7. Hôtel Régence
8. Hôtel Acacias
9. Hôtel Voltaire

10. Restaurants Le 16, Au Bryn du Thym & La Paillotte
11. Bistrot à Vins Restaurant
12. La Bohème Rest.
13. La Cuisine de Comptoir Rest.
14. Café de la Major (Coffee/Tea)
15. Le Grillon Rest.
16. L'Atelier Restaurant
17. Soleilei Ice Cream

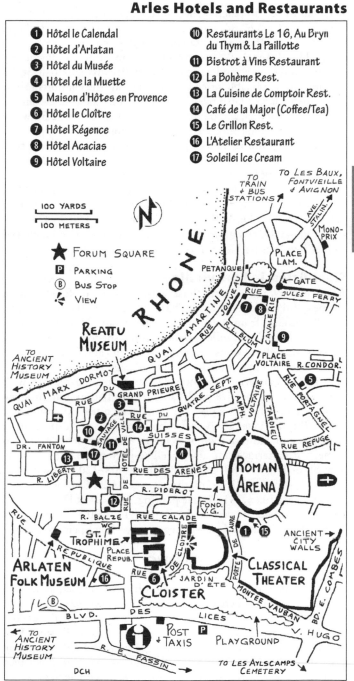

Arles

between towers to reach 5 rue Marius Jouveau; tel. 04 90 96 39 85, fax 04 90 96 67 64, www.hotel-regence.com, contact@hotel-regence.com). The gentle Nouvions speak some English.

$ Hôtel Acacias** just off place Lamartine and inside the old city walls, is a modern pastel paradise. Its smallish, well-maintained, reasonably priced rooms have all the comforts (Sb or Db-€46–55, larger Db-€62–71, extra bed-€15, air-con, elevator, 1 rue Marius Jouveau, tel. 04 90 96 37 88, fax 04 90 96 32 51, www.hotel-acacias.com, contact@hotel-acacias.com).

$ Hôtel Voltaire* rents 12 small and spartan rooms with ceiling fans and nifty balconies overlooking a caffeine-stained square. Located a block below the Arena, it's perfect for starving artists. Smiling owner Mr. Ferran (fur-ran) loves the States (his dream is to travel there), and hopes you'll add to his postcard collection (D-€28, Ds-€32, Db-€38, 1 place Voltaire, tel. 04 90 96 49 18, fax 04 90 96 45 49, levoltaire@aol.com). They also serve lunch and dinner (see "Eating," later in this chapter).

Near Arles, in Fontvieille

Many drivers, particularly those with families, prefer staying in the peaceful countryside, which has easy access to the area's sights. Just 10 minutes from Arles and Les Baux (and 20 minutes from Avignon), little Fontvieille slumbers in the shadows of its big-city cousins (though it has its share of restaurants and boutiques). See also "Sleeping—In or near Les Baux" on page 74.

$$$ Le Peiriero*** is a pooped parent's dream come true, with a grassy garden, massive pool, table tennis, badminton, massage parlor, indoor children's play area, and even a few miniature golf holes. The spacious family loft rooms, capable of sleeping up to five, have full bathrooms on both levels. This complete retreat also comes with a terrace café and a well-respected restaurant (streetside Sb or Db-€90–98, gardenside Db-€108–120, Db with terrace-€125–135, loft-€170–210, dinner *menu*-€29, €34 for breakfast and dinner, air-con, Wi-Fi, free parking, just east of Fontvieille on road to Les Baux, 34 avenue des Baux, tel. 04 90 54 76 10, fax 04 90 54 62 60, www.hotel-peiriero.com, info@hotel-peiriero.com).

EATING

You can dine well in Arles on a modest budget—in fact, it's hard to blow a lot on dinner here (most of my listings have *menus* for €22 or less). The bad news is that restaurants here change regularly, so double-check my suggestions. All restaurants I list (except Bistrot à Vins and La Bohème) have outdoor seating. Before dinner, go local on place du Forum and enjoy a *pastis*. This anise-based apéritif is served straight in a glass with ice, plus a carafe of water—dilute to taste.

For **picnics,** a big, handy Monoprix supermarket/department store is on place Lamartine (Mon–Sat 8:30–19:25, closed Sun).

On or near Place du Forum

Great atmosphere and mediocre food at fair prices await on place du Forum. By all accounts, the garish, yellow Café Van Gogh is worth avoiding. A half-block below the Forum, on rue du Dr. Fanton, lies a lineup of more tempting restaurants (including the first three listed below).

Le 16, with warm ambience inside and out, is an affordable place to enjoy a fresh salad (€8, bright and creative) or a one-course dinner (their "bull and red rice" is popular). They also offer a daily *plat du jour,* a two-course €14 *formule,* and a seasonal *menu* (closed Sat–Sun, 16 rue du Dr. Fanton, tel. 04 90 93 77 36).

La Paillotte, a few doors down, features soft tablecloths under wood-beamed comfort inside, a nice terrace outside, and fine regional cuisine at affordable prices. It's quite popular with tourists (€18–30 *menus,* closed Wed, 28 rue du Dr. Fanton, tel. 04 90 96 33 15).

Au Bryn du Thym, almost next door, has long been reliable and specializes in traditional Provençal cuisine. Arrive early for an outdoor table (€19 *menu,* closed Tue, 22 rue du Dr. Fanton, tel. 04 90 49 95 96).

Bistrot à Vins is for wine addicts who love matching food and drink. This comfortable *bistrot* is run by affable Ariane. She speaks English and offers simple, tasty dishes designed to highlight her reasonably priced wines—many available by the glass (closed Mon, 2 rue du Dr. Fanton, tel. 04 90 52 00 65).

La Bohème seems lost a block above the Forum. Here, you'll be greeted by gentle Nicholas. You'll dine under a long, vaulted ceiling in a restaurant with good budget options (€15 vegetarian *menu,* €20 Provençal *menu,* closed Sun–Mon, 6 rue Balze, tel. 04 90 18 58 92). While you may see an occasional tour group here, they usually leave by 19:30.

At **La Cuisine de Comptoir,** locals abandon Provençal décor and pretend they're urbanites in Paris. This cool little bistro serves light €9 *tartine* dinners—a cross between pizza and bruschetta served with soup or salad (closed Sun, just off place du Forum's lower end at 10 rue de la Liberté, tel. 04 90 96 86 28).

Café de la Major is the place to go to recharge with some serious coffee or tea (closed Sun, 7 bis rue Réattu, tel. 04 90 96 14 15).

Near the Roman Arena

For about the same price as on place du Forum, you can enjoy regional cuisine with a point-blank view of the Arena. Because they change regularly, the handful of (mostly) outdoor eateries that overlook the Arena are pretty indistinguishable.

Le Grillon—with good salads, crêpes, and *plats du jour* for €9–12—has been the most reliable (closed Wed, at the top of Arena on rond point des Arènes, tel. 04 90 96 70 97).

The recommended **Hôtel le Calendal** (see "Sleeping," above) hosts an all-you-can-eat salad-and-pasta bar (€15, daily 12:00–15:00); the selection is as good as the quality. Retreat from the city and enjoy a healthy lunch in the hotel's palm-shaded garden (just above Arena at 5 rue Porte de Laure, tel. 04 90 96 11 89).

The recommended **Hôtel Voltaire** (see "Sleeping," page 61) serves a nothing-fancy three-course dinner (or lunch) for €11 and hearty salads for €8–10—try the *salade fermière* (1 place Voltaire, tel. 04 90 96 49 18).

A Gastronomic Dining Experience

L'Atelier is so intriguing that people travel great distances just for the experience of dining here. Diners fork over €55 (lunchers spoon out €38) and trust Chef Jean-Luc Rabanel to create a memorable meal (which he does). There is no menu, just an onslaught of about 20 delicious taste sensations served on artsy dishes.

Don't plan on a quick dinner and don't come for the setting—it's a contemporary shoebox-shaped dining room, but several outdoor tables are also available. The get-to-know-your-neighbor atmosphere means you can't help but join the party (closed Mon–Tue, best to book ahead, friendly servers will hold your hand through this palate-widening experience, 50 yards downhill from place de la République at 7 rue des Carmes, tel. 04 90 91 07 69, www.rabanel.com).

And for Dessert...

Soleilei has Arles' best ice cream, with all-natural ingredients and unusual flavors such as *fadoli*—olive oil (open daily, across from recommended Le 16 restaurant at 9 rue du Dr. Fanton).

TRANSPORTATION CONNECTIONS

From Arles by Train to: Paris (17/day, 2 direct TGVs—4 hrs, 15 transfer in Avignon—5 hrs), **Avignon Centre-Ville** (11/day, 20 min, less frequent in the afternoon), **Nîmes** (9/day, 30 min), **Orange** (4/day direct, 35 min, more frequently with transfer in Avignon), **Aix-en-Provence Centre-Ville** (10/day, 2 hrs, requires at least 1 transfer in Marseille), **Marseille** (20/day, 1–2 hrs), **Cassis** (7/day, 2 hrs), **Carcassonne** (8/day, 2.5–4 hrs, 5 with transfer in Nîmes or Narbonne), **Beaune** (10/day, 4.5 hrs, 9 with transfer in Nîmes or Avignon and Lyon), **Nice** (11/day, 3.75–4.5 hrs, most require transfer in Marseille), **Barcelona** (2/day, 6 hrs, transfer in Montpellier), **Italy** (3/day, transfer in Marseille and Nice; from Arles, it's 4.5 hrs to Ventimiglia on the border, 8 hrs to Milan, 9.5 hrs to Cinque Terre, 11 hrs to Florence, and 13 hrs to Venice or Rome).

By Bus to: Avignon TGV (11/day, 1 hr, by SNCF bus—take the faster train from the Centre-Ville station instead), **Nîmes** (6/day, 1 hr), **St. Rémy-de-Provence** (3/day Mon–Sat only, none Sun, 50 min), **Fontvieille** (6/day, 10 min), **Camargue/ Stes-Maries-de-la-Mer** (6/day Mon–Sat, 3/day Sun, 1 hr). The bus stops in Arles' Centre-Ville at 16–24 boulevard Georges Clemenceau (2 blocks below main TI, next to Café le Wilson). Bus info: tel. 04 90 49 38 01 (unlikely to speak English).

Les Baux can be tricky to reach by bus out of peak season (usually July–Aug only, 6/day, 35 min, €4 one-way). For other ideas, see "Getting to Les Baux" on page 69 of the next chapter. In a pinch, a taxi to Les Baux costs €32 each way (€40 after 19:00; tel. 04 90 96 90 03).

NEAR ARLES

*Les Baux, St. Rémy, and
the Camargue*

The diverse terrain around Arles harbors many worthwhile and easy day trips. The medieval ghost town of Les Baux haunts the eerie Alpilles Mountains, while chic and compact St. Rémy-de-Provence awaits just over the hills, offering Roman ruins and memories of Vincent van Gogh. For an entirely different experience, the flat Camargue knocks on Arles' southern door with saltwater lakes, rice paddies, flamingos, wild horses, and wild black bulls.

Planning Your Time

Because public transportation in this area is sparse, these sights are easiest to reach by car, taxi, or minivan tour. For a fine one-day road trip from Arles or Avignon, spend the morning in Les Baux (visiting before the crowds), have lunch in sleepy St. Rémy, then explore the nearby sights and the **Roman aqueduct of Barbegal** in the afternoon. Non-drivers can do the same day trip (without the aqueduct) by bus and taxi. If you have more time or are a nature or bird-watching buff, head for the Camargue.

Les Baux

The hilltop town of Les Baux crowns the rugged Alpilles (ahl-pee) Mountains, evoking a tumultuous medieval history. Here, you can imagine the struggles of a strong community that lived a rugged life—thankful more for their top-notch fortifications than for their dramatic views. While mobbed with tourists most of the day, Les Baux rewards those who arrive by 9:00 or after 17:00. (While the hilltop citadel's entry closes at the end of the day, once you're inside, you're welcome to live out your fondest

Near Arles

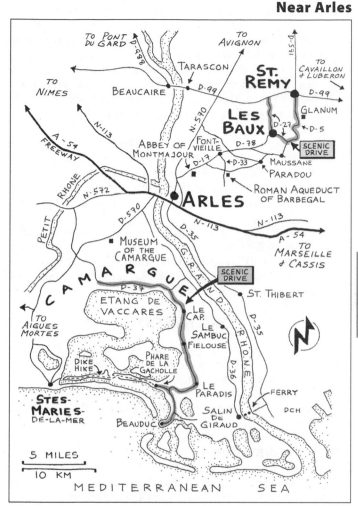

medieval fantasies all night long.) Sunsets are dramatic, the castle is brilliantly illuminated after dark, and nights in Les Baux arc pin-drop peaceful.

Getting to Les Baux

By Car: Les Baux is a 20-minute drive from Arles: Follow signs for *Avignon*, then *Les Baux*. Drivers can combine Les Baux with St. Rémy (15 min away) and the ruined Roman aqueduct of Barbegal (both described later in this chapter).

By Foot: Les Baux is a beautiful-but-strenuous four-hour hike from St. Rémy; see "Hike to Les Baux" on page 80. Note that this hike is prohibited from July through mid-September because of the risk of fire.

By Bus: From Arles, the direct bus service to Les Baux runs only during July and August (6/day, 35 min, €4 one-way, via Abbey of Montmajour, Fontvieille, and Paradou). To go directly to Les Baux (not including St. Rémy) from Arles at other times of the year, take the bus to Maussane (6/day Mon–Sat, none on Sun, 20 min, €4 one-way), and taxi from Maussane to Les Baux (allow €10 one-way).

You can also combine Les Baux and St. Rémy into a worthwhile day trip from Arles or Avignon. From either city, take the bus to St. Rémy (50 min, €4 one-way, from Arles: 3/day Mon–Sat April–Oct, none Sun or Nov–March; from Avignon: 6/day Mon–Sat, none Sun); then take a taxi to Les Baux from there (figure €15 one-way).

By Taxi: Figure €32 for a taxi one-way from Arles (€40 after 19:00, tel. 06 80 27 60 92).

By Minivan or "Hop On/Off" Tour: The best option for many is an excursion tour, which can be both efficient and economical (see page 36).

ORIENTATION

Les Baux is actually two visits in one: castle ruins perched on an almost lunar landscape, and a medieval town below. See the castle, then savor or blitz the lower town on your way out. The town, which lives entirely off tourism, is packed with shops, cafés, and tourist knickknacks. This polished-stone gauntlet of boutiques is a Provençal dream-come-true for shoppers.

Tourist Information

The TI is on the main drag into town (daily 9:30–12:30 & 14:00–17:30, tel. 04 90 54 34 39, www.lesbauxdeprovence.com). Ask about ticket combo deals (like the castle ruins and Cathédrale d'Images), and if you'll be doing a lot of sightseeing, consider the €13.50 **Les Baux Jours pass,** which covers the castle ruins, the Cathédrale d'Images, and the Yves Brayer Museum (saves €5.50 if you visit all three).

Arrival in Les Baux

Drivers must pay €4 to park. As you enter, take a ticket, then drive as close to the top of the parking lot as you can. Pay at the machine just below the town entry (next to telephone, WC, and bakery).

Walk up the cobbled street into town, where you're greeted first by the TI. From here, the main drag leads directly to the castle—just keep going uphill (a 10-min walk).

SIGHTS

The Castle Ruins (The "Dead City")

The sun-bleached ruins of the "dead city" of Les Baux are carved into, out of, and on top of a rock 650 feet above the valley floor.

Many of the ancient walls of this striking castle still stand as a testament to the proud past of this once-feisty village.

Cost and Hours: €7.50, includes good audioguide, daily July–Aug 9:00–20:00, Easter–June and Sept–Oct 9:00–19:00, Nov–Easter 9:30–17:00. Those inside the castle when the entry closes can stay as long as they like. From mid-July through late August, the mountaintop is enlivened by medieval pageantry and tournaments.

History: Imagine the importance of this citadel in the Middle Ages, when the Lords of Baux were notorious warriors. (How many feudal lords could trace their lineage back to one of the "three kings" of Christmas-carol fame, Balthazar?) In the 11th century, Les Baux was a powerhouse in southern France, controlling about 80 towns. The Lords of Baux fought the counts of Barcelona for control of Provence...and eventually lost. But while in power, these guys were mean. One ruler enjoyed forcing unransomed prisoners to jump off his castle walls.

In 1426, Les Baux was incorporated into Provence and France. Not accustomed to subservience, Les Baux struggled with the French king, who responded by destroying the fortress in 1483. Later, Les Baux regained some importance and emerged as a center of Protestantism. Arguing with Rome was a high-stakes game in the 17th century, and Les Baux's association with the Huguenots brought destruction again in 1632 when Cardinal Richelieu (under King Louis XIII) demolished the castle. Louis rubbed salt in the wound by billing Les Baux's residents for his demolition expenses. The once-powerful town of 4,000 was forever crushed.

In the old olive mill where you buy your ticket, study the models of the town before its 17th-century destruction. Take full advantage of the included audioguide—it narrates 30 stops while you wander where you like, keying in the number for any sight that interests you.

As you wander out on the windblown field, past kid-thrilling medieval siege weaponry, try to imagine 4,000 people living up here. Notice the water-catchment system (a slanted field that caught rainwater and drained it into a cistern—necessary during

Les Baux

1. Hostellerie de la Reine Jeanne
2. Le Mas d'Aigret
3. Le Mas de l'Esparou B&B
4. To Le Mazet des Alpilles B&B
5. Renaissance Window
6. City Hall

NOT TO SCALE

TO ST. REMY VIA MOST SCENIC ROUTE

CAVES DE SARRAGAN

CATHEDRALE D'IMAGES

MUSEUM OF SANTONS

CHAPEL OF PENITENTS

EYGUIERES GATE

YVES BRAYER MUSEUM

PLACE LOUIS JOU

R. PORTE MAGE

CEM.

ST. VINCENT

RUE DE LA CALADE

UPHILL!

GRAND RUE F. MISTRAL

TO ARLES & FONTVIEILLE

CHAPEL

RUE TRENCAT

TICKETS & ENTRY TO "DEAD CITY"

R. NEUVE

RUE DES FOURS

R. DE LORME

CASTLE RUINS

CLIFFS

TO ST. REMY

PDCH

P – PARKING
↖↗ – VIEW

TO MAUSSANE, PARADOU, ABBEY DE MONTMAJOUR, ARLES, 4 & BARBEGAL

a siege). In the little chapel across from the entry, the slide show *(Van Gogh, Gauguin, and Cézanne: Painting in the Land of the Olive Trees)* provides a relaxing 10-minute interlude (plays constantly; no words—just images and music).

For the most sensational views, climb to the blustery top of the citadel. Hang on. The mistral wind just might blow you away.

Lower Town

After your castle visit, you can shop and eat your way back through the new town. Or you can escape the crowds by taking the first left as you leave the castle, continuing downhill, and checking out these minor but worthwhile sights as you descend:

Yves Brayer Museum (Musée Yves Brayer)—This enjoyable museum lets you peruse three floors of paintings (van Gogh–like Expressionism, without the tumult) by Yves Brayer (1907–1990), who spent his final years here in Les Baux. Like van Gogh, Brayer was inspired by all that surrounded him. Brayer picked up inspiration from his travels through Morocco, Spain, and the rest of the Mediterranean world (€4, daily 10:00–12:30 & 14:00–18:30, tel. 04 90 54 36 99). Pick up the descriptive English sheet at the entry.

• *Next door is...*

St. Vincent Church—This 12th-century Romanesque church was built short and wide to fit the terrain. The center chapel on the right (partially carved out of the rock) houses the town's traditional Provençal processional chariot. Each Christmas Eve, a ram pulled this cart—holding a lamb, symbolizing Jesus, and surrounded by candles—through town to the church.

• *Around the corner (to the left as you leave the church) are public WCs. Directly in front of the church is a vast view, making clear the strategic value of this rocky bluff's natural fortifications. A few steps away is the...*

Chapel of Penitents—Notice the nativity scene painted by Yves Brayer, illustrating the local legend that says Jesus was born in Les Baux. Leaving the church, turn left. Wash your shirt in the old-town "laundry"—with a pig-snout faucet and 14th-century stone washing surface designed for short women.

• *Heading downhill on rue de la Calade, you'll pass cafés with wonderful views, the town's fortified wall, and one of its two gates. After passing a free (and curiously evangelical) "museum of aromas and perfumes," you hit the awe-inspiring...*

Museum of Santons—This free museum displays a collection of *santons*, popular folk figurines that decorate local Christmas mangers. Notice how the nativity scene "proves" once again that Jesus was born in Les Baux. These painted clay dolls show off local dress and traditions. Find the old couple leaning heroically into the mistral.

• *If you choose to visit the main drag through town (grand rue Frédéric Mistral), you'll find the following sights. The first is halfway up to the castle entry.*

Manville Mansion City Hall—The 15th-century city hall the red-and-white flag of Monaco, a reminder that the Grimaldi family (who have long ruled the tiny principality of Monaco) owned Les Baux until the French Revolution (1789). In fact, in 1982, Princess Grace Kelly and her royal husband, Prince Rainier Grimaldi, came to Les Baux to receive the key to the city.

Across the street and 20 yards farther up, the fine 1571 **Renaissance window,** marking the site of a future Calvinist museum, stands as a reminder of this town's Protestant history. This was probably a place of Huguenot worship—the words carved into the lintel, *Post tenebras lux,* were a popular Calvinist slogan: "After the shadow comes the light."

Near Les Baux

A half-mile beyond Les Baux, D-27 leads to dramatic views of the hill town. There are pullouts and walking trails at the pass, and two sights that fill cool, cavernous caves in former limestone quarries dating back to the Middle Ages. (The limestone is easy to cut, but gets hard and nicely polished when exposed to the weather.) Speaking of quarries, in 1821, the rocks and soil of this area were found to contain an important mineral for the making of aluminum. It was named after the town: bauxite.

Caves de Sarragan—The best views of Les Baux are from this parking lot, occupied by the Sarragan Winery (which invites you in for a taste). While this place looks like it's designed for groups, the friendly, English-speaking staff welcomes individuals (free, daily April–Sept 10:00–12:00 & 14:00–19:00, Oct–March until 18:00, tel. 04 90 54 33 58).

Cathédrale d'Images—This similar cave nearby offers a mesmerizing sound-and-slide show. Its 48 projectors flash countless images set to music on the quarry walls as visitors wander around. The 2008 program features the life of Vincent van Gogh (€7.50, daily March–Dec 10:00–18:00, closed Jan–Feb, tel. 04 90 54 42 65). Dress warmly, since the cave is cool.

D-27 continues to St. Rémy, allowing for a handy loop trip (to complete the loop, return from St. Rémy to Les Baux via D-5).

SLEEPING

In or near Les Baux

$$$ **Le Mas d'Aigret*****, on the road to St. Rémy, is a well-run, lovely refuge that crouches just past Les Baux. Lie on your back and stare up at the castle walls rising beyond the swimming pool or enjoy sensational valley views from the groomed terraces (Db with no view-€95, larger Db with balcony and view-€145, Tb/Qb-€200–230, two cool troglodyte rooms-€190–230, half-pension option with big breakfast and good dinner-€39, air-con, rooms have some daytime road noise, tel. 04 90 54 20 00, fax 04 90 54 44 00, www.masdaigret.com, contact@masdaigret.com, Dutch Marieke and French Eric).

$$ **Le Mas de l'Esparou** *chambre d'hôte*, a few minutes below Les Baux toward Paradou, is welcoming and kid-friendly, with three spacious rooms, a big swimming pool, table tennis, and distant views of Les Baux. Sweet Jacqueline loves her job, and her lack of English only makes her more animated (Db-€62, extra bed-about €16, includes breakfast, cash only, between Les Baux and Maussane les Alpilles on D-5, look for white sign with green lettering, tel. & fax 04 90 54 41 32).

Sleep Code

(€1 = about $1.30, country code: 33)
S = Single, **D** = Double/Twin, **T** = Triple, **Q** = Quad, **b** = bathroom, **s** = shower only, ***** = French hotel rating system (0–4 stars). Unless otherwise noted, credit cards are accepted and English is spoken.

To help you easily sort through these listings, I've divided the rooms into three categories, based on the price for a standard double room with bath:

$$$ **Higher Priced**—Most rooms €80 or more.
$$ **Moderately Priced**—Most rooms between €55–80.
$ **Lower Priced**—Most rooms €55 or less.

For more accommodations in this area, see page 80

$$ Hostellerie de la Reine Jeanne**, an exceptional value, is a good place to watch the sun rise and set from Les Baux. Run by Gaelle and Marc, this place offers a handful of comfy rooms are above a busy (and good value) restaurant (standard Ds-€50, standard Db-€56, Db with view deck-€65, cavernous family suite-€100, air-con in most rooms, ask for *chambre avec terrasse*, good *menus* from €16, 150 feet to your right after entry to the village of Les Baux, tel. 04 90 54 32 06, fax 04 90 54 32 33, www.la-reinejeanne .com, reine.jeanne@wanadoo.fr).

$ Le Mazet des Alpilles is a small home with three tidy, air-conditioned rooms just outside the unspoiled village of Paradou, five minutes below Les Baux. It may have space when others don't (Db-€55, ask for largest room, includes breakfast, cash only, air-con, child's bed available, pleasant garden, follow brown signs from D-17, in Paradou look for route de Brunelly, tel. 04 90 54 45 89, www.alpilles.com/mazet.htm, lemazet@wanadoo.fr). Sweet Annick speaks just enough English.

Sights Between Les Baux and Arles

The following stops are easiest for drivers.
Abbey of Montmajour—This brooding hulk of a ruin, just a few minutes' drive from Arles toward Les Baux, was once a thriving abbey and a convenient papal retreat (c. A.D. 950). Today, the vacant abbey church is a massive example of Romanesque architecture (€7; May–Aug daily 10:00–18:30; Sept–April Tue–Sun 10:00–17:00, closed Mon; tel. 04 90 54 64 17). For more on abbeys,

see "Medieval Monasteries" on page 186.

The surrounding fields were a favorite of van Gogh's, who walked here from Arles to paint his famous wheat fields. Now they're rice fields, which wouldn't have looked nearly as good on canvas.

▲**Roman Aqueduct of Barbegal**—To be all alone with evocative Roman ruins, drivers can take a quick detour to the crumbled arches of ancient Arles' principal aqueduct. Coming from Arles, take D-17 toward Fontvieille, then, 1.5 miles before Fontvieille, follow signs for *L'Aqueduc Romain* on D-82 (it's signed coming from Fontvieille to Arles as well, on the left). In less than two miles, park at the pullout (no sign, just after *Los Pozos Blancos* sign, where the ruins of the aqueduct cross the road). Leave no valuables visible in your car; the gravel twinkles with the remains of broken car windows.

Follow the dirt path to the right through the olive grove and along the aqueduct ruins for 200 yards. Approaching the bluff with the grand view, you'll see that the water canal split into two troughs: One takes a 90-degree right turn and heads for Arles; the other goes straight to the bluff and over, where it once sent water cascading down to power eight grinding mills. Romans grew wheat on the vast fields you see from here, then brought it down to the mega-watermill of Barbegal. Historians figure that this mill produced enough flour each day to feed 12,000 hungry Romans. If you saw the model of this eight-tiered mill in Arles' Ancient History Museum (see page 49), the milling is easy to visualize—making a visit here quite an exciting experience.

Returning to your car, find the broken bit of aqueduct—it's positioned like a children's playground slide—and take a look at the waterproofing mortar that lined all Roman aqueducts.

St. Rémy-de-Provence

Sophisticated and lively St. Rémy gave birth to Nostradamus and cared for a distraught artist. Today, it caters to shoppers. A few minutes from the town center, you can visit the once-thriving Roman city called Glanum, the mental ward where Vincent van Gogh was sent after lopping off his lobe, and an art center dedicated to his memory. Best of all is the chance to elbow your way through its raucous Wednesday market (until 12:30). A racecourse-like ring road hems in a pedestrian-friendly

center that's well-stocked with fine foods, pottery boutiques, art galleries, and the latest Provençal fashions.

Getting to St. Rémy

By Car: From Les Baux, St. Rémy is a spectacular 15-minute drive over the hills and through the woods. Roads D-5 and D-27 each provide scenic routes between these towns, making a loop drive between them worthwhile. The most scenic approach is on D-27; from Les Baux, take the road that passes the Cathédrale d'Images; from St. Rémy to Les Baux, follow signs for *Tarascon*, and you'll see the D-27 turnoff to Les Baux in a few miles. Parking in St. Rémy is tricky; it's easiest at the TI lot (€1/3 hrs, free Mon–Sat 12:00–14:00 and all day Sun). Parking on place Charles de Gaulle is always free, but farther from the center (leave the ring road on avenue Frédéric Mistral).

By Bus: Buses run from Arles (3/day Mon–Sat April–Oct, none Sun or Nov–March) and Avignon (6/day Mon–Sat, none Sun) to St. Rémy (either trip is about €4 and 50 min). If arriving at St. Rémy by bus, get off on the ring road at the stop called République. The TI is just a block up avenue Maillane (facing the street, it's to your right).

By Taxi: From Les Baux, figure on €15 one-way; from Avignon, allow €35 (tel. 06 80 27 60 92 or 06 09 52 71 54). St. Rémy's four taxis park on place de la République, next to the bus stop.

ORIENTATION

From St. Rémy's center, it's a 20-minute walk along a busy road with no sidewalk to Glanum and the St. Paul Monastery (van Gogh's mental hospital).

Tourist Information

The TI is two blocks toward Les Baux from the ring road (May–Sept Mon–Sat 9:00–12:30 & 14:00–19:00, Sun 10:00–13:00; Oct–April Mon–Sat 9:00–12:00 & 14:00–18:00, closed Sun Nov–March, tel. 04 90 92 05 22, www.saintremy-de-provence.com). At the TI, pick up a town map, information, and a map tracing van Gogh's favorite painting locations with in situ copies of the painted scenes (described below, the *Starry Night* panel is just outside the TI), hiking maps, and bus schedules. Ask about walking tours (see below). They'll also call a taxi for you.

TOURS

Get information at the TI about English **walking tours** (€6.50, 90 min, departs TI at 10:00 most days; tours of the town usually on Sat and Mon; van Gogh tour usually on Tue, Thu, and Fri; requires reservation). Skip the overpriced **Citypod audioguide,** a quick 30-minute tour of the town (€5, at TI).

SIGHTS AND ACTIVITIES

St. Rémy's best attractions are outside the town center: The ruins at Glanum and the Vincent van Gogh sights nearby. This cluster of sights is a 15-minute walk south of the TI. If you're driving, you can usually park for free at the St. Paul Monastery and walk five minutes to Glanum from there (or pay €3 to park at the Glanum site).

▲Glanum Ruins

These crumbling stones are the foundations of a Roman market town, located at the crossroads of two ancient trade routes between Italy and Spain. This important town had grand villas and temples, a basilica, a forum, a wooden dam, aqueducts, and more. A massive Roman arch and tower stand proud and lonely near the ruins' parking lot. The arch marked the entry into Glanum, and the tower is a memorial to the grandsons of Emperor Augustus Caesar. The setting is stunning, though shadeless, and the small museum at the entry sets the stage well.

While the ruins are, well...ruined, they remind us of the range and prosperity of the Roman Empire. Along with other Roman monuments in Provence, they paint a more complete picture of Roman life (the city was about seven times larger than the ruins you see). The free English handout is helpful, and the exhibits in the entry help you reconstruct the site, but eager Romanophiles will want to spring for the €7 guidebook. Inside the ruins, signs give basic English explanations at key locations, and the view from the belvedere justifies the effort (€6.50, under 18 free, daily April–Aug 9:00–19:00, Sept–May 10:30–17:00, parking-€3, tel. 04 90 92 23 79).

Tracing Van Gogh's Steps

For more on Vincent van Gogh's time in this region, see page 56 in the Arles chapter.

St. Paul Monastery (Le Monastère St. Paul de Mausole)—Just below Glanum is the still-functioning mental hospital (Clinique St. Paul) that treated Vincent van Gogh from 1889 to 1890. Pay €4 and enter Vincent's temporarily peaceful world: a small chapel, intimate cloisters, a re-creation of his room, and a small lavender field with six (of my favorite) paintings copied on large poster boards. It's worth reading the thoughtful English explanations about Vincent's tortured life. Amazingly, he painted 150 works in his 53 weeks here—none of which remain anywhere nearby today. The contrast between the utter simplicity of his room (and his life) and the

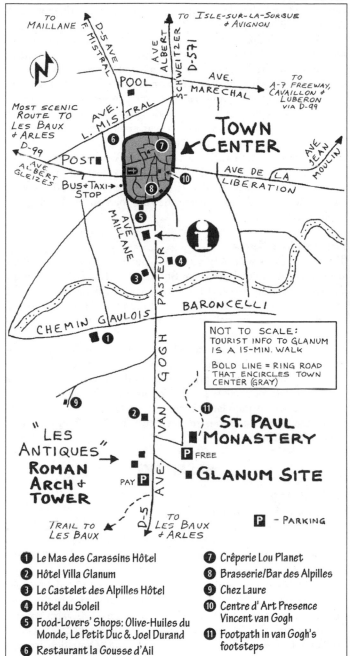

1. Le Mas des Carassins Hôtel
2. Hôtel Villa Glanum
3. Le Castelet des Alpilles Hôtel
4. Hôtel du Soleil
5. Food-Lovers' Shops: Olive-Huiles du Monde, Le Petit Duc & Joel Durand
6. Restaurant la Gousse d'Ail
7. Crêperie Lou Planet
8. Brasserie/Bar des Alpilles
9. Chez Laure
10. Centre d'Art Presence Vincent van Gogh
11. Footpath in van Gogh's footsteps

multimillion-dollar value of his paintings today is jarring. The site is managed by Valetudo, a center specializing in art therapy (daily April–Aug 9:30–18:45, Sept–March 10:00–16:45, tel. 04 90 92 77 00). A footpath that leads from the complex back into town is dotted with 21 panels of Vincent's works—some located right where he painted them (the TI has a map with a list of the reproductions).

Centre d'Art Présence Vincent van Gogh—In St. Rémy's center, you'll find this ongoing tribute to the painter, which features a small room of reproductions and a video presentation (with English subtitles). The theme changes each year, though the subject always remains Vincent van Gogh. Upstairs is a rotating exhibit that reflects the enormous influence of Vincent's work on contemporary artists. You'll also find a worthwhile collection of works by Cubist precursor Albert Gleizes (€3.50, Tue–Sun 10:00–13:00 & 15:00–19:00, closed Mon, inside the ring road on rue Estrine, tel. 04 90 92 34 72).

Hike to Les Baux

These directions will help you find your way on the lovely-but-strenuous four-hour hike from St. Rémy to Les Baux (for more details and a map, ask at TI). Note that this hike is only allowed from mid-September through June. (In hotter months, the path is closed because of the risk of fire.) Make sure to wear good shoes and take plenty of water with you.

Start from the signposted slope opposite the Glanum entry. Follow the goat path up into the mountain and arrive at the chimney. Go down the iron ladder, and you'll come to a lake. Walk around the lake on the left-hand side, turning left along the *Mas de Gros* cart track. A mile later, turn right on Sentier des Crêtes, and follow the yellow markings to Les Baux. You'll end on the paved road in Val d'Enfer.

SLEEPING

In St. Rémy
(€1 = about $1.30, country code: 33)

$$$ Le Mas des Carassins*, a 15-minute walk from the center, is impeccably run by friendly Michel and Pierre. Luxury is affordable here. Your hosts pay careful attention to every detail, from the generously sized pool and gardens to the muted room decor and optional €28 weekday-only dinner (standard Db-€122, deluxe Db-€153, Db with terrace-€175, suite-€200, extra bed-€20, includes breakfast, air-con, table tennis, look for signs 200 yards toward Les Baux from TI, 1 Chemin Gaulois, tel. 04 90 92 15 48, fax 04 90 92 63 47, www.hoteldescarassins.com, info@hoteldescarassins .com). Reservations are smart here—its 14 rooms fill fast.

$$$ Hôtel Villa Glanum*** is a modern hotel on the main road (some traffic noise) across from the St. Paul Monastery and the Glanum ruins. It's a 15-minute walk from the town center with tight, but well-maintained rooms. The best rooms, which come with higher rates, are in bungalows around the pretty pool and lush gardens (Db-€72–95, Tb-€100, Qb-€120, cheaper off-season, 46 avenue van Gogh, tel. 04 90 92 03 59, fax 04 90 92 00 08, www .villaglanum.com, villa.glanum@wanadoo.fr).

$$ Le Castelet des Alpilles*** is way Old World, but the location is good (a few blocks toward Les Baux from the TI), the price is fair, and the rooms are plenty comfortable. Most are big and airy, and the balcony rooms have views of the Alpilles (Db-€68, Db with air-con and view balcony-€95, Tb-€110, 6 place Mireille, tel. 04 90 92 07 21, fax 04 90 92 52 03, www.castelet-alpilles.com, hotel.castel.alpilles@wanadoo.fr).

$$ Hôtel du Soleil**, an easy walk from St. Rémy's center, is a budget traveler's refuge, with simple, spotless rooms clustered around a pleasant courtyard and pool (standard Sb/Db-€57, bigger Sb/Db-€74, Tb-€75–90, 3 rooms have small terraces, 2-room apartment-€85, no air-con, Internet access and Wi-Fi, easy parking, a block above the TI at 35 avenue Pasteur, tel. 04 90 92 00 63, fax 04 90 92 61 07, www.hotelsoleil.com, contact@hotelsoleil .com).

EATING

The town is packed with fine restaurants, each trying to outdo the other. Join the evening strollers and compare. For some good food-shopping options, see the "Food-Lovers' Guide to St. Rémy" sidebar.

La Gousse d'Ail is no secret, but even so, it's a reliable and warm place for a mini-splurge (*menus* from €32, closed Thu, on the ring road just after the turnoff to Maillane at 6 boulevard Marceau, tel. 04 90 92 16 87).

Crêperie Lou Planet, on pleasant place Favier, is cheap and peaceful, with outdoor seating in summer, delicious crêpes, and good salads. Owner Jean has been here for 24 years and still hasn't changed the menu (daily April–Sept 12:00–22:00, behind Hôtel de Ville).

Brasserie/Bar des Alpilles sits on the ring road offering a great salad selection and good, standard café fare (daily lunch and dinner, 21 boulevard Victor Hugo, tel. 04 90 92 0 17).

Near Arles

Food-Lovers' Guide to St. Rémy

Wednesday is market day in St. Rémy, but you don't have to fast until then. Foodies will appreciate the three shops gathered on the ring road in St. Rémy, near the turnoff to Les Baux.

Start at **Olive-Huiles du Monde,** where you can saddle up to a wine bar–like setting and sample the best olive oil and vinegar in the area. The friendly staff speaks English and is happy to spoon up samples of three olive oils and two surprisingly tasty vinegars. Check out the fine display of other products made from olive oil and the good truffle display (daily 10:00–12:30 & 15:00–19:00, 16 boulevard Victor Hugo, tel. 04 90 15 02 33).

Le Petit Duc, across the road, offers a remarkable introduction to antique cookies. Let friendly owner Anne, who speaks English (or her sidekick, Marie, who tries), take you on a tour (daily 10:00–13:00 & 15:00–19:00, 7 boulevard Victor Hugo, tel. 04 90 92 08 31).

Just one whiff of **Joel Durand**'s chocolate will lure chocoholics inside. Ask for a sample and learn the letter-coded system. The lavender is surprisingly good (daily 9:30–12:30 & 14:30–19:30, 3 boulevard Victor Hugo, next door to Le Petit Duc; tel. 04 90 92 38 25).

Chez Laure is a simple, local, and relaxed outdoor restaurant. It's located a mile from St. Rémy in a park-like setting with toys available for kids (open daily, lunch *menu*–€10, dinner *menu*–€18, on route du Lac, tel. 04 90 92 51 99). To get to the restaurant, look for signs between the Glanum ruins and the TI (see map on page 79).

The Camargue

The Camargue region occupies the vast delta of the Rhône River, and is one of Europe's most important wetlands. This marshy area exists where the Rhône splits into two branches (big and little), just before it flows into the Mediterranean. Over the millennia, a steady flow of sediment has been deposited at the mouth of the rivers—thoroughly landlocking villages that once faced the sea.

Since World War II, large northern tracts of the Camargue have been converted to rice fields, and today the delta is a major producer of France's rice and salt. Because the salt marshes were long considered useless, the land has been relatively untouched, leaving a popular nature destination today.

The Camargue Regional Nature Park is a protected and

"wild" area, where pink flamingos, wild bulls, nasty boars, nastier mosquitoes, and the famous white horses wander freely through lagoons and tall grass.

In this nature reserve, graceful pink flamingos and other bird species flourish, attracting birdwatchers from all over the world. Once an endangered species, several thousand flamingos migrate from here each fall, heading to warmer climates and then returning in March to pink up the Camargue.

The black bulls are raised for bullfights (by local cowboys called *gardians*) and eventually end up on plates in Arles' restaurants. The *gardians*, who have patrolled the Camargue on local horses for centuries, add a Wild West aura to the region.

The Camargue's unique, small, but rugged horses—born brown or black, later turning light gray or white—comprise one of the oldest breeds in the world, and may have existed in the area since prehistoric times.

The Camargue's subtle wetlands beauty makes it a worthwhile joyride, but not a must-see sight. The marshy scenery—particularly along the Etang de Vaccarès (a birder's paradise)—is unique in France, and the experience is downright fun if you see a clumsy flamingo in flight. The occasional bulls and wild horses add to the enjoyment, but for me, this is basically a big swamp—interesting to drive through, with a few roadside walkabouts, and worthwhile only if you're a birder or in Arles for awhile. The Camargue appeals mostly to Europeans, for whom such expansive areas of wilderness are rare, and to naturalists (tel. 04 90 97 86 32, www.parc-camargue.fr, info@parc-camargue.fr).

Getting to the Camargue

There are several ways to experience the Camargue: horseback, mountain bikes, and jeep safaris. All three options are available in Stes-Maries-de-la-Mer (see next page), and jeep safaris are also offered from Arles (ask at TI). Hiking is not popular in the Camargue, as there are few good trails (check www.coastalguide.to/camargue). The best biking is across the Digue (dike) to Phare de la Gacholle (see below).

There are two main **driving routes** from Arles through the Camargue: to Stes-Maries-de-la-Mer (see below), and toward Salin de Giraud (which I prefer). Here's my favorite route: Leave Arles on D-570 toward Stes-Maries-de-la-Mer, passing the Camarguais Museum (listed below). Then follow D-37 toward Salin de Giraud and Le Sambuc as it skirts the Etang de Vaccarès lagoon. The lagoon itself is off-limits, but this area has some of the finest views. Turn right off D-37 onto the tiny road at Villeneuve, following La Capelière and La Fiélouse.

This stretch is the best I found, with pullouts and viewing

stands. A small exhibit and walking trail are provided at La Capelière (small fee), with some English information on the Camargue. Pick up their good Camargue map, which shows walking routes, called *Ballade Naturalistes*. Birders can look at the register and see what birds have been spotted recently (observations in English are in red). The drive past La Capelière is pretty for another few miles. If you're into this experience, you can continue all the way to the Phare de La Gacholle lighthouse, where a seven-mile biking/hiking trail leads to Ste-Maries-de-la-Mer, crossing a dike located along the Mediterranean, between sand dunes and wetlands.

Buses serve the Camargue (stopping at Camarguais Museum and Stes-Maries-de-la-Mer) from Arles' bus station (6/day Mon–Sat, 3/day Sun, 1 hour, tel. 04 90 96 36 25). In Stes-Maries-de-la-Mer, walk from the stop to the church (10 min) to get oriented. There are several parking lots and plenty of on-street parking for drivers.

SIGHTS

Camarguais Museum (Musée Camarguais)—In a traditional Camargue barn on the road to Stes-Maries-de-la-Mer, this folk museum does a good job of describing the natural features and traditions of the Camargue. The costumes, tools, and helpful exhibits are all well-described in English, but the two-mile nature trail has information only in French (€5, May–Sept daily 9:00–18:00; Oct–April Wed–Mon 10:00–1700, closed Tue; 8 miles from Arles on D-570 toward Stes-Maries-de-la-Mer at Mas du Pont de Rousty farmhouse, tel. 04 90 97 10 82).

Stes-Maries-de-la-Mer—At the western end of the Camargue lies this whitewashed, Spanish-feeling seafront town with acres of flamingos, bulls, and horses at its doorstep. The place is so popular that it's best avoided on weekends and during holidays. It's a French Coney Island—a trinket-selling, perennially windy place.

The town is also famous as a mecca for Gypsies (more appropriately known as Roma). Every May, Roma from all over Europe pile in their caravans and migrate to Stes-Maries-de-la-Mer to venerate the statue of St. Sarah (a Roma leader who, according to tradition, welcomed Mary Magdalene here after Jesus' death). The impressive spectacle is like a sprawling flea market spilling out from the town. Avoid the women with flowers, who often cluster near the church—they want your money, not your friendship.

The town of Stes-Maries-de-la-Mer has little to offer except its beachfront promenade, bullring, and towering, five-belled, fortified church. The church interior is worth a look for its unusual decorations and artifacts, including the statue of St. Sarah (church entry free, €2 to climb to roof for Camargue and sea views).

Most tourists come to take a horse, jeep, or bike into the Camargue—and there's no lack of outfits ready to take you for a ride. The TIs in Arles (see page 45) and Stes-Maries-de-la-Mer have long lists (Stes-Maries-de-la-Mer TI open daily April–Sept 9:00–19:00, until 20:00 in summer, Oct–March 9:00–17:00, tel. 04 90 97 82 55, www.saintesmaries.com). You can rent **bikes** and get advice on the best route at Le Vélo (19 rue de la République, tel. 04 90 97 74 56). **Jeep** excursions run about €30/for 2.5 hours; Camargue-Decouverte is one of many outfits based in Arles (1 rue Emile Fassin, tel. 04 90 96 69 20, www.camargue-decouverte .com).

Aigues-Mortes—This strange walled city, on the western edge of the Camargue (20 miles from Nîmes), was built by Louis IX as a jumping-off point for his Crusades to the Holy Land. Although Aigues-Mortes was a strategically situated royal port city, it was actually never near the sea—ships reached it via canals that were dug through an immense lagoon. Today, its tall towers and thick fortifications seem oddly out of place, surrounded by nothing but salt marshes and flamingos. The name "Aigues-Mortes" means "Dead Waters," which says it all. Skip it unless you need more souvenirs and crowded streets, although drivers can detour to Aigues-Mortes, between Nîmes and Arles, for a quick-and-easy taste of the Camargue. Aigues-Mortes and Nîmes are linked by buses (6/day, 50 min) and trains (6/day, 45 min).

AVIGNON

Famous for its nursery rhyme, medieval bridge, and brooding Palace of the Popes, contemporary Avignon (ah-veen-yohn) bustles and prospers behind its mighty walls. During the 68 years (1309–1377) that Avignon starred as the *Franco Vaticano*, it grew from a quiet village into a thriving city. With its large student population and fashionable shops, today's Avignon is an intriguing blend of medieval history, youthful energy, and urban sophistication. Street performers entertain the international crowds who fill Avignon's ubiquitous cafés and trendy boutiques. If you're here in July, be prepared for the rollicking theater festival. (Reserve your hotel far in advance.) Clean, sharp, and popular with tourists, Avignon is more impressive for its outdoor ambience than for its museums and monuments. See the Palace of the Popes, and then explore the city's thriving streets and beautiful vistas from the parc des Rochers des Doms.

ORIENTATION

The cours Jean Jaurès, which turns into rue de la République, runs straight from the Centre-Ville train station to place de l'Horloge and the Palace of the Popes, splitting Avignon in two. The larger eastern half is where the action is. Climb to the parc des Rochers des Doms for a fine view, enjoy the people scene on place de l'Horloge, meander the back streets (see my "Discovering Avignon's Back Streets" self-guided walk, below), and lose yourself in a quiet square. Avignon's shopping district fills the traffic-free streets where rue de la République meets place de l'Horloge.

Tourist Information

The main TI is between the Centre-Ville train station and the old town, at 41 cours Jean Jaurès (April–Oct Mon–Sat 9:00–18:00, until 19:00 in July, Sun 9:00–17:00; Nov–March Mon–Fri 9:00–18:00, Sat 9:00–17:00, Sun 10:00–12:00; tel. 04 32 74 32 74, www.avignon-tourisme.com). From April through mid-October, a branch TI office, called Espace Ferruce, is usually open at St. Bénezet Bridge (but it's slow, with just one person working).

At either TI, get the good tear-off map and pick up the free and handy *Guide Pratique* (info on car and bike rental, hotels, and museums). Also pick up the free **Avignon Passion Pass** (valid 15 days, for up to five people). Get the pass stamped when you pay full price at your first sight, and then receive reductions at the others; for example, €2 less at the Palace of the Popes and €3 less at the Petit Palais. The pass comes with the Avignon "Passion" map and guide, which includes several good (but tricky-to-follow) walking tours.

The TI offers informative, two-hour English **walking tours** of Avignon (€10–15, €8 with Avignon Passion Pass; April–Oct daily at 10:00, Nov–March on Sat only; depart from main TI, Sun departures from ticket room at Palace of the Popes; themes vary daily). The TI also offers information and bookings for bus excursions to popular regional sights, including the wine route, the Luberon, and the Camargue (see "Tours of Provence" on page 36).

Arrival in Avignon

By Train

Avignon has two train stations, the TGV (linked to downtown by frequent shuttle buses) and Centre-Ville.

TGV Station (Gare TGV)

To get to the city center, the best and most inexpensive option is to take a shuttle bus (described below).

Services: There is no baggage check here, though you can check your bags at the Centre-Ville station (see below). A taxi ride between the TGV station and downtown Avignon costs about €13. For car rentals, take the south exit *(sortie sud)* to find the *location de voitures* (for driving directions to other destinations from this station, see "By Car," below).

Shuttle Bus to Downtown Avignon: To get to the city shuttle bus *(navette)* that will take you to the Avignon's center, go out the north exit *(sortie nord)*, down the stairs, and to the left. Look for an information booth, and across from it, the shuttle bus or the stop marked *Navette/Avignon Centre*. The shuttle bus leaves frequently (3/hr, 15 min, €1.10, buy tickets at info booth at TGV station or from the driver). You'll arrive at a stop located three blocks from the city's main TI (described above, down cours Jean Jaurès).

Shuttle Bus to the TGV Station: In Avignon, the shuttle-bus *(navette)* stop is just inside the city walls, in front of the post office on cours Président Kennedy, near the Centre-Ville station.

Centre-Ville Station (Gare Avignon Centre-Ville)

All non-TGV trains serve the central station. To reach the town center, walk out of the train station and through the city walls onto cours Jean Jaurès. The TI is three blocks down, at #41.

Services: You can check bags here—exit the station to the left and look for *consignes* sign (daily May–Sept 6:00–22:00, Oct–April 7:00–19:00).

Getting to the Bus Station: The bus station *(gare routière)* is 100 yards to the right of the Centre-Ville station as you leave (beyond and below Ibis Hôtel).

By Bus

The dingy bus station is located just east of the Centre-Ville train station; to get to Avignon's sights, follow the walking directions explained above.

By Car

Drivers entering Avignon should follow *Centre-Ville* and *Gare SNCF* (train station) signs. Park in the parking structure next to the Centre-Ville station (€10/half-day, €11.50/day). Free parking is available near the city walls (on boulevard Saint-Roch near Porte de la République), though a new parking garage is under construction that will eliminate some of this free parking. To park in the underground garage at the Palace of the Popes, follow the signs from the riverside road (boulevard St. Lazare) just past St. Bénezet Bridge. Leave nothing in your car. Hotels have advice for smart overnight parking.

If you're renting a car at the TGV station and heading off to Arles, St. Rémy-de-Provence, Les Baux, or the Luberon, start by leaving the TGV station and following signs to *Avignon Sud*, then *La Rocade*. You'll soon see exits to Arles (best for St Rémy and Les Baux as well), and Cavaillon (for Luberon villages).

Helpful Hints

Book Ahead for July: During the July theater festival, rooms are rare—reserve very early or stay in Arles (see page 61) or St. Rémy (page 80).

Internet Access: Consider **Webzone** (Mon–Sat 10:00–23:00, Sun 12:00–22:00, 3 rue St. Jean le Vieux on place Pie, tel. 04 32 76 29 47) or at nearby **Chez W@M** (Mon–Thu 8:00–20:00,

Festival d'Avignon

The last thing Avignon needs is an excuse to party. Still, every July since 1947, a theater festival envelops Avignon, creating a Mardi Gras–like atmosphere. Contemporary theater groups come from throughout Europe, and each year the festival showcases a different theater director or artist. The program is announced in May, and most tickets are booked immediately—hotels are 80 percent full by March. The festival is indoors, but venues overflow into the streets. The organizers need 20 different locations for the performances, from actual theater spaces to small chapels to the inner courtyard of the Palace of the Popes, which seats 2,000. There's also a "fringe festival," called Avignon-Off, which adds another 100 venues and countless amateur performances. In July, the entire city is a stage, with mimes, fire-breathers, singers, and musicians filling the streets. Most of the performances are in French, some are occasionally in English, and many dance performances don't require language at all (www.festival-avignon .com and www.avignon-off.org).

Fri–Sat 8:00–23:00, Sun 8:00–18:00, 34 rue Bonneterie, tel. 04 90 86 19 03), or ask your hotelier for the nearest Internet café.

English Bookstore: Try **Shakespeare Bookshop** (Tue–Sat 9:30–12:00 & 14:00–18:30, closed Sun–Mon, 155 rue Carreterie, in Avignon's northeast corner, tel. 04 90 27 38 50).

Baggage Storage: You can leave your bags at the Centre-Ville train station (see "Centre-Ville Station," above).

Laundry: The launderette at 66 place des Corps-Saints, where rue Agricol Perdiguier ends, has English instructions and is handy to most hotels (daily 7:00–20:00).

Grocery Store: **Shopi** is central and has long hours (Mon–Sat 7:00–21:00, Sun 9:00–12:00, 2 blocks from the TI, toward place de l'Horloge on rue de la République).

Bike Rental: You can rent a bike or a scooter near the bus station at **Provence Bike** (52 boulevard Saint-Roch, tel. 04 90 27 92 61). You'll enjoy riding on the Ile de la Barthelasse, but bike riding is better in Isle-sur-la-Sorgue (page 163) and Vaison la Romaine (page 137).

Car Rental: The TGV station has the car-rental agencies (open long hours daily).

Tourist Trains: Two little trains, designed for tired tourists, leave regularly from the Palace of the Popes (mid-March–mid-Oct daily 10:00–19:00, tel. 06 11 35 06 66, www.petittrainavignon .com). One does a town tour (€7, 3/hr, 45 min, English commentary) and the other choo-choos you sweat-free to the

Avignon at a Glance

▲▲**Palace of the Popes** Fourteenth-century Gothic palace built by the popes who made Avignon their home. **Hours:** Mid-March–Oct daily 9:00–19:00, until 20:00 July and Sept, until 21:00 in Aug, Nov–mid-March daily 9:30–17:45.

▲▲**Parc des Rochers des Doms** Park and ramparts at the hilltop where Avignon was first settled, with great views of the Rhône River Valley and the famous broken bridge. **Hours:** Daily April–Sept 7:30–20:00, Oct–March 7:30–18:00.

▲▲**St. Bénezet Bridge** The "pont d'Avignon" of nursery-rhyme fame, once connecting Vatican territory to France. **Hours:** Mid-March–Oct daily 9:00–19:00, until 20:00 July and Sept, until 21:00 in Aug, Nov–mid-March daily 9:30–17:45.

▲▲**Scenic Squares** Numerous hide-and-seek squares ideal for postcard-writing and people-watching—pick your favorite: place des Corps-Saints, place St. Pierre, place des Châtaignes (adjacent to place St. Pierre), place Crillon, place St. Didier (near recommended Caveau du Théâtre Restaurant), and the big place Pie (see map on page 92).

▲**Tower of Philip the Fair** Massive tower across St. Bénezet Bridge, featuring the best view over Avignon and the Rhône

top of the park, high above the river (€1 one-way, schedule depends on demand, no commentary).

Shuttle Boat: A free shuttle boat plies back and forth across the river (as it did in the days when the town had no functioning bridge) from near St. Bénezet Bridge (daily July–Aug 11:00–21:00, Sept–June roughly 11:00–18:00, 3/hr). It drops you on the peaceful Ile de la Barthelasse, with its riverside restaurant (see page 107), grassy walks, and bike rides with city views. If you stay on the island for dinner, check the schedule for the last return boat—or be prepared for a pleasant 25-minute walk back to town.

Commanding City Views: Walk or drive across Daladier Bridge (pont Daladier) for a great view of Avignon and the Rhône River (there's a good walking path across the bridge, along the river). You can enjoy other impressive vistas from the top of parc des Rochers des Doms, the tower cafeteria in the Palace of the Popes, and from the end of the famous, broken St. Bénezet Bridge.

basin. **Hours:** April–Sept daily 10:00–12:30 & 14:00–18:30; Oct–Nov and March Tue–Sun 10:00–12:00 & 14:00–17:00, closed Mon; closed Dec–Feb.

Petit Palace Museum "Little palace" displaying the Church's collection of medieval Italian painting and sculpture. **Hours:** June–Sept Wed–Mon 10:00–13:00 & 14:00–18:00, closed Tue; Oct–May Wed–Mon 9:30–13:00 & 14:00–17:30, closed Tue.

Synagogue Thirteenth-century synagogue rebuilt in a Neo-classical Greek-temple style. **Hours:** Mon–Fri 10:00–12:00 & 15:00–17:00, closed Sat–Sun.

Fondation Angladon-Dubrujeaud Museum with a small but enjoyable Post-Impressionist collection, including art by Cézanne, van Gogh, Daumier, Degas, and Picasso. **Hours:** May–Nov Tue–Sun 13:00–18:00, closed Mon; Dec–April Wed–Sun 13:00–18:00, closed Mon–Tue.

Calvet Museum Fine-arts museum with a good collection and no English descriptions. **Hours:** Wed–Mon 10:00–13:00 & 14:00–18:00, closed Tue.

Avignon

SELF-GUIDED WALKS

Combine these two walks—one ("Welcome to Avignon") covering the major sights, and the other ("Discovering Avignon's Back Streets") along the roads less taken—to get beyond the surface of this historic city.

▲▲Welcome to Avignon

This walk connects Avignon's best sights.

• *Start your tour where the Romans did, on place de l'Horloge, in front of City Hall (Hôtel de Ville).*

Place de l'Horloge: This café square was the town forum during Roman times and the market square through the Middle Ages. (Restaurants here offer good people-watching, but they also have less ambience and low-quality meals—you'll find better squares elsewhere to hang your beret in.) Named for a medieval clock tower that the City Hall now hides, this square's present popularity arrived with the trains in 1854. Walk a few steps to the center of the square, and look down the main drag, rue de la

Avignon

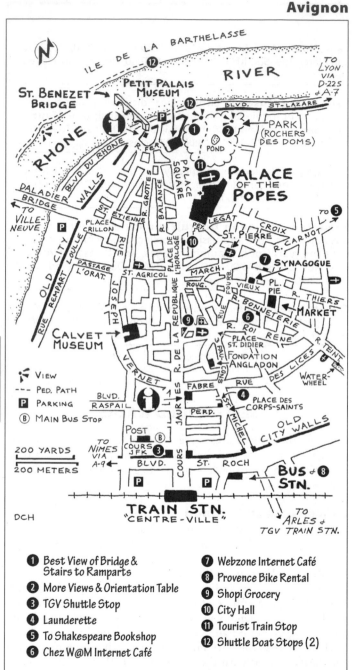

Avignon (vertical side tab)

Legend:
- View
- --- Ped. Path
- **P** Parking
- Ⓑ Main Bus Stop

200 YARDS
200 METERS

DCH

1 Best View of Bridge & Stairs to Ramparts
2 More Views & Orientation Table
3 TGV Shuttle Stop
4 Launderette
5 To Shakespeare Bookshop
6 Chez W@M Internet Café

7 Webzone Internet Café
8 Provence Bike Rental
9 Shopi Grocery
10 City Hall
11 Tourist Train Stop
12 Shuttle Boat Stops (2)

République. When the trains came to Avignon, proud city fathers wanted a direct, impressive way to link the new station to the heart of the city (just like in Paris)—so they plowed over homes to create rue de la République and widened place de l'Horloge. This main drag's Parisian feel is intentional—it was built not in the Provençal manner, but in the Haussmann style that is so dominant in Paris (for example, buildings have slate roofs rather than tile).

• *Walk past the carousel (public WCs behind). You'll see the Palace of the Popes looming large over the buildings. Veer right, and continue into...*

Palace Square (Place du Palais): This grand square is surrounded by the forbidding Palace of the Popes, the Petit Palais, and the cathedral. In the 1300s, the Vatican moved the entire headquarters of the Catholic Church to Avignon. The Church bought Avignon and gave it a complete makeover. Along with clearing out vast spaces like this square and building this three-acre palace, the Church erected more than three miles of protective wall, with 39 towers, "appropriate" housing for cardinals (read: mansions), and residences for the entire Vatican bureaucracy. The city was Europe's largest construction zone. Avignon's population grew from 6,000 to 25,000 in short order. (Today, 13,000 people live within the walls.) The limits of pre-papal Avignon are outlined on city maps: Rues Joseph Vernet, Henri Fabre, des Lices, and Philonarde all follow the route of the city's earlier defensive wall.

The Petit Palais (Little Palace) seals the uphill end of the square and was built for a cardinal; today, it houses medieval paintings (museum described below). The church just to the left of the Palace of the Popes is Avignon's cathedral. It predates the Church's purchase of Avignon by 200 years. Its small size reflects Avignon's modest, pre-papal population. The gilded Mary was added in 1854, when the Vatican established the doctrine of her Immaculate Conception. Mary is purposefully taller than the Palace of the Popes. The Vatican never accepted what it called the "Babylonian Captivity," and had a bad attitude about Avignon long after the pope was definitively back in Rome.

Directly across the square from the palace's main entry stands a cardinal's residence built in 1619. Its fancy Baroque facade was a visual counterpoint to the stripped-down Huguenot aesthetic of the age. During this time, Provence was a hotbed of Protestantism—but, buried within this region, Avignon was a Catholic stronghold.

Notice the stumps in front of the Conservatoire National de Musique. Nicknamed *bites*, slang for the male anatomy, they effectively keep cars from double-parking in areas designed for people. Many of the metal ones slide up and down by remote control to let privileged cars come and go.

Avignon

• *You can visit the massive Palace of the Popes (described on the next page) now, but it works better to visit that palace at the end of this walk, then continue directly to my next "Back Streets" walk. Now is a good time to take in the...*

Petit Palace Museum (Musée du Petit Palais): This palace displays the Church's collection of mostly medieval Italian painting (including one delightful Botticelli) and sculpture. All 350 paintings deal with Christian themes. A visit here before going to the Palace of the Popes helps furnish and populate that otherwise barren building (€6, €3 with Avignon Passion Pass; June–Sept Wed–Mon 10:00–13:00 & 14:00–18:00, closed Tue; Oct–May Wed–Mon 9:30–13:00 & 14:00–17:30, closed Tue; at north end of Palace Square, tel. 04 90 86 44 58).

• *From Palace Square, we'll head up to the rocky hilltop where Avignon was first settled, then down to the river. With this short loop, you can enjoy a park, hike to a grand river view, walk a bit of the wall, and visit Avignon's beloved broken bridge—an experience worth ▲▲. Begin by hiking (or taking the tourist train—see "Helpful Hints," earlier in this chapter) up to the...*

Parc des Rochers des Doms: While the park itself is a delight—with a sweet little café and public WCs—don't miss the climax (rated ▲▲): a panoramic view of the Rhône River Valley and the broken bridge. You'll find a huge terrace in the north side of the park, with an orientation table and information plaques, but views that are inferior to the smaller viewpoint described below (park gates open daily April–Sept 7:30–20:00, Oct–March 7:30–18:00).

For the best views (and the favorite make-out spot for local teenagers), find the small terrace past the park café and behind the odd zodiac display. An orientation table explains the view. On a clear day, the tallest peak you see, with its white limestone cap, is Mont Ventoux ("Windy Mountain"). St. André Fortress (across the river) was built by the French in 1360, shortly after the pope moved to Avignon, to counter the papal incursion into this part of Europe. The castle was in the kingdom of France. Avignon's famous bridge was a key border crossing, with towers on either end—one French and one Vatican.

• *From this viewpoint, take the stairs (closed at night) down to the tower. As the stairs spiral down, just before St. Bénezet Bridge, catch a glimpse of the...*

Ramparts: The only bit of the rampart you can walk on is just beyond the tower (access from St. Bénezet Bridge). When the pope came in the 1360s, small Avignon had no town wall...so he built one. What you see today was restored in the 19th century.

• *When you come out of the tower on street level, exit outside the walls and walk left to find the bridge's entrance (it's outside the walls on boulevard du Rhône).*

St. Bénezet Bridge (Pont St. Bénezet): This bridge (rated ▲▲), whose construction and location were inspired by a shepherd's religious vision, is the "pont d'Avignon" of nursery-rhyme fame. The ditty (which you've probably been humming all day) dates back to the 15th century: *Sur le pont d'Avignon, on y danse, on y danse, sur le pont d'Avignon, on y danse tous en rond* ("On the bridge of Avignon, we will dance, we will dance, on the bridge of Avignon, we will dance all in a circle").

But the bridge was a big deal even outside of its kiddie-tune fame. Built between 1171 and 1185, it was the only bridge crossing

the mighty Rhône in the Middle Ages. It was damaged several times by floods and subsequently rebuilt, until 1668, when most of it was knocked down by a disastrous icy flood. The townsfolk decided not to rebuild this time, and for more than a century, Avignon had no bridge across the Rhône. While only four arches survive today, the original bridge was huge: Imagine a 22-arch, 3,000-foot-long bridge extending from Vatican territory to the lonely Tower of Philip the Fair, which marked the beginning of France. A Romanesque chapel on the bridge is dedicated to St. Bénezet. While there's not much to see on the bridge, the audioguide included with your ticket tells a good story. It's also fun to be in the breezy middle of the river with a fine city view.

Cost and Hours: €4, €3.30 with Avignon Passion Pass, €12 combo-ticket includes Palace of the Popes, mid-March–Oct daily 9:00–19:00, until 20:00 July and Sept, until 21:00 in Aug, Nov–mid-March daily 9:30–17:45—same hours as the Palace of the Popes, last entry 1 hour before closing, tel. 04 90 27 51 16. The ticket booth is housed in what was a medieval hospital for the poor (funded by bridge tolls). Admission includes a small museum about the song of Avignon's bridge and your only chance to walk a bit of the ramparts (enter both from the tower).

• *To get to the Palace of the Popes from here, exit left, turn left again back into the walls (following signs to* Palais des Papes*), then go right onto rue Ferruce. After a block, look for the brown signs leading you left under the passageway, and up the stairs to Palace Square and the...*

Palace of the Popes (Palais des Papes): In 1309, a French pope was elected (Pope Clement V). At the urging of the French king, His Holiness decided he'd had enough of unholy (and dangerous) Italy. So he loaded up his carts and moved to Avignon for a secure rule under a supportive king. The Catholic Church literally bought Avignon (then a two-bit town), and popes resided here until 1403. Meanwhile, Italians demanded a Roman pope, so from

1378 on, there were twin popes, one in Rome and one in Avignon, causing a schism in the Catholic Church that wasn't fully resolved until 1417.

A visit to the mighty yet barren papal palace (rated ▲▲) comes with an audioguide that leads you along a one-way route and does a credible job of overcoming the lack of furnishings. It teaches the basic history while allowing you to tour at your own pace.

As you wander, ponder that this palace—the largest surviving Gothic palace in Europe—was built to accommodate 500 people as the administrative center of the Vatican and home of the pope. This was the most fortified palace of the age (remember, the pope left Rome to be more secure). You'll walk through the pope's personal quarters (frescoed with happy hunting scenes), see models of how the various popes added to the building, and learn about its state-of-the-art plumbing. The rooms are huge. The "pope's chapel" is twice the size of the adjacent Avignon cathedral.

While the last pope checked out in 1417, the Vatican owned Avignon until the French Revolution in 1789. During this interim period, the pope's "legate" (official representative...normally a nephew) ruled Avignon from this palace. Avignon residents, many of whom had come from Rome, spoke Italian for a century after the pope left, making it a linguistic island within France. In the Napoleonic age, the palace was a barracks, housing 1,800 soldiers. You can see cuts in the wall where high ceilings gave way to floor beams. Climb the tower (Tour de la Gâche) for a grand view and windswept café.

A room at the end of the tour is dedicated to the region's wines, of which they claim the pope was a fan. Sniff "Le Nez du Vin"—a black box with 54 tiny bottles designed to develop your "nose." (Blind-test your travel partner.) The nearby village of Châteauneuf-du-Pape is where the pope summered in the 1320s. Its famous wine is a direct descendant of his wine. You're welcome to taste here (€6 for three fine wines and souvenir tasting cup).

Cost and Hours: €9.50, €7.50 with Avignon Passion Pass, €12 combo-ticket includes St. Bénezet Bridge, daily mid-March–Oct daily 9:00–19:00, until 20:00 July and Sept, until 21:00 in Aug, Nov–mid-March 9:30–17:45—same hours as St. Bénezet Bridge, last entry 1 hour before closing, tel. 04 90 27 50 74, www.palais-des-papes.com.

• *You'll exit at the rear of the palace, where my "Back Streets" walking tour begins (see below). Or, to return to Palace Square, make two rights after exiting the palace.*

▲▲Discovering Avignon's Back Streets

Use the map in this chapter or the TI map to navigate this easy, level, 30-minute walk. This self-guided tour begins in the small square (place de la Mirande) behind the Palace of the Popes. If you've toured the palace, this is where you exit. Otherwise, from the front of the palace, follow the narrow, cobbled rue Peyrollerie, carved out of the rock, around the palace on the right side as you face it.

• *Our walk begins at the...*

Hôtel la Mirande: Located on the square, Avignon's finest hotel welcomes visitors. Find the atrium lounge and consider a coffee break amid the understated luxury (€11 afternoon tea served daily 15:00–18:00, includes a generous selection of pastries). Inspect the royal lounge and dining room (recommended on page 107); cooking courses are offered in the basement below. Rooms start at €300.

• *Turn left out of the hotel and left again on rue Peyrollerie (Coppersmiths Street), then take your first right on rue des Ciseaux d'Or. On the small square ahead you'll find the...*

Church of St. Pierre: The original chestnut doors were carved in 1551, when tales of New World discoveries raced across Europe. (Notice the Indian headdress, top center.) The fine Annunciation (lower right) shows Gabriel giving Mary the exciting news in impressive Renaissance 3-D. Now take 10 steps back from the door and look way up. The tiny statue breaking the skyline of the church is the pagan god Bacchus, with oodles of grapes. What's he doing sitting atop a Christian church? No one knows.

• *Follow the alley to the left, which was covered and turned into a tunnel during the town's population boom. It leads into what was the cloister of St. Pierre—named for chestnut trees (place des Châtaignes), but now replaced by plane trees. The practical atheists of the French Revolution destroyed the cloister, leaving only faint traces of the arches along the church side of the square. For recommended restaurants near the Church of St. Pierre, see page 104. Continue around the church.*

With the church on your right, cross busy place Carnot to the Banque Chaix. The classy 15th-century building across the lane to the right, with its beams showing, is a rare vestige from the Middle Ages. Notice how the building widens the higher it gets. A medieval loophole based taxes on ground-floor square footage—everything above was tax-free. Walking left down the pedestrian street, rue des Fourbisseurs (Street of the Animal Furriers), notice how the top floors almost meet. Fire was a constant danger in the Middle Ages, as flames leapt easily from one home to the next. In fact, the lookout guard's primary responsibility was watching for fires, not the enemy. Virtually all of Avignon's medieval homes have been replaced by safer structures.

• *Turn left on the traffic-free rue du Vieux Sextier (Street of the Balance, for weighing items); another left under the first arch leads 10 yards along rue B. Lyon to Avignon's...*

Synagogue: Jews first arrived in Avignon with the Diaspora (exile) of the first century. Avignon's Jews were nicknamed "the Pope's Jews" because of the protection that the Vatican offered to Jews expelled from France. While this synagogue dates from the 1220s, in the mid-19th century it was completely rebuilt in a Neoclassical, Greek-temple style by a non-Jewish architect. This is the only synagogue under a rotunda that you'll see anywhere. The ark holding the Torah is in the east, next to a list of the Jews who were deported from here to Auschwitz in 1942, after Vichy France was overtaken by the Nazis. To visit the synagogue, press the buzzer and friendly Rabbi Moshe Amar will be your guide (Mon–Fri 10:00–12:00 & 15:00–17:00, closed Sat–Sun, 2 place Jerusalem).

• *From here, retrace your steps to rue du Vieux Sextier. Cross it, then go through the arch and down the yellow alley. Turn left on rue de la Bonneterie (Street of Hosiery), which leads to the big, boxy...*

Market (Les Halles): In 1970, the town's open-air market was replaced by this modern one. Step inside for a sensual experi-

ence of organic breads, olives, and festival-of-mold cheeses. The rue des Temptations cuts down the center. Cafés and cheese shops are on the left—as far as possible from the stinky fish stalls on the right. Follow your nose away from the fish and have a coffee with the locals, or exit to big place Pie and find a seat at one of the many cafés there. Enjoy the lively atmosphere on this open square and the unexpected view of the market's green wall. The vegetation reflects the changes of seasons and helps mitigate its stark exterior (market open Tue–Sun until 13:00, closed Mon).

• *Continue on for five minutes from Les Halles on rue de la Bonneterie, which eventually becomes...*

Rue des Teinturiers: This "Street of the Dyers" is Avignon's headquarters for all that's hip. You'll pass the Grey Penitents chapel. The facade shows the GPs, who dressed up in robes and pointy hoods to do their anonymous good deeds back in the 13th century (long before the KKK dressed this way).

As you stroll, you'll see the work of amateur sculptors, who have carved whimsical car barriers out of limestone. Earthy cafés, galleries, and a small stream (a branch of the Sorgue River) with waterwheels line this tie-dyed street. This was the cloth industry's dyeing and textile center in the 1800s. Those stylish Provençal fabrics and patterns you see for sale everywhere started here, after a pattern imported from India.

For trendy restaurants on this atmospheric street, see page 106.

• *Farther down rue des Teinturiers, you'll come to the...*

Waterwheel: Standing here, imagine the Sorgue River—which hits the mighty Rhône in Avignon—being broken into sev-

eral canals in order to turn 23 such wheels. In about 1800, waterwheels powered the town's industries. The little cogwheel above the big one could be shoved into place, kicking another machine into gear behind the wall. (For more on the Sorgue River and its waterwheels, see my self-guided walk of Isle-sur-la-Sorgue, page 164.) Across from the wheel at #41 is **La Cave Breysse,** offering regional wines by the glass and good lunch fare (see page 106).

• *To return to the real world, double back on rue des Teinturiers and turn left on rue des Lices, which traces the first medieval wall. (*Lices *is the no-man's-land along a wall.) You'll pass a four-story arcaded building that was a home for the poor in the 1600s, an army barracks in the 1800s, a fine-arts school in the 1900s, and a deluxe condominium today (much of this neighborhood is going high-class residential). Eventually you'll return to rue de la République, Avignon's main drag.*

SIGHTS

Most of Avignon's top sights are covered by the walking tours, above. With more time, consider these options.

In Avignon

Fondation Angladon-Dubrujeaud—Visiting this museum is like being invited into the elegant home of a rich and passionate art collector. It mixes a small but enjoyable collection of art from Post-Impressionists (including Paul Cézanne, Vincent van Gogh, Honoré Daumier, Edgar Degas, and Pablo Picasso) with re-created art studios and furnishings from many periods. It's a quiet place with a few superb paintings (€6, €4 with Avignon Passion Pass; May–Nov Tue–Sun 13:00–18:00, closed Mon; Dec–April

Wed–Sun 13:00–18:00, closed Mon–Tue; 5 rue Laboureur, tel. 04 90 82 29 03, www.angladon.com).

Calvet Museum (Musée Calvet)—This fine-arts museum impressively displays its good collection, without a word of English explanation (€6, €3 with Avignon Passion Pass, Wed–Mon 10:00–13:00 & 14:00–18:00, closed Tue, on quieter west half of town at 65 rue Joseph Vernet, antiquities collection a few blocks away at 27 rue de la République—same hours and ticket, tel. 04 90 86 33 84).

Near Avignon, in Villeneuve-lès-Avignon

▲**Tower of Philip the Fair (Tour Philippe-le-Bel)**—Built to protect access to St. Bénezet Bridge in 1307, this massive tower offers the finest view over Avignon and the Rhône basin. It's best late in the day (€2, €1 with Avignon Passion Pass; April–Sept daily 10:00–12:30 & 14:00–18:30; Oct–Nov and March Tue–Sun 10:00–12:00 & 14:00–17:00, closed Mon; closed Dec–Feb; tel. 04 32 70 08 57). To reach the tower from Avignon, you can drive (5 min, cross Daladier Bridge, follow signs to Villeneuve-lès-Avignon); take a boat (Bateau-Bus departs from Mireio Embarcadère near Daladier Bridge); or take bus #11 (2/hr, catch bus across from Centre-Ville train station, in front of post office, on cours Président Kennedy).

SLEEPING

Hotel values are better in Arles. Avignon is particularly popular during its July festival (see sidebar on page 89), when you must book ahead (expect inflated prices). Also note that only a few hotels have elevators—specifically, the first three listed near place de l'Horloge.

Sleep Code

(€1 = about $1.30, country code: 33)
S = Single, **D** = Double/Twin, **T** = Triple, **Q** = Quad, **b** = bathroom, **s** = shower only, ***** = French hotel rating system (0–4 stars). Unless otherwise noted, credit cards are accepted and English is spoken.

To help you easily sort through these listings, I've divided the rooms into three categories, based on the price for a standard double room with bath:

\$\$\$ Higher Priced—Most rooms €85 or more.
  \$\$ Moderately Priced—Most rooms between €65–85.
    \$ Lower Priced—Most rooms €65 or less.

Near Avignon's Centre-Ville Station

The first three listings are a 10-minute walk from the main train station; turn right off cours Jean Jaurès on rue Agricol Perdiguier.

$$ Hôtel Colbert** is a good midrange bet with a variety of rooms in many sizes and a sweet little patio. Your efficient hosts—Patrice, Annie, and *le chien* Brittany—care for this restored manor house and its cozy public spaces (Sb-€45–60, Db-€60–75, Tb-€83–90, air-con, Wi-Fi, parking-€9, 7 rue Agricol Perdiguier, tel. 04 90 86 20 20, fax 04 90 85 97 00, www.lecolbert-hotel.com, contact@avignon-hotel-colbert.com).

$ Hôtel du Parc* is a spotless value with white walls, tiny bathrooms, and stone accents. It's scrupulously managed by entertaining Avignon native Madame Rous, who bakes her own bread and pastries for breakfast—and even made the bedspreads by hand (S-€28, Ss-€38, D-€39, Ds-€47–54, Ts-€65, no TVs or phones, tel. 04 90 82 71 55, fax 04 90 85 64 86, hotel.parc@modulonet.fr). This place is cheaper and sharper than Hôtel le Splendid, across the street.

$ Hôtel le Splendid* rents 17 small, musty-but-cheery rooms with good beds, ceiling fans, and small bathrooms. Your room comes with a smile from Madame Prel-Lemoine (Sb-€43–46, Db-€55–65, bigger Db with air-con-€61–71, three Db apartments-€80, extra person-€10, discounts for stays longer than one week, 17 rue Agricol Perdiguier, tel. 04 90 86 14 46, fax 04 90 85 38 55, www.avignon-splendid-hotel.com).

$ Hôtel Boquier** offers 12 quiet, modest rooms under wood beams at fair prices, though this may change after their major renovation (Db-€50–60, Tb-€72, Qb-€90, extra bed-€10, parking-€7, near the TI at 6 rue du portail Boquier, tel. 04 90 82 34 43, fax 04 90 86 14 07, www.hotel-boquier.com, contact @hotel-boquier.com).

In the Center, near Place de l'Horloge

$$$ Hôtel d'Europe****, with Avignon's most prestigious address, lets peasants sleep royally—if you get one of the 15 surprisingly reasonable "standard rooms." Enter a fountain-filled courtyard, linger in the lounges, and enjoy every comfort. The hotel is located on the handsome place Crillon, near the river (standard Db-€142, spacious Db standard-€172, first-class Db-€240, deluxe Db-€340, superior Db-€455, breakfast-€25, elevator, Internet access, garage-€16, near Daladier Bridge at 12 place Crillon, tel. 04 90 14 76 76, fax 04 90 14 76 71, www.heurope.com, reservations@heurope.com). The hotel's restaurant is Michelin-rated (one star) and serves an upscale €50 *menu* in its formal dining room or front courtyard.

$$$ Hôtel Mercure Cité des Papes*** is a modern chain hotel within spitting distance of the Palace of the Popes. It has

Avignon

Avignon Hotels

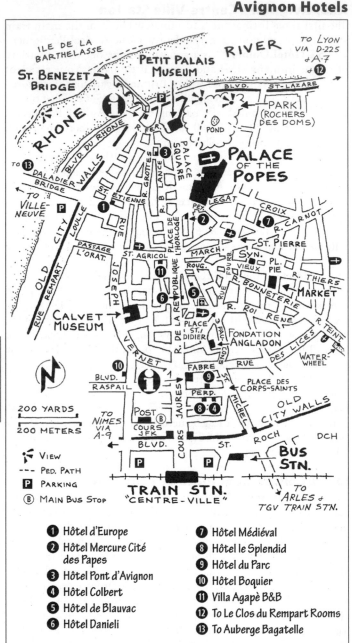

1. Hôtel d'Europe
2. Hôtel Mercure Cité des Papes
3. Hôtel Pont d'Avignon
4. Hôtel Colbert
5. Hôtel de Blauvac
6. Hôtel Danieli
7. Hôtel Médiéval
8. Hôtel le Splendid
9. Hôtel du Parc
10. Hôtel Boquier
11. Villa Agapè B&B
12. To Le Clos du Rempart Rooms
13. To Auberge Bagatelle

89 smartly designed, smallish rooms, air-conditioning, elevators, and all the comforts (Sb-€108, Db-€118, up to €138 during holiday weekends and the July festival, many rooms have views over place de l'Horloge, 1 rue Jean Vilar, tel. 04 90 80 93 00, fax 04 90 80 93 01, www.mercure.com, h1952@accor.com).

$$$ Hôtel Pont d'Avignon*, just inside the walls near St. Bénezet Bridge, is part of the same chain as the Hôtel Mercure Cité des Papes, with the same prices for its 87 rooms (direct access to a garage makes parking easier than at the other Mercure hotel, elevator, on rue Ferruce, tel. 04 90 80 93 93, fax 04 90 80 93 94, www.mercure.com, h0549@accor.com).

$$ At Hôtel de Blauvac, friendly owner Veronica offers 16 mostly spacious, high-ceilinged rooms (many with an additional upstairs loft), a sky-high atrium and Internet access for a fee. It's a faded old manor home near the pedestrian zone, with reliable noise at night (Sb-€67–77, Db-€72–82, Tb-€87–97, Qb-€102, €10 less off-season, 1 block off rue de la République at 11 rue de la Bancasse, tel. 04 90 86 34 11, fax 04 90 86 27 41, www.hotel -blauvac.com, blauvac@aol.com).

$$ Hôtel Danieli is a *Hello Dolly* fluffball of a place, renting 29 colorful and simple rooms on the main drag to lots of tour groups (Sb-€70, Db-€80, Tb-€90, Qb-€100, 17 rue de la République, tel. 04 90 86 46 82, fax 04 90 27 09 24, www.hotel-danieli-avignon .com, hoteldanieli@wanadoo.fr, kind owner Madame Shogol).

$$ Hôtel Médiéval is burrowed deep a few blocks from the Church of St. Pierre. Built as a cardinal's home, this massive stone mansion has a small garden and friendly managers. It has 35 wood-paneled, mostly air-conditioned, unimaginative rooms (Sb-€47, Db-€57–72, larger Db-€81–88, Tb-€88, kitchenettes available but require 3-night minimum stay, Wi-Fi, 5 blocks east of place de l'Horloge, behind Church of St. Pierre at 15 rue Petite Saunerie, tel. 04 90 86 11 06, fax 04 90 82 08 64, www.hotelmedieval.com, hotel.medieval@wanadoo.fr, Mike).

Chambres d'Hôte

$$$ Villa Agapè, just off busy place de l'Horloge (right in the center of town), is an oasis of calm and good taste. Run by friendly Madame de La Pommeraye, the villa has three handsomely decorated rooms, a peaceful courtyard, lovely public spaces, and a soaking pool to boot (Db-€100–150, extra person-€30, includes breakfast, 2-night minimum, Internet access and Wi-Fi, from place de l'Horloge it's one block down on left above the pharmacy at 13 rue St. Agricol—ring buzzer, tel. & fax 04 90 85 21 92, mobile 06 07 98 71 30, www.villa-agape.com, michele@villa-agape.com). For a weeklong stay, ask about renting her entire house, where you get Madame's room, study, and kitchen (€2,500–3,300).

$$$ Le Clos du Rempart, while less central, is still within the walls and worth considering. Madame Assad, another Parisian refugee, rents two rooms and one apartment on a pleasant courtyard decorated in a Middle Eastern theme, complete with a hammock (Db-€90–120 depending on season and room size, 2-bedroom apartment for 4 with kitchen-€150–230, apartment cheaper by the week, includes breakfast, air-con, 1 parking spot in garage, a 20-min walk from the Centre-Ville station at 35–37 rue Crémade, call for directions, tel. & fax 04 90 86 39 14, www.closdurempart.com, aida@closderempart.com).

Sleeping Cheaply near Avignon

$ Auberge Bagatelle's hostel offers dirt-cheap beds, a lively atmosphere, café, grocery store, launderette, great views of Avignon, and campers for neighbors (D-€38, dorm bed-€16, across Daladier Bridge on Ile de la Barthelasse, bus #10 from main post office, tel. 04 90 86 71 31, fax 04 90 27 16 23, www.aubergebagatelle.fr, auberge.bagatelle@wanadoo.fr).

EATING

Skip the overpriced places on place de l'Horloge (Les Domaines and La Civette near the carousel are the least of the evils here) and find a more intimate location for your dinner. Avignon has many delightful squares filled with tables ready to seat you (including place des Corps-Saints—see page 107).

Near the Church of St. Pierre

The church has enclosed squares on both sides, offering outdoor yet intimate ambience.

L'Epicerie, located on a small, unpretentious square, serves the highest-quality and highest-priced cuisine around the Church of St. Pierre (€20–25 *plats*, closed Sun, cozy interior good in bad weather, 10 place St. Pierre, tel. 04 90 82 74 22).

Pass under the arch by L'Epicerie restaurant and enter enchanting place des Châtaignes, a tasty commotion of tables from four restaurants: **Crêperie du Cloître** (big salad and main-course crêpe for about €14, closed Sun–Mon); **Restaurant Nem,** tucked in the corner (Vietnamese, family-run, *menus* from €12); and **Pause Gourmande** (lunch only, €9 *plats du jour*, always a veggie option, closed Sun). Just through the arch, past Pause Gourmande, is **La Goulette,** offering Tunisian specialties like couscous and tagine (slow-cooked meals in a special pot) for €19 (closed Mon).

Avignon Restaurants

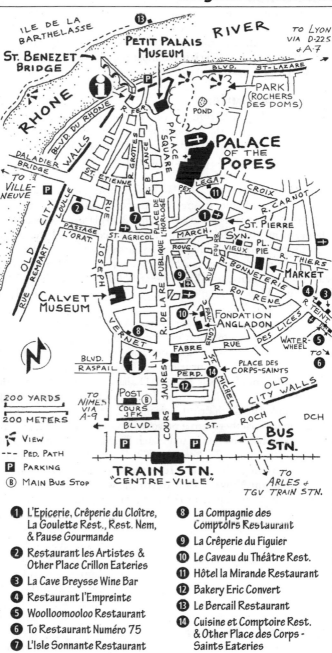

1. L'Epicerie, Crêperie du Cloître, La Goulette Rest., Rest. Nem, & Pause Gourmande
2. Restaurant les Artistes & Other Place Crillon Eateries
3. La Cave Breysse Wine Bar
4. Restaurant l'Empreinte
5. Woolloomooloo Restaurant
6. To Restaurant Numéro 75
7. L'Isle Sonnante Restaurant
8. La Compagnie des Comptoirs Restaurant
9. La Crêperie du Figuier
10. Le Caveau du Théâtre Rest.
11. Hôtel la Mirande Restaurant
12. Bakery Eric Convert
13. Le Bercail Restaurant
14. Cuisine et Comptoire Rest. & Other Place des Corps-Saints Eateries

Place Crillon

This large and trendy open square just off the river provides more atmosphere than quality. Several cafés offer inexpensive bistro fare with *menus* from €16, *plats* from €12, and many tables to choose from. **Restaurant les Artistes** is most popular (daily until 22:30, 21 place Crillon, tel. 04 90 82 23 54).

Rue des Teinturiers

While a bit of a walk from the center, this street has a wonderful concentration of eateries popular with the natives. It's a youthful and trendy area, recently spiffed up with a canalside ambience and little hint of tourism. I'd survey the four eateries listed here before choosing.

La Cave Breysse is a fun and colorful stop for a lunch salad, or a good pause before dinner. Midday or evening, Christine and Tim would love to serve you a fragrant €2.50 glass of regional wine. Choose from the blackboard by the bar that lists all the bottles open today. You're welcome to take yours out and sit by the canal. In the evening, this place is a hit with the young local crowd for its wine (flexible hours, usually Tue–Sat 12:00–14:30 & 18:00–22:30, closed Sun–Mon, no food in evening; across from waterwheel at 41 rue des Teinturiers).

L'Empreinte is good for North African cuisine. Choose a table in its tent-like interior, or sit canalside on the cobbles (copious couscous for €11–20, take-out and veggie options available, open daily, 33 rue des Teinturiers, tel. 04 32 76 31 84).

Woolloomooloo was named, Dada-style, for the aboriginal term for "little black kangaroo." It's a funky and young-spirited eatery...think van Gogh drunk on rum-and-fruit punch. The food—while slopped together from a precooked buffet—is hearty, creative, and a good value. You'll mix and match from a very fun menu (€18/1 course and a drink, €21/2 courses, €28/3 courses, open daily, frequent jazz evenings, 16 rue des Teinturiers, tel. 04 90 85 28 44).

Restaurant Numéro 75 is worth the walk, filling the Pernod mansion (of *pastis* liquor fame) and a large, romantic courtyard with outdoor tables. The menu is limited to Mediterranean cuisine, but everything's *très* tasty. It's best to go with the options offered by your young, black-shirted server (three entrées, plus a fish and a meat main; 2-course lunch *menu* with wine and coffee-€20; dinner *menus*: €25/main course and dessert, €27/appetizer and main course, €33/3 courses; Mon–Sat 12:00–14:00 & 20:00–22:00, closed Sun, 75 rue Guillaume Puy, tel. 04 90 27 16 00).

Elsewhere in Avignon

At **L'Isle Sonnante,** join chef Boris and his wife Anne to dine intimately in their charming one-room *bistrot*. You'll choose from a small menu offering only fresh products and be served by owners who care (*menus* from €27, closed Sun–Mon, 100 yards from the carousel on place de l'Horloge at 7 rue Racine, tel. 04 90 82 56 01, best to book ahead).

La Compagnie des Comptoirs is the brainchild of famous twin-brother chefs who established a following in southern France with their inventive cuisine. Enter a Mediterranean world of cool bars, smart interiors, and a dazzling courtyard. This is where young Avignon professionals enjoy foods from the Mediterranean basin (allow €45 for dinner with wine, 83 rue Joseph Vernet, tel. 04 90 85 99 04).

La Crêperie du Figuier has good crêpes and salads that won't break the bank (dinner crêpe or salad for €11, daily July–Aug, otherwise closed Sun–Mon, 3 rue du Figuier, tel. 04 90 82 60 67).

Le Caveau du Théâtre invites relaxed diners to share a glass of wine or dinner at one of a few sidewalk tables. Its wild posters decorate a carefree interior (€13 *plats*, €19 *menus*, fun ambience for free, closed Sun, 16 rue des Trois Faucons, tel. 04 90 82 60 91).

Hôtel la Mirande is the ultimate Avignon splurge. Reserve ahead here for understated elegance and Avignon's top cuisine (€35 lunch *menu*, €105 dinner tasting *menu*, closed Tue–Wed, behind Palace of the Popes, 4 place de la Mirande, tel. 04 90 86 93 93, fax 04 90 86 26 85).

Bakery Eric Convert has excellent bread and sandwiches for lunch. Here you'll find a great selection of breads, including olive, Roquefort, orange chocolate, and dark Russian, and all varieties of baguettes and mouthwatering pastries (closed Sun, 45 cours Jean Jaurès, tel. 04 90 85 80 62).

Dining on the Square: On the pleasing **place des Corps-Saints,** you'll find several relaxed and reasonable eateries with tables sprawling under big plane tress. Try **Cuisine et Comptoire** (closed Sun, tel. 04 90 82 18 39).

Across the River

Le Bercail offers a fun opportunity to get out of town (barely) and take in *le fresh air* with a terrific riverfront view of Avignon, all while enjoying inexpensive Provençal cooking served in big portions. Book ahead, as this restaurant is popular (*menus* from €16, serves late, daily April–Oct, tel. 04 90 82 20 22).

To get there, take the small shuttle boat (located near St. Bénezet Bridge) to the Ile de la Barthelasse, turn right, and walk five minutes. As the boat usually stops running at about 18:00 (except in July–Aug, when it runs until 21:00), you can either taxi home or walk 25 minutes along the pleasant riverside path and over Daladier Bridge.

TRANSPORTATION CONNECTIONS

Trains

Remember, there are two train stations in Avignon: the suburban TGV station and the Centre-Ville station in the city center (€1.10 shuttle buses connect to both stations, 3/hr, 15 min). Only the Centre-Ville station has baggage check (see "Arrival in Avignon," page 87). Car rental is available at the TGV station. Some cities are served both by slower local trains from the Centre-Ville station and by faster TGV trains from the TGV station; I've listed the most convenient stations for each trip.

From Avignon's Centre-Ville Station by Train to: Arles (11/day, 20 min, less frequent in the afternoon), **Orange** (10/day, 15 min), **Nîmes** (14/day, 30 min), **Isle-sur-la-Sorgue** (10/day on weekdays, 5/day on weekends, 30 min), **Lyon** (10/day, 2 hrs, also from TGV station—see below), **Carcassonne** (8/day, 7 with transfer in Narbonne, 3 hrs), **Barcelona** (2/day, 6 hrs, transfer in Montpellier).

From Avignon's TGV Station to: Nice (20/day, 13 of which are via TGV, 4 hrs, most require transfer in Marseille), **Marseille** (10/day, 1 hr), **Aix-en-Provence TGV** (10/day, 25 min), **Lyon** (12/day, 1.5 hrs, also from Centre-Ville station—see above), **Paris'** Gare de Lyon (9/day in 2.5 hrs, 6/day in 3–4 hrs with change), **Paris'** Charles de Gaulle airport (7/day, 3 hrs).

Buses

The bus station *(gare routière)* is just past and below the Ibis Hôtel, to the right as you exit the train station (information desk open Mon–Fri 10:15–13:00 & 14:00–18:00, Sat 8:00–12:00, closed Sun, tel. 04 90 82 07 35). Nearly all buses leave from this station. The biggest exception is the SNCF bus service from the Avignon TGV station to Arles (11/day, 1 hr—the train is a much better option). The Avignon TI has schedules. Service is reduced or nonexistent on Sundays and holidays. Check your departure time beforehand and make sure to verify your destination with the driver.

From Avignon by Bus to Pont du Gard: Buses leave regularly for Pont du Gard (4/day, 50 min; more with inconvenient transfer), but the schedule doesn't work well for day-trippers from Avignon—the way the return buses are timed, you get either far too little time there (20 min) or a bit too much (5 hrs). For a more worthwhile day trip, see my suggested train/bus excursion that combines Nîmes and the Pont du Gard (page 110).

By Bus to Other Regional Destinations: Uzès (4/day Mon–Sat, none Sun, 1 hr), **St. Rémy-de-Provence** (6/day, 50 min, handy way to visit its Wed market); **Orange** (hourly, 55 min), **Isle-sur-la-Sorgue** (6/day Mon–Sat, fewer on Sun, 45 min); **Vaison**

la Romaine, Nyons, Sablet, and Séguret (2–3/day during school year, called *période scolaire*, 1/day otherwise and 1/day from TGV station, 75–90 min); Gordes (via Cavaillon, 1/day, not on Wed or Sun, 2 hrs, spend the night or taxi back to Cavaillon); Lourmarin (3/day, 90 min).

NEAR AVIGNON

Nîmes, Pont du Gard, and Uzès

While Avignon lacks Roman monuments of its own, some of Europe's most impressive Roman sights are an easy, breezy day trip away. The Pont du Gard aqueduct is a magnificent structure to experience, as is the city it served 2,000 years ago, Nîmes, which wraps a variety of intriguing Roman monuments together in a bustling, bigger-city package. The pedestrian-friendly town of Uzès, between Nîmes and the Pont du Gard, offers a refreshing break from power monuments and busy cities. Combining these three sights makes a memorable day trip into the Languedoc region. Traveling by car, you'll drive scenic roads (particularly D-979 between Uzès and Nîmes) that show off the rugged *garrigue* landscape that this area is famous for.

Planning Your Time

If you've got the time, consider getting away from the tourists and spending a night in classy Nîmes or relaxing Uzès. If you're on a tighter schedule, don't worry—this region's sights are easy to cover in a day trip from Avignon, even without a car.

For a great all-day excursion, take a morning train from Avignon to Nîmes (leave at about 9:00 from Avignon's Centre-Ville station) and follow my self-guided walking tour. Then take the 13:00 bus from Nîmes to Pont du Gard, which gives you enough time to enjoy the aqueduct and its museum before catching a 16:00 bus to Uzès. Wind down with an evening stroll through Uzès, and take the last bus from Uzès back to Avignon at 18:30. This lands you back at Avignon at 19:25—just in time for dinner (see "Transportation Connections" on page 108 for more details). These connections work everyday but Sunday (when buses are too infrequent); be sure to double-check schedules at Avignon's TI before you head out. Have cash on hand for bus tickets (bus and

Near Avignon

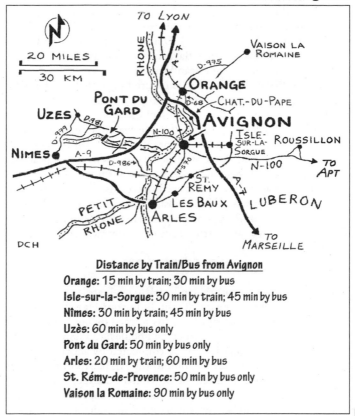

Distance by Train/Bus from Avignon

Orange: 15 min by train; 30 min by bus

Isle-sur-la-Sorgue: 30 min by train; 45 min by bus

Nîmes: 30 min by train; 45 min by bus

Uzès: 60 min by bus only

Pont du Gard: 50 min by bus only

Arles: 20 min by train; 60 min by bus

St. Rémy-de-Provence: 50 min by bus only

Vaison la Romaine: 90 min by bus only

train fares for these trips come to about €35), and verify your destination with the driver when you board.

If you'd rather not leave Avignon quite so early in the morning, skip Uzès and take the 12:05 bus from Avignon, arriving at Pont du Gard at 12:50. Then take the 14:45 bus from there to Nîmes (where trains run hourly back to Avignon).

Nîmes

Nîmes joins Arles and Avignon on the list of central Provence's "big three." While Arles and Avignon have more touristic appeal, Nîmes—which feels richer and surer of itself—is completely lacking in overnight tourists. This thriving town of classy shops and serious businesses is studded with world-class Roman monuments. (And if you've visited the magnificent Pont du Gard, you must be curious where all that water went.)

Since the Middle Ages, Nîmes has exported a famous fabric: The word *denim* actually comes from here ("denim"—from *de Nîmes*, meaning "from Nîmes"). Denim caught on in the United States in the 1800s, when a Bavarian immigrant, Levi Strauss, exploited its use in the American West.

Today, Nîmes is officially considered part of the Languedoc region (for administrative purposes only), yet historically the town has been a key player in the evolution of Provence. Only 30 minutes by train from Arles or Avignon (€8 one-way to either), and three hours from Paris on the TGV, Nîmes is worth a visit if you want a taste of today's urban Provence. The city keeps its clean, peaceful, and pedestrian-polished old center a secret for its well-heeled residents. (Locals admit they don't need the tourist money as much as other Provençal towns.) While most visitors understandably prefer sleeping in Arles or Avignon, a night here provides a good escape from tourist crowds and a truer taste of a Provençal city.

ORIENTATION

Nîmes has no river or natural landmark to navigate by, so it's easy to become disoriented. For a quick visit, limit yourself to the manageable triangle within the ring of roads formed by boulevard Victor Hugo, boulevard Amiral Courbet, and boulevard Gambetta.

The town's landmarks can be connected by short walks: It's five minutes from the train station to the Arena, 10 minutes from the Arena to the Roman temple of Maison Carrée, and 10 minutes from Maison Carrée to either the Castellum or the Fountain Garden. Apart from seeing this handful of ancient monuments, appreciate the city's virtually traffic-free old center—a delight for browsing, strolling, sipping coffee, and people-watching.

Tourist Information

The helpful TI is a few steps out the front door and across the street from Maison Carrée (Mon–Fri 8:30–19:00, Sat 9:00–19:00, Sun 10:00–18:00, 6 rue Auguste, tel. 04 66 58 38 00, www.ot-nimes.fr). Pick up the excellent *Discovering Nîmes* pamphlet, which includes a map with a description of the city's sights and museums, and a worthwhile old-town walk. You can also rent an MP3-player audioguide for a walking tour of Old Nîmes (€8/1 player, €10/2 players, leave ID as deposit).

Arrival in Nîmes

By Train and Bus: Trains and buses use the same station, which is handy for travelers who want to combine Pont du Gard with Nîmes. There is no baggage check. Confirm return schedules before leaving the station, as service can be sparse. The bus information office is in the rear of the train station (Mon–Fri 7:30–12:30 & 14:00–18:30, closed Sat–Sun). Television screens near the bus information office display departure times (still, it's a good idea to verify times with a clerk at the information booth).

The Arena is a five-minute walk straight out of the train station. Head up the left side of avenue Feuchères, veer left at the end of the street, then curve right and you'll see the Arena. The Maison Carrée and TI are a pleasant 10-minute stroll from the Arena through Nîmes' traffic-free old town.

By Car: Follow signs for *Centre-Ville* and *TI*, then *Arènes*, and pay to park underneath the Arena.

Helpful Hints

Summer Thursdays: The "Jeudi de Nîmes" (Thursdays of Nîmes) tradition turns the entire old center of town into a festival of shops, street music, and liveliness Thursday nights in July and August from 18:00 until late.

Internet Access: An Internet café is behind Maison Carrée at 25 place du Maison Carrée (daily 10:00–24:00, lots of young gamers).

Laundry: There's a clean launderette at 14 rue Nationale (daily 7:00–21:00).

Taxi and Tours: Call 04 66 29 40 11 for a cab or for an English-language tour of Nîmes by taxi (up to 6 people).

Car Rental: Avis and others are at the train station (tel. 04 66 29 66 36).

Train Tickets: The small SNCF Boutique office—centrally located in the old town—is an easy place to check schedules or buy train tickets without having to go to the station (Tue–Sat 8:30–18:50, closed Sun–Mon, 11 rue de l'Aspic).

Local Guide: Sylvie Pagnard is a delightful local guide whose walking tours are top quality and top price. She does regional tours and has a car (€130/3 hrs, €350/8 hrs, tel. 04 66 20 33 14, mobile 06 03 21 37 33, sylviepagnard@aol.com).

Tourist Train: The tourist train will save your soles (€5, daily April–Oct, nearly hourly at the bottom of the hour, doesn't run Nov–March, 35 min, departs from esplanade with fountain in front of Arena).

View and WCs: Ride the glass elevator to the top-floor café of the Museum of Contemporary Art for a great view over the ancient Maison Carrée and a quiet break above the world. The museum is in the glass building that faces the monument, and the elevator is inside near the front door (Tue–Sun 10:00–18:00, closed Mon). The basement has good WCs (same hours as café).

SELF-GUIDED WALK

Welcome to Nîmes

I've described Nîmes' best sights below in a logical walking order for a good, daylong visit, starting from the Arena (near the train station, with easy parking underground). Most of the sights I mention are free; the major exception is the Arena.

▲▲Arena (Amphithéâtre)

Nîmes' Arena dates from about A.D. 100 and is more than 425 feet in diameter and 65 feet tall. Considered the best-preserved arena of the Roman world, it's a fine example of Roman engineering...

and propaganda. In the spirit of "give them bread and circuses," it was free. No gates, just 60 welcoming arches, numbered to allow entertainment-seekers to come and go freely. The agenda was to create a populace that was thoroughly Roman—enjoying the same activities and entertainment, all thinking as one (not unlike Americans' nationwide obsession with the same reality-TV shows). The 24,000 seats could be filled and emptied in minutes (through passageways called *vomitoires*).

Climb to the very top—it's a rare opportunity to enjoy the view from the nosebleed seats of a Roman arena. An amphitheater is literally a double theater: two theaters facing each other, designed so that double the people could view a *Dirty Harry* spectacle (without the fine acoustics provided by the back wall of a theater stage). You may think of this as a "colosseum," but that's not a generic term. Rome's Colosseum was a one-of-a-kind arena—named for a colossal statue of Nero that stood nearby.

The floor where the action took place was the *arena* (literally, "sand"—which absorbed the blood, as in bullfights today). The Arena's floor, which covered passages and storage areas underneath, came with the famous elevator for surprise appearances of wild animals. (While Rome could afford exotic beasts from the tropics, places like Nîmes made do with snarling local beasts... bulls, wild boars, lots of bears, and so on.) The standard fight was as real as professional wrestling is today—mostly just crowd-pleasing. Thumbs down and kill the guy? Maybe in Rome, but only rarely (if ever) here.

After Rome fell, and stability was replaced by Dark Age chaos, a huge structure like this was put to good use—bricked up

Near Avignon

Nîmes

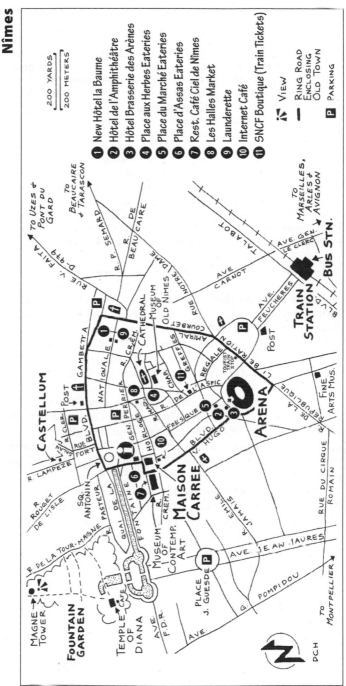

200 YARDS
200 METERS

1 New Hôtel la Baume
2 Hôtel de l'Amphithéâtre
3 Hôtel Brasserie des Arènes
4 Place aux Herbes Eateries
5 Place du Marché Eateries
6 Place d'Assas Eateries
7 Rest. Café Ciel de Nîmes
8 Les Halles Market
9 Launderette
10 Internet Café
11 SNCF Boutique (Train Tickets)

— VIEW

— RING ROAD
ENCLOSING
OLD TOWN

P PARKING

Near Avignon

Roman Nîmes

Born a Celtic city (about 500 B.C.), Nîmes joined the Roman Empire in the first century B.C. Because it had a privileged status within the Roman Empire, Nîmes was never really considered part of the conquered barbarian world. It rated highly enough to merit one of the longest protective walls in the Roman world and to have a 30-mile-long aqueduct (Pont du Gard) built to serve its growing population.

Today, the physical remains of Roman Nîmes testify to its former importance. The city's emblem—a crocodile tied to a palm tree—is a reminder that Nîmes was a favorite retirement home for Roman officers who conquered Egypt. (The crocodile is Egypt, and the palm tree symbolizes victory.) All over town, little bronze croc-palm medallions shine on the sidewalks. In the City Hall, 400-year-old statues of crocodiles actually swing from the top of a monumental staircase.

and made a fortress (just like the Roman Arena in Arles). In the 13th century, after this region was incorporated into France, the Arena became a gated community housing about 700 people—with streets, plumbing, even gardens on the top level. Only in 1809 did Napoleon decide to scrape away the people and make this a historic monument, thus letting the ancient grandeur of Roman France shine.

Since 1850, Nîmes' Arena has been a venue for spectacles, even Spanish-style bullfights. An inflatable dome added in 1988 provides a roof over the lower seats (from the glass half-walls down), giving the city a winter venue of 7,000 seats for ice-skating, opera, and concerts. Acts from Elton John to Depeche Mode have played here.

Cost and Hours: €8, includes audioguide, daily April–Oct 9:00–17:30, June–Aug until 19:00, Nov–March closes at 16:30, last ticket sold 45 min before closing, may close for special events—check at TI. Buy the €10 combo-ticket if you plan to visit the Maison Carrée and the Tour Magne (tower in the Fountain Garden—not worth the climb).

• *From the Arena, head to Maison Carrée via a stroll through Nîmes' "conservation zone"—the Old City. From opposite the Arena's ticket office, follow rue des Arènes into place du Marché and the heart of the...*

▲▲Old City

Those coming to Nîmes only for its famous Roman sights are pleasantly surprised by its carefully preserved old center. Here, you can study how elements in the buildings from the medieval and Renaissance times artfully survive: Shop interiors incorporate medieval brick with stone arches; windows expose Gothic finery; and Renaissance staircases grace peaceful courtyards.

Place du Marché has an inviting café ambience, including a wispy palm-tree-and-crocodile fountain. **Le Courtois Café/ Pâtisserie** is the class act of the square—check out its old-time interior. It's been family-run since 1892. If you have a sweet tooth, try the house specialty, a dipped-in-chocolate *nélesko* (somewhere between a cake and a cookie—the oldest recipe of the house); or a Nîmes specialty, *caladon* (literally, "cobble"—like on the street; a hard honey-and-almond cookie; café open daily 8:00–19:30, tel. 04 66 67 20 09).

• *Leave the square, heading to the right on rue des Broquiers, then turn left on rue de l'Aspic, the town's primary shopping spine. Rue de l'Aspic leads to place de l'Horloge, the center of the old town. From here, pedestrian-friendly streets take off in all directions, including directly to Maison Carrée (described below). Follow rue de la Madeleine to the...*

▲Place aux Herbes

This inviting square is the site of Nîmes' oldest market. Marking the center of the old town, it's a good hub for a bit of sightseeing. There are several good places to eat on or near the square (see "Eating," below). Also consider the next four sights, each of which either faces the square or is within a block of it:

Nîmes Cathedral

While its Romanesque facade survives from the 12th century, the cathedral's interior—gutted over centuries of dynastic squabbles, Reformation, and revolution—is unremarkable neo-Romanesque, mostly from the 19th century.

Museum of Old Nîmes

One floor of a 17th-century bishop's palace with a humble exhibition on life in the city, this museum starts with the Middle Ages and provides the best chance to bring the intriguing architectural remnants of historic Nîmes to life. You'll also learn the story of indigo, 19th-century denim wear, and early Levis (free, no English, Tue–Sun 10:00–18:00, closed Mon, tel. 04 66 76 73 70).

Covered Produce Market

Les Halles Centre Commerciale (a block past the cathedral) looks like a big, black, and modern parking garage, but the ground floor is a thriving, colorful market hall, well worth exploring (daily until 13:00).

Near Avignon

Old-Time Spice Shop

L'Huilerie Epicerie is a charming time warp displaying spices and herbs, oils, and candy. Just a block off the square (at 10 rue des Marchands), it's worth a quick visit. To revel in more of Nîmes' medieval atmosphere, find the nearby Passage du Vieux Nîmes.

• *When you're ready to move on, return to place de l'Horloge and follow rue de l'Horloge just behind the clock tower to the...*

▲▲Maison Carrée

This temple rivals Rome's Pantheon as the most complete and beautiful building that survives from the Roman Empire. (There's

nothing inside but a tacky 3-D history movie, described below. Instead, focus on its magnificent exterior.) The temple survived in part because it's been in constant use for the last thousand years—as a church, City Hall, private stable, archives during the Revolution, people's art gallery after the Revolution (like Paris' Louvre), and finally as the monument you visit today. It's a textbook example of a "pseudo-peripteral temple" (surrounded by columns, half of which support the roof over a porch, and half of which merely decorate the rest of the building) and a "six-column temple" (a standard proportion—if it's six columns wide, it must be 11 columns deep).

The lettering across the front is long gone, but the tiny surviving "nail holes" presented archaeologists with a fun challenge: Assuming each letter would leave a particular series of nail holes as evidence, derive the words. Archaeologists agree that this temple was built to honor Caius and Lucius, the grandsons (and adopted sons) of Emperor Augustus. And from this information, they date the temple from the year A.D. 4.

Maison Carrée (literally, "Square House"—named before they had a word for "rectangle") was the centerpiece of a fancy plaza surrounded by a U-shaped commercial, political, and religious forum. This marked the core of Roman Nîmes. As was the case in all Roman temples, only the priest went inside. Worshippers gathered for religious rituals at the foot of the steps. Climb the steps as a priest would—starting and ending with your right foot... *dexter* (from the Latin for "right") rather than *sinister* ("left"). Put your right foot forward for good karma.

Inside, the *Heroes of Nîmes* **movie** tells the story of six heroic locals, each vying to be "the most heroic citizen of noble

Nîmes." While entertaining, this 3-D film—covering 2,000 years in 20 minutes—insults the building it fills (€4.50, every 30 min, soundtrack in Latin and French, with English subtitles).

The modern building facing the temple is Nîmes' **Carrée d'Art** ("Square of Art"), designed by British architect Norman Foster. It's home to the city's Museum of Contemporary Art (Tue–Sun 10:00–18:00, closed Mon, good view café and WCs—see "Helpful Hints," on page 113).

• *If you haven't visited the TI yet, do it now (across the street from Maison Carrée; see page 112). Then walk down rue Molière with the Museum of Contemporary Art on your left. Dogleg right until you hit the canal, then follow the canal left until you reach the...*

▲The Spring of Nemo in the Fountain Garden

Centuries before the Romans arrived in Nîmes, the Spring of Nemo was here (named, like the town itself, for a Celtic god). When the Romans built a shrine to Emperor Augustus around the spring, rather than bulldoze the Nemo temple, they built alongside it and welcomed Nemo into their own pantheon (as was their more-gods-the-merrier tradition). Today, the spring remains, though the temple is gone.

Walk into the center of the Fountain Garden (Jardin de la Fontaine) and look into the canal. In the early 1700s, Nîmes needed a reliable source of water for its textile industry—to power its mills and provide water for the indigo dyes for the fabric *serge de Nîmes* (denim). About 1735, the city began a project to route a canal through the city and discovered this Roman temple. The city eventually agreed to fund a grander project that ultimately resulted in what you see today: a lavish Versailles-type park, complete with an ornate system of canals and boulevards. This was just 50 years after the construction of Versailles and, to the French, this place has a special significance. These were the first grand public gardens not meant for a king, but for the public. The industrial canals built then still wind throughout the city.

• *Hiding behind trees in the back-left corner of Fountain Garden, find the...*

▲▲Temple of Diana

This first-century "temple," which modern archaeologists now believe was more likely a Roman library, has long been considered one of the best examples of ancient stonework. Its roof—a round Roman barrel vault laced together with still-visible metal pegs—survived until a blast during the Catholic–Protestant Wars of Religion in the 1500s.

At first glance, all the graffiti is obnoxious. But it's actually part of the temple's story. For centuries, France had a highly esteemed guild of stone-, metal-, and woodworkers called the Compagnon, founded by Gothic-church builders in the Middle Ages. As part of their almost mystic training, these craftsmen would visit many buildings—including the great structures of antiquity (such as this one)—for inspiration. Walk through the side aisle for a close look at the razor-accurate stonework and the 17th-, 18th-, and 19th-century signatures of the Compagnon craftsmen who this building inspired. Notice how their signatures match their era—no-nonsense "Enlightened" chiseling of the 18th century gives way to ornate script in the Romantic 19th century.

Cost and Hours: The park and temple are free and open daily (April–mid-Sept 7:30–22:00, mid-Sept–March 7:30–18:30). Skip the hike up to Tour Magne (at top of gardens), which has two remaining levels of a Roman tower; the view is worth neither the sweat nor the €3 fee. Instead, have a well-deserved coffee break or snack at the park's café, located next to the Temple of Diana.

• *To reach the next described sight (about a 15-min walk away), turn left out of the park onto quai de la Fontaine, merge onto busy boulevard Gambetta, and then turn left on rue du Fort, which leads (after a jog to the left up rue de la Lampèze) to the....*

Castellum

This exposed excavation site shows a modest-looking water distribution tank that was the grand finale of the 30-mile-long Pont du Gard aqueduct.

Discovered in the 1850s, this is one of only two known Roman distribution tanks (the other is in Pompeii). The water needs of Roman Nîmes grew beyond the capacity of its local springs. Imagine the jubilation on the day (in A.D. 50) that this system was finally operational. Suddenly, the town had an abundance of water—for basic needs as well as for fun extras like public fountains. Notice the big hole marking the end of the aqueduct, a pool, and two layers of water distribution holes. The lower holes were for top-priority needs, providing water via stone and lead pipes to the public wells that graced neighborhood squares. The higher holes—which got wet only when the supply was plentiful—routed water to the homes of the wealthy, to public baths, and to nonessential fountains. The excavation site is free to visit (daily April–Oct 7:30–22:00, Nov–March 7:30–18:00; for more on this impressive example of Roman engineering, see "Pont du Gard," page 122).

Sleep Code

(€1 = about $1.30, country code: 33)
S = Single, **D** = Double/Twin, **T** = Triple, **Q** = Quad, **b** = bathroom,
s = shower only, ***** = French hotel rating system (0–4 stars).
Unless otherwise noted, credit cards are accepted and English
is spoken.

To help you easily sort through these listings, I've divided
the rooms into three categories, based on the price for a standard double room with bath:

$$$ **Higher Priced**—Most rooms €85 or more.
 $$ **Moderately Priced**—Most rooms between €60–85.
  $ **Lower Priced**—Most rooms €60 or less.

SLEEPING

$$$ **New Hôtel la Baume*****, a few blocks from the cathedral,
has 34 ample and well-designed rooms with every comfort. This
beautiful Renaissance building dates from the 1600s (Sb-€105,
Db-€130–145, Tb-€160, air-con, elevator, 21 rue Nationale, tel.
04 66 76 28 42, fax 04 66 76 28 45, www.new-hotel.com/labaume,
nimeslabaume@new-hotel.com).

$$ **Hôtel de l'Amphithéâtre**** is ideally located, a spear's toss
from the Arena. It's quiet—unless there's a concert at the Arena—
with well-kept rooms run by helpful Hervé and Nathalie (small
Db-€53–63, larger Db-€65–80, no elevator, 3 of the 15 rooms have
air-con, 4 rue des Arènes, tel. 04 66 67 28 51, fax 04 66 67 07 79).

$ **Hôtel Brasserie des Arènes*** occupies a privileged location
facing the Arena. Its 11 rooms above a modern café—some with
kitchenettes—provide one-star comfort at fair rates (Db-€35–45,
Tb-€40–50, 4 boulevard des Arènes, tel. 04 66 67 23 05, fax 04 66
67 76 93, www.brasserie-arenes.com, hotel@brasserie-arenes.com).

EATING

Enjoy the classiness of Nîmes by lunching on one of its fine
squares.

Place aux Herbes: This square, beautifully situated in the
shadow of the cathedral, boasts several popular and hardworking
bistros. **Restaurant ô Délices** and **Le Petit Moka** both serve fresh
salads, crêpes, and *tartines.*

Place du Marché: A block from the Arena, this square is home
to **Mogador Café,** serving tasty, light lunches (salads, crêpes,

and lots of veggies), and **Le Courtois Café/Pâtisserie,** with its trademark desserts (described on page 117).

Place d'Assas: A block from Maison Carrée is a modern square where the young and dynamic meet at **Le Cosy Wine** for finger food and a glass of *vin.* To dine on traditional cuisine, head to **La Source d'Assas,** or to **La Bodeguita** for Mediterranean–Spanish cooking.

Overlooking the Maison Carrée: **Restaurant Café Ciel de Nîmes** fills a terrace atop the city's Norman Foster–designed contemporary art gallery, offering diners great views of the Roman temple. Facing the temple, you'll see the terrace atop the modern building on your right (€8 *plats du jour,* €12 salads, €15 3-course workday lunch special, Tue–Sun 10:00–18:00, closed Mon, place de la Maison Carrée, tel. 04 66 36 71 70).

TRANSPORTATION CONNECTIONS

Trains and buses depart from the same station in Nîmes (see "Arrival in Nîmes," page 112). If traveling by bus, plan to arrive early at the station to double-check your schedule. Ask at the information office for the next bus to your destination and which stand it leaves from (most likely to your right as you walk outside). If the information office is closed, get your ticket from the driver (who probably won't have change for big bills). No route numbers are displayed on the buses, so verify your destination with the driver.

From Nîmes by Train to: Arles (9/day, 30 min), **Avignon** (14/day, 30 min), **Aigues-Mortes** in the Camargue (6/day, 45 min), **Carcassonne** (8/day, 2.5 hrs, transfer in Narbonne), **Paris** (10/day, 3 hrs).

By Bus to: Uzès (10/day Mon–Fri, 6/day Sat, 2/day Sun, 1 hr, €8), **Pont du Gard** (8/day Mon–Sat, 2/day Sun and off-season, 45 min, €7; check return times before you leave, tel. 04 66 29 27 29, www.stdgard.com), **Aigues-Mortes** in the Camargue (6/day, 50 min), **Arles** (6/day, 1 hr).

Pont du Gard

Throughout the ancient world, aqueducts were like flags of stone that heralded the greatness of Rome. A visit to this sight still works to proclaim the wonders of that age. This perfectly preserved Roman aqueduct was built as the critical link of a 30-mile canal that, by dropping one inch for every 350 feet, supplied nine million gallons of water per day (about 100 gallons per second) to Nîmes—one of ancient Europe's largest cities. Though most of the aqueduct is on or below the ground, at the Pont du Gard it spans a canyon on a massive bridge—one of the most remarkable surviving Roman ruins anywhere.

Getting to Pont du Gard

The famous aqueduct is between Remoulins and Vers-Pont du Gard on D-981, 17 miles from Nîmes and 13 miles from Avignon.

By Car: Pont du Gard is an easy 25-minute drive due west of Avignon on N-100 and D-981 (follow signs to *Nîmes*, then *Pont du Gard*) and 45 minutes northwest of Arles (via Tarascon). The handy Rive Gauche parking is off D-981 (the road from Remoulins to Uzès). (Parking is also available on the Rive Droite side, but it's farther away from the museum.) If going to Arles from Pont du Gard, follow signs to *Nîmes* (not Avignon), then follow D-986.

By Bus: Buses run to Pont du Gard (on the Rive Gauche side) from Nîmes, Uzès, and Avignon. Combining Pont du Gard with Nîmes and/or Uzès makes a good day-trip excursion from Avignon (see "Planning Your Time," at the beginning of this chapter).

Most buses stop at the traffic roundabout 300 yards from the aqueduct (in summer, however, buses coming from Avignon drive into the Pont du Gard site and stop at the parking lot's ticket booth). At the roundabout, the stop for buses going from Avignon and to Nîmes is on the far side of the roundabout; the stop for buses going from Nîmes and to Avignon is on the same side as the Pont du Gard (to the left as you enter the traffic circle from the Pont du Gard; see map on page 124). Make sure you're waiting for the bus on the correct side of the traffic circle, and use your hand to signal the bus to stop for you (otherwise, it'll chug on by). Buy your ticket when you get on, and verify your destination with the driver.

To catch buses from Pont du Gard to Uzès, use the same roundabout stop as buses coming from Avignon. In summer, however, when buses from Avignon deviate into the Pont du Gard parking lot, you need to walk out to the far side of the roundabout and find the Uzès stop.

By Taxi: From Nîmes, it's a €35 taxi ride to Pont du Gard (tel. 04 66 29 40 11).

ORIENTATION

There are two riversides to Pont du Gard: the Left Bank (Rive Gauche) and Right Bank (Rive Droite). Park on the Rive Gauche, where you'll find the museums, ticket booth, ATM, cafeteria, WCs, and shops—all built into a modern plaza. You'll see the aqueduct in two parts: first, the fine museum complex, then the actual river gorge spanned by the ancient bridge.

Cost: While it's free to see the aqueduct itself, the various

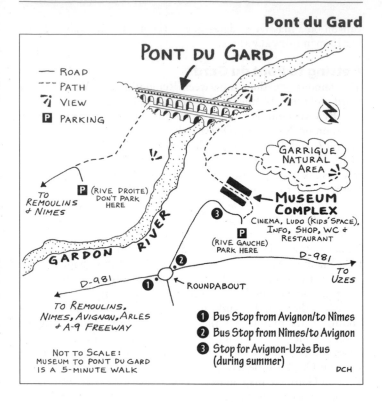

optional activities cost extra: parking (€5), museum (€7), corny film (€4), and a kids' space called *Ludo* (€5, scratch-and-sniff experience in English of various aspects of Roman life and the importance of water). The new extensive outdoor *garrigue* natural area, featuring historic crops and landscapes of the Mediterranean, is free (though €4 buys you a helpful English booklet). During summer months, a nighttime sound-and-light show plays against Pont du Gard. All these attractions are designed to give the sight more meaning—and they do—but for most visitors, only the museum is worth paying for. The **€12 combo-ticket**—which covers all sights and parking—is a no-brainer for drivers, and the best bet for most visitors. Families save even more money with the €24 family ticket (covers two parents and up to four kids). If you get a combo-ticket, check the movie schedule; the romancing-the-aqueduct 25-minute film is silly, but it offers good information in a flirtatious French–Mediterranean style...and a cool, entertaining, and cushy break.

Hours: The museum is open May–Sept Tue–Sun 9:30–19:00, Mon 13:00–19:00; Oct–April closes at 17:00; closed two weeks in Jan. The aqueduct itself is free and open until 1:00 in the morning, as is the parking lot.

Information: Tel. 08 20 90 33 30, www.pontdugard.fr.

Canoe Rental: Consider seeing Pont du Gard by canoe. Collias Canoes will pick you up at Pont du Gard (or elsewhere, if prearranged) and shuttle you to the town of Collias. You'll float down the river to the nearby town of Remoulins, where they'll pick you up and take you back to Pont du Gard (€18 per person, €9 for kids under 12, usually 2 hours, though you can take as long as you like, good idea to reserve the day before in July–Aug, tel. 04 66 22 85 54).

Plan Ahead for Swimming: Pont du Gard is perhaps best enjoyed on your back and in the water—bring along a swimsuit, and sandals for the rocks.

SIGHTS

▲**Museum**—The state-of-the-art museum's multimedia approach (well-presented in English) shows how water was an essential part of the Roman "art of living." You'll see examples of lead pipes, faucets, and siphons; walk through a rock quarry; and learn how they moved those huge rocks into place and how those massive arches were made. While actual artifacts from the aqueduct are few, the exhibit shows the immensity of the undertaking as well as the payoff. Imagine the excitement as this extravagant supply of water finally tumbled into Nîmes. A relaxing highlight is the scenic video helicopter ride along the entire 30-mile course of the structure, from its start at Uzès all the way to the Castellum in Nîmes.

▲▲▲**Viewing the Aqueduct**—A park-like path leads to the aqueduct. Until a few years ago, this was an actual road—adjacent to the aqueduct—that had spanned the river since 1743. Before you cross the bridge, pass under it and hike about 300 feet along the riverbank for a grand viewpoint from which to study the second-highest standing Roman structure.

(Rome's Colosseum is only 6 feet taller.)

This was the biggest bridge in the whole 30-mile-long aqueduct. It seems exceptional because it is: The arches are twice the width of standard aqueducts, and the main arch is the largest the Romans ever built—80 feet (so it wouldn't get its feet wet). The bridge is about 160 feet high and was originally about 1,100 feet long. Today, 12 arches are missing, reducing the length to 790 feet.

While the distance from the source (in Uzès) to Nîmes was only 12 miles as the eagle flew, engineers chose the most economical route, winding and zigzagging 30 miles. The water made the trip in 24 hours with a drop of only 40 feet. Ninety percent of the aqueduct is on or under the ground, but a few river canyons like this required bridges. A stone lid hides a four-foot-wide, six-foot-tall chamber lined with waterproof mortar that carried the stream for more than 400 years. For 150 years, this system provided Nîmes with good drinking water. Expert as the Romans were, they miscalculated the backup caused by a downstream corner, and had to add the thin extra layer you can see just under the lid to make the channel deeper.

The bridge and the river below provide great fun for holiday-goers. While parents suntan on rocks, kids splash into the gorge from under the aqueduct. Some daredevils actually jump from the aqueduct's lower bridge—not knowing that crazy winds scrambled by the structure cause painful belly flops (and sometimes even accidental deaths). For the most refreshing view, float flat on your back underneath the structure.

The appearance of the entire gorge changed in 2002, when a huge flood flushed lots of greenery downstream. Those floodwaters put Roman provisions to the test. Notice the triangular-shaped buttresses at the lower level—designed to split and divert the force of any flood *around* the feet of the arches rather than *into* them. The 2002 floodwaters reached the top of those buttresses. Anxious park rangers winced at the sounds of trees crashing onto the ancient stones...but the arches stood strong.

The stones that jut out—giving the aqueduct a rough, unfinished appearance—supported the original scaffolding. The protuberances were left, rather than cut off, in anticipation of future repair needs. The lips under the arches supported wooden templates that allowed the stones in the round arches to rest on something until the all-important keystone was dropped into place. Each stone weighs four to six tons. The structure stands with no mortar—taking full advantage of the innovative Roman arch, made strong by gravity.

Hike over the bridge for a closer look. Across the river, a high trail (marked *panorama*) leads upstream and offers commanding views. On the exhibit side of the structure, a trail marked *Accès l'Aqueduc* leads up to surviving stretches of the aqueduct. For a peaceful walk alongside the top of the aqueduct (where it's on land and no

longer a bridge), follow the red-and-yellow markings. Remains of this part are scant because of medieval cannibalization—frugal builders couldn't resist the precut stones as they constructed local churches. The ancient quarry (about a third of a mile downstream on the exhibit side) may be open to the public in 2008.

Uzès

Like Nîmes and Pont du Gard, this intriguing, less-trampled town is officially in Languedoc, not Provence. Uzès (oo-zehs) feels like

it must have been important—and it was, as a bishopric from the fifth century until 1789. It's best seen slowly on foot, with a long coffee break in its arcaded and mellow main square, place aux Herbes (not so mellow during the colorful Wednesday morning and even bigger all-day Saturday markets).

By car, Uzès is 10 minutes from Pont du Gard (allowing a quick side-trip—best after dark to see the aqueduct illuminated), and 30 minutes from Nîmes and Avignon. It offers a welcome, small-town break from serious sightseeing. Go local and overnight here. Arrive on Tuesday or Friday nights to enjoy the next morning's market.

The town itself—traffic-free and tastefully restored—is the sight. In spite of all those bishops, there are no important museums. You can follow the TI's self-guided walking tour, but skip the dull and overpriced Palace of the Duché de Uzès (€12, French-only tour). The unusual, circular tower called Tour Fenestrelle is all that remains of a 12th-century cathedral. Even if you're not a plant enthusiast, pop into the Medieval Garden, a "living herbarium" with plants thought to have curative qualities. The garden is at the foot of the King's and Bishop's towers. The €3 entrance fee includes a little shot of lemongrass tea lovingly delivered by the volunteers who care for this sight (April–Sept daily 14:00–18:00 plus 10:30–12:30 on Sat–Sun and daily in July–Aug, until 17:00 in Oct, closed Nov–March, English handout and some information posted, tel. 04 66 22 38 21).

Getting to Uzès

Uzès is a short hop west of Pont du Gard. It's well-served by bus from Nîmes (10/day Mon–Fri, 6/day Sat, 2/day Sun, 1 hour, €8), but less so from Avignon (4/day Mon–Sat, none Sun, 1 hour, stops at Pont du Gard).

Near Avignon

Tourist Information

At the TI on the ring road, pick up the brief self-guided *Tour of Historic Town* brochure in English (June–Sept Mon–Fri 9:00–18:00, Sat–Sun 10:00–13:00 & 14:00–17:00; Oct–May Mon–Fri 9:00–12:30 & 14:00–18:00, Sat 10:00–13:00, closed Sun; on ring road on place Albert 1er, tel. 04 66 22 68 88, www.uzes-tourisme.com).

SLEEPING

$$$ Hôtel du Général d'Entraigues*** is a classy, 15th-century, stone-cozy hotel with 38 rooms. It combines traditional and modern touches with a terrific flowery terrace and pool (Db-€70–170, most about €100, air-con, place de l'Evêché, tel. 04 66 22 32 68, fax 04 66 22 57 01, www.hoteldentraigues.com, entraigues @leshotelsparticuliers.com).

$$$ L'Hostellerie Provençale*** is an intimate place with nine thoughtfully appointed rooms a block outside the ring road. It's well-known for its adorable and delectable restaurant (Db-€75–135, 4-course dinner *menus* from €30, 1 rue de la Grande Bourgade, tel. 04 66 22 11 06, fax 04 66 75 01 03, www.hostellerieprovencale.com, contact@hostellerieprovencale.com).

$$$ Chambres d'Hôtes de Charme, a block from the ring road, offers elegant digs in a graceful old stone building surrounding a lovely garden and pool (Db-€90–120, includes breakfast, cash only, 15 rue de la Petite Bourgade, tel. 04 66 57 29 26, www.auquinze.com, auquinze@wanadoo.fr).

EATING

When the weather cooperates, it's hard to resist dining on place aux Herbes, which is lined with appealing café options. **La Renaissance** is a fair bet, with salads, pizzas, and *plats du jour* for about €10–13, plus a €20 *menu* (open daily for lunch and dinner, 6 place aux Herbes, tel. 04 66 03 11 82). **Terroires,** on the other side of the square, is a culinary treasure serving modern, light cuisine such as *tartines*, tapas, and great salads, all made with regional products (€13 *plats*, closed Mon). To dine well indoors, find the restaurant **La Parenthèse** in the recommended **Hostellerie Provençale** (closed Mon–Tue, see above).

ORANGE AND THE CÔTES DU RHÔNE

The sunny Côtes du Rhône wine road—one of France's best—starts at Avignon's doorstep. It winds north through an appealingly rugged, mountainous landscape carpeted with vines, peppered with warm stone villages, and presided over by the Vesuvius-like Mont Ventoux. The wines of the Côtes du Rhône (grown on the *côtes*, or hillsides, of the Rhône River Valley) are easy on the palate and on your budget. But this hospitable place offers more than famous wine—its hill-capping villages inspire travel posters, and its vistas are unforgettable. Yes, there are good opportunities for enjoyable wine-tasting, but there is also a soul to this area...if you take the time to look.

Located 20 minutes north of Avignon, the ancient town of Orange has vineyards at its doorstep. But it's because of its remarkably well-preserved Roman Theater that Orange gets (and deserves) the attention.

Planning Your Time

Vaison la Romaine is the small hub of this region, offering limited bus connections with Avignon and Orange, bike rental, and a mini-Pompeii in the town center. Nearby, you can visit the impressive Roman Theater in Orange, drive to the top of Mont Ventoux, follow my self-guided driving tour of Côtes du Rhône villages and wineries, and pedal to nearby towns for a breath of fresh air. The vineyards' centerpiece, the Dentelles de Montmirail mountains, are laced with a variety of exciting trails ideal for hikers.

To explore this area, allow two nights for a good start. Drivers should head for the hills (read the self-guided driving tour on page 148 before deciding where to stay). Those without wheels find that Vaison la Romaine is the only practical home base (or, maybe better, consider a minivan tour for this area; see "Getting Around the Côtes du Rhône—By Tour," below).

Getting Around the Côtes du Rhône

By Car: Pick up the Michelin Local maps #332 or #528 to navigate your way around the Côtes du Rhône. (Landmarks like Dentelles de Montmirail and Mont Ventoux make it easier to get your bearings.) I've described my favorite driving route on page 148. If your plan is to connect the Côtes du Rhône with the Luberon, do it scenically via Mont Ventoux (follow signs to *Malaucène*, then to *Mont Ventoux*, allowing 2 hours to Roussillon). This route is one of the most spectacular in Provence.

By Bus: Buses run to the Côtes du Rhône from Orange and Avignon (2–3/day, 45 min from Orange, 90 min from Avignon) and connect several wine villages (including Gigondas, Sablet, and Beaumes de Venise) with Vaison la Romaine and Nyons to the north. Another line runs from Vaison la Romaine to Carpentras, serving Le Crestet, Malaucène, and Le Barroux (2/day, tel. 04 90 36 09 90). Both routes provide scenic rides through this area.

By Train: Trains get you as far as Orange (from Avignon: 10/day, 15 min), where buses make the 45-minute trip to Vaison la Romaine (see above).

By Tour: Two companies—**Wine Safari** and **Taxi des Oliviers**—can expertly guide you through this tricky-without-a-car region. **Lieutaud** offers big-bus excursions from Arles and Avignon to Vaison la Romaine and Orange. For details on these companies, see "Tours of Provence," page 36.

Côtes du Rhône Market Days

Monday: Bedoin (good market, between Vaison la Romaine and Mont Ventoux)

Tuesday: Vaison la Romaine (great market with produce and antiques/flea market)

Wednesday: Malaucène (good and less-touristy market with produce and antiques/flea market, near Vaison la Romaine), Buis les Barronies (on recommended loop drive north into the Drôme Provençale), and Sault (handy if you're driving to the Luberon area)

Thursday: Nyons (great market with produce and antiques/flea market) and Vacqueyras

Friday: Châteauneuf-du-Pape (small market) and Carpentras (big market)

Saturday: Valréas (small market north of Vaison la Romaine)

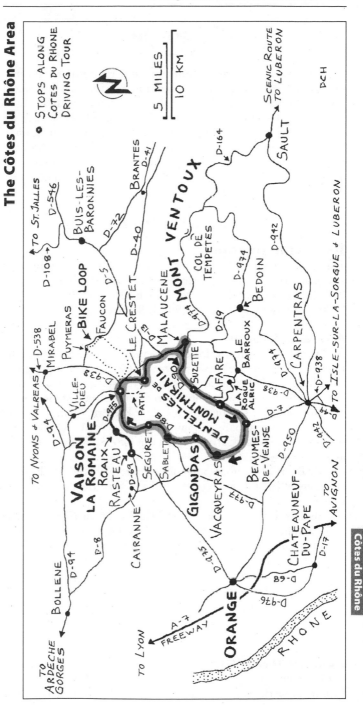

The Côtes du Rhône Area

○ Stops Along Côtes du Rhône Driving Tour

5 MILES
10 KM

Orange

Orange is notable for its Roman arch and grand Roman Theater. Orange was a thriving city in ancient times—strategically situated on the Via Agrippa, connecting the important Roman cities of Lyon and Arles. It was actually founded as a comfortable place for Roman army officers to enjoy their retirement. Even in Roman times, career military men retired after only 20 years. Does the emperor want thousands of well-trained, relatively young guys hanging around Rome? No way. What to do? "How about a nice place in the south of France...?"

ORIENTATION

Tourist Information

The unnecessary TI is located next to the fountain and parking area at 5 cours Aristide Briand (April–Sept Mon–Sat 9:30–19:00, Sun 10:00–13:00 & 14:00–18:30; Oct–March Mon–Sat 10:00–13:00 & 14:00–17:30, closed Sun; tel. 04 90 34 70 88).

Arrival in Orange

By Train: Orange's **train station** is a level 15-minute walk from the Roman Theater (or a €8 taxi ride, tel. 06 09 51 32 25). The recommended Hôtel de Provence across from the station will keep your bags (see below). To walk into town from the train station, head straight out of the station (down avenue Frédéric Mistral), merge left onto Orange's main shopping street (rue de la République), then turn left on rue Caristie; you'll run into the Roman Theater's massive stage wall.

By Bus: Buses drop you at place Pourtoules, two blocks from the Roman Theater (walk to the hill and turn right to reach the theater).

By Car: Drivers follow *Centre-Ville* signs, then *Théâtre Antique* signs, and park as close to the Roman Theater's huge wall as possible; the easiest option is Parking Théâtre Antique (by the fountain and the TI). Those coming from the autoroute will land here by following *Centre-Ville* signs; others should follow *Centre-Ville* signs then *Tourist Information* signs to find this parking. To reach the theater, walk to the hill and turn left.

SIGHTS

▲▲**Roman Theater (Théâtre Antique)**—Orange's ancient theater is the best-preserved in existence, and the only one in Europe with its acoustic wall still standing. (Two others in Asia Minor

Orange

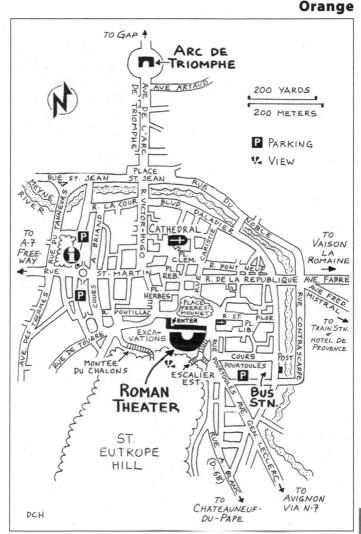

TO GAP

ARC DE TRIOMPHE

AVE ARTAUD

AVE. DE L'ARC DE TRIOMPHE

200 YARDS
200 METERS

P PARKING
⅄ VIEW

PLACE ST. JEAN

RUE ST. JEAN

MEYNE RIVER

TO A-7 FREE-WAY

R. LA COUR

RUE DU TANNEURS

R. VICTOR HUGO

J. BRIAND

BLVD. DALADIER

CATHEDRAL

RUE DU NOBLE

TO VAISON LA ROMAINE

PL. CLEM.

R. CARISTIE

R. PONT NEUF

RUE ST-MARTIN

COURS A. BRIAND

PL. REB.

R. DE LA REPUBLIQUE

AVE. FABRE

AVE. FRED. MISTRAL

PL. HERBES

R. PONTILLAC

PLACE FRERES MOUNET

RUE DE TOURRE

ENTER

EXCA-VATIONS

R. ST. FLOR.

PL. LIB.

RUE CONTRASCARPE

TO TRAIN STN. + HOTEL DE PROVENCE.

AVE. DES HIERMES

MONTÉE DU CHALONS

⅄
ESCALIER EST

RUE POURTOULES

COURS POURTOULES

Post

ROMAN THEATER

BUS STN.

ST. EUTROPE HILL

RUE A. BLANC (D-68)

AVE. GEN. LECLERC

TO CHATEAUNEUF-DU-PAPE

TO AVIGNON VIA N-7

DCH

also survive.)

After you enter (to the right of the actual theater), you'll see a huge dig—the site of the Temple to the Cult of the Emperor.

Climb the steep stairs to the top of the theater to appreciate the acoustics (eavesdrop on people by the stage) and contemplate the idea that 2,000 years ago, Orange residents enjoyed grand spectacles with high-tech sound and lighting effects—such as simulated thunder, lightning, and rain. The glass-and-iron stage roof is new and was designed to protect the stage wall and improve acoustics. It was built by the Eiffel Engineering Company (yes, the same folks who built the tower).

A grandiose Caesar overlooks everything. If it seems like you've seen this statue before, you probably have. Countless sculptures identical to this one were mass-produced in Rome and shipped throughout the empire to grace buildings like this theater for propaganda purposes. To save money on shipping and handling, only the heads of these statues were changed with each new ruler. The permanent body wears a breastplate emblazoned with the imperial griffon (body of a lion, head and wings of an eagle) that only the emperor could wear. When a new emperor came to power, new heads were made in Rome and shipped off throughout the empire to replace the pop-off heads on all these statues. (Imagine George W. Bush's head on Bill Clinton's body. Now pop off W.'s head and pop on anybody else's—except Hillary's.)

Archaeologists believe that a puny, vanquished Celt was included at the knee of the emperor, touching his ruler's robe respectfully—a show of humble subservience to the emperor. It's interesting to consider how an effective propaganda machine can con the masses into being impressed by their leader.

The horn has blown. It's time to find your seat: row two, number 30. Sitting down, you're comforted by the "EQ GIII" carved into the seat (Equitas Gradus #3...three rows for the Equestrian order). You're not comforted by the hard limestone bench (thinking it'll probably last 2,000 years). The theater is filled with 10,000 people. Thankfully, you mix only with your class, the nouveau riche—merchants, tradesmen, and city big shots. The people seated above you are the working-class, and way up in the "chicken roost" section is the scum of the earth—slaves, beggars, prostitutes, and youth hostellers. Scanning the orchestra section (where the super-rich sit on real chairs), you notice the town dignitaries hosting some visiting VIPs.

Okay, time to worship. They're parading a bust of the emperor from its sacred home in the adjacent temple around the stage. Next is the ritual animal sacrifice called *la pompa* (so fancy, future generations will use that word for anything full of such...pomp). Finally, you settle in for an all-day series of spectacles and dramatic entertainment. All eyes are on the big stage door in the middle—where the Julia Roberts and Tom Hanks of the day will appear. (Lesser actors come out of the side doors.)

Côtes du Rhône

The play is good, but many come for the halftime shows—jugglers, acrobats, and striptease dancers. In Roman times, the theater was a festival of immorality. An ancient writer commented, "The vanquished take their revenge on us by giving us their vices through the theater."

With an audience of 10,000 and no amplification, acoustics were very important. At the top of the side walls, a slanted line of stones marks the position of a long-gone roof—not to protect from the weather, but to project the voices of the actors into the crowd. For further help, actors wore masks with leather caricature mouths that functioned as megaphones.

The Roman Theater was all part of the "give them bread and circuses" approach to winning the support of the masses (not unlike today's philosophy of "give them tax cuts and Fox News"). The spectacle grew from 65 days of games per year when the theater was first built (and when Rome was at its height) to about 180 days each year by the time Rome finally fell.

Cost and Hours: Theater entry-€8, April–Sept daily 9:00–18:00, until 19:00 in summer, until 17:00 Oct–March, tel. 04 90 51 17 60.

Information: Your ticket includes a worthwhile audio-guide, a 13-minute film (English subtitles), and entrance to the small museum across the street (Musée d'Art et d'Histoire). Pop in to see a few theater details and a rare grid used as the official property-ownership registry—each square represented a 120-acre plot of land. Vagabonds wanting to see the theater for free can hike up nearby stairs (*escalier est* off rue Pourtoules is closest) to view it from the bluff high above.

Cafés: A shaded café-filled square hides a block across from the theater up rue Ségond Weber.

▲**Roman "Arc de Triomphe"**—Technically the only real Roman arches of triumph are in Rome's Forum, built to commemorate various emperors' victories. The great Roman arch of Orange is actually a municipal arch erected (about A.D. 19) to commemorate a general, named Germanicus, who protected the town. The 60-foot-tall arch is on a noisy traffic circle (north of city center, on avenue Arc de Triomphe).

SLEEPING

$$ Hôtel de Provence**, at the train station, is pleasant, air-conditioned, and affordable (Db-€60, restaurant and café, 60 avenue Frédéric Mistral, tel. 04 90 34 00 23, fax 04 90 34 91 72, www.hoteldeprovence84.com, hoteldeprovence84@wanadoo.fr).

Côtes du Rhône

TRANSPORTATION CONNECTIONS

From Orange by Train to: Avignon (10/day, 15 min), **Arles** (4/day direct, 35 min, more with transfer in Avignon), **Lyon** (16/day, 2 hrs).

By Bus to: Châteauneuf-du-Pape (1/day, none Sun, 30 min), **Vaison la Romaine** (2–3/day, 45 min), **Avignon** (hourly, 55 min). Buses to Vaison la Romaine and other wine villages depart from the big square, place Pourtoules (turn right out of the Roman Theater and right again on rue Pourtoules).

Châteauneuf-du-Pape

This most famous of the Côtes du Rhône wine villages is busy with tourists eager to sample its famous product and stroll its climbing lanes. While I prefer the less-famous wine villages farther

north (described under "The Best of the Côtes du Rhône Villages," page 147), this welcoming, wine-drenched town makes an easy day trip from Avignon, and works well with a visit to nearby Orange.

Châteauneuf-du-Pape means "New Castle of the Pope," named for the pope's summer retreat—now a ruin capping the beautiful-to-see but little-to-do hill town (more interesting during the Friday market). Wine-loving popes planted the first vines here in the 1300s. The pope's crest is embossed on all bottles of this deservedly famous wine.

Approaching from Avignon, signs announce, "Here start the vineyards of Châteauneuf-du-Pape." Pull over and stroll into a vineyard with a view of the hill town. Notice the rocky soil—perfect for making a good wine grape. Those stones retain the sun's heat (plentiful here) and force the vines to struggle, resulting in a lean grape—lousy for eating, but ideal for producing strong wines (see "Côtes du Rhône Wines," page 42). Eight different grapes are blended to make the local specialty, which has been strictly controlled for 80 years. Grenache is the most prominent grape in the blend. A white wine is also available (blend of five grapes), but the reds are best.

The **Wine Museum** (Musée du Vin) provides useful background for your Côtes du Rhône exploration (free, daily 9:00–12:00

& 14:00–18:00, on route d'Avignon, at start of the village if coming from Avignon, tel. 04 90 83 70 07). After a brief self-guided tour of the winemaking process (English explanations in the notebooks reward good students), enjoy a tasting. You'll need to tell them what you want; see "French Wine Lingo," page 41. For a clear contrast, taste a "ready-to-drink" wine (*prêt à boire;* pret ah bwar), then a wine from "old vines" (*vieille vignes;* vee-yay-ee veen-yuh).

A handy way to sample this prestigious product is to find the **Cave du Verger des Papes.** Drive to the very top of the village, following brown *Château* signs (fine views at the top), and park at the ruined castle. A short walk down the path into the village leads to this *cave,* where Guy and Jean-Baptiste are dying to help you understand the wines of Châteauneuf-du-Pape. Speaking fluent English and offering wines from 50 different producers, they offer an ideal introduction to the area wines in their stone-vaulted tasting cellar (careful—they're also good salesmen). You'll taste two whites and four reds, and if you like what you taste, they can ship directly to your home at fair rates (March–Dec daily 10:00–19:00, closed Jan–Feb, tel. 04 90 83 50 94, www.caveduverger.com). If it's lunchtime, consider a meal at the restaurant of the same name (run by the same folks), with reasonable prices and a pleasing patio.

The town **TI** has a long list of other wineries that welcome visitors (Mon–Sat 9:00–12:30 & 14:00–18:00, closed Sun, place du Portail, tel. 04 90 83 71 08).

Vaison la Romaine

With quick access to vineyards, villages, and Mont Ventoux, this lively little town of 6,000 makes a great base for exploring the Côtes du Rhône region by car or by bike. You get two villages for the price of one: Vaison la Romaine's "modern" lower city is like a mini-Arles, with worthwhile Roman ruins, a lone pedestrian street, and too many cars. The car-free medieval hill town looms above, with meandering cobbled lanes, a dash of art galleries and cafés, and a ruined castle with a good view from its base. (Vaison la Romaine is also a good place to have your hair done, since there are more than 20 hairdressers in this small town.)

Côtes du Rhône

ORIENTATION

The city is split in two by the Ouvèze River. The Roman Bridge connects the more modern lower town (Ville-Basse) with the hill-capping medieval upper town (Ville-Haute).

Vaison la Romaine

Côtes du Rhône

- ① Hôtel le Beffroi
- ② L'Evêché Chambres
- ③ Hôtel la Fête en Provence
- ④ Hôtel Burrhus
- ⑤ La Bartavelle Restaurant
- ⑥ Le Bateleur Restaurant
- ⑦ Le Tournesol Restaurant
- ⑧ Brasserie du Siècle
- ⑨ View Crêperie & Pizzeria
- ⑩ Bike Rental
- ⑪ Launderette
- ⑫ To Car Rental
- ⑬ Bus to Avignon/Orange
- ⑭ Bus from Avignon/Orange
- ⑮ To Séguret by Bike or Car

Tourist Information

The superb TI is in the lower city, between the two Roman ruin sites, at place du Chanoine Sautel (Mon–Sat 9:00–12:00 & 14:00–17:45, Sun 9:00–12:00, closed Sun Oct–April, tel. 04 90 36 02 11, www.vaison-la-romaine.com). Say *bonjour* to *charmante* and ever-so-patient Valerie—get bus schedules, ask about festivals and evening programs, and pick up information on walks from Vaison la Romaine. The TI sells a helpful €7 guide to biking, *Parcours Cyclo Touristiques,* with detailed maps for several bike tours ranging from easy half-day trips to all-day pedals. They also sell guides for the many mountain-biking trails nearby. The guides are in French, but consist mostly of maps with little text to guide you.

Arrival in Vaison la Romaine

By Bus: The unmarked bus stop to Orange and Avignon is in front of the Cave la Romaine winery. Buses from Orange or Avignon drop you across the street (2–3/day, 45 min from Orange, 90 min from Avignon). Tell the driver you want the stop for the Office de Tourisme. When you get off the bus, walk five minutes down avenue Général de Gaulle to reach the TI and recommended hotels.

By Car: Follow signs to *Centre-Ville,* then *Office de Tourisme;* park free across from the TI. Most parking is free in Vaison la Romaine.

Helpful Hints

Market Day: Sleep in Vaison la Romaine on Monday night, and you'll wake to an amazing Tuesday market. But be warned: Mondays are quiet, and the town's two best restaurants are closed. If you do spend a Monday night, avoid parking at market sites or you won't find your car where you left it.

Internet Access: Find **Brasserie du Siècle** near the recommended Hôtel Burrhus on place Montfort (daily 7:00–1:00 in the morning, tel. 04 90 36 00 19).

Laundry: The self-service **Laverie la Lavandière** is on cours Taulignan, near avenue Victor Hugo (daily 8:00–22:00). The friendly owners, who work next door at the dry cleaners, will do your laundry while you sightsee—when you pick up your laundry, thank them with a small tip (dry cleaners open Mon–Sat 9:00–12:00 & 15:00–19:00, closed Sun).

Bike Rental: Try **Mag 2 Roues,** in the lower town on cours Taulignan (tel. 04 90 28 80 46).

Taxi: To call a taxi, dial 04 90 46 81 36 or 06 22 28 24 49.

Car Rental: Wallgreen has a few cars for rent at Vaison Pneus (avenue Marcel Pagnol, tel. 04 90 28 73 54).

Local Guide: Let sincere and knowledgeable Anna-Marie Melard

Côtes du Rhône

bring those Roman ruins to life for you (€40/80-min tour, tel. 04 90 36 50 48).

SIGHTS AND ACTIVITIES

In Vaison la Romaine

Roman Ruins—Ancient Vaison la Romaine had a treaty that gave it the preferred "federated" relationship with Rome (rather than simply being a colony). This, along with a healthy farming economy (olives and vineyards), made it a most prosperous place...as a close look at its sprawling ruins demonstrates. About 6,000 people called Vaison la Romaine home 2,000 years ago. When the barbarians arrived, the Romans were forced out, and the townspeople fled into the hills (see sidebar on page 150). Here's something to ponder: The town has only recently reached the same population as during its Roman era.

Vaison la Romaine's Roman ruins are split by a modern road into two sites: Puymin and La Villasse. Each is well-presented, offering a good picture of life during the Roman Empire. Visit **Puymin** first. Inside the site, climb the hill to the museum (exhibits explained in English loaner booklet). Behind the museum is a 6,000-seat theater (just enough seats for the number of residents). Nearest the entry are the scant but impressive remains of a sprawling mansion. Back across the modern road in **La Villasse,** you'll explore a "street of shops" and the foundations of more houses.

Cost and Hours: €8 Roman ruins combo-ticket includes both ruins, a helpful audioguide, and the cloister at the Notre-Dame de Nazareth cathedral (see below); daily March–May 10:00–18:00, June–Sept 9:30–18:00, Oct–Feb 10:00–12:00 & 14:00–17:00.

Lower Town (Ville-Basse)—Vaison la Romaine's nondescript modern town stretches from its car-littered main square, place Montfort. The cafés grab the north side of the square, conveniently sheltered from the prevailing mistral wind, enjoying the generous shade of the ubiquitous plane *(platane)* trees (cut back each year to form a leafy canopy). A few blocks away, the stout **Notre-Dame de Nazareth** cathedral—with an evocative cloister—is a good example of Provençal Romanesque (cloister entry-€1.50, covered by €8 Roman ruins combo-ticket—see above). The pedestrian-only Grand Rue is a lively shopping street leading to the small river gorge and the Roman Bridge.

Roman Bridge—The Romans cut this sturdy, no-nonsense vault into the canyon rock 2,000 years ago, and it has survived ever since. Until the 20th century, this was the only way to cross the Ouvèze River. The metal plaque on the wall *(Crue du 22-09-92)* shows the high-water mark of the record flood that killed 30 people and washed away the valley's other bridges. The flood swept away the modern top of this bridge...but couldn't budge the 55-foot Roman arch.

Upper Town (Ville-Haute)—While there's nothing of particular importance to see in the fortified medieval old town atop the hill, the cobbled lanes and charming fountains make you want to break out a sketchpad. Vaison la Romaine had a prince-bishop since the fourth century. He came under attack by the Count of Toulouse in the 12th century. Anticipating a struggle, the prince-bishop abandoned the lower town and built a château on this rocky outcrop (about 1195). Over time, the rest of the townspeople followed, vacating the lower town and building their homes at the base of the château behind the upper town's fortified wall.

To reach the upper town, hike up from the Roman Bridge (passing memorials for both world wars) through the medieval gate, under the lone tower crowned by an 18th-century wrought-iron bell cage. The château is closed, but a steep, uneven trail to it rewards you with a fine view.

▲Market Day—In the 16th century, the pope gave Vaison la Romaine market-town status. Each Tuesday since then, the town has hosted a farmers' market. Today, merchants gather with gusto, turning the entire place into a festival of produce and Provençal products. This Tuesday-morning market is one of France's best, but it can challenge those who suffer from claustrophobia. Be warned that parking is a real headache unless you arrive early (see "Helpful Hints," earlier in this chapter; and "Market Day," in the Shopping chapter).

Wine-Tasting—Cave la Romaine, a five-minute walk up avenue Général de Gaulle from the TI, offers a variety of great-value wines from nearby villages in a pleasant, well-organized tasting room (daily 8:30–13:00 & 14:00–19:00, avenue St. Quenin, tel. 04 90 36 55 90).

Hiking—The TI has good information on relatively easy hikes into the hills above Vaison la Romaine. It's about 90 minutes to the tiny hill town of Le Crestet, though great views begin immediately. To find this trail, drive or walk up past the upper town (with the castle just on your left), find the *chemin des Fontaines*, and stay the course as far as you like. Cars are not allowed on the road after about a mile. Consider taking the bus (2/day, 5 min) or a taxi to Le Crestet, and walking back (see "Le Crestet," later in this chapter).

Biking—This area is not particularly flat, and it's often hot and windy, making bike-riding a dicey option. But if it's calm, the five-mile ride to cute little Villedieu is a delight (the bike route is signed along small roads). With a little more energy, you can pedal beyond Villedieu on the lovely road to Mirabel (ask in Villedieu for directions). Or get a good map and connect the following villages for an enjoyable 11-mile loop ride: Vaison la Romaine, St. Romain-en-Viennois, Puyméras (with a recommended restaurant—see page 158), Faucon, and St. Marcellin-lès-Vaison. The TI has good information on mountain-biking trails.

Near Vaison la Romaine
▲Mont Ventoux and Lavender

The drive to Mont Ventoux is worth ▲▲▲ if skies are crystal-clear, or in any weather from late June to early August, when the lavender blooms. It also provides a scenic connection between the Côtes du Rhône villages and the Luberon. Allow an hour to drive to the top of this 6,000-foot mountain, where you'll be greeted by cool temperatures, crowds of visitors, and acres of white stones.

Mont Ventoux is Provence's rooftop, with astonishing Pyrénées-to-Alps views—but only if it's clear (which it usually isn't). But even under hazy skies, it's an interesting place. The top combines a barren and surreal lunar landscape, with souvenirs, bikers, and hikers. All that chalky mess you see was once the bottom of a sea. Miles of poles stuck in the rock identify the route (the top is usually snowbound Dec–April). **Le Vendran** restaurant (near the old observatory and Air Force control tower) offers snacks and meals with commanding views. An orientation board is available on the opposite side of the mountaintop.

Between Mont Ventoux and the Luberon, you'll pass through several climate zones and astonishingly diverse landscapes. The scene alternates between rocky canyons, lush meadows, and wildflowers. Thirty minutes east of Mont Ventoux, lavender fields forever surround the rock-top village of **Sault** (pronounced "soh"), which produces 40 percent of France's lavender essence. Sault is a welcoming town in any season which goes unnoticed by most hurried travelers. It's a slow-down-and-smell-the-lavender kind of place, with a relaxing, sociable "mountain market" on Wednesdays.

Getting to Mont Ventoux: To reach Mont Ventoux from Vaison la Romaine, go to Malaucène on D-938, then wind up D-974 for 40 minutes to the top (or take D-19 to pleasant little Bedoin, with a fun Monday market; from there, D-974 offers a longer, prettier route to the top). If continuing to Sault (worthwhile only when the lavender blooms) or on to the Luberon (worthwhile anytime—see next chapter), follow signs to *Sault*, then *Gordes*. The *Les Routes de la Lavande* brochure suggests driving and walking routes in the area (available online at www.routes-lavande.com or at Sault TI, tel. 04 90 64 01 21).

Lavender

Whether or not you travel to Provence during the late-June and July lavender blossom, you'll see examples of this par-  ticularly local product everywhere—in shops, on tables in restaurants, and in your hotel room. And if you do come during lavender season, you'll experience one of Europe's great color events, where rich fields of purple lavender meet equally rich yellow fields of sunflowers. While lavender season is hot, you'll find the best fields in the cooler hills, since the flowers thrive at higher altitudes. The flowers are harvested in full bloom (beginning in mid-July), then distilled to extract the oils for making soaps and perfume. For a good explanation of this process, visit the Museum of Lavender in Coustellet (see page 184 in the Luberon chapter).

While lavender seems like an indigenous part of the Provence scene, it wasn't cultivated here until about 1920, when it was imported by the local perfume-makers. Since lavender is not native to Provence, growing it successfully requires great care. Three kinds of lavender are grown in Provence: true lavender (traditionally used by perfume makers), spike lavender, and lavandin (a cloned hybrid of the first two). Today, a majority of Provence lavender fields are lavandin—which is also mass-produced at factories, a trend that is threatening to put the true lavender grower out of business.

Some of the best lavender fields bloom near Vaison la Romaine. Lavender blooms later the higher you go; the ones described here are listed from lowest to highest elevations. For an impressive display, drive north of Vaison la Romaine and ramble the tiny road between Valréas and Vinsobres (D-190 and D-46). You'll see more beautiful fields along D-538 between Nyons and Dieulefit, and still more if you climb Mont Ventoux to Sault (see the previous page).

▲Drôme Provençale Loop Drive

Follow this loop drive north into the Drôme Provençale to get away from popular tourist areas and combine gorgeous scenery on a big scale with overlooked towns and villages. This loop is ideal on Thursdays, when it's market day in Nyons; and good on Wednesdays, when it's market day in Buis les Barronies. If the wind is howling, the drive provides some protection, as you'll be in and out of gorges and along mountain slopes. Allow most of a day for this drive, particularly if it's market day in Nyons.

From Vaison la Romaine, drive to **Nyons,** an attractive mid-size town set along a river and against the hills. Here you'll find a handsome Roman bridge with views, an olive mill, a lavender distillery, a handful of walking streets, and an arcaded square—all with few tourists. Nyons is famous for its rollicking Thursday market (until 12:30) and for producing France's best olives—which you can taste at its *Coopérative* (daily 9:00–12:00 & 14:00–19:00, on place Olivier de Serres, tel. 04 75 26 95 00).

From Nyons, head for the hills following signs to *Gap* on D-94, then follow signs to *St. Jalles* on D-64. Little **St. Jalles** hovers above the road with a pretty Romanesque church (usually closed), two cafés (Café de Lavande overhangs the river, providing a pleasing backdrop for a drink, lunch, or a snack), and a small winery making crisp whites and easy-to-drink reds (Domaine de Rieu Frais, Mon–Sat 10:00–12:00 & 14:00–18:00, closed Sun).

From St. Jalles, cross the bridge following D-108 to Buis les Barronnies, and start your ascent up and over the rocky mountains. Prepare for miles of curves, sensational views, and no guardrails. Drop down (err, drive down) and meet the Ouvèze River, then follow it into bustling **Buis les Barronnies** (with all the services, including many cafés and a nice old town to stroll). Buis les Barronnies is the linden tree capital of France and hosts an earthy outdoor market on Wednesdays with produce and crafts.

From Buis les Barronnies, continue south on D-5 (notice the rock fin that crowns the town as you leave), then make a left toward Eygaliers on D-72. Follow this slow, serpentine road along the back-side of Mont Ventoux and go all the way to the jewel of this trip: **Brantes,** one of Provence's most spectacularly located villages. Stop here for some fresh air, a stroll, and a look at the local pottery. Then follow signs back to *Vaison la Romaine* along the faster, less curvy D-40.

▲Ardèche Gorges (Gorges de l'Ardèche)

These gorges, which wow visitors with abrupt, chalky-white cliffs, follow the Ardèche River through immense canyons and thick forests. To reach the gorges from Vaison la Romaine, drive west 45 minutes, passing through Bollène and Pont Saint-Esprit to Vallon Pont d'Arc (the tourist hub of the Ardèche Gorges). From Vallon Pont d'Arc, you can canoe along the peaceful river through some of the canyon's most spectacular scenery and under the rock arch of Pont d'Arc (half-day, all-day, and 2-day trips possible), and learn about hiking trails that get you above it all (**TI** tel. 04 75 88 04 01, www.vallon-pont-darc.com). If continuing north toward Lyon, connect Privas and Aubenas, then head back via the

---

Sleep Code

(€1 = about $1.30, country code: 33)
S = Single, **D** = Double/Twin, **T** = Triple, **Q** = Quad, **b** = bathroom, **s** = shower only, * = French hotel rating system (0–4 stars). Unless otherwise noted, credit cards are accepted and English is spoken.

To help you sort easily through these listings, I've divided the rooms into three categories based on the price for a standard double room with bath:

$$$ Higher Priced—Most rooms €85 or more.
$$ Moderately Priced—Most rooms between €55–85.
$ Lower Priced—Most rooms €55 or less.

---

autoroute. Endearing little Balazuc—a village north of the gorges, with narrow lanes, flowers, views, and a smattering of cafés and shops—makes a fine stop.

SLEEPING

Hotels in Vaison la Romaine are a good value. Those in the medieval upper town (Ville-Haute) are quieter, cozier, cooler, and a 15-minute walk uphill from the parking lot next to the TI. If you have a car, consider staying in one of the charming Côtes du Rhône villages near Vaison la Romaine (see page 156). If staying at one of the first three places, follow signs to *Cité Médiévale* and park just outside the upper village entry (driving into the Cité Médiévale itself is a challenge, with tiny lanes and nearly impossible parking).

$$$ Hôtel le Beffroi*** hides deep in the upper town, just above a demonstrative bell tower (you'll hear what I mean). It's a 16th-century, red-tile-and-wood-beamed-cozy place with nary a level surface. The rooms—split between two buildings a few doors apart—are Old World comfy, and some have views. You'll also find classy public spaces, a garden with view tables (light meals available in the summer), a small pool with more views, and animated Nathalie at the reception (standard Db-€85–105, superior Db-€135, Tb-€160, rue de l'Evêché, tel. 04 90 36 04 71, fax 04 90 36 24 78, www.le-beffroi.com, info@le-beffroi.com). The hotel's restaurant offers *menus* from €30.

$$$ L'Evêché Chambres, almost next door to le Beffroi in the upper town (look for the ivy), is a five-room, melt-in-your-chair B&B. The owners (the Verdiers) own the art boutique across the street, have an exquisite sense of interior design, and are passionate

Côtes du Rhône

about books, making this place feel like a cross between a library and an art gallery (Sb-€70–80, standard Db-€80–90, Db suite-€105–130, the *solanum* suite is worth every euro, Tb-€110–150, Internet access and Wi-Fi, rue de l'Evêché, tel. 04 90 36 13 46, fax 04 90 36 32 43, http://eveche.free.fr, eveche@aol.com).

$$ Hôtel la Fête en Provence, conveniently located for drivers at the upper entry to the medieval upper town, offers a variety of room shapes and sizes. All the rooms are chiffon-comfortable, and several have small kitchenettes. Rooms are located around a calming courtyard, and there's a pool and Jacuzzi next door (standard Db-€68, bigger Db with king-size bed and bath-€98, extra person-€15, cash only, Cité Médiévale, tel. & fax 04 90 36 36 43, www.hotellafete-provence.com, fete-en-provence@wanadoo.fr). Their apartment (€110) sleeps up to six people, and comes with a kitchenette and sitting area.

$ Hôtel Burrhus** is part art gallery, part funky hotel—and the best value in the lower town. It's a central, laid-back, go-with-the-flow place, with a broad terrace over the raucous place Montfort (for maximum quiet, request a back room). Its floor plan will confound even the ablest navigator. The bigger, newer rooms—which come with cool colors and contemporary décor—are worth the extra euros (Db-€47–54, new Db-€58–70, extra bed-€15, air-con in some rooms, free Internet access and Wi-Fi, 1 place Montfort, tel. 04 90 36 00 11, fax 04 90 36 39 05, www.burrhus.com, info @burrhus.com).

EATING

Vaison la Romaine is a small town with a handful of good, popular places—arrive by 19:30 or reserve a day ahead, particularly on weekends. You can eat very well on a moderate budget in the lower town, or go for medieval ambience rather than memorable food in the atmospheric upper town (which has a view *crêperie* and an air-conditioned pizzeria, open daily and with fair prices). And if it's summer, a light dinner in the **Hôtel le Beffroi** garden is just right (recommended under "Sleeping," earlier in this chapter). With a car, it's well worth venturing to nearby Côtes du Rhône villages to eat (see page 158). Wherever you dine, begin with a fresh glass of Muscat from the nearby village of Beaumes de Venise.

La Bartavelle is a fine place to savor traditional French cuisine in the lower town. Owner Berangère (bear-ahn-zher), has put together a tourist-friendly mix-and-match menu of local options. You get access to the top-end selections even on the €20 bottom-end *menu*—just fewer courses (closed Mon, small terrace outside, air-con and pleasant interior, reserve ahead, 12 place de Sus Auze, tel. 04 90 36 02 16).

Le Bateleur, almost on the river, serves fine Provençal cuisine in a more formal setting. English-speaking owners, Jean-François and his wife Fabienne, are popular hosts; reserve ahead if you can (€16 lunch *menu,* €28 and €38 dinner *menus,* closed Mon year-round and Thu Oct–May, air-con, near Roman Bridge at 1 place Théodore Aubanel, tel. 04 90 36 28 04).

Le Tournesol offers the best €18 dinner value in town, with mostly Provençal dishes and friendly service. I love the *aubergine feuilleté* (eggplant puff pastry) and lamb with cheese. Show this book in 2008 to get a free *kir* (daily June–Oct, Nov–May closed Tue–Wed, 30 cours Taulignan, tel. 04 90 36 09 18, owner Patrick speaks a little English).

TRANSPORTATION CONNECTIONS

The most central bus stop is at Cave Vinicole.

From Vaison la Romaine by Bus to: Avignon (2–3/day, 90 min), **Orange** (2–3/day, 45 min), **Nyons** (2–3/day, 45 min), **Le Crestet** (2/day, 5 min), **Carpentras** (2/day, 45 min). Bus info: tel. 04 90 36 05 22.

The Best of the Côtes du Rhône Villages

Officially, the Côtes du Rhône vineyards follow the Rhône River from just south of Lyon to Avignon. Our focus is the southern section of the Côtes du Rhône, centering on the small area between Châteauneuf-du-Pape and Vaison la Romaine. This area is best toured by car. My self-guided driving tour (below) starts in the village of Séguret, continues on to wine-happy Rasteau, then returns to Vaison la Romaine and winds clockwise around the Dentelles de Montmirail, visiting the mountaintop village of Le Crestet, adorable little Suzette, and the renowned wine villages of Beaumes de Venise and Gigondas. I've listed several wineries *(domaines)* along the way. Before you go, study up with "Provençal Wine Tasting 101," page 40. Even if wine isn't your thing, don't miss this easy loop.

Planning Your Time

While seeing the Côtes du Rhône is possible as a day trip by car from Arles or Avignon, you'll have a more relaxing and intimate experience if you sleep in one of the villages (my favorite accommodations are listed on page 156).

With a car, the best one-day plan is to take the driving

tour below (allow an entire day for the 80-mile round-trip from Avignon). Try to get the first two stops done before lunch (most wineries are closed 12:00–14:00), then complete the loop in the afternoon. In addition to closing at lunchtime, some wineries are also closed on Sundays, holidays, and during the harvest (mid-Sept). This route is picnic-friendly, but there are few shops along the way—stock up before you leave.

Getting Around the Côtes du Rhône Villages

This area is clearly easiest if you have wheels. Without a car, it's tougher, but a representative sampling is doable by **bike** (for ideas, see "Biking" on page 141); on **foot** (taxi to Séguret, then walk through vineyards to Sablet, continue by foot to Gigondas, and taxi back); or by **bus** (2–3 buses/day from Avignon and Orange stop at some Côtes du Rhône villages; consider taking the bus one way, then returning by taxi). For less effort and more expense, **Wine Safari** and **Taxi des Oliviers** are happy to follow this route (see "Tours of Provence," page 36).

SELF-GUIDED DRIVING TOUR

Welcome to the Wine Road

This tour introduces you to the characteristic best of the Côtes du Rhône wine road. While circling the rugged Dentelles de Montmirail mountain peaks, you'll experience all that's unique about this region: its natural beauty, glowing limestone villages, inviting wineries, and rolling hills of vineyards. As you drive, notice how some vineyards grow at angles—they're planted this way to compensate for the strong effect of the mistral wind.

This trip provides a crash course in Rhône Valley wine, an excuse to meet the locals who make the stuff, and breathtaking scenery—especially late in the day, when the famous Provençal sunlight causes colors to absolutely pop.

Our tour starts just south of Vaison la Romaine in little Séguret. This town is best for a visit early or late, when it's quieter. (If you get a late start or prefer ending your tour here, begin the tour in Le Crestet—stop #3—and save the first two stops for last.)
• *From Vaison la Romaine, the easiest way to reach Séguret is to follow signs for Orange, then look for the turnoff to Séguret in a few minutes. By bike, or for a more scenic drive, go to the river in Vaison la Romaine, then follow signs downriver to Séguret. Once you've arrived, park in the lot.*

❶ Séguret

Blending into the hillside with a smattering of shops, two cafés, made-to-stroll lanes, and a natural spring, this hamlet is

Côtes du Rhône Driving Tour

① Séguret

② Domaine des Girasols Winery

③ Le Crestet

④ La Col de la Chaîne

⑤ Suzette

⑥ Domaine de Coyeux Winery

⑦ Domaine de Durban Winery

⑧ Gigondas

understandably popular. Séguret makes for a good coffee or dinner stop (restaurants recommended on page 158).

Séguret's name comes from the Latin word *securitas* (meaning "secure"). The bulky entry arch came with a massive gate, which reinforced the message of village's name. In the Middle Ages, Séguret was patrolled 24/7—they never took their *securitas* for granted. To appreciate how the homes' outer walls provided security in those days, stroll down the main drag, keep right, then take one of the tunnel exits to the right. These exit passages, or *poternes*, were needed in periods of peace to allow the town to

The Life of a Hill Town in Provence

Heat-seeking northerners have made Provence's hill towns prosperous and worldly. But before the 1960s, nobody wanted to live in these sun-drenched, rock-top settings. Like lost ships in search of safe harbor, people took refuge here only out of necessity.

When the Romans settled Provence (125 B.C.), they brought stability to the warring locals, and hill-towners descended en masse to the Roman cities (such as Arles, Orange, Nîmes, and Vaison la Romaine). There they enjoyed theaters, fresh water from aqueducts, and commercial goods brought via the Roman road that stretched from Spain to Italy (passing along the northern edge of the Luberon).

When Rome fell (A.D. 476), barbarians swept in to rape and pillage, forcing locals back up into the hills, where they'd stay for almost 1,000 years. These "Dark Ages" were when many of the villages we see today were established. Most grew up around castles, since peasants depended on their lord for security. The hill-towners gathered stones from nearby fields and built their homes side by side to form a defensive wall, terracing the hillsides to maximize the scarce arable land. They would gather inside heavy stone Romanesque churches to pray for salvation. Medieval life was not easy behind those walls—there were barbarians, plagues, crop failures, droughts, thieves, wars, and the everyday battle with gravity.

Just when they thought the coast was clear to relocate down below, France's religious wars (1500s) chased the hill-towners back up. As Protestants and Catholics duked it out, hilltop villages prospered, welcoming refugees. Little Séguret (pop. 100 today) had almost 1,000 residents; the village of Mérindol (near Avignon) sprouted from nowhere; and Fort de Buoux (near Apt, nothing but ruins today) was an impregnable fortress (see page 192). The turmoil of the Revolution (1789) continued to make the above-the-fray hill towns desirable.

Over the next century, hill towns slept peacefully as the rest of France modernized. Most of the hill towns you'll visit housed between 200 and 600 people and were self-sufficient, producing just what was needed (farmers, lawyers, and telemarketers were

expand below.

Back in the village, find Séguret's open washbasin *(lavoir),* a hotbed of social activity and gossip over the ages. The basins behind the fountain were reserved for washing animals (which outnumbered residents in the Middle Ages); the larger ones (on the left) were for laundry only. Public washbasins like this were used right up until World War II. Find the community bread oven *(four banal),* used for festivals and celebrations. Consider climbing at equilibrium). Many town fountains and communal washrooms date from this time. Animals were everywhere, outnumbering humans four to one.

But 20th-century life down below required fewer stairs—and was closer to the convenience of trains, planes, and automobiles. So after World War I, down the hill-towners moved. To build in the flatlands, they pillaged the hill towns' stones, roof tiles, you name it, leaving those villages in ruin. By mid-century, most of these lovely villages became virtual ghost towns (in 1965, Le Crestet had but 15 residents—less than a third of its current still-tiny population).

In recent years, hill towns have bounced back. Lavender production took off, and the government launched irrigation projects. But most of all, real estate boomed as Parisians, northern Europeans, and (to a lesser extent) North Americans discovered the rustic charm of hill-town life. They invested huge sums—far more than most locals could afford—to turn ancient stone structures into modern vacation homes (in most cases, buying several houses and combining them into one). Today's hill towns survive in part thanks to these outsiders' deep pockets.

Today, most villages have organizations to preserve their traditions and buildings (such as Les Amis de Séguret, or "Friends of Séguret"). Made up of older residents, groups like these raise money, sponsor festivals and dances, and even write collective histories of their villages. Many fear that younger folks won't have the motivation to carry on this tradition.

But hope springs eternal, as there appears to be a movement of locals back to these villages. Some northerners are finding hill-town life less romantic as their knee replacements fail. Meanwhile, the popularity of organic produce makes it financially viable for hill-town farmers with smaller plots to pursue their healthy dreams of living off the land. Finally, the Internet has allowed some hill-towners to live in remote villages and telecommute, rather than move into bigger cities. Could the cycle be restarting? Armed with their laptops, will hill-towners once again prosper when the next wave of barbarians comes?

to the unusual 12th-century church for views. This rock-sculpted church is usually closed, but it's worth a look from the outside. High above, on the top of the hill, a castle once protected Séguret. All that's left is a tower that you can barely make out from a distance. A four-star hotel/restaurant with more views lies behind the church. At Christmas, this entire village transforms itself into one big crèche scene (a Provençal tradition that has long since died out in other villages).

• *From Séguret, follow D-88 down to Roaix and turn left on D-975, passing through the village. A well-marked turnoff between Roaix and Rasteau leads uphill to...*

❷ Domaine des Girasols

Friendly Françoise, her American husband John (both speak English), or mama (Marie-Elizabeth, speaks "a leetle" English) will take your palate on a tour of some of my favorite wines. This is the ideal place to get oriented, because the helpful owners produce a wide variety of wines and understand Americans. Papa Joyet bought this winery about 14 years ago, trading a vegetable business in the big city of Lyon for vineyards in little Rasteau. The setting is postcard-perfect, their wines are now available in the US, and son-in-law John (a big Oakland Raiders fan) studied winemaking in the Napa Valley. Mama made those beautiful quilts you see in the tasting room (Mon–Sat 9:00–12:00 & 14:00–18:00, Sun by appointment only, tel. 04 90 46 11 70).

• *Next, return to Vaison la Romaine and follow signs toward Carpentras. You'll soon come to Le Crestet (on D-938). Look for signs to the right, leading up to* Le Village—*it's five minutes to ridge-top...*

❸ Le Crestet

This village—founded after the fall of the Roman Empire, when laws were nonexistent and people gathered in high places like this for protection from marauding barbarians—followed the usual hill-town evolution (see sidebar). The outer walls of the village did double duty as ramparts and house walls. The castle above (from about A.D. 850) provided a final safe haven when the village was attacked.

The Bishop of Vaison la Romaine was the first occupant, lending little Le Crestet a certain prestige. With about 500 residents in 1200, Le Crestet was a very important town in this region, reaching its zenith in the mid-1500s, when 660 people called it home. Le Crestet began its gradual decline when the bishop moved to Vaison la Romaine in the 1600s, though the population remained fairly stable until World War II. Today, about 35 people live within the walls year-round (about 55 during the summer).

As you drive up to Le Crestet, stop by Charley Schmitt's house to pick up his well-done self-guided tour in English (on the road up to the village, it's the first house on the right after passing the *No Bus Allowed* sign; look for the small solar panel over his door). White-haired Charley has spent the last 40 years of his life studying and sketching this village, and he knows every stone. He's 87, speaks no English (his daughter translated the walking tour), and would be honored to sell you his brochure for €3.

Walking-tour brochure in hand, park at the entry of the

village and wander the peaceful lanes. Appreciate the amount of work it took to put these stones in place. Notice the elaborate water channels. Le Crestet was served by 18 cisterns in the Middle Ages, and disputes over water were a common problem. The peaceful church (might be closed, €0.50 turns the lights on) has a beautiful stained-glass window behind the altar. Imagine hundreds of people living here, and animals roaming everywhere. Get to the top of town. The village's only business, café-restaurant **Le Panoramic,** has an upstairs terrace with a view that justifies the name...even if the food is overpriced and mediocre (see page 158).

Walkers can return to Vaison la Romaine along a scenic footpath. The trail leaves from the very top of the village, at the upper, non-château end. Look for the brown sign, which indicates that it's eight kilometers (5 miles) to Vaison la Romaine, and—in a few steps—turn right, following the yellow sign that shows it's 5.1 kilometers (3 miles) to Vaison la Romaine.

• *Drivers can carry on and reconnect with the road below, following signs to Malaucène. Look for the huge* boules *courts as you near Malaucène (on your left). As you enter Malaucène, turn right on D-90 (direction: Suzette) just before the gas station. As you climb to the mountain pass, look for signs on the left to* La Col de la Chaîne *(Chain Pass). From this point on, the scenery gets better fast.*

❹ The Dentelles de Montmirail

Get out of your car at the pass (about 1,500 feet) and enjoy the breezy views. Wander about. The peaks in the distance—thrusting up like the back of a stegosaurus or a bad haircut (you decide)—are the Dentelles de Montmirail, a small range running just nine miles basically north to south and reaching 2,400 feet in elevation. This region's land is constantly shifting. Those rocky tops were the result of a gradual uplifting of the land, then were blown bald by the vicious mistral wind. Below, pine and oak trees mix with scotch broom, which blooms brilliant yellow from April to June. The village below the peaks is Suzette (you'll be there soon). The yellow-signed hiking trail leads to the castle-topped village of Le Barroux (3.5 miles, mostly downhill).

The scene is lovely and surprisingly undeveloped. You can thank the lack of water for the absence of more homes or farms in this area. Water is everything in this parched region, and if you don't have ready access to it, you can't build or cultivate the land. (Some farmers have drilled down 1,300 feet to try to find water.) With no water at hand, farmers here lie awake at night worrying about fire. Hot summers, dry pines, and windy days make a scary recipe for fast-traveling fires.

Now turn around and face Mont Ventoux. Are there clouds in the horizon? You're looking into the eyes of the Alps (behind

Ventoux), and those "foothills" help keep Provence sunny.

• *Time to push on. You'll pass countless yellow trail signs along this drive. (The Dentelles provide fertile ground for walking trails.) Barely up the road is a small lavender field (see sidebar on page 143). To sleep nearby, try **La Ferme Dégoutaud,** just ahead (see page 157). With the medieval castle of Le Barroux topping the horizon in the distance (off to the left), drive on to little...*

❺ Suzette

Tiny Suzette floats on its hilltop, with a small 12th-century chapel, one café, a handful of residents, and the gaggle of houses where they live. Park in Suzette's lot, below, then find the big orientation board above the lot (Rome is 620 kilometers—or 385 miles—away). Look out to the broad shoulders of Mont Ventoux. At 6,000 feet, it always seems to have some clouds hanging around. The top looks like it's snow-covered; if you drive up there you'll see it's actually white stone (see page 142).

Look to the village. Suzette's homes once lived in the shadow of an imposing castle, destroyed during the religious wars of the mid-1500s. **Les Coquelicots** café makes a perfect lunch or drink stop (see page 159); if it's warm, consider returning for dinner. Good picnic tables lie just past Suzette if you brought your own food. Back across the road from the orientation table is a tasting room for **Château Redortier** wines (English brochure and well-explained list of wines provided; skip their white, but try the good rosé and two reds).

• *If you're enjoying the views and can't get enough of this landscape, consider adding this 20-minute detour from Suzette: Drive down to Le Barroux, then loop back to D-90 via the rock-swirled village of La Roque Alric, and rejoin our route in La Fare (see below).*

Otherwise, continue from Suzette in the direction of Beaumes de Venise. You'll drop down into the lush little village of La Fare. Just after La Fare lies a worthwhile wine-tasting opportunity...

❻ Domaine de Coyeux

The private road winds up and up to this impossibly beautiful setting, with the best views of the Dentelles I found. Olive trees line the final approach, and *Le Caveau* signs lead to a modern tasting room (you may need to ring the buzzer). These wines have earned their excellent reputation. Start with the dry Muscat, then try their delectable Côtes du Rhône Villages red, and finish with their trademark sweet Muscat (wines range from €7–11 per bottle, Mon–Sat 10:00–12:00 & 14:00–18:00, closed Sun, tel. 04 90 12 42 42, some English spoken). After tasting, take time to wander about the vineyards.

• *Drive on toward Beaumes de Venise. On the way, **Restaurant le***

Cicadas

In the countryside, listen for *les cigales*. They sing in the heat and are famous for announcing the arrival of summer. (Locals say their song also marks the coming of the tourists...and more money.) People here love these ugly, long-winged bugs, an integral part of Provençal life. You'll see souvenir cicadas made out of every material possible. If you look closely—they are well-camouflaged—you can find live specimens on tree trunks and branches. Cicadas live for about two years, all but the last two weeks of which are spent quietly underground as larvae. But when they go public, their nonstop chirping begins with each sunrise and doesn't stop until sunset.

Redortier is worth considering for a bite (see page 159). You'll drop out of the hills as you approach Beaumes de Venise. To find the next winery, keep right at the first Centre-Ville *sign as the road bends left, then carefully track* Domaine de Durban *signs for three incredibly scenic miles to...*

❼ Domaine de Durban

In this stunning setting, equally *charmante* Nathalie or Sylvie will take your taste buds on a tour. This *domaine* produces appealing whites, reds, and Muscats. Start with the 100 percent Viognier, then try their Viognier–Chardonnay blend. Their rosé is light and refreshing (and less than €4 a bottle). Next, their two reds are very different from each other: One is fruity, and the other—aged in oak—is tannic (both could use another year before drinking but seemed fine to me). Finish with their popular Muscat de Venise (wines cost €4–10 per bottle, Mon–Sat 9:00–12:00 & 14:00–18:30, closed Sun, tel. 04 90 62 94 26). Picnics are not allowed, though strolling amid the gorgeous vineyards is.

• *Retrace your route to Beaumes de Venise, turn left at the bottom, then make a quick right and navigate through Beaumes de Venise, following signs for* Vacqueyras. *At a big roundabout, you'll pass Beaumes de Venise's massive* **cave coopérative,** *which represents many growers in this area (big selection, but too slick for my taste; daily 8:30–12:30 & 14:00–19:00). Continue following signs for* Vacqueyras (*a famous wine village with another* cave coopérative), *and then signs for* Gigondas *and* Vaison par la route touristique. *Follow signs to the TI and park on or near the tree-shaded square.*

❽ Gigondas

This town produces some of the region's best red wines and is ideally situated for hiking, mountain-biking, and driving into the mountains. The info-packed **TI** has a list of welcoming wineries, *chambres d'hôte,* and good hikes or drives (Mon–Sat 10:00–12:00 & 14:00–18:00, closed Sun, place du Portail, tel. 04 90 65 85 46). The €2.50 *Chemins et Sentiers du Massif des Dentelles* hiking map is helpful, though not critical, since routes are well-signed. Route #1 is an ideal one-hour walk above Gigondas to superb views from the Belvedere du Rocher du Midi (route #2 extends this hike into a 3-hour loop). At the least, take a short walk through the streets above the TI—the church is an easy destination with good views over the heart of the Côtes du Rhône vineyards.

Several good tasting opportunities await you on the main square. **Le Caveau de Gigondas** is best, where Sandra and Barbara await your visit with a large and free selection of tiny bottles for sampling, filled directly from the barrel (daily 10:00–12:00 & 14:00–18:30, 2 doors down from TI, tel. 04 90 65 82 29). Here you can compare wines from a variety of private producers in an intimate, low-key surrounding. The provided list of wines is helpful. Because of a self-imposed gag rule (so they don't favor the production of a single winery in this co-op showcase), it's best to know what you want (see "French Wine Lingo," page 41).

You'll find a small grocery store and several eating options in the village. Diagonally across from the TI, the shaded red tables of **Du Verre à l'Assiette** ("From Glass to Plate") entice lunchtime eaters with a terrific interior ambience (€10 salads, €13 *plats,* €15 mixed plate of meats and salad, closed Mon, place du Village, tel. 04 90 12 36 64). To dine very well or to sleep nearby, find **Hôtel les Florets,** a half-mile above town (closed Wed, see the next page).
• *From Gigondas, follow signs to the circular wine village of Sablet—with generally inexpensive yet tasty wines (the TI and wine cooperative share a space in the town center)—then past Séguret and back to Vaison la Romaine, where our tour ends.*

SLEEPING

(€1 = about $1.30, country code: 33)

Along the Côtes du Rhône

These accommodations are along the self-guided driving tour route described above. They offer a great opportunity for drivers who want to experience rural France and get better values.

Near Vaison la Romaine

These five accommodations are within a 10-minute drive of Vaison la Romaine.

$$$ Domaine de Cabasse*** is a lovely spread flanked by vineyards at the foot of Séguret (with a walking path to the village).

Winemaking is their primary business (tastings possible), though the hotel is well-run by its relaxed staff. The 13 rooms have retained a simple Old World feel. All the rooms have decks, and a big pool and bikes are at your disposal. From the entry gate—which opens automatically...and slowly—the place appears more formal than it is (Db-€110–150, Tb/Qb-€120–155, on D-23 between Sablet and Séguret, tel. 04 90 46 91 12, fax 04 90 46 94 01, www.domaine -de-cabasse.fr, info@domaine-de-cabasse.fr). The restaurant offers a mouthwatering, though limited, dinner *menu* (€32) served inside or out. (Hotel guests start with an apéritif.)

$$$ **Hôtel Les Florets****, a half-mile above Gigondas, is surrounded by pine trees at the foothills of the Dentelles de Montmirail. It comes with a huge terrace that van Gogh would have loved, thoughtfully designed rooms, and an exceptional restaurant (Db-€98–113, Tb-€115–135, annex rooms are best, Gigondas, tel. 04 90 65 85 01, fax 04 90 65 83 80, www.hotel -lesflorets.com, accueil@hotel-lesflorets.com). For more details about the hotel's restaurant, see page 159.

$$$ **Domaine de Tilleuls*****, 10 minutes from Vaison la Romaine in workaday Malaucène, is a splendid, moderately priced refuge, and the most family-friendly place I list. (Welcoming owners Arnaud and Dominique have three kids.) Its 20 country-modern rooms fill an old farmhouse, overlooking lovely grounds with namesake linden trees *(tilleuls)*, a sandbox, toys, and a large pool. If you missed market day in Vaison la Romaine, sleep here Tuesday night and wake to a bustling market (Db-€78–88, Tb/Qb-€115, well-signed in Malaucène on the route to Mont Ventoux, tel. 04 90 65 22 31, fax 04 90 65 16 77, www.hotel -domainedestilleuls.com, info@hotel-domainedestilleuls.com). An Internet café is close by.

$$ **L'Ecole Buissonnière Chambres** is run by an engaging Anglo-French team, Monique and John, who share their peace and quiet 10 minutes from Vaison la Romaine. This creatively restored farmhouse has three character-filled, half-timbered rooms, and convivial public spaces. Getting to know John, who has lived all over the south of France and even worked as a *gardian* (cowboy) in the Camargue, is worth the price of the room—he's also generous with his knowledge of the area. The outdoor kitchen allows guests to picnic in high fashion in the tranquil garden (Db-€54–60, Tb-€68–75, Qb-€84–90, includes breakfast, cash only, between Villedieu and Buisson on D-75, tel. 04 90 28 95 19, ecole .buissonniere@wanadoo.fr).

In or near Suzette
$$ **La Ferme Dégoutaud,** a 20-minute drive from Vaison la Romaine, is a splendidly situated and utterly isolated *chambre d'hôte*

about halfway between Malaucène and Suzette (well-signed, a mile down a dirt road). Friendly Véronique (minimal English) rents three farm-rustic rooms with many thoughtful touches, a view pool, and table tennis (Db-€63–68, includes breakfast, tel. & fax 04 90 62 99 29, www.degoutaud.fr, le.degoutaud@wanadoo.fr). If you plan to spend a week, inquire about her apartments. Ask and she'll cook you dinner—€23 for the homemade works, including drinks.

EATING

Along the Côtes du Rhône

Drivers enjoy a wealth of country-Provençal dining opportunities in rustic settings, handy to many of the rural accommodations. Many of these eateries are described in the self-guided driving tour route explained above; I've listed them by distance from Vaison la Romaine (nearest to farthest). Most are within a five-minute drive of Vaison la Romaine.

La Girocedre is an enchanting place to eat lunch or dinner if you have a car and it's nice outside. Just three picturesque miles from Vaison la Romaine in adorable Puyméras, this place offers a complete country-Provençal package: outdoor tables placed just-so in a lush garden, warm interior decor, and mouthwatering, Provençal cuisine (*menus* from €24, closed Mon, tel. 04 90 46 50 67).

Auberge d'Anaïs, at the end of a dirt road 10 minutes from Vaison la Romaine, is another find—and a true Provençal experience. Outdoor tables gather under cheery lights with grand views and reliable cuisine. Ask for a table *sur la terrasse* (€9 lunch *menu*, good dinner *menus* from €16, closed Mon, tel. 04 90 36 20 06). From Vaison la Romaine, follow signs to *Carpentras*, then *St. Marcellin*; signs will guide you from there.

Le Panoramic, in hill-capping Le Crestet, serves average salads, pizzas, and *plats* for more than you should spend at what must be Provence's greatest view tables (open daily for lunch and dinner, tel. 04 90 28 76 42). Come for a drink and view, but if you're really hungry, eat elsewhere. Drivers should pass on the first parking lot in Le Crestet and keep climbing to park at place du Château. The restaurant is to your right as you face the view.

Loupiotte is a cheap and cheerful roadside café-restaurant between Vaison la Romaine and Malaucène, below Le Crestet. It's a good place for families, serving pizza (try *le végétarienne*), pasta, salads, and *plats*—consider the grilled lamb with vegetables and fries (closed Mon, tel. 04 90 36 29 50).

Domaine de Cabasse lets you dine surrounded by vineyards at a relaxed wine estate/hotel. Even with its limited-selection €31 *menu*, it more than merits the short drive from Vaison la Romaine (see hotel listing, page 156).

Le Grand Pré has the best (and most expensive) cuisine I list in this area. Fresh off its Michelin-star rating, this place is small and elegant, with a small outside terrace (*menus* from about €50, closed Tue, closed Sun–Thu Nov–Feb, on D-975 in Roaix, between Vaison la Romaine and Rasteau, tel. 04 90 46 18 12).

Hôtel les Florets, in Gigondas, is a traditional, family-run place that's worth the drive. Dinners are a sumptuous blend of classic French cuisine and Provençal accents, served with class by English-speaking Thierry. The marvelous terrace makes your meal even more memorable (*menus* from €26, restaurant closed Wed; see hotel listing, page 157).

La Maison Bleue, on Villedieu's adorable little square, is a pizza-and-salad place with great outdoor ambience. Skip it if the weather forces you inside (open for lunch and dinner, closed Wed, tel. 04 90 28 97 02).

Les Coquelicots, a small café-restaurant surrounded by vines and views in minuscule Suzette, is a sweet place. The food is scrumptious (owner/chef Frankie insists on fresh products) and the setting is memorable. Try the *omelet au chèvre* for lunch (€10), or splurge for a more elaborate *plat* (€18–20, usually closed Tue–Wed May–Sept, then open weekends only Oct–April; tel. 04 90 65 06 94).

Restaurant le Redortier, off a short dirt road between Suzette and Beaumes de Venise, is the real thing: unspoiled and unpretentious, with outdoor tables flanked by cozy interior dining. The owners are new, so things might change, but give it a look (*menus* from €20, salads and *plats,* arrive by 13:30 for lunch, tel. 04 90 65 07 16).

HILL TOWNS OF THE LUBERON

Not Quite a Year in Provence

The Luberon region, stretching 30 miles along a ridge of rugged hills east of Avignon, hides some of France's most appealing hill towns and sensuous landscapes. Those intrigued by Peter Mayle's books love joyriding through the region, connecting I-could-live-here villages, crumbled castles, and meditative abbeys. Mayle's bestselling *A Year in Provence* describes the ruddy local culture from an Englishman's perspective as he buys a stone farmhouse, fixes it up, and adopts the region as his new home. His book is a great read while you're here.

The Luberon terrain in general (much of which is a French regional natural park) is as appealing as its villages. Gnarled vineyards and wind-sculpted trees separate tidy stone structures from abandoned buildings—little more than rock piles—that seem to challenge city slickers to fix them up. White rock slabs bend along high ridges, while colorful hot-air balloons survey the sun-drenched scene from above.

The wind is an integral part of life here. The infamous mistral wind, finishing its long ride in from Siberia, hits like a hammer (see sidebar on page 7).

Planning Your Time

There are no obligatory museums, monuments, or vineyards in the Luberon. Treat this area like a vacation from your vacation. Downshift your engine. Brake for the views, and get out of your car to take a walk.

To enjoy the ambience of the Luberon, you'll want at least two nights and a car (only Isle-sur-la-Sorgue—and, to a lesser extent, Lourmarin—are accessible by train or bus). Allow a half-day for Isle-sur-la-Sorgue if it's market day (less time if not) and a full day for the Luberon villages. For the ultimate Luberon experience,

The Luberon

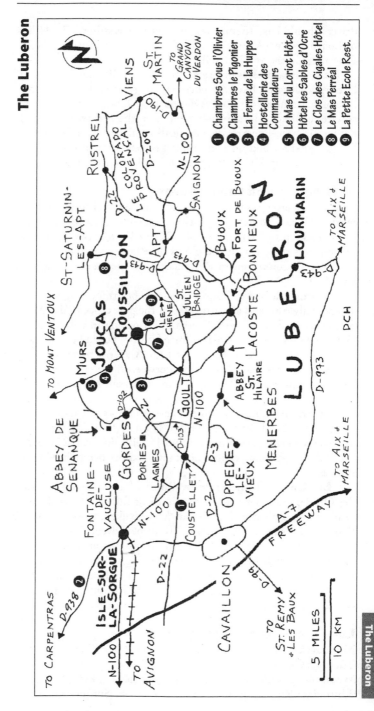

1 Chambres Sous l'Olivier
2 Chambres le Pigonier
3 La Ferme la Huppe
4 Hostellerie des Commandeurs
5 Le Mas du Loriot Hôtel
6 Hôtel les Sables d'Ocre
7 Le Clos des Cigales Hôtel
8 Le Mas Perréal
9 La Petite Ecole Rest.

drivers should base themselves in or near Roussillon. The village of Lourmarin works well as a southern base for visiting Aix-en-Provence, Cassis, and Marseille.

If you lack wheels or prefer streams to hills, stay in Isle-sur-la-Sorgue, located halfway between Avignon and the Luberon. Adequate train service from Avignon and Marseille, and some bus service, connect Isle-sur-la-Sorgue with the real world. Mostly flat terrain, tree-lined roads, and nearby villages make Isle-sur-la-Sorgue good for biking. Determined travelers can also take a bus from Avignon or Aix-en-Provence to reach Lourmarin.

Getting Around the Luberon

By Car: Luberon roads are scenic and narrow. With no big landmarks, it's easy to get lost in this area—but getting lost is the point. Pick up the Michelin Local Map #332 to navigate. If connecting this region with the Côtes du Rhône, consider doing so via Mont Ventoux—one of Provence's most spectacular routes (see page 142).

By Bus: Isle-sur-la-Sorgue is easy by bus from Avignon, with several daily trips and a central stop at the post office (6/day Mon–Sat, fewer on Sun, 45 min). Buses link Lourmarin with Avignon (3/day, 90 min) and Aix-en-Provence (75 min, bus to Pertuis leaves 3/day, transfer there to bus bound for Aix-en-Provence, 2/hr), making it a workable village stop between these cities. Without a car or minivan tour, I'd skip the more famous hill towns of the Luberon.

By Train: Trains get you to Isle-sur-la-Sorgue (station called "L'Isle–Fontaine de Vaucluse") from Avignon (10/day on weekdays, 5/day on weekends, 30 min) or from Marseille (8/day, 1–2 hours). If you're day-tripping by train, check return times before leaving the station.

By Minivan Tour: Friendly Roland Vanove—and his **Taxi des Oliviers** tour service—offers half- or full-day English tours of his native Luberon. Dutchman Mike Rijken, who runs **Wine Safari**, offers similar services (see "Tours of Provence" on page 36).

By Bike: Hardy bikers can ride from Isle-sur-la-Sorgue to Gordes, then to Roussillon, connecting other villages in a full-day loop ride (30 miles round-trip to Roussillon and back, with lots of hills). Other appealing villages are closer to Isle-sur-la-Sorgue and offer easier biking options (see "Biking" on page 168).

Luberon Area Market Days

Monday: Cavaillon (produce and antiques/flea market)
Tuesday: Gordes and Lacoste (both small)
Wednesday: Sault (produce and antiques/flea market)
Thursday: Roussillon (cute) and Isle-sur-la-Sorgue (good, but

smaller than its Sunday market)

Friday: Lourmarin (very good) and Bonnieux (pretty good)

Saturday: Apt (huge produce and antiques/flea market)

Sunday: Isle-sur-la-Sorgue (granddaddy of them all, produce and antiques/flea market) and Coustellet (very good and less touristy)

Isle-sur-la-Sorgue

This sturdy market town—literally, "Island on the Sorgue River"—sits within a split in its crisp, happy little river. It's a workaday town

with too many cars and some unpolished edges, but makes a good base for exploring the Luberon and Avignon (30 min to each by car) and can work for exploring the Côtes du Rhône (50 min to Vaison la Romaine).

After the arid cities and villages elsewhere in Provence, the presence of water at every turn is a welcome change. In Isle-sur-la-Sorgue—called the "Venice of Provence"—the Sorgue River's extraordinarily clear and shallow flow divides like cells, producing water, water everywhere. The river is essential to the region's economy. The fresh spring water of the many branches of the Sorgue has provided ample fish, nourishment for crops, and power for key industries for centuries. Today, antique shops power the town's economy—every other shop seems to sell some kind of antique.

ORIENTATION

While Isle-sur-la-Sorgue is renowned for its market days (Sun and Wed), it's otherwise a pleasantly average town with no important sights and a steady trickle of tourism. It's calm at night and downright dead on Mondays.

Tourist Information

The TI has information on hiking and biking, and a line on rooms in private homes, all of which are outside the town (Mon–Sat

9:00–13:00 & 14:30–18:00, Sun 9:00–13:00, in town center next to church, tel. 04 90 38 04 78, www.ot-islesurlasorgue.fr, office -tourisme.islesur-sorgue@wanadoo.fr).

Arrival in Isle-sur-la-Sorgue

By Car: Traffic is a mess and parking is a headache on market days (all day Sunday and Thursday mornings). Circle the ring road and look for parking signs, or give up and find the pay lot behind the post office (PTT). There are also several lots just west of the roundabout, with roads to Carpentras and Fontaine-de-Vaucluse. You'll also pass freestyle parking on roads leaving the city. Don't leave anything visible in your car.

By Train: Remember that the train station is called "L'Isle–Fontaine de Vaucluse." To reach my recommended hotels, walk straight out of the station and turn right on the ring road.

By Bus: The bus from Avignon drops you at the post office (PTT), a block from the recommended Hôtel les Névons.

Helpful Hints

Internet Access: Try **Internet Station,** across from the church and TI and a block down rue Danton at #3 (tel. 04 90 20 03 28).

Laundry: It's just off the pedestrian street rue de la République, at 23 impasse de l'Hôtel de Palerme (daily 8:00–20:30).

Supermarket: A well-stocked **Spar** market is on the main ring road, near the Peugeot Car shop and the train station (Mon–Sat 9:00–12:00 & 15:00–19:00, Sun 15:00–19:00). A smaller **Casino** market is more central on pedestrian rue de la République (Tue–Sun 7:30–12:30 & 15:30–19:30).

Bike Rental: Isles 2 Roues, by the train station, rents bikes (€14/ day, must show your passport, 10 avenue de la Gare, tel. 04 90 38 19 12).

Taxi: Call tel. 06 09 06 92 06 or 06 08 09 19 49.

Public WC: There's a good WC in the parking lot between the post office (PTT) and the Hôtel les Névons.

Hiking: The TI has good information on area hikes; most trails are accessible by short drives, and you can use a taxi to get there.

SELF-GUIDED WALK

Wandering Isle-sur-la-Sorgue

The town has crystal-clear water babbling under pedestrian bridges stuffed with flower boxes, and its old-time carousel is always spinning. For this walk, navigate by the town's splintered streams and nine mossy waterwheels, which, while still turning, power only

Isle-sur-la-Sorgue

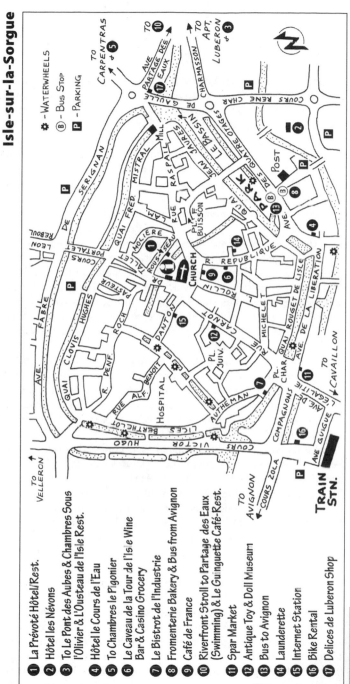

✿ – WATERWHEELS
Ⓑ – BUS STOP
P – PARKING

1. La Prévoté Hôtel/Rest.
2. Hôtel les Névons
3. To Le Pont des Aubes & Chambres Sous l'Olivier & L'Ousteau de l'Isle Rest.
4. Hôtel le Cours de l'Eau
5. To Chambres le Pigonier
6. Le Caveau de la Tour de l'Isle Wine Bar & Casino Grocery
7. Le Bistrot de l'Industrie
8. Fromenterie Bakery & Bus from Avignon
9. Café de France
10. Riverfront Stroll to Partage des Eaux (Swimming) & Le Guinguette Café-Rest.
11. Spar Market
12. Antique Toy & Doll Museum
13. Bus to Avignon
14. Launderette
15. Internet Station
16. Bike Rental
17. Delices de Luberon Shop

memories of the town's wool and silk industries.

• *Start your tour at the church next to the TI—where all streets seem to converge—and make forays into the town from there. Go first to the church.*

Notre-Dame des Anges: This 12th-century church has a festive Baroque interior and seems overgrown for today's town. Walk in. The curls and swirls and gilded statues date from an era that was all about Louis XIV, the Sun King. This is propagandist architecture, designed to wow the faithful into compliance. (It was made possible thanks to profits generated from the town's river-powered industries.) When you enter a church like this, the heavens should open up and assure you that whoever built it had unearthly connections.

• *Wander down rue Danton, in front of the church, to lose the crowds and find...*

Three Waterwheels: These big, forgotten waterwheels have been in business here since the 1200s, when they were first used for grinding flour. Paper, textile, silk, and woolen mills would later find their power from this river. At its peak, Isle-sur-la-Sorgue had 70 waterwheels like this, and in the 1800s, the town competed with Avignon as Provence's cloth-dyeing and textile center. Those stylish Provençal fabrics and patterns you see for sale everywhere were made possible by this river.

• *Double back to the church, turn left under the arcade, then find the small stream just past the TI. Breakaway streams like this run under the town like subways run under Paris. Take a right on the first street after the stream; it leads under a long arch (along rue J. J. Rousseau). Follow this straight, and veer slightly right at place F. Buisson to the main river, then follow it left. You'll come to...*

Le Bassin: Literally translated as a "pond," this is where the Sorgue River enters the town and separates into many branches. Track as many branches as you can see (Frank Provost hides a big one), and then find the round lookout point for the best perspective (carefully placed lights make this a beautiful sight after dark). Fishing was the town's main industry until the waterwheels took over. In the 1300s, local fishermen provided the pope with his fresh-fish quota. They either trapped them in nets or speared them while standing on skinny, flat-bottomed boats. You'll find streets named after the fish they caught—including rue de l'Aiguille (literally, "Eel Street") and rue des Ecrevisses ("Crayfish Street").

The sound of the rushing water reminds us of the power that rivers can generate. With its source (a spring) a mere five miles away, the Sorgue River never floods and has a constant flow and temperature in all seasons. Isle-sur-la-Sorgue was able to prosper in the Middle Ages in spite of its location (situated in a flat valley), thanks to the natural protection this river provided. Walls with big moats once ran along the river, but they were destroyed during the French Revolution.

• *Cross the busy roundabout, and walk to the orange Delices de Luberon store. Stop at the entryway tasting table to sample its scrumptious tapenade selection. Walk behind the store to find the river and take a refreshing...*

Riverfront Stroll: Follow the main river upstream, along the bike/pedestrian lane, as far as you like. The little road meanders about a mile, following the serene course of the river, past waterfront homes and beneath swaying trees, all the way to Hôtel le Pescador and a riverside café (Le Guinguette—see "Eating," later in this chapter). The wide and shallow Partage des Eaux, where the water divides before entering Isle-sur-la-Sorgue, is perfect for a refreshing swim on a hot day.

SIGHTS AND ACTIVITIES

In Isle-sur-la-Sorgue

▲▲**Market Days**—The town erupts into a carnival-like market frenzy each Sunday and Thursday, with hardy crafts and local produce. The Sunday market is astounding and famous for its antiques; the Thursday market is more intimate (see market tips on page 162). Find a table at the Café de France and enjoy the scene.

Antique Toy and Doll Museum (Musée du Jouet et de la Poupée Ancienne)—The town's lone sight is a fun and funky toy museum with more than 300 dolls displayed in three small rooms (€3.50, kids-€1.50; June–Sept Mon–Fri 13:00–17:30, Sat–Sun 11:00–17:00; Oct–May Sat–Sun 11:00–17:00, closed Mon–Fri; 26 rue Carnot).

Near Isle-sur-la-Sorgue

Fontaine-de-Vaucluse—You'll read and hear a lot about this village, impressively located at the source of the Sorgue River, where the medieval Italian poet Petrarch mourned for his love, Laura. The river seems to magically appear from nowhere (the actual source is a murky, green water hole) and flows through the town past a lineup of cafés, souvenir shops, and too many tourists. While the setting is beautiful—with cliffs jutting to the sky and a ruined castle above—the trip is worth it only if the spring is flowing. Ask your hotelier and arrive early or late to avoid crowds. It's a good bike ride here from Isle-sur-la-Sorgue (about four miles).

Arriving by car, you'll pay €3 to park, and then walk about 20 minutes along the sparkling river to *la source* (the spring), located in a cave at the base of the cliff. (It's an uphill hike for the last part.) The spring itself is the very definition of anticlimactic, unless it's surging. At those times, it's among the most prolific water producers in the world, with a depth no one has yet been able to determine.

The path to the spring is lined with distractions. The **Monde Souterrain** offers 40-minute guided walks through reproduced caverns; it's skippable for everyone but avid spelunkers (€5.50, daily 10:00–12:00 & 14:00–18:00, in French only, English handouts, tel. 04 90 20 34 13). The **Musée d'Histoire 1939–1945** seems out of place here, but it does a good job explaining life in France during the German occupation and Vichy collaboration (€3.50, June–Sept Wed–Mon 10:00–12:00 & 14:00–18:00, Oct–May Wed–Mon until 17:00, closed Tue year-round, many interesting exhibits, essential and free audioguide in English, tel. 04 90 20 24 00). A worthwhile and relevant detour is the **Moulin à Papier,** a reproduction of a 17th-century paper mill. Here, you'll see the value of harnessing the river's power. In the mill, a 22-foot-diameter paddle wheel turns five times a minute, driving hammers that pound paper for up to 36 hours (free, open daily 9:00–19:00).

Canoe Trips on the Sorgue—A better reason to travel to Fontaine-de-Vaucluse is to canoe down the river. If you're really on vacation, consider this five-mile, two-hour trip. A guide escorts small groups in canoes, starting in Fontaine-de-Vaucluse and ending in Isle-sur-la-Sorgue; you'll return to Fontaine-de-Vaucluse via shuttle bus (call for departure times: Canoe Evasion, €19, tel. 04 90 38 26 22; and Kayaks Verts, €19, tel. 04 90 20 35 44). While a shuttle bus will pick you up in Isle-sur-la-Sorgue, con-

sider renting a bike and riding one-way, and then canoeing back. (Provence Vélos can arrange bike pickup or drop-off—see "Bike Rental," page 164.)

Biking—These towns make easy biking destinations from Isle-sur-la-Sorgue: Velleron (5 miles north, flat, a tiny version of Isle-sur-la-Sorgue with waterwheels, fountains, and an evening farmer's market Mon–Sat 18:00–20:00); Lagnes (3 miles east, mostly flat, a pretty and well-restored hill town with views from its ruined château); and Fontaine-de-Vaucluse (5 miles northeast, gently uphill, described above). Allow 30 miles and many hills for the round-trip ride to Roussillon. (Isle-sur-la-Sorgue bike-rental companies are listed under "Helpful Hints," on page 164.)

SLEEPING

In Isle-sur-la-Sorgue

Pickings are slim for good sleeps in Isle-sur-la-Sorgue, though the few I've listed provide solid values.

Sleep Code

(€1 = about $1.30, country code: 33)
S = Single, **D** = Double/Twin, **T** = Triple, **Q** = Quad, **b** = bathroom,
s = shower only, ***** = French hotel rating system (0–4 stars).
Unless otherwise noted, credit cards are accepted and English
is spoken.

To help you sort easily through these listings, I've divided
the rooms into three categories based on the price for a standard double room with bath:

$$$ **Higher Priced**—Most rooms €85 or more.
$$ **Moderately Priced**—Most rooms between €55–85.
$ **Lower Priced**—Most rooms €55 or less.

$$$ La Prévôté*** has the town's highest-priced digs. Its
five meticulously decorated rooms—located above a classy restau-
rant—are each decorated in earth tones, with high ceilings, a few
exposed beams, and beautiful furnishings. Séverine manages the
hotel while chef-hubby Jean-Marie controls the kitchen (standard
Db-€130, larger Db-€150, suite Db-€170, no air-con or elevator,
Internet access and Wi-Fi, rooftop deck with Jacuzzi, no parking,
one block from the church at 4 rue J. J. Rousseau, tel. & fax 04 90
38 57 29, www.la-prevote.fr, contact@la-prevote.fr).

$$ Hôtel les Névons**, two blocks from the center (behind
the post office), is concrete motel-modern outside. Inside, how-
ever, it does everything right, with eager-to-please staff and two
wings to choose from: the new wing, with cavernous and cushy
rooms, or the old wing, with puce halls and more modest, cheaper
(but good enough) rooms. There are several family suites and a roof
deck with 360-degree views around a small pool (old wing—Db-
€56–62; new wing—huge Db-€64–74, Tb-€75–84, Qb-€85–95;
air-con, Internet access, easy parking, 205 chemin des Névons, tel.
04 90 20 72 00, fax 04 90 20 56 20, www.hotel-les-nevons.com,
info@hotel-les-nevons.com).

$$ Le Pont des Aubes Chambres has two huggable rooms in an
old, green-shuttered farmhouse right on the river a mile from town.
Borrow a bike or a canoe. From here, you can cross a tiny bridge and
walk 15 minutes along the river into Isle-sur-la-Sorgue, or cross the
street to the recommended L'Ousteau de l'Isle restaurant. Charming
Martine speaks English, while husband Patrice speaks smiles
(Db-€70, Tb-€85, 1-room apartments-€310–350/week, cash only,
a mile from town toward Apt, next to Pain d'Antin Boulangerie at
189 route d'Apt, tel. & fax 04 90 38 13 75, http://perso.wanadoo.fr/
lepontdesaubes, patriceaubert@wanadoo.fr).

The Luberon

$ Hôtel le Cours de l'Eau is a gruff place with bargain beds above a café. It's sufficiently clean and nearly quiet; it's also the closest of my recommended hotels to the train station (Db-€40–48, on ring road opposite Café de la Sorgue at place Gambetta, tel. & fax 04 90 38 01 18, no English spoken).

Near Isle-sur-la-Sorgue

$$$ Chambres Sous l'Olivier, located five minutes east of Isle-sur-la-Sorgue, is well-situated for exploring the hill towns of the Luberon and Isle-sur-la-Sorgue. Its six lovely, comfortable rooms are housed in a massive, 150-year-old farmhouse with lounges that you and your entire soccer team could spread out in. Julien and Carole take care of your every need, and they'll cook you a full-blown dinner with wine for €27 per person (Db-€80–130, 3-room suite-€180, cash only, pool, route d'Apt, tel. 04 90 20 23 54 or 04 90 20 33 90, www.chambresdhotesprovence.com, souslolivier @wanadoo.fr). It's below Isle-sur-la-Sorgue, about 40 minutes from Avignon toward Apt on D-22; look for signs 200 yards after the big sign to *le Mas du Grand Jonquier* on the right.

$$ Chambres le Pigeonnier is run by gracious Corinne, who welcomes guests to a flawless, modern refuge with two rooms by a wonderful garden and pool. The rooms are top quality: One is low-ceilinged and opens onto the pool, while the other *(la Cabane)* is a smashing two-room unit. The bigger unit is rented on a weekly basis (€480), but it's available on a daily basis if it's not booked up—and it's worth asking for (Db-€66–84, Tb-€92, includes breakfast, cash only, 135 impasse les Costières, tel. 04 90 20 77 92, mobile 06 21 83 26 82, www.lepigeonnier-provence.com, corinne.manni@wanadoo.fr). From Isle-sur-la-Sorgue, follow signs to Carpentras, go 1.1 kilometers—about three-quarters of a mile (past the McDonald's), turn right on the tiny road marked *Les Costières,* and cross the minuscule bridge. Turn left on the first road—it's the third home on the left.

EATING

Inexpensive restaurants are easy to find in Isle-sur-la-Sorgue, but consistent quality is another story. The two restaurants I list (La Prévôté and L'Ousteau de l'Isle) are both fair values, but neither is cheap. For inexpensive meals, I prefer trolling the riverside cafés for today's catch. Dining on the river is a unique experience in this arid land famous for its hill towns, and shopping for the perfect table is half the fun. Also consider a riverside picnic (the Fromenterie bakery, listed below, stocks mouthwatering quiche and more).

Begin your dinner with a glass of wine at the cozy **Le Caveau**

The Luberon

de la Tour de l'Isle (part wine bar, part wine-and-cheese shop, open Tue–Sat until about 20:00, closed Sun–Mon, 12 rue de la République, tel. 04 90 20 70 25).

Le Bistrot de l'Industrie is less central, but is one of the better values lining the river for basic café fare (closed Mon–Tue, near the train station on quai de la Charité, tel. 04 90 38 00 40).

La Prévôté is a place to really do it up. Its dining room is covered in wood beams, the outdoor patio is peaceful, and the place feels country-classy but not stuffy. A branch of the Sorgue runs through the restaurant, visible through glass windows (*menus* from €43, save room for amazing cheese platter, closed Tue–Wed, 4 rue J. J. Rousseau, on narrow street that runs along left side of church as you face it, tel. 04 90 38 57 29).

L'Ousteau de l'Isle, located in a Provençal farmhouse a mile from the town center, has a modern interior and lovely seating outside (request a table *sur la terrasse*). Serving regional cuisine with a modern twist, it draws a loyal clientele (dinner *menus* from €27, lunch *menu* for €17, closed Tue–Wed, 147 chemin de Bosquet, tel. 04 90 20 81 36). From Isle-sur-la-Sorgue's center, follow signs toward Apt, and turn right at Pain d'Antin Boulangerie; or walk 20 minutes along the river and cross the small bridge to chemin de Bosquet.

The **Fromenterie** bakery next to the post office (PTT) sells decadent quiche, monster sandwiches, desserts, wine, and other drinks—in other words, everything you need to picnic (open daily until 20:00).

At **Le Guinguette,** experience a decent riverside meal or snack in a dreamy Partage des Eaux (parting of the waters) setting (€15 *plats*, closed Mon; follow directions for "Riverfront Stroll" at the end of my self-guided walk earlier in this chapter; tel. 04 90 38 10 61).

The Heart of the Luberon

A 15-minute drive east of Isle-sur-la-Sorgue lies this protected area, where canyons and ridgelines rule, and land developers take a back seat. Here, still-proud hill towns stand guard over long-forgotten valleys, while carefully managed vineyards (producing mostly inexpensive wines) play hopscotch with cherry groves, lavender fields, and cypress trees.

Peter Mayle's *A Year in Provence* nudged tourism in this area into overdrive. A visit to Mayle's quintessential Provence includes many of the popular villages and sights described in this chapter. While the hill towns can be seen as subtly different variations on the same theme, each has a distinct character. Look for differences:

The Luberon

the color of shutters, the pattern of stones, the way flowers are planted, or the number of tourist boutiques. Every village has something to offer—it's up to you to discover and celebrate it.

Stay in or near Roussillon. By village standards, Roussillon is always lively. When restaurant-hunting, read descriptions of the villages in this chapter—many good finds are embedded in the countryside. For aerial views high above this charmed land, consider a hot-air balloon trip (see page 177).

Planning Your Time

With a car and one full day, I'd linger in Roussillon in the morning, visit the St. Julien Bridge, then have lunch nearby in Lacoste or Bonnieux (suggestions on page 185). After lunch, continue the joyride to Ménerbes and Oppède-le-Vieux, then return through Coustellet and Gordes. With a second full day, I'd start by climbing the Fort de Buoux and lunch nearby (suggestions offered). After lunch, continue to Saignon and Viens, then loop back via St-Saturnin-lès-Apt.

I've described sights at each of the stops listed above, but you'll need to be selective, because you can't see them all. Read through your options and choose the ones that sound most interesting to you. Remember that the best sight is the dreamy landscape between the villages.

Roussillon

With all the trendy charm of Santa Fe on a hilltop, photogenic Roussillon requires serious camera and café time (and €2 for parking). Roussillon has been a protected village since 1943 and

has benefited from a complete absence of modern development. An enormous deposit of ochre gives the earth and its buildings that distinctive red color and provided this village with its economic base until shortly after World War II. This place is popular; it's best to visit early or late in the day.

ORIENTATION

Roussillon sits atop Mont Rouge (Red Mountain) at about 1,000 feet above sea level. The village curls around this hospitable mountain, and the exposed ochre cliffs are a short walk south.

The Luberon

Roussillon

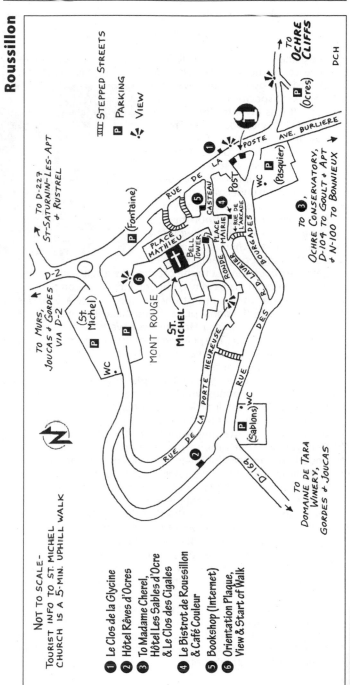

NOT TO SCALE—
TOURIST INFO TO ST. MICHEL
CHURCH IS A 5-MIN. UPHILL WALK

① Le Clos de la Glycine
② Hôtel Rêves d'Ocres
③ To Madame Cherel,
Hôtel Les Sables d'Ocre
& Le Clos des Cigales
④ Le Bistrot de Roussillon
& Café Couleur
⑤ Bookshop (Internet)
⑥ Orientation Plaque,
View & Start of Walk

STEPPED STREETS
P PARKING
↯ VIEW

TO D-227
ST-SATURNIN-LES-APT
& RUSTREL

TO MURS,
JOUCAS & GORDES
VIA D-2

D-2

(St.
Michel)

P

WC

MONT ROUGE

ST.
MICHEL

BELL
TOWER

PLACE
MATHIEU

RUE DE

RUE
CASTEAU

PLACE
MAIRIE

⑤

④

← RUE DE
L'ARCADE

POST

LA

①

POSTE

WC

P
(Pasquier)

AVE. BURLIERE

DCH

TO
OCHRE
CLIFFS

P
(Ocres)

TO ③,
OCHRE CONSERVATORY,
D-104 TO GOULT & APT
& N-100 TO BONNIEUX

P
(Fontaine)

RUE RONDE

R. LAVIERE

RUE DES BOURGADES

RUE DE LA PORTE HEUREUSE

RUE
DES

P
(Sablons) WC

②

D-169

TO
DOMAINE DE TARA
WINERY,
GORDES & JOUCAS

The Luberon

Boules (Pétanque)

The game of *boules*—also called *pétanque*—is the horseshoes of Provence and the Riviera. It's played in every village, almost exclusively by men, on level dirt areas kept specifically for this purpose. It was invented here in the early 1900s, and today every French boy grows up playing *boules* with Papa and *Ton-Ton* (Uncle) Jean. It's a social-yet-serious sport, and endlessly entertaining to watch—even more so if you understand the rules.

Boules is played with heavy metal balls (*boules,* about the size of baseballs) and a small wooden target ball (*le cochonnet,* about the size of a ping-pong ball). Whoever gets their *boule* closest to the *cochonnet* wins. It's most commonly played in teams of two, though individual competition and teams of three are not uncommon. (There are *boules* leagues and professional players who make little money but are national celebrities.) Most teams have two specialists, a *pointeur* and a *tireur*. The *pointeur* goes first and tries to lob his balls as close to the target as he can. The *tireur*'s job is to blast away opponent's *boules*.

Here's the play-by-play: Each player gets three *boules*. A coin toss determines which team goes first. The starting team scratches a small circle in the dirt, in which players must stand (with both feet on the ground) when launching their *boules*. Next, the starting team tosses the *cochonnet* (about 6–10 yards)—that's the target. The *boule* must be tossed underhand, and can be rolled, thrown sky-high, or rocketed at its target. Most lob it like a slow pitch in softball, with lots of backspin. The starting team's *pointeur* shoots, then the other team's *pointeur* shoots until he gets closer. Once the second team lands a *boule* closer, the first team is back up. If the opposing team's *boule* is very near the *cochonnet,* the *tireur* will likely attempt to knock it away. If the team decides that they can lob one in closer, the *pointeur* shoots.

Once all *boules* have been launched, the tally is taken. This is where it gets tense, as the difference in distance often comes down to millimeters. Faces are drawn, lips are pursed, and eyes are squinted as teams try to sort through the who's-closer process. I've seen all kinds of measuring devices, from shoes to belts to tape measures. The team with the ball closest to the target receives one point, and the teams keep going until someone gets 13 points.

Two parking lots are available: one on the northern edge (by the recommended Hôtel Rêves d'Ocres) and another on the southern flank, closer to the ochre cliffs. If you approach from Gordes or Joucas, you'll end up at the northern lot. If you're coming from N-100 and the south, you'll park at the southern lot (but don't park there on Wednesday night, because Thursday is Roussillon's market day). Leave nothing valuable showing in your car.

Tourist Information

The little TI is in the center, between the two parking lots and across from the David restaurant. Leaf through their good binders describing area hotels and *chambres d'hôte*. Walkers should get info on trails from Roussillon to nearby villages (April–Oct Mon–Sat 10:00–12:00 & 14:00–17:30, closed Sun except in summer; Nov–March Mon–Sat 14:00–17:30, closed Sun; tel. 04 90 05 60 25).

Helpful Hints

An ATM is next to the TI, and Internet access is available at the bookshop—*librairie*—on the main square (daily 10:00–18:00).

SELF-GUIDED WALK

Welcome to Roussillon

This quick walk will take you through Roussillon's village to its ochre cliffs.

• *To begin this walk, climb a few minutes from either parking lot (passing the Hollywood set–like square under the bell tower and the church) to the summit of...*

▲The Village

Find the orientation plaque and the dramatic viewpoint, often complete with a howling mistral. During the Middle Ages, a castle stood where you are, on the top of Mont Rouge, and protected the village below. While nothing remains of the castle today, the strategic advantage of this site is clear: You can see forever. Count how many villages you can identify, and then notice how little sprawl there is in the valley below. Because the Luberon is a natural reserve (Parc Naturel Régional du Luberon), development is strictly controlled.

A short stroll down leads to the church. Duck into the pretty 11th-century Church of St. Michel, and appreciate the natural air-conditioning and the well-worn center aisle. The white interior suggests that the stone came from elsewhere.

On leaving the church, look across the way to the derelict building, a reminder of Roussillon's humble roots. After World War II, when the demand for ochre faded, this became a dusty, poor village. Residents fled for an easier life below, with level streets and modern conveniences, making the economy even worse. Abandoned buildings such as this presented a serious problem—until the tourists discovered Roussillon, and people began reinvesting in the village.

• *Continue down to the village.*

Notice the clamped-iron beams that shore up old walls. Examine the different hues of yellow and orange. These lime-finished exteriors, called *chaux* (literally "limes"), need to be redone about every 10 years. Locals choose their exact color...but in this town of ochre, it's never white. The church tower that you walk under once marked the entrance to the fortified town.

See how local (or artsy) you can look as you walk in what must be the most scenic village square in Provence (place de la Mairie) and watch the river of shoppers. Is anyone playing *boules* at the opposite end? You could paint the entire town without ever leaving the red-and-orange corner of your palette. Many do. While Roussillon receives its share of day-trippers, evenings are romantically peaceful on this square. The bookshop on the square's corner has some English books, Internet access, and a view terrace on the top floor (daily 10:00–18:00).

• *With the cafés on your right, drop downhill past the gauntlet of shops and turn right past the TI to find the parking lot just beyond. For centuries, animals grazed here. It was later turned into a school playground. When tourists outnumbered students, it became a parking lot. Walk past the parking lot with the cliffs on your left and find the...*

▲▲Ochre Cliffs

Roussillon was Europe's capital for ochre production until World War II. A stroll to the south end of town, beyond the upper parking lot, will show you why: Roussillon sits on the world's largest known ochre deposit. A brilliant orange path leads through the richly colored ochre canyon, explaining the hue of this village (€2, ask about combo-tickets with the Ochre Conservatory—described below; daily 9:00–17:30, until 19:00 in summer; beware—light-colored clothing and orange powder don't mix).

Ochre is a made of iron oxide and clay. When combined with sand, it creates the yellowish-red pigments you see in the buildings around you. While ochre is also produced in the US and Italy, the quality of France's ochre is considered tops.

The value of Roussillon's ochre cliffs was known in Roman times. Once excavated, the clay ochre was rinsed with water to separate it from sand, and bricks of the stuff were dried and baked for deeper hues. The procedure for extracting the ochre did not change much over 2,000 years, until ochre mining became industrialized in the late 1700s. Used primarily for wallpaper and linoleum, ochre use reached its zenith just before World War II. (After that, cheaper substitutes took over.)

SIGHTS AND ACTIVITIES

In and near Roussillon

Ochre Conservatory (Conservatoire des Ocres et Pigments Appliqués)—If the ochre cliffs inspire you, consider this colorful, interesting exposition, about a half-mile below Roussillon toward Apt on D-104. One-hour tours of a reconstructed ochre factory explain how ochre is converted from an ore to a pigment, from extraction to shipping (€5, ask about combo-ticket with ochre cliffs, tours usually daily at 11:00, 14:00, 15:00, and 16:00, only in French but short English handout available, great gift shop, tel. 04 90 05 66 69, www.okhra.com).

Domaine de Tara Winery—Just below Roussillon on the road to Joucas, you'll pass this easygoing, ivy-covered winery featuring Côtes de Ventoux wines (Mon–Sat 9:00–18:00, closed Sun, tel. 04 90 05 74 87).

Hot-Air Balloon Flight—Ply the calm morning air above the Luberon in a hot-air balloon. The Montgolfières–Luberon outfit has two flight options: the Four-Star Flight (€255, 1.5 hours in balloon, allow 3 hours total, includes picnic and champagne) and the economy-class Tourist Flight (€160, 45 min, includes glass of bubbly). For either flight, meet on the main road below Joucas at 7:00 (reserve a few days ahead, maximum 12 passengers, tel. 04 90 05 76 77, fax 04 90 05 74 39).

Goult Bigger than its sister hill towns, this surprisingly quiet village seems content to be away from the tourist path. Wander up the hill to the panoramic view and windmill, and consider its many good restaurants—where you won't have to compete with tourists for a table. **La Bartavelle** is the best in town and has reasonable prices. When it's warm, tables spill along a quiet alley (*menus* from €39, closed Tue–Wed, rue du Cheval Blanc, tel. 04 90 72 33 72).

SLEEPING

(€1 = about $1.30, country code: 33)

In Roussillon

The TI posts a list of hotels and *chambres d'hôte*. Parking is free in Roussillon—if you sleep in a hotel here, ask your hotelier where to park. The village offers three good-value accommodations—conveniently, one for each price range.

$$$ **Le Clos de la Glycine****** provides Roussillon's four-star accommodations, with nine gorgeous rooms located dead-center

The Luberon

in the village (Db-€124–155, big Db-€175, loft suite with deck and view-€260, Wi-Fi, located at the restaurant David, across from the TI on place de la Poste, tel. 04 90 05 60 13, fax 04 90 05 75 80, www.luberon-hotel.com, le.clos.de.la.glycine@wanadoo.fr).

$$ Hôtel Rêves d'Ocres**, the first building you pass coming from Gordes and Joucas, is a solid value, run by eager-to-help Sandrine and Yvan. It's ochre-colored, warm, and comfortable, with 16 mostly spacious rooms (eight have view terraces) and a lounge where you can stretch out (Sb-€56, Db without balcony-€76, Db with balcony-€82, Tb-€95, air-con, route de Gordes, tel. 04 90 05 60 50, fax 04 90 05 79 74, www.hotel-revesdocres.com, hotelrevesdocres@wanadoo.fr).

$ Madame Cherel rents rooms that are just this side of a youth hostel. A common view terrace and good reading materials are available, and the beds have firm mattresses (D-€42–46, includes breakfast, cash only, 3 blocks from upper parking lot, between the gas station and school, La Burlière, tel. 04 90 05 71 71, mulhanc@hotmail.com). Chatty and sincere Cherel speaks English, is a wealth of regional travel tips, and rents mountain bikes to guests (€15/day).

Near Roussillon

The next two listings, for drivers only, are most easily found by turning north off N-100 at the *Roussillon/Les Huguets* sign. It's the second turn-off to Roussillon coming from Avignon. Joucas, St-Saturnin-lès-Apt, and Lacoste (all described below) also have good beds near Roussillon.

$$ Hôtel Les Sables d'Ocre** is a modern resort kind of place, with 22 motel-esque rooms, a big pool, the greenest grass in Provence, air-conditioning, and fair rates (Db-€66, spring for the Db with garden balcony-€80, Tb loft-€95–115, a half-mile after leaving Roussillon towards Apt at intersection of D-108 and D-104, tel. 04 90 05 55 55, fax 04 90 05 55 50, www.roussillon-hotel.com, sablesdocre@free.fr).

$$ Le Clos des Cigales, run by friendly Philippe, has five newly built, blue-shuttered, stylish bungalows. Two are doubles, three are two-room suites with tiny kitchenettes, and all have private patios facing a big pool. When you arrive, you'll understand the name—the cacophony from the *cigales* (cicadas) is deafening (Db-€82, Tb-€115, Qb-€130, includes breakfast, ping pong, hammock, 5 min from Roussillon towards Goult on D-104, tel. & fax 04 90 05 73 72, www.leclosdescigales.com, philippe.lherbeil @wanadoo.fr).

EATING

In Roussillon

Choose ambience over cuisine if dining in Roussillon, and enjoy any of the eateries on the main square. It's a festive place, where children dance while parents dine, and dogs and cats look longingly for leftovers. Restaurants change with the mistral here—what's good one year disappoints the next. Consider my suggestions and go with what looks best (or look over my recommendations in other Luberon villages). One of the two places listed below is always open. Look also at the hotels listed in Joucas (below)—all offer quality cuisine at fair prices, just a few minutes' drive from Roussillon.

Le Bistrot de Roussillon is the most consistent value on the square, with excellent salads (try the *salad du bistrot*) and *plats* for the right price, a breezy terrace in back, and helpful David and Yann in charge (daily, tel. 04 90 05 74 45).

Café Couleur sits next door, offering similar atmosphere and prices, but less-steady quality (daily, tel. 04 90 05 62 11).

Joucas

This understated, quiet, and largely overlooked village slumbers below the Gordes buzz. Vertical stone lanes with carefully

arranged flowers and well-restored homes play host to occasional artists and a smattering of locals. There's not much to do or see here, except eat, sleep, and relax. Joucas has one tiny grocery, one café, one pharmacy, a good kids' play area, and two good-value accommodation options. Sleep here for a central location and utter silence. For views, walk past the little fountain in the center and up the steep lanes as high as you want.

Several **hiking** trails leave from Joucas. Gordes and Roussillon are each three miles away, uphill. Serious hikers can take the three-mile hike to Murs, though it's easier in the other direction (yellow signs point the way from the top of the village). You don't have to go far to enjoy the natural beauty on this trail.

SLEEPING AND EATING

In and near Joucas

Each of these hotels comes with a good restaurant.

$$$ La Ferme de la Huppe*** has a Gordes address, but it's closer physically and spiritually to Joucas. This small, farmhouse-elegant hacienda is an excellent mini-splurge if food matters. Sincere owners Gerald and Charlotte will make you feel at home. Ten low-slung rooms gather on two levels behind the stylish pool. The decor is understated and rustic, and the service can be *laissez-faire*—the owners devote most of their attention to the restaurant (which is a good thing). Dinners poolside or in the cozy dining room are memorable (small Db-€85, bigger Db-€105–125, much bigger Db-€145–165, includes breakfast, €45 dinner *menu* changes daily, restaurant closed Wed–Thu, air-con, Wi-Fi; between Joucas and Gordes on D-156 road to Goult, just off D-2; tel. 04 90 72 12 25, fax 04 90 72 01 83, www.lafermedelahuppe.com, charlotte.gerald@lafermedelahuppe.com).

$$$ Le Mas du Loriot is another worthwhile, almost-in-Joucas value. Charming owners Alain and Christine have carved the ideal escape out of an olive grove, with eight soothing rooms, private terraces, a generous pool, and home-cooked dinners—all at fair prices and with a view to remember (Db-€100–130, extra bed-€20, €28 four-course dinners available three nights a week, Internet access, on D-102 between Joucas and Murs, tel. 04 90 72 62 62, fax 04 90 72 62 54, www.masduloriot.com, hotel @masduloriot.com).

$$ Hostellerie des Commandeurs**, run by soft Sophie, has modern, comfortable, and clean rooms in the village of Joucas. It's kid-friendly, with a big pool and a sports field/play area next door. The relaxed restaurant offers tasty cuisine at very fair prices (*menus* from €18). Ask for a south-facing room *(coté sud)* for the best views (Db-€55–58, extra bed-€16, above park at village entrance, tel. 04 90 05 78 01, fax 04 90 05 74 47, www.lescommandeurs.com, hostellerie@lescommandeurs.com).

More Luberon Towns

Le Luberon is packed with appealing villages and beautiful scenery, but it has only a handful of must-see sights. I've grouped them by area to make your sightseeing planning easier (see map on page 161). Busy N-100 slices like an arrow through the heart of the Luberon, dividing the region in half. The more popular and visited section lies above N-100 (with Roussillon and Gordes), while the villages to the south seem a bit less trampled.

The busiest sights are in and near Gordes; I've listed those first, to encourage you avoid afternoon crowds. Beyond that, you're free to connect the stops however you please. (I've chosen not to provide fixed directions, since the order matters little.) Rambling the Luberon's spaghetti network of small roads is a joy. None of the sights listed below are must-sees, but all are close to each other. Pick up a good map (the Michelin Local Map #332 works for me). But remember, getting lost in the Luberon is half the fun.

Gordes and Nearby Sights

For the last 40 years, Gordes has been the most touristy and trendy town in the Luberon—creating gridlock and parking headaches (come early). In the 1960s, Gordes was a virtual ghost town of derelict buildings. But now it's thoroughly renovated and filled with people who live in a world without calluses. Many Parisian big shots and wealthy foreigners have purchased and restored older homes here, putting property values out of sight for locals.

Still, the village's setting is striking. As you approach Gordes, make a hard right at the impressive view of the village (you'll find some parking along the small road). Beyond here, the village has little of interest, except its many boutiques and its Tuesday market (which ends at 13:00). The town's 11th-century castle houses a mildly interesting collection of contemporary art.

There are two worthwhile sights near Gordes—the Abbey Notre-Dame de Sénanque and the Village des Bories—both well-marked from Gordes and described below.

SIGHTS

Near Gordes
Abbey Notre-Dame de Sénanque—This still-functioning and beautifully situated Cistercian abbey was built in 1148 as a back-to-basics reaction to the excesses of Benedictine abbeys. The Cistercians strove to be separate from the world, and to recapture the simplicity, solitude, and poverty of the early Church. To succeed required industrious self-sufficiency—a skill that these monks had. Their movement spread and colonized Europe with a new form of Christianity. By 1200, there were more than 500 such monasteries and abbeys in Europe.

The Luberon

Luberon Restaurants that Justify the Trip

Many of the restaurants in the countryside around Roussillon are worth a detour. Read my descriptions of the eateries below (most are described in greater detail elsewhere in the chapter, as noted), and remember that Isle-sur-la-Sorgue is a manageable 30-minute drive from Roussillon.

Ideal for Dinner

La Ferme de la Huppe is a country-classy farmhouse with inventive cuisine and a menu that changes daily. Those willing to trust the chef will have an exquisite dining experience. You can dine poolside or inside (€45 *menus*, closed Wed–Thu, between Joucas and Gordes—a 5-min drive from Roussillon; see page 180).

Hostellerie des Commandeurs is inexpensive, traditional, friendly, and a solid value (€18 *menus*, closed Wed, in Joucas—a 5-min drive from Roussillon; see page 180).

Le Fournil, in Bonnieux, has marvelous food, a postcard-perfect terrace, and outdoor tables around a tranquil fountain. The interior is uninviting, so book an outside table or skip it (€20 lunch *menu*, €40 dinner *menus*, closed Mon, well-signed next to the TI in Bonnieux; see page 185).

La Petite Ecole, located in a renovated little schoolhouse, is where locals go for fine cuisine at affordable prices. The perfect team, host Denis and chef Sophie, enthusiastically welcome travelers and locals into their simple restaurant. This place offers a real experience—the food is fresh and very Provençal. There's a pleasant terrace in front or a small interior (€18 and €24 *menus*, closed Sun–Mon, call ahead to dine inside, below Roussillon on N-100 in Le Chêne, tel. 04 32 52 16 41).

Hôtel le St. Hubert, located in an appealing village, has nice views and few—if any—Americans (€27 *menus*, closed Thu, in St-Saturnin-lès-Apt—a 15-min drive from Roussillon; see page 190).

La Bartavelle, with a mostly local clientele in an untouristy and unspoiled town, has terrific cuisine (*menus* from €39, closed Tue–Wed, rue du Cheval Blanc in Goult—a 10-min drive from

The abbey is best appreciated from the outside, and is worth the trip for its splendid and remote setting alone. Come early or late, stop at a pullout for a bird's-eye view as you descend, then wander the abbey's perimeter with fewer tourists. In late June through much of July, the lavender fields that surround the abbey make a breathtaking picture.

The abbey itself is only open for tours (in French only, about 6/day Mon–Sat, 1 hour, limited to 50 people so call ahead or check their website) and to attend Mass (Sun at 10:00, Mon at 8:30, Tue–Sat at 12:00). The tour will show you Sénanque's purposefully simple

Roussillon; see page 177).

Le Bistrot de Roussillon, on the village square with a terrace out back, has excellent salads and *plats* priced just right (open daily; see page 179).

Le Mas du Loriot is a small hotel where owner/chef Christine provides a take-it-or-leave-it *menu* three nights a week. Her elegant dining room has views over the Luberon. Reservations are a must (€28 *menu*, on D-102 between Joucas and Murs; see page 180).

Best Places to Lunch

Le Fournil in Bonnieux (with a half-price lunch *menu*) and **Le Bistrot de Roussillon**—both listed for dinner, above—are also good lunch stops.

Bar/Restaurant de France, in Lacoste, is an easygoing eatery with sensational view tables and good *plats*, omelets, and salads for about €10 (daily for lunch only, at the Ménerbes end of Lacoste; see page 187).

L'Auberge de la Loube is the ultimate country/Provençal experience, but makes for a long after-dinner drive, so it's best for a relaxing lunch (€22 lunch *menus*, €30 dinner *menus*, closed Sun evening and all day Mon and Thu, in Buoux—20-min drive from Roussillon; see page 193).

L'Auberge des Sequins is a corner of paradise awaiting those who survive the climb to Fort de Buoux (light meals, snacks, or *menus* from €21, open daily; see page 192).

Le Petit Café serves simple and cheap lunches with views of the castle ruins in the forgotten hamlet of Oppède-le-Vieux (open daily; see page 189).

Le Petit Jardin Café, in remote Viens, offers an unpretentious lunch or dinner stop, with cozy interior tables, a garden terrace, and reasonable prices *(menu du jour*-€12 on weekdays, more elaborate €20 *menu* on weekends, lunch served 12:00–14:00, closed Wed, see page 191).

church, small cloisters, refectory, and a *chauffoir* (small heated room where monks could copy books year-round). A small monastic community still resides here (€4.60 admission includes tour, good bookshop open Mon–Sat 10:00–12:00 & 13:30–18:00, Sun 14:00–18:00, tel. 04 90 72 05 72, www.senanque.fr). For more on monasteries, see the "Medieval Monasteries" sidebar on page 186.

If your next destination is near Roussillon, Bonnieux, or Apt, leave the abbey the opposite way you arrived, following signs to *Gordes*, then *Roussillon*, then follow *Murs* and *Joucas*...and enjoy the ride.

Village des Bories—A stone-bordered dirt road sets the mood for this open-air museum. The vertical stones you see on the walls as you approach the site were used for counterweight to keep these walls, built without mortar, intact.

The "village" you tour is composed of dry-laid stone structures, proving that there has always been more stone than wood in this rugged region. Stone villages like this predated the Romans—some say by 2,000 years. This one was inhabited for 200 years (from about 1600 to 1800). You'll also see *bories* (dry-stone huts) in fields, now used to store tools or hay. A look around these hills confirms the supply of building materials: The trees are small and gnarled (not good for construction), but white stone lies everywhere.

The "village" is composed of five "hamlets." You'll duck into several homes and see animal pens, a community oven, and more (identified in English). Study the "beehive" stone-laying method and imagine the time it took to construct. The villagers had no scaffolds or support arches—just hammers and patience (€5.50, buy €4 booklet of English translations to learn more, daily June–Sept 9:00–20:00, Oct–May 9:00–17:30, tel. 04 90 72 04 39).

A free shuttle bus runs from the center of Gordes to Village des Bories (Mon–Fri, no buses Sat afternoon or all day Sun, call 04 90 72 02 08 to reserve a seat and arrange pickup location).

Bouillon Olive Mill and Museum of Glass (Moulin des Bouillons and Musée de l'Histoire du Verre)—This fun museum park is a true Back Door experience. Find an hour and give it over to two charming women who will explain to you (in fine English) the mill and the museum. Start with Carole at the olive mill, which has been in use for more than 2,000 years. You'll learn about this ancient practice, including how olive oil and its products are made. The Roman remains are cool, but take a back seat to the massive, 400-year-old oak olive press.

Then, scamper through a small park with chickens and modern sculpture to the bunker-like Museum of Glass. Here, Béatrice will teach you about the historic importance of glass from Roman times to contemporary glassblowing. You'll learn about the medieval art of stained glass and see modern glass made by the museum's benefactor, Madame Frédérique Duran (€3.50 each, €5 for both, April–Oct Wed–Mon 10:00–12:00 & 14:00–18:00, closed Tue, by appointment in winter, tel. 04 90 72 22 11). It's well-signed between Gordes, Coustellet, and St. Pantaleon on D-148.

Museum of Lavender (Musée de la Lavande)—Located halfway between Gordes and Isle-sur-la-Sorgue in Coustellet, this surprisingly interesting museum does a fine job of explaining the process of lavender production with interesting exhibits and good English information (via an audioguide, a film, and posted explanations at the exhibits). It's popular with tour groups, smells great inside, and offers the ultimate "if they made it with lavender, we sell it" gift shop (€5, daily 10:00–12:00 & 14:00–18:00, in Coustellet just off N-100 toward Gordes, tel. 04 90 76 91 23).

Villages and Sights South of Roussillon

These villages and sights below Roussillon and N-100 feel less visited than places north of this busy road. You'll need a good half-day to visit them all. They work well in the order described below, with a relaxed lunch in Bonnieux or Lacoste (see "Luberon Restaurants that Justify the Trip" sidebar, page 182). The first sight is situated south of Roussillon, where D-108 crosses N-100.

St. Julien Bridge (Pont St. Julien)—This small, three-arched bridge survives as a testimony to Roman engineers—and to the importance

of this rural area 2,000 years ago. It's the only surviving bridge on what was once the main road from northern Italy to Provence—the primary route used by Roman armies. This 215-foot-long Roman bridge was built from 27 B.C. to A.D. 14. Mortar had not yet been invented, so (as with the Pont du Gard) stones were carefully set in place. Amazingly, the bridge survives today, having outlived Roman marches, hundreds of floods, and decades of automobile traffic. A new bridge finally rerouted traffic from this beautiful structure in 2005.

Be sure to walk below the bridge. Notice how thin the layer of stone seems between the arch tops and the road. Those open niches weren't for statues, but instead allowed water to pass through when the river ran high. (At its current trickle, it's hard to fathom.) Walk under an arch and examine the pockmarks in the side—medieval thieves in search of free bronze stole the clamps.

Bonnieux—Spectacular from a distance, this town disappoints up close. It lacks a pedestrian center, though the Friday-morn-
ing market briefly creates one.
Bonnieux boasts several excellent restaurants, including **Le
Fournil;** reserve ahead for this
reliable place. They serve creative Provençal specialties in a
warm setting (€20 lunch *menu,*

Medieval Monasteries

France is littered with medieval monasteries, and Provence is no exception. Most have virtually no furnishings (they never had many), which leaves the visitor with little to reconstruct what life must have been like in these cold stone buildings a thousand years ago. A little history can help breathe life into these important yet underappreciated monuments.

After the fall of the Roman Empire, monasteries arose as refuges of peace and order in a chaotic world. While the pope got rich and famous playing power politics, monasteries worked to keep the focus on simplicity and poverty. Throughout the Middle Ages, monasteries were mediators between Man and God. In these peacefully remote abbeys, Europe's best minds struggled with the interpretation of God's words. Every sentence needed to be understood and applied. Answers were debated in universities and contemplated in monasteries.

St. Benedict established the Middle Ages' most influential monastic order (Benedictine) in Monte Cassino, Italy, in A.D. 529. He scheduled a rigorous program of monastic duties that combined manual labor with intellectual tasks. His movement spread north and took firm root in France, where the abbey of Cluny (Burgundy) eventually controlled more than 2,000 dependent abbeys and vied with the pope for control of the Church. Benedictine abbeys grew dot-com rich, and with wealth came excess (such as private bedrooms with baths). Monks lost sight of their purpose and became soft and corrupt. In the late 1100s, the determined and charismatic St. Bernard rallied the Cistercian order by going back to the original rule of St. Benedict. Cistercian abbeys thrived as centers of religious thought and exploration from the 13th through the 15th centuries.

€40 dinner *menus*, closed Mon, eat outside by the fountain or skip it, next to TI at 5 place Carnot, tel. 04 90 75 83 62).

Lacoste—Little Lacoste slumbers across the valley from Bonnieux in the shadow of its looming castle. Climb through this photogenic village of arches and stone paths, passing American art students (from the Savannah College of Art and Design) showing their work. Support an American artist, learn about their art, and then keep climbing and climbing to the ruined castle base. The view of Bonnieux from the base of Lacoste's castle is as good is it gets.

The Marquis de Sade (1740–1814) lived in this castle for more than 30 years. Author of pornographic novels, he was notorious for hosting orgies behind these walls, and for kidnapping peasants for scandalous purposes. He was eventually arrested and imprisoned for 30 years, and thanks to him, we have a word to describe his favorite hobby—sadism. Today, clothing designer Pierre Cardin is

Cistercian abbots ran their abbeys like little kingdoms, doling out punishment and food to the monks, and tools to peasant farmers. Abbeys were occupied by two groups: the favored monks from aristocratic families (such as St. Bernard) and a larger group of lay brothers from peasant stock, who were given the heaviest labor and could join only the Sunday services.

Monks' days were broken into three activities: prayer, reading holy texts, and labor. Monks lived in silence and poverty with few amenities—meat was forbidden, as was cable TV. In summer, they ate two daily meals; in winter, just one. Monks slept together in a single room on threadbare mats covering solid-rock floors.

With their focus on work and discipline, Cistercian abbeys became leaders of the medieval industrial revolution. Among the few literate people in Europe, monks were keepers of technological knowledge—about clocks, waterwheels, accounting, foundries, gristmills, textiles, and agricultural techniques. Abbeys became economic engines that helped drive France out of its Middle Aged funk.

As France (and Europe) slowly got its act together in the late Middle Ages, cities re-emerged as places to trade and thrive. Abbeys gradually lost their relevance in a brave new humanist world. Kings took over abbot selection, further degrading the abbeys' power, and Gutenberg's movable type made monks obsolete. The French Revolution closed the book on abbatial life, with troops occupying and destroying many abbeys. The still-functioning Abbey Notre-Dame de Sénanque, near Gordes, is a rare survivor.

spending a fortune renovating the castle in lavish fashion, complete with a concert hall. Some locals whisper that he's the Marquis de Sade reincarnated.

If you need inexpensive digs and find Lacoste appealing, **Café de Sade** is spotless, with six basic rooms above a little restaurant (D-€36, Db-€50, family room-€65, dorm beds-€15, cash only, sheets €4 extra in dorm only, tel. 04 90 75 82 29, fax 04 90 75 95 68). A good bakery with pizza slices and drinks is nearby. If you need a café with killer views, walk to the other end of Lacoste and find the **Bar/Restaurant de France**'s outdoor tables overlooking Bonnieux (daily, lunch only, tel. 04 90 75 82 25).

Abbey St. Hilaire—A dirt road off D-103 between Lacoste and Ménerbes leads down to this long-forgotten and pint-size abbey. There's a pure church and a cute little cloister, but it's not really much to see—instead, there's more to experience. The tranquility and isolation sought by monks 800 years ago is still palpable, and it might be just what you need after experiencing the crowds in some of these villages. Once a Cistercian outpost for the bigger abbey at Sénanque, Abbey St. Hilaire is now owned by Carmelite Friars. Pick up the English handout, contribute to the abbey's well-being (free entry, donation requested), and wander around. The lone stone bench in front is picnic-ready, and a rugged WC is cut into the rock (across the courtyard). Leave nothing valuable in your car at this remote site.

Ménerbes—Ménerbes is (in)famous as the village that drew author Peter Mayle's attention to this region, but offers little of interest for most. To experience Provence pre-tourism, wander into **Café du Progrès**' time-warp interior (the original café, not the outdoor extension that spills into the parking area). Ponder a region that in the last 30 years has experienced such a dramatic change. In 1970, the Luberon was unknown to most travelers. Locals led simple lives and had few ambitions (as depicted in the film *Manon des Sources* and the *Jean de Florette* movies). They blame the theater festival in Avignon for bringing directors here every year, who then recreated perfect Provençal villages on film. (Gordes was first.) Parisians, Swiss, Brits, and eventually Americans followed, willing to pay any price for their place in the Provençal sun. Property taxes increased—as did the cost of *une bière* at the corner café—and all too soon, villagers found themselves with few affordable options... except for cafés like this.

To explore Ménerbes, follow signs to *Eglise* and walk 10 minutes to the squat Romanesque church (closed) and graveyard (more great views in all directions and a stone bench for picnics). You're face-to-face with the Grand Luberon ridge. Notice the quarry carved into its side, where the stone for this village came from. Foodies can duck into the snazzy **Maison de la Truffe et du Vin,** which offers "truffle discovery workshops" (call for schedule, tel. 04 90 72 52 10).

Corkscrew Museum (Musée du Tire-Bouchon)—This exhibit, between Ménerbes and Oppède-le-Vieux, is worth a stop if you're a corkscrew enthusiast or want to taste their worthwhile wines (Domaine de la Citadelle). They have 1,200 corkscrews on display in glass cases and a well-stocked gift shop (€4 for the "museum," includes tasting, daily 10:00–12:00 & 14:00–19:00).

Oppède-le-Vieux—This windy barnacle of a town clings to its hillside like a baby to its mother. There's one boutique, two cafés, and a dusty main square at the base of a short, ankle-twisting climb to a pretty little church and ruined castle. This off-the-beaten-path fixer-upper of a village was completely abandoned in the early 1900s, and today has a ghost town–like feel. The village has a rugged character and shows little inclination for boutiques and smart hotels. It's ideal for those looking to perish in Provence.

Consider a light lunch at one of the town's two cafés (**Le Petit Café** serves cheap lunches with views of the castle ruins—daily, tel. 04 90 76 74 01) and plan your ascent to the castle. It's 20 minutes straight up, but the Luberon views justify the effort. (After making this walk, you'll understand why locals abandoned it for level terrain.) Walk under the central arch of the building across from the café and climb. At the fork, either way works (right is a bit easier). Find the little church terrace. From here, tiled rooftops paint a delightful picture with the grand panorama; the flat plain of the Rhône delta is visible to the left. The colorful **Notre-Dame d'Alidon church** (1588) is generally open, except at lunch (depends on village volunteers). Pick up the English text and imagine having to climb this distance every Sunday—your entire life. Go behind the church and notice the flowers growing from the stone. From here, mountain goats can climb on what remains of the castle. (But be careful—there are no rails.)

To find Oppède-le-Vieux from N-100, follow signs to *Oppède-le-Village*, then head to Oppède-le-Vieux and drive towards le Grand Luberon massif. You'll be forced to park a few hundred yards from the village, for which you'll get to pay €2.

Villages and Sights East of Roussillon: La Provence Profonde

Provence is busy with tourists, but there are still plenty of characteristic and less-discovered spots to explore. The area east of Roussillon feels peaceful and less touristed—come here to get a sense of how most villages were before they became "destinations." Here are the key sights in the order that you'll pass them coming from Roussillon. Allow a full day to complete this loop. If all you have is a half-day, head straight for the Fort de Buoux (see map on page 161).

St-Saturnin-lès-Apt—Most tourists pass by this pleasant town (with a lively Sunday market) on their way to more famous destinations. I couldn't find a souvenir shop. Ditch your car below the main entry to the town (just below the old city) and walk up the main drag (rue de la République). You'll come to a striking church (usually closed) that's a fine example of Provençal Romanesque, with a tall, rounded spire. From here, look for *Le Château* signs pointing up the steps. The ruined "château" grows right out of the rock, making it difficult to tell the man-made from the natural. Climb as high as the sun allows with no shade—the green arrows guide you up. It's a scamperer's paradise, with views that rank among the best village-top vistas I found in Provence. The small chapel at the very top is closed, so there's no reason to climb all the way up. To get back down, find your way through the small opening to the little dam.

For an overnight stay, try **Le Mas Perréal,** where American Kevin and his Parisian wife Elisabeth left no stone unturned when restoring this lovely farmhouse just outside St-Saturnin-lès-Apt. It features sumptuous rooms, a pool, American-size breakfasts that change daily, and no language barrier (Db-€115–130, includes breakfast, tel. 04 90 75 46 31, fax 04 90 04 88 08, www.masperreal .com, elisabeth-kevin@masperreal.com). From Avignon, take N-100 toward Apt, then go north on D-943 and turn left before Moulin d'Huile d'Olive.

Hôtel le St. Hubert is centrally located in the village, with a cozy café wallpapered with wine labels on one side (salads and *plats*) and a classier view restaurant on the other (*menus* from €27, café and restaurant closed Thu). The hotel has eight basic rooms above (Db-€60, tel. 04 90 75 42 02, fax 04 90 75 49 90).

Le Colorado Provençal—This park has ochre cliffs similar to Roussillon's, but they're spread over a larger area, with well-signed trails. So if you'd like to hike in orange sand through Bryce Canyon–like rocks, follow signs to the town of *Rustrel*, the gateway to Le Colorado Provençal.

Rustrel has two parking lots. Skip the sprawling lot on the main road with the big signs—it leaves you 15 minutes from the trails. The lower-profile and more convenient *Parking Municipal* at the trailhead is 200 yards toward Apt from the big parking lot (look for signs to *Colorado Provençal*, allow €5 for parking).

For the best walk, cross the little footbridge and follow either the Cheminée de Fée or the Sahara trail. (Trails are color-coded and easy to follow, allow about 30–40 min for each with modest elevation gain; Cheminée de Fée is more impressive, but steeper.) Light-colored clothing is a bad choice. Signs remind you to please remain on the trails and not to climb the cliffs.

Viens—Located about 15 minutes uphill and east of Le Colorado Provençal (turn right when leaving Colorado), this village is where

locals go to get away. With a
setting like this, it's surprising
that modest Viens is not more
developed. The panoramas
are higher and more vast than
around Roussillon (with some
lavender fields), and the vegetation is more rugged. Walk
the streets of the old town
(bigger than it first appears)
and visit the few shops scat-

tered about. Find the courtyard of the old château and the lone
stone arch overlooking the view. This is how Gordes must have
looked before it became chic.

Le Petit Jardin Café, just below the town's only phone booth,
offers an unpretentious lunch or dinner stop, with cozy interior
tables, a garden terrace, and reasonable prices (*menu du jour*-€12
on weekdays, more elaborate €20 *menu* on weekends, lunch served
12:00–14:00, closed Wed, tel. 04 90 75 20 05). There's a small
grocery store and a bakery a few blocks past the café, toward St.
Martin de Castillon.

To reach the next village (Saignon), follow signs to *St. Martin
de Castillon*, then turn right on N-100 toward Apt.

Saignon—Sitting high atop a rock spur, you'll look down upon
Apt, a city of only 11,500, which from here looks like a megalopolis
after all these tiny villages. If you need a break, climb Le Rocher
Belvedere (The Belvedere Rock) for grand views over lavender
fields. Park as high as you feel comfortable driving, and follow *Le
Rocher* signs up to this "ship's prow" (about three stories of stairs to
the top). You'll find several cafés, a cushy hotel, and a grocery store
in the linear village's center.

Buoux

Buoux (pronounced "boox"), a way-off-the-beaten-path village,
is home to two memorable restaurants and Provence's without-a-
doubt best ruined castle. A trip to this far-flung corner rewards
with rocky canyons, acres of lavender, and few tourists. Start early
and climb to the castle before the heat rises, then have a long, well-
earned lunch nearby (recommendations provided).

Buoux is south of Apt on D-113 between Saignon and
Lourmarin. Ambitious travelers can combine a visit to Buoux with
Lourmarin and Bonnieux.

SIGHTS

▲▲Fort de Buoux

The remains of this remote, ridge-top castle are a playground for energetic lovers of crumbled ruins and grand views. You need good legs and stable shoes to navigate the steep, uneven footing.

Floating like a cloud above the valleys below, the fort is easy to miss—it blends with the limestone rock cliffs that dominate the landscape. The long, rocky outcrop has been inhabited since prehistoric times, but today it's like a ruined Les Baux without the tourists. In the Middle Ages, it was home to hundreds of residents and a powerful castle that controlled a vast area. Like Les Baux, the fort was destroyed in the 1500s during the wars of religion (it was a Protestant base) and again in the 1600s by a paranoid King Louis XIII (see "The Life of a Hill Town in Provence" on page 150).

Madame la Caretaker lives in the flowery house where you buy your ticket (€3). Get the English map and start climbing. The map suggests a one-way route through the rocky ruins. You'll start with what's left of the village, then scramble around rock piles along the long outcrop to the castle remains, which once housed hundreds of residents. You'll climb around the remains of homes, a church, cisterns, and medieval storage silos.

The unforgettable highlight of this castle is a three-story stone spiral staircase. Cut into the cliffs, it leads back down to the base (follow the faded white arrows as you leave the ruins). The staircase is steep and has no handrails and big steps, so be very careful—or return the way you came.

Getting There: To reach the fort from Apt and the north, drive through Buoux, pass L'Auberge de la Loube, drop down, and follow signs to *Fort de Buoux* (and *L'Auberge des Sequins*). If you're coming from the south, you'll see a turnoff to the fort before the village of Buoux. Park in the dirt lot and walk about 15 minutes up a dirt road to the foot of the fort.

EATING

In Buoux

L'Auberge des Sequins is a stone's throw from the parking area for the fort. It's a lush, Shangri-la kind of place at the end of the valley with drinks, snacks, and meals, and makes a perfect post-fort stop (daily, tel. 04 90 74 16 37).

L'Auberge de la Loube is up the road in Buoux village and offers the ultimate in Provençal country-coziness. Plan to stay a while and enjoy the superb cuisine and setting (indoors or out). You'll understand why it was one of Peter Mayle's favorites (allow €22 for lunch—more on Sun, €30 for dinner, closed Sun evening and all day Mon and Thu, tel. 04 90 74 19 58).

Lourmarin

The southernmost Luberon village of Lourmarin has a fine Friday market, a well-preserved Renaissance château on its fringe, and an enchanting town center. Lourmarin feels strangely peaceful and happy, away from the more-visited villages in the heart of the Luberon. Existentialist writer Albert Camus *(The Stranger)* lived in Lourmarin in the 1950s, lending it a certain fame that persists today. Author Peter Mayle lives here now, adding to the village's cachet. Lourmarin makes a good base for touring the southern Luberon, Aix-en-Provence, and even Marseille and Cassis (if you're willing to drive a bit farther). From here, you can tour big cities, beaches, and castles, returning every night to the comfort of your village.

Tourist Information: The TI is located across from the soccer field and the château on avenue Philippe de Girard (Mon–Sat 10:00–12:30 & 15:00–18:00, closed Sun, tel. 04 90 68 10 77).

Getting There: Three buses per day link Lourmarin to Avignon (90 min), and to Aix-en-Provence (75 min, bus to Pertuis leaves 3/day, transfer there to bus bound for Aix-en-Provence, 2/hr).

Theft Alert: There has been a rash of break-ins at car lots in Lourmarin. Park centrally, and leave nothing visible in your car.

SIGHTS AND ACTIVITIES

Château de Lourmarin—The château offers a rare look (in this region) inside a Renaissance château—more common in the Loire Valley. You can tour the château on your own, with the help of its decent English handout and posted explanations (€5.50, daily 10:00–11:30 & 14:30–17:30, tel. 04 90 68 15 23).

Friday Market—This little town erupts into a market frenzy every Friday until 13:00. Sleep here Thursday night and awake to the commotion, arrive early, or prepare for a good walk from your car.

SLEEPING

In Lourmarin

Try to sleep here on a Thursday, so you can awake to Friday's market. These two good-value *chambres d'hôte* sit across from each other in the center.

$$ Villa St. Louis is a cross between a museum, a fine old manor home, and a garage sale. Its fun and slightly eccentric owners add charm to a place packed with character. Mapie (short for Marie-Pierre) runs the show with a knowledge of fluent English and a knowledge of the area that the TI would envy. The big backyard is ideal for a siesta (hammock provided) and picnics. The rooms are like grandma's, and there's a common room with a fridge (Db-€60–70, includes breakfast, cash only, 35 rue de Henri Savournin, tel. 04 90 68 39 18, fax 04 90 68 10 07, www .villasaintlouis.com, villasaintlouis@wanadoo.fr).

$$ Les Chambres de la Cordière is a fine getaway located almost across the street. Amiable Françoise's goal is to make you feel at home. Five cozy rooms are tucked into the village's oldest building (c. 1582), with a small, photogenic courtyard and welcoming cats (Db-€70, Tb-€85, Qb-€100, includes breakfast, cash only, rue Albert Camus, tel. & fax 04 90 68 03 32, www.cordiere .com, cordiereluberon@aol.com).

EATING

In Lourmarin

All roads seem to converge on the postcard-perfect intersection near **Café de la Fontaine,** where you can enjoy a light meal or snack inside or out—or choose from several other nearby cafés. To eat well in Lourmarin, book a romantic table at the feminine **Restaurant l'Antiquaire** (€30 *menu*, closed Sun–Mon, indoors only but air-con, a block up from Café de la Fontaine on 9 rue du Grand Pré, tel. 04 90 68 17 29). If you've had it with Provençal cuisine, **Le Bistrot Lyonnais** offers a change, with ambience and cuisine from Lyon and outdoor seating (€16 *plats*, €25 *menu*, closed Sun and Thu, 2 avenue Philippe de Girard, tel. 04 90 68 29 74). Across the street, **La Recreation** features a welcoming terrace and regional cuisine with a vegetarian emphasis (€14 *plats*, €23 *menus,* closed Wed except in summer, next to the TI on avenue Philippe de Girard, tel. 04 90 68 23 73).

MARSEILLE, CASSIS, AND AIX-EN-PROVENCE

In the rush to get between Avignon and the Riviera, most travelers zip through the eastern fringe of Provence. That's too bad, as this area offers compelling cities and a strikingly beautiful coastline, all in a tight package. I cover three different-as-night-and-day places, each worthy of a slice of your time. Marseille is an untouristy, semiseedy-but-vibrant port city with 2,600 years of history. The nearby coastal village of Cassis offers the perfect antidote to the big city. And just inland, popular and polished Aix-en-Provence is the yin to Marseille's yang, with beautiful people to match its lovely architecture.

Marseille

Those who think of Marseille as the "Naples of France"— a big, gritty, dangerous port—missed the boat. Today's Marseille (mar-say), while hardly pristine, is closer to the "Barcelona of France." It's a big, gritty port, *sans* question, but it has a distinct culture, a proud spirit, a new prosperity, and a populace determined to clean up its act. They have lots of work to do, and they're off to a good start. Thousands of Marseille's historic buildings are undergoing a massive renovation program, and a new tramway system is under construction.

France's second-biggest city (and Europe's third-largest port) nurtures a history that goes back to ancient Greek times—and challenges you to find its charm. Marseille is a world apart from France's other leading cities (such as Paris and Lyon). It's amazing to think that Marseille has no essential sight to visit. The city itself is the sight, the streets are its paintings, and the happy-go-lucky residents provide its ambience.

You're likely to hear as much Arabic as French. The influence

Marseille, Cassis, and Aix-en-Provence

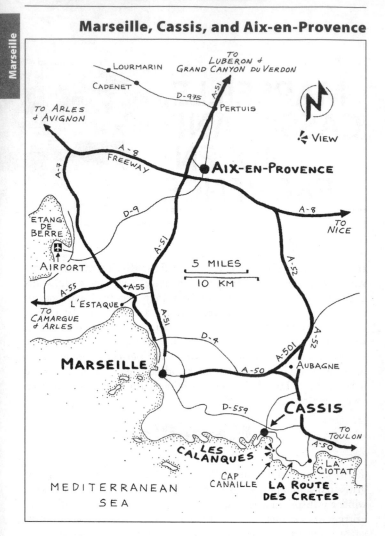

of immigrants is huge; more than 25 percent of the city's population came from countries in North Africa. These migrants have created residential ghettos where nary a word of French is uttered—infuriating anti-immigrant French people who fear that this may be the destiny for the rest of "their" country.

While most tourists leave Marseille off their itinerary—it's not their idea of the French Riviera—it would be a shame to come to the south of France and not experience the region's leading city. By train or car, it's made-to-order for a quick visit. And with the TGV line making it just a three-hour trip from Paris, this much-maligned city seems eager to put on a welcoming face.

Planning Your Time

For a four-hour tour of Marseille that covers the basics, walk from the train station down La Canebière, wander around the Old Port on quai du Port, climb to the La Charité Museum (ideal lunch café), find the cathedral, then return to the port and take the shuttle ferry across to the new town (with the best eating options). Finally, take a bus, tourist train, or taxi up to Notre-Dame de la Garde before returning to the station.

ORIENTATION

Although Marseille sprawls, keep it simple and focus on the area immediately around the Old Port (Vieux Port). A main boulevard (La Canebière) meets the colorful Old Port at a cluster of small (and skippable) museums and the TI. The characteristic Panier district is the old town, blanketing a hill that tumbles down to the Old Port. The harborside is a lively, broad promenade lined with inviting eateries, amusements, and a morning fish market. Everything described here (except the church on the hill) is within a 30-minute walk of the train station.

A sleek new tramway line should be completed by 2008, though you won't find use for it.

Tourist Information

The main TI is right at the **port** (Mon–Sat 9:00–19:00, Sun 9:00–17:00, 4 La Canebière, tel. 04 91 13 89 00, www.marseille -tourisme.com), with a branch office at the **train station** (Mon–Fri 10:00–12:30 & 13:00–17:00, closed Sat–Sun). At either TI, pick up the good city map, the flier with a self-guided walk through the old town, and fliers on each of the museums.

Ask about occasional walking tours in English and the worthwhile 2.5-hour English **taxi tours,** which are available anytime and arranged through the main TI (€66 for up to 4 people).

Arrival in Marseille

By Train: St. Charles Station (Gare St. Charles) is modern and user-friendly (but under eternal renovation). Everything you want (except taxis and the subway, which are well signed) is along or outside of track A. There's a good cafeteria, WCs (€0.50), a baggage check (daily 7:15–22:00), and a quiet waiting area. Exiting by track A to Square Narvik, you'll find a TI (pick up a free city map; closed Sat–Sun), airport buses, car rental, and Hôtel Ibis (all but the TI to the left as you exit). To get from the station to the Old Port, you can walk, take the Métro, or catch a taxi.

By foot, it's a 15-minute downhill gauntlet—past filthy streets and questionable shops—from the station to the Old

Marseille at a Glance

▲**Marine Museum** Grandiose building with small exhibit on the city's maritime history. **Hours:** June–Sept Tue–Sun 10:00–18:00, Oct–May Tue–Sun 10:00–17:00, closed Mon.

Marseille History Museum Shows off the city's remarkable history with artifacts from Caesar to Louis XIV. **Hours:** Mon–Sat 12:00–19:00, closed Sun.

▲**Old Port** Economic heart of town, featuring lots of boats and a fish market, all protected by two impressive fortresses. **Hours:** Port—always open; fish market—daily until 13:00.

▲**La Charité Museum** Housed in a beautiful building with Celtic, Greek, Roman, and Egyptian artifacts, plus temporary exhibits. **Hours:** June–Sept Tue–Sun 11:00–18:00, Oct–May Tue–Sun 10:00–17:00, closed Mon.

▲**Notre-Dame de la Garde** Marseille's landmark sight: a huge Romanesque–Byzantine basilica, towering above everything, with panoramic views. **Hours:** Daily in summer 7:00–20:00, until 19:00 in winter.

Cathédrale de la Nouvelle Major Impressive striped cathedral with floor and wall mosaics. **Hours:** Daily 10:00–12:00 & 14:00–18:00.

Arab Markets Taste of North Africa in downtown Marseille. **Hours:** Open long hours daily.

Fashion Museum Sparse collection of dresses from the last half-century. **Hours:** June–Sept Tue–Sun 11:00–18:00, Oct–May Tue–Sun 10:00–17:00, closed Mon.

Château d'If Island with fortress-turned-prison, featured in Alexandre Dumas' *The Count of Monte Cristo*. **Hours:** Boats depart quai des Belges on the hour 9:00–17:00.

Port. Leave the station through the exit at track A, veer right, and admire the view from atop the stairs (Toto, we're not in Cassis anymore). That's Notre-Dame de la Garde overlooking the city. Walk down the stairs and straight on boulevard d'Athènes, which becomes boulevard Dugommier. Turn right at McDonald's onto the grand boulevard, La Canebière, which leads directly to the port and the main TI.

By **Métro,** it's an easy two stops from the train station to the port: Go down the escalator opposite track E and buy a ticket (from the machines or inside the *Accueil* office, €1.70 ticket is good for 1 hour of travel on Métro and buses, all-day pass costs €4.50). Descend the long escalator, and take the blue line #1 (direction La Timone) to Vieux Port. Following *Sortie la Canebière* exit signs, you'll pop out at the TI (and smell the fish market). To return to the station from here, take the train (direction: La Rose) two stops and get off at the stop called Gare SNCF.

By **taxi,** allow €8 to the port and €10 to Notre-Dame de la Garde—though cabbies may refuse these short trips if business is hopping (tel. 04 91 02 20 20).

By Car: Drivers who are good in big, crazy cities can reasonably navigate Marseille. Leaving the autoroute, signs to *Vieux Port, Centre-Ville,* and *Office du Tourisme* take you right to the port. At the port, turn left and let the blue *P* signs direct you into an underground lot with 625 spaces (locals claim pay lots are patrolled and safe).

By Plane: Marseille's airport (Aéroport Marseille–Provence), 25 minutes from the city center, is small and easy to navigate (tel. 04 42 14 14 14, www.marseille.aeroport.fr). Shuttle buses run to the St. Charles train station (€9, 3/hr, 25 min) and to Aix-en-Provence (stops at Aix-en-Provence's TGV station or bus station, 2/hr, 30 min, www.rdt13.fr).

Helpful Hints

Pickpockets: Be on guard. Marseille is one of the few cities in France where you might run into Roma (Gypsy) thieves. Looking like beggars, they're usually raggedly dressed barefoot kids, or a mom with a baby, who hold up newspapers or cardboard to distract you as they pick your pocket. Be firm and rude if you must, but don't let them near you. Big-city thieves thrive in crowds and target tourists. Wear your money belt, and assume any commotion is a smokescreen for theft.

Internet Access: Try the **Info-Café,** two blocks from the TI (daily, 1 quai de Rive-Neuve, tel. 04 91 33 53 05).

Car Rental: All the major companies are represented at St. Charles Station (see "Arrival in Marseille," earlier in this chapter).

Le Petit Train: Helpful little tourist trains with skimpy recorded information make two handy routes through town. Both leave at least hourly from the port (across from TI). One train, called the Vieux Marseille, toots you through the Panier district (€5, 40 min, April–Oct only). The other saves you the 30-minute climb to the Notre-Dame de la Garde's fantastic view (€5, allow 60 min round-trip, including 30 min to visit the church, runs daily, April–Oct every 20 min from

10:00–12:20 & 13:40–18:20, March and Nov every 30 min, Dec–Feb 5/day, tel. 04 91 25 24 69, www.petit -train-marseille.com).

Soccer Matches: *Le football* is to Marseille what American football is to Green Bay: Frenzied fans go crazy and star-worship is always temporary. One of the best-ever soccer players (Zinédine Zidane) was raised here. On my last visit, 30,000 Marseille fans were boarding trains to Paris for the France finals. If you're here during soccer season (end of July to mid-May), consider getting tickets to a match (every other Sat, tickets start at €15, ask at TI or at the OM Café on the port). To get to the soccer stadium (Stade Vélodrome), take Métro line 2 (direction: Ste. Marguerite) to the stop called Point du Prado. The TI also offers visits to the stadium in July and August (ask at TI).

SIGHTS

I've listed these sights in roughly the order that you come to them as you approach the Old Port on La Canebière. I've also included some commentary to help you connect the dots.

Along La Canebière

The boulevard La Canebière (pronounced "can o' bee-air") with its new facelift—the classy tramway—is the celebrated main drag

of Marseille. Strolling this stubby thoroughfare, you feel surrounded by a teeming and diverse city. Two blocks before the harbor, you'll find three museums and a stylish shopping district (you'll reach them in the order listed below). The boulevard dead-ends at the Old Port's fish market and TI.

Arab Markets—Marseille's huge Moroccan, Algerian, and Tunisian populations give the city a special spice. For a taste of Africa, leave La Canebière by turning left at the second street onto rue Longue des Capucins. Suddenly you're immersed in an exotic and fragrant little medina filled with commotion. For a more sprawling Arab market, explore the lanes around boulevard d'Athènes near the train station (such as rue des Convalescents).

French Fashion—On the right side of La Canebière, the **Fashion Museum** (Musée de la Mode) is as skimpy as most of its dresses, with two rooms full of creative and colorful outfits from the 1950s to today (€3; June–Sept Tue–Sun 11:00–18:00, Oct–May Tue–Sun 10:00–17:00, closed Mon; 11 La Canebière, in Espace Mode Mediterranée).

For more fashion, cross La Canebière, continue across place du Général de Gaulle (passing the merry-go-round), and find the tiny rue de la Tour, Marseille's self-proclaimed "rue de la Mode." It's lined with shops proudly displaying the latest fashions, mostly from local designers. Just beyond that is the 1920s Art Deco facade of Marseille's opera house.

▲**Marine Museum and Chamber of Commerce**—Near the end of La Canebière, cross back across the street and approach the tall and grandiose Chamber of Commerce building. Step inside (free entry) and take in the grand 1860s interior. A relief on the ceiling shows great moments in Marseille's history and a large court with a United Nations of plaques, reminding locals how their commerce comes from trade around the world.

The small ground-floor exhibit on the city's maritime history starts (to the right as you enter) with an impressive portrait of Emperor Napoleon III (who called for the building's construction) and his wife. Sketches show the pomp surrounding its grand opening. The next room traces the growth of the city through charts of its harbor, and the following rooms display models of big ships over the centuries (€2; June–Sept Tue–Sun 10:00–18:00, Oct–May Tue–Sun 10:00–17:00, closed Mon; tel. 04 91 39 33 33).

Marseille History Museum (Musée d'Histoire de Marseille)—Come here for a French-only introduction to Marseille's remarkable history, including the remains of an old Roman ship and bits of a Greek vessel—both found here (no English, €2, Mon–Sat 12:00–19:00, closed Sun, in the Centre Bourse, a modern shopping center behind the Chamber of Commerce, tel. 04 91 90 42 22, www.marseille.fr).

• *The TI is just down the street from the Marine Museum. After checking in at the TI, cross the big street and get close to the...*

Old Port (Vieux Port)

Protected by two impressive fortresses at its mouth, Marseille's Vieux Port has long been the economic heart of town. These citadels were built in the 17th century under Louis XIV, supposedly to protect the city. But locals figured the forts were actually designed to keep an eye on Marseille—a city that was essentially autonomous until 1660, and a challenge to thoroughly incorporate into

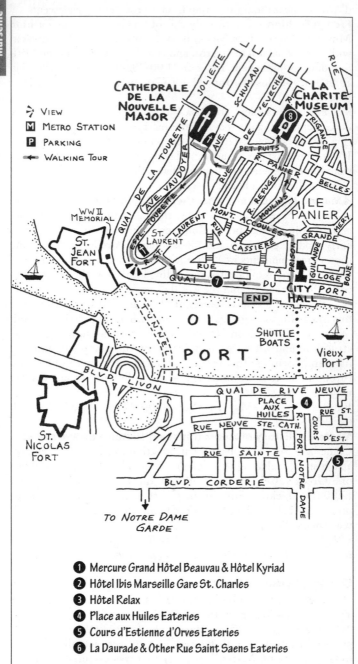

Marseille

1 Mercure Grand Hôtel Beauvau & Hôtel Kyriad
2 Hôtel Ibis Marseille Gare St. Charles
3 Hôtel Relax
4 Place aux Huiles Eateries
5 Cours d'Estienne d'Orves Eateries
6 La Daurade & Other Rue Saint Saens Eateries

7 Le Souk & Les Galinettes Chez Madie Restaurants
8 La Charité Museum Café
9 Arab Markets
10 Internet Café
11 Le Petit Trains Departure Point
12 Boat Dock for Château d'If & Islands of Frioul

Marseille

the growing kingdom of France.

Today, the serious shipping is away from the center, and the Old Port is the happy domain of pleasure craft. The fish market along quai des Belges (where you're standing) thrives each morning (unless the mistral wind kept the boats home the day before). The stalls are gone by 13:00, but the smells linger. Looking out from here, Le Panier (the old town) rises to your right. The harborfront below Le Panier was destroyed in 1943 by the Nazis, who didn't want a tangled refuge for resistance fighters so close to the harbor. Today, it's rebuilt as modern condos and trendy restaurants.

• *Walk around the right side of the port and find the small ferry dock (La Ligne du Ferry Boat) that crosses the port. You'll be back here soon. But for now, turn around and find Hôtel de Ville.*

Le Panier District (Old Town)

Until the mid-19th century, Marseille was just the hill-capping old town and its fortified port. Today, that old town is the best place to find the town's soul. The ornate **City Hall** (Hôtel de Ville) stands across from the three-masted sailboat and the little shuttle ferry. Its bust of Louis XIV overlooks the harbor. Rue de la Prison leads behind the City Hall and up the hill. At the crest of the hill—the highest point in the old town—you'll find the peaceful place des Moulins. It's named for the 15 windmills that used to spin and grind from this windy summit. (Today, only the towers of three can be seen.)

• *Walk up the broad stairway, passing the City Hall, turn left at the top, then track the brown signs to* Vieille Charité. *As you walk, read the thoughtful English-information plaques posted on iron stands at points of historic interest.*

▲**La Charité Museum (Centre de la Vieille Charité)**—Now a museum, this was once a poorhouse. In 1674, the French king

decided that all the poor people on the streets were bad news. He built a huge triple-arcaded home to house a thousand needy subjects. In 1940, the famous architect Le Corbusier declared it a shame that such a fine building was so underappreciated. Today, the striking building—wonderfully renovated and beautiful in its arcaded simplicity—is used as a collection of art galleries surrounding a Pantheon-esque church.

The pediment of the church features the figure of Charity taking care of orphans (as the state did with this building). She's flanked by pelicans (symbolic of charity, for the way they actually pick flesh from their own bosom to feed their hungry chicks). The ground floor outside the church houses temporary exhibits. Upstairs, you'll find rooms with interesting collections of Celtic (c. 300 B.C.), Greek, and Roman artifacts from this region. There's also a surprisingly good Egyptian collection, and masks from Africa and the South Pacific (€2–5 depending on exhibits; June–Sept Tue–Sun 11:00–18:00, Oct–May Tue–Sun 10:00–17:00, closed Mon; idyllic restaurant/bar, tel. 04 91 14 58 80).

• *From La Charité, cross the cobbled triangular square, turn right on rue du Petit Puits, and follow the street down, veering left, then right, to find...*

Cathédrale de la Nouvelle Major—This astonishing striped cathedral seems lost out here away from the action and above the nondescript cruise-ship port. The cathedral, built in the late 1800s, looks striking from the outside and has a Byzantine feel inside, with impressive floor and wall mosaics (daily 10:00–12:00 & 14:00–18:00).

• *Return to the Old Port by walking up the tree-lined esplanade de la Tourette. A brilliant view terrace awaits at the bend.*

View Terrace—Wow! Here you get a fine city panorama with Notre-Dame de la Garde presiding, and a closer look at the twin forts protecting the entrance to the Old Port. The ugly, boxy building marked "monument" at the base of the fort (below and to your right) is a memorial to those lost during the Nazi occupation of the city in World War II.

• *Continue down the steps back to the Old Port.*

From the Old Port to the New Town

Halfway along the promenade (quai du Port), at the City Hall, you'll see the fun little **shuttle boat** that ferries locals across the harbor to the new town (€0.50 each way; if you want a one-way ticket, say "ah-lay-samp-luh"; every 10 min 7:00–19:20). Note the unusual two-way steering wheel as you sail. You'll dock in the new town—which, because of the 1943 bombings, is actually older than the "old" town along the harborfront.

Directly in front of the ferry landing, you'll find popular bars and brasseries, good for a quick meal or memorable drink. Wander in along the place aux Huiles, make your way left, and find a smart pedestrian zone crammed with cafés and restaurants (see "Eating," page 207).

• *Consider a pilgrimage up to Notre Dame de la Garde.*

Overlooking the Old Port

▲Notre-Dame de la Garde—Crowning Marseille's highest point, 500 feet above the harbor, is the city's landmark sight. This massive Romanesque–Byzantine basilica, built in the 1850s during the reign of Napoleon III, is a harmonious collection of domes, gold, and mosaics. The monumental statue of Mary and the Baby Jesus towers above everything (Jesus' wrist alone is 42 inches around, and the statue weighs nine tons). While the interior is elegant (daily in summer 7:00–20:00, until 19:00 in winter, cafeteria and WCs just below the view terrace), people come here mostly for the commanding city view. This hilltop has served as a lookout, as well as a place of worship, since ancient times.

To get to the church, you can hike 30 minutes from the harbor, catch a taxi (about €10), hop on bus #60 (stop is on the port, opposite the TI on the quai des Belges), or ride the tourist train from the harborfront (see "Helpful Hints" on page 199).

Offshore Islands

Château d'If—When King François I visited Marseille in the 16th century, he realized the potential strategic importance of a fort on the uninhabited island just outside the harbor. His château was finished in 1531. The impregnable fortress, which never saw battle, became a prison—handy for locking up Protestants during the Counter-Reformation. Among its illustrious inmates was José Faria, a spiritualist priest who was the idol of Paris and whom Alexandre Dumas immortalized in *The Count of Monte Cristo*. Since 1890, the château has been open to the public. Tour boats take tourists to this French Alcatraz, where the required two-hour stay will leave you sensitive to the count's predicament. I'd skip this prison (€10 round-trip, €5 château entry, 30-min trip, usually depart daily on the hour 9:00–17:00, get the latest at the TI).

Islands of Frioul—These islands, which offer a nature break from the big city with a few hiking paths and cafés, are another 15 minutes away (round-trip with Château d'If-€10, boats run daily on the half-hour 9:30–17:30, get the latest at the TI).

SLEEPING

Stay in Marseille only if you want a true urban experience. Hotel values and ambience are better 20 minutes away in Cassis (see page 214).

$$$ Mercure Grand Hôtel Beauvau**** lets you pay way too much to buy away the gritty reality outside your door (Db-€180, view Db-€250, Wi-Fi in little lobby, 4 rue Beauvau, tel. 04 91 54 91 00, fax 04 91 54 15 76, h1293@accor.com).

Sleep Code

(€1 = about $1.30, country code: 33)
S = Single, **D** = Double/Twin, **T** = Triple, **Q** = Quad, **b** = bathroom,
s = shower only, ***** = French hotel rating system (0–4 stars).
Unless otherwise noted, credit cards are accepted and English
is spoken.

To help you sort easily through these listings, I've divided
the rooms into three categories based on the price for a standard double room with bath:

$$$ **Higher Priced**—Most rooms €90 or more.
$$ **Moderately Priced**—Most rooms between €60–90.
$ **Lower Priced**—Most rooms €60 or less.

$$$ Hôtel Ibis Marseille Gare St. Charles**, with 180 rooms
(which are often fully booked), is a worthwhile value because it's
right at the train station—on the left as you exit (Db-€90, extra
bed-€10, check for deals on their website, air-con, elevator, Square
Narvick, tel. 04 91 95 62 09, fax 04 91 50 68 42, www.ibishotel
.com, h1390@accor.com).

$$ Hôtel Kyriad**, a block off the port behind the TI, is a
shade musty but offers relative quiet and livable comfort at good
rates (Db-€78, Db with king-size bed and bath–€85, Tb-€105,
elevator, 6 rue Beauvau, tel. 04 91 33 02 33, fax 04 91 33 21 34,
kyriad.vieux-port@wanadoo.fr).

$ Hôtel Relax*, run by sweet Houria (pronounced "oo-ree-
ah," which means "Liberty" in Arabic—she's Algerian) and her
family, feels more like a B&B and is a terrific budget stay. Despite
its downtown location, it has no traffic noise and a lobby any poodle
would love. Book this place way ahead. Half the rooms overlook a
classy square—worth requesting—as the back-side rooms can be
gloomy (back-side Db-€50, Db on square-€55, rooms have small
bathrooms, air-con, Wi-Fi, just 2 blocks off harbor on place de
l'Opéra at 4 rue Corneille, tel. 04 91 33 15 87, fax 04 91 55 63 57,
www.hotelrelax.fr, hotelrelax@free.fr).

EATING

In the New Town: For the best combination of trendiness, variety, and a fun people scene, consider eating in the new town, on
or near quai de Rive-Neuve (on the left side of the Old Port as
you look out to sea). Look for the place aux Huiles, the cours
d'Estienne d'Orves, and rue Saint-Saens for a melting pot of
international eateries ranging from giant salads and fresh seafood

to crêpes, Vietnamese dishes, Belgian waffles, and buffalo wings. Don't expect high cuisine here, but the ambience can't be beat. **La Daurade** is a worthwhile place for fresh seafood at fair prices served in a fine setting (€18 *menus*, closed Wed, 36 rue Saint Saëns, tel. 04 91 33 82 42).

Near the Old Port: For good views *en terrasse*, go to the other side of the port. Consider a real Moroccan dinner at **Le Souk** (€18 couscous and *tagine* dishes, intimate and authentic interior, closed Mon, 100 quai du Port, tel. 04 91 91 29 29). If you must have bouillabaisse, try **Les Galinettes Chez Madie** (€22 *menu*, €35/person for bouillabaisse, closed Sun, 138 quai du Port, tel. 04 91 90 40 87).

Near La Charité: **La Charité Museum** has a lovely, quiet courtyard café (lunch only).

TRANSPORTATION CONNECTIONS

Marseille is well-served by TGV and local trains, and is the hub for many smaller stations in eastern Provence.

From Marseille by Train to: Cassis (20/day, 25 min), **Aix-en-Provence** Centre-Ville station (18/day, 35 min), **Nice** (18/day, 2.5 hrs), **Arles** (20/day, 1–2 hrs), **Avignon** (10/day, 1 hr), **Paris** (hourly, 3–3.25 hrs), **Isle-sur-la-Sorgue** (8/day, 1–2 hrs).

From Marseille's Train Station by Bus to: Marseille Airport (3/hr, 20 min), **Cassis** (8/day, 50 min), **Aix-en-Provence** (4/hr, 50 min).

From Marseille's Métro Castellane to: Cassis (10/day, 40 min).

Cassis

Crouching in awe of impossibly high cliffs, Cassis (kah-see) is an unpretentious port town that offers travelers a sunny time-out from their busy vacation. Two hours away from the fray of the Côte d'Azur, Cassis is a poor man's St-Tropez. Outdoor cafés line the small port on three sides, where boaters clean their crafts as they chat up café clients. Cassis is popular with the French and close enough to Marseille to be busy on weekends and all summer. Come to Cassis to dine portside, swim in the glimmering-clear water, and explore its rocky *calanques* and fjord-like inlets.

ORIENTATION

The Massif du Puget mountain hovers over little Cassis, with hills spilling down to the port. Cap Canaille cliff rises from the southeast and the famous fjord-like *calanques* hide along the coast northwest of town. Hotels, restaurants, and boats line the attractive little port.

Tourist Information

The TI is in the modern building in the middle of the port among the boats (Mon–Sat 9:00–12:30 & 14:00–18:00, Sun 10:00–12:00, longer hours in summer, quai des Moulins; tel. 08 92 25 98 92—this toll line costs €0.34/min, push 2 to talk to an agent; www .cassis.fr). If going to Marseille, pick up a map here.

Arrival in Cassis

By Train: Cassis' hills forced the train station to be built two miles away. Most weekday trains are met by buses that will take you into town (€0.80, 14/day Mon–Fri, 6/day Sat, none on Sun, ask at station if you don't see one, 10-min trip into Cassis). Taxis cost about €10 with baggage to most hotels (taxis usually meet arriving trains; if not, call 04 42 01 78 96, a phone cabin is outside the train station). Otherwise, it's a 45-minute walk into town (turn left out of the station and follow signs).

By Bus: Regional buses (including those from Marseille) drop you off a five-minute walk from the port (turn right on avenue P. Lariche).

By Car: There are two exits from the autoroute for Cassis; the second (coming from Aix-en-Provence) costs €1 more in tolls but saves you 10 minutes, provides easy access to La Route des Crêtes (described below under "Sights and Activities"), and offers memorable views. The hills above Cassis make navigating here a challenge. Hotels are signed, though the blue signs can be tricky to follow, so pay attention. Hotel parking is minimal, and the traffic is worse the closer you get to the port. Outside of summer, drivers arriving by 10:00 can usually find curbside parking (about €1/hour, free 18:00–9:00); latecomers will probably need to park in one of the well-marked pay lots above the port (**Parking de la Viguerie** is closest but often full, and their *Abonnés* entrance is for locals only). On busy holiday weekends, and every day from late June through early September, the city provides free parking with shuttle service from **Parking les Gorguettes** high above the town (well-signed).

Helpful Hints

Market Days: The market hops on Wednesdays and Fridays until 12:30 (on the streets around the Hôtel de Ville).

Beaches: Cassis' beaches are pebbly. The big beach behind the TI is sandier than others, though aqua-shoes still help. You can rent a mattress with a towel (about €15/day) and paddleboats (about €10/hr). Underwater springs just off the Cassis shore make the water clean, clear, and a bit cooler than at other beaches.

Cassis

Internet Access: Two Internet cafés are a few blocks from the port on rue de la Viguerie, near Parking la Viguerie: **Europrim** (Mon–Fri 8:30–12:00 & 14:00–18:30, closed Sat–Sun, rue de la Viguerie 7, tel. 04 42 01 98 28) and **Cassis Télécom** (Mon–Sat 9:00–12:00 & 15:00–19:00, closed Sun, a block uphill at rue de la Viguerie 28, tel. 04 42 98 81 94).

Laundry: Walk up rue Victor Hugo, then find 9 rue Autheman (daily 9:00–19:30, self-serve or full-serve).

Grocery Store: The **Casino** market is next door to Hôtel le Liautaud (daily 8:30–12:30 & 15:30–19:00, Sun until 18:00).

Wine Tasting: Le Chai Cassidain is a wine bar where young Russian Anastasia welcomes visitors with red-leather stools and a good selection of regional wines. Buy by the bottle or by the glass (daily 10:00–13:00 & 16:00–19:00, 4 blocks from port at 6 rue Séverin Icard, tel. 04 42 01 99 80).

Taxi: Call 04 42 01 78 96.

Bike and Vehicle Rentals: Fouad Grairi has bikes, scooters, and Smart cars (€80/day for car, 26 rue Abbé Cabrol, tel. 06 26 96 13 22, grairiincassis@aol.com).

Tourist Train: The little white *train touristique*, with commentary in French and English, will take you on a worthwhile 45-minute circuit out to the peninsula on the Port-Miou *calanque* and back (€5, April–Oct, afternoons only, catch it next to Hôtel Lieutaud on the port).

SELF-GUIDED TOUR

Cassis Visual Tour from the Port

Find a friendly bench in front of Hôtel le Golfe—or, better, enjoy a drink at their café—and read this quick town intro.

Cassis was born more than 2,500 years ago (on the hill with the castle ruins, across the harbor). Ligurians, Phoenicians, maybe Greeks, certainly Romans, and plenty of barbarians all found this spot to their liking. Parts of the castle date from the eighth century, and the **fortress walls** were constructed in the 13th century to defend Cassis against seaborne barbarian raids. The Michelin family recently sold the fortress to investors who wanted to turn it into a luxury hotel. Cassis' planning commission had other ideas.

In the 18th century, when things got safer, people moved their homes back to the waterfront. Since then, Cassis has made its

Cassis

① Best Western Hôtel la Rade
② Hôtel le Golfe
③ Hôtel le Clos des Arômes
④ Hôtel Cassitel
⑤ Hôtel Laurence
⑥ To Mahogany Hôtel de la Plage & Le Jardin d'Emile Hôtel
⑦ El Sol, L'Oustau de la Mar & La Canaille Restaurants
⑧ Le Grand Large Rest.
⑨ Le 8 et Demi Café & Grand Marnier Crêpes

⑩ La Girondole Restaurant
⑪ Le Chai Cassidain Wine Bar
⑫ Europrim Internet Café
⑬ Telecom Internet Café
⑭ Launderette
⑮ Casino Supermarket
⑯ Tourist Train (Afternoon Only)
⑰ To Fouad Graïri (Smart Car Rental)
⑱ Motorboat Rental & WC
⑲ Pedal Boat Rental

living through fishing, quarrying its famous white stone, producing well-respected white wines—which, conveniently, pair well with the local seafood dishes, and *bien sûr*, with tourists like us.

With improvements in transportation following the end of World War II, tourism rose gradually in Cassis, though crowds are still sparse by Riviera standards. While foreigners overwhelm nearby resorts, Cassis is popular mostly with the French, and still feels unspoiled. The town's protected status limits the height of the buildings along the harbor as well as the crass development you see elsewhere on the coast. Its **harbor** is home to some nice boats... but they're chump change compared to the glitzier harbors farther east.

The big **cliff** towering above the castle hill is Cap Canaille. Europe's highest maritime cliff, it was sculpted by receding glaciers (wrap your brain around that concept), and today drops 1,200 feet straight down. You can—and should—drive or taxi along the top for sensational views (see "La Route des Crêtes," below). Return to this bench at sunset, when the Cap glows a deep red.

Walk to your right, then veer left on top of the short wall in front of the public WCs. The rocky shore over your right shoulder looks cut away just for sunbathers. But Cassis was once an important **quarry,** and stones were sliced right out of this beach for easy transport to ships. The Statue of Liberty's base sits on this rock, and even today, Cassis stone remains highly valued throughout the world...but yesterday's quarrymen have been replaced by today's sunbathers.

SIGHTS AND ACTIVITIES

▲▲▲The *Calanques*

Calanques (kah-lahnk) are the narrow inlets created by the prickly extensions of cliffs that border the shore. Until you see the intimate beaches and exotic fjords of translucent blue water, it's hard to understand what all the excitement is about. You can hike, or cruise by boat or kayak, to many *calanques,* all of which are located along the 13 miles of coast between Cassis and Marseille. Bring water, sunscreen, and anything else you need for the day, as there's nary a baguette for sale. Don't dawdle—  to limit crowds, the most popular *calanques* can be closed by 11:00 in high season (July–mid-Sept) and on weekends. The TI can give you plenty of advice about enjoying the *calanques.*

Boats offer trips of various lengths (3 *calanques*-€13, 2/hr, 45 min; 5 *calanques*-€15, 3/day, 65 min; 8–10 *calanques*-€16–20, 1–3/day, 2 hrs; tel. 04 42 01 90 83, http://calanques-cassis.com). The three-*calanques* tour seems most popular. Tickets are sold (and boats depart) from a small booth on the TI side of the port. *Prochain départ* means "next departure."

Hardy souls can **hike** to three of the *calanques* (Port-Miou, Port-Pin, and d'En-Vau)—though shade is nonexistent, and maps lack detail (verify route as you go). For most, the best *calanque* by foot is Calanque Port-Pin, about an hour from Cassis (30 min after the linear, boat-lined Calanque Port-Miou). It's intimate and well-forested, with a small beach.

If you leave early, the most spectacular *calanque* to hang out at is **Calanque d'En-Vau.** In high season, access is strictly controlled, and this *calanque* is closed by about 11:00. From Cassis, hiking is the most reliable option. At the TI, get a map and ask about the trail conditions. Start along the road behind the Hôtel le Golfe and walk past the Plage du Bestouan, continuing to the Calanque Port-Miou along the avenue des Calanques. You'll join the primary *GR (Grande Randonnée)* trail at the Port-Miou Calanque and walk with the sea to your left, following red, white, and green markers (painted on rocks, trees, etc.).

There is a boat option, but it's not necessarily easier (€16, 2/hr, less for one-way tickets). Boats can drop you on a cliff, provided you're wearing appropriate shoes (short jump) and the sea is calm—but it's a steep, treacherous hike down to the beach for inexperienced climbers, and an even more difficult hike back up—a bad idea for most. If you *really* want to do this, you can buy a one-way ticket and hike back to Cassis (take the inland route and avoid the more difficult hike up the cliff). Sea currents can make boat drop-off difficult—verify that you can get off at Calanque d'En-Vau before buying your ticket.

To explore the *calanques* on your own, you can rent a **kayak** (about €25/half-day) or a small **motorboat** (€100/half-day, €140/day, €700 cash or credit-card imprint as deposit, no special boat license needed for the small boats; at Loca'Bato office, a few steps away from Hôtel le Golfe; tel. 04 42 01 27 04). Other options include **kayak tours** (sunset tour-€25 per person, half-day tour-€35, full-day tour-€55, tel. 06 12 95 20 12, www.provencekayakmer.fr) and **skippered boat rental** (up to 8 people, about €250/half-day, €440/day, ask at TI).

Above Cassis

▲▲**La Route des Crêtes**—If you have a car, or are willing to spring for a taxi (€30 for a good 45-min trip, 4 people per taxi) or a Smart-car rental (see "Helpful Hints," page 199), you must take this remarkable drive. Ride straight up to the top of Cap Canaille and toward the next town, La Ciotat. It's a twisty road, providing access to numbingly high views over Cassis and the Mediterranean. From Cassis, follow signs to *La Ciotat/Toulon*, then *La Route des Crêtes*. The towns just east of Cassis (La Ciotat, Bandol, etc.) do not merit a detour. This road is occasionally closed (because of strong winds or road repair), though you can usually get partway up (check at the TI before renting a car for this).

SLEEPING

(€1 = about $1.30, country code: 33)

Cassis hotels are relaxed places with less polish but lower rates than those on the Côte d'Azur. Some close from November to March, but those that stay open offer good discounts. All are busy on weekend and summer nights, when many can come with late-night noise. Book early for sea views and bring earplugs. Most hotels have a few invaluable parking spots that you can reserve when booking your room.

Near the Port or in Town

$$$ Best Western Hôtel la Rade*** lies on a busy road above the northwest corner of the port, with good views from its lovely poolside deck. It rents small, simple, and pricey rooms with air-conditioning (Db-€118, bigger Db-€155, apartments-€225, free Internet access and Wi-Fi, route des Calanques, 1 avenue de Dardanelles, tel. 04 42 01 02 97, fax 04 42 01 01 32, www.hotel-cassis.com, larade@hotel-cassis.com).

$$ Hôtel le Golfe**, over a relaxed (but not late-night) café, has good rates, air-conditioning, friendly English-speaking Michele at the desk, and the best views of the port. Half of its basic-but-cute, little, blue-and-yellow rooms come with port views and small balconies and are worth booking ahead (Db with view and possible noise-€80–95, Db without view-€70–85, rates depend on time of year, extra bed-€16, 2 extra beds-€23, 3 parking spaces-€6/day, nearby garage-€8/day, 3 place Grand Carnot, tel. 04 42 01 00 21, fax 04 42 01 92 08).

$$ Hôtel le Clos des Arômes** is for those who don't need to be right on the port and prefer a quieter retreat. This place has appealing ambience with public spaces you can stretch out in. *Très provençal,* it has a big courtyard terrace and a good restaurant. It's run by service-oriented manager Julien and his capable staff, Cédric and Rénault (like the car). The rooms have old furnishings, so-so beds, dim lighting, and no air-conditioning (some have ceiling fans), but the place works in spite of these things (Sb-€50, standard Db-€75, bigger Db-€85, Tb/Qb-€95, Internet access and Wi-Fi, near Parking la Viguerie at 10 rue Abbé Paul Mouton, tel. 04 42 01 71 84, fax 04 42 01 31 76, www.le-clos-des-aromes.com, cannot reserve by e-mail).

$$ Hôtel Cassitel**, located on the harbor over a loud café (particularly noisy on weekends), has decent rooms with air-conditioning and Wi-Fi. The harborview rooms come with night noise (standard Db-€72, large Db-€92, extra bed-€13, garage-€12/day, place Clemenceau, tel. 04 42 01 83 44, fax 04 42 01 96 31, www.hotel-cassis.com, cassitel@hotel-cassis.com).

$ **Hôtel Laurence**** offers Cassis' best budget beds, in small but clean, tasteful, and air-conditioned rooms. Some come with decks and views. You must call a few days ahead to confirm your reservation (Db-€44–64, Db with balcony-€65–80, Db with view terrace-€75–86, extra bed-€13, cash only, closed in winter, 2 blocks off the port beyond Hôtel Cassitel at 8 rue de l'Arène, tel. 04 42 01 88 78, fax 04 42 01 81 04, www.cassis-hotel-laurence.com, contact@cassis-hotel-laurence.com).

On the Plage du Bestouan

The next two hotels are a 10-minute walk from the port on the next beach west, the Plage du Bestouan. Easy parking makes them good for drivers.

$$$ **Mahogany Hôtel de la Plage***** has a big modern exterior, lackluster lobby, and well-conceived rooms at acceptable rates (rooms with decks and sea view-€165, much bigger suite-like rooms without view-€145, includes breakfast, air-con, Plage du Bestouan, tel. 04 42 01 05 70, fax 04 42 01 34 82, www.hotelmahogany.com, info@hotelmahogany.com).

$$$ **Le Jardin d'Emile**** is a villa-hotel located below the Mahogany Hôtel de la Plage. It's a charming little refuge with rich colors inside and out, plush rooms, and a green garden. Six of the seven rooms have decks, and three have sea views (Db-€135–145, includes breakfast, air-con, Plage du Bestouan, tel. 04 42 01 80 55, fax 04 42 01 80 70, www.lejardindemile.fr, provence @lejardindemile.fr).

EATING

Shop the lineup of tempting restaurants along the port, consider the recommended places below, and then decide for yourself. You can have a simple crêpe or go all-out for bouillabaisse with the same great view. Arrive by 19:30 for the view tables. Picnickers can enjoy a "beggars' banquet" at the benches at Hôtel le Golfe or on the beach (small grocery stores open until 19:00).

Dining Portside

The first three places offer €23–25 *menus* and are ideally situated side by side, allowing diners to comparison shop. I've enjoyed good meals at each of them.

El Sol is sharp and popular with discerning diners (closed Mon, 20 quai des Baux, tel. 04 42 01 76 10).

L'Oustau de la Mar is a good choice, with a loyal following, fair prices, and welcoming owner Dominique. Try the *dos de loup de mer à la crème d'olives*—a whitefish smothered in a delectable sauce (closed Thu, 20 quai des Baux, tel. 04 42 01 78 22).

Le Canaille specializes in fresh seafood platters (closed Wed, 22 quai des Baux, tel. 04 42 01 72 36).

Le 8 et Demi serves crêpes, pizza, salads, and good Italian gelato on plastic tables with front-and-center portside views (closed Thu, 8 quai des Baux).

The **Grand Marnier crêpe stand** cooks delicious dessert crêpes to go—the Grand Marnier crêpe rules. This is ideal for strollers (next to recommended Le 8 et Demi restaurant).

Dining Away from the Port

Le Clos des Arômes, listed above in "Sleeping," is the place to come for a refined, candlelit dinner. Dine on a lovely terrace and let Julien take care of your every need (€25 *menu*, open daily, tel. 04 42 01 71 84).

Le Grand Large owns the scenic beachfront next to the TI. Come here for a quiet drink before dinner, or to dine seaside rather than portside (€24 *menu*, open daily, Plage de Cassis, tel. 04 42 01 81 00).

La Girondole is an easy place for families, with inexpensive pizza and salads. It's a block off the port and popular with locals (open daily in summer, closed Tue off-season, 1 rue Thérèse Rastit, tel. 04 42 01 13 39).

TRANSPORTATION CONNECTIONS

While the train station is two miles from the port, shuttle buses meet most trains on weekdays (plus a few on Sat morning, but none on Sun), and taxis are reasonable (about €10 into the center, tel. 04 42 01 78 96). All destinations below require a transfer in Marseille.

From Cassis by Train to: Marseille (20/day, 25 min), **Aix-en-Provence** (12/day, 1.5 hrs, transfer in Marseille), **Arles** (7/day, 2 hrs), **Avignon** (7/day, 2 hrs), **Nice** (14/day, 3 hrs, transfer in Toulon or Marseille), **Paris** (7/day, 4 hrs).

Aix-en-Provence

Aix-en-Provence is famous for its beautiful women and ability to embrace the good life. It was that way when the French king made the town his administrative capital of Provence, and it's that way today. For a tourist, Aix-en-Provence (the "Aix" is pronounced "X") is happily free of any obligatory turnstiles. And there's not a single ancient sight to see. It's just a wealthy town filled with 140,000 people—most of whom, it seems, know how to live well and look good. Aix-en-Provence's 40,000 students (many from other countries) give the city a youthful energy and its well-deserved nickname, "Sex-en-Provence."

ORIENTATION

Aix-en-Provence can be seen in an hour's stroll from the TI or train station. Cours Mirabeau (the grand central boulevard) divides the stately, quiet Mazarin Quarter from the lively and *très* chic old town. In the old town, several squares (hopping with markets several days a week—see "Helpful Hints," below) are laced together by fine pedestrian shopping lanes that lead to the cathedral.

Tourist Information
The TI anchors the west end of cours Mirabeau at La Rotonde traffic circle. You'll feel like you're taking out a loan here, with individual desks and chairs for each information agent. Get a city map and the walking-tour brochure *In the Footsteps of Cézanne,* which also gives you an overview of excursions in the area (Mon–Sat 8:30–19:00, Sun 10:00–13:00 & 14:00–18:00, longer hours in the summer, shorter hours in the winter, 2 place du Général de Gaulle, tel. 04 42 16 11 61, www.aixenprovencetourism.com). They sponsor town walks a few times a week in English (€8).

Arrival in Aix-en-Provence
By Train: Aix-en-Provence has two train stations: Centre-Ville, near the city center; and the outlying TGV station. Neither has luggage storage.

Arrival at the Centre-Ville Station: It's a breezy 10-minute stroll to the TI and pedestrian area (walk straight up avenue Victor Hugo, turn left at first intersection, still on Victor Hugo; TI is on the left when you reach La Rotonde, the big traffic circle).

Arrival at Aix-en-Provence TGV Station: Shuttle buses *(navettes)* connect the distant, futuristic TGV station with Aix-en-Provence's city-center bus station, described below (€4, 3/hr, 15 min; from the tracks, follow signs for *Navette–Aix Centre* to the end of the hall and downstairs; buses leave from an underpass below the tracks). If you're headed to the TGV station, note that the *navettes* usually depart from stall #4 at the bus station (schedule posted).

By Bus: From the bus station *(gare routière)*, it's a gritty 10-minute walk to the TI: Head to the roundabout and turn left

Aix-en-Provence

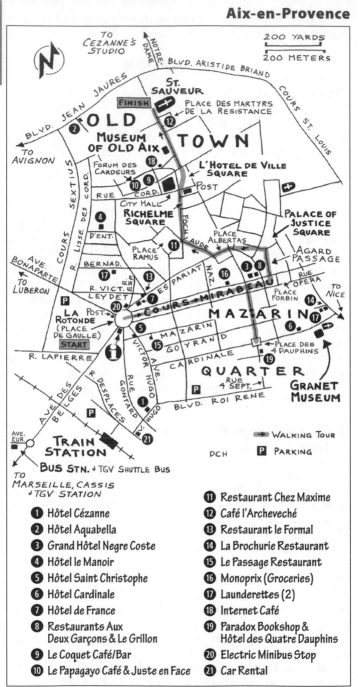

1. Hôtel Cézanne
2. Hôtel Aquabella
3. Grand Hôtel Negre Coste
4. Hôtel le Manoir
5. Hôtel Saint Christophe
6. Hôtel Cardinale
7. Hôtel de France
8. Restaurants Aux Deux Garçons & Le Grillon
9. Le Coquet Café/Bar
10. Le Papagayo Café & Juste en Face
11. Restaurant Chez Maxime
12. Café l'Archevéché
13. Restaurant le Formal
14. La Brochurie Restaurant
15. Le Passage Restaurant
16. Monoprix (Groceries)
17. Launderettes (2)
18. Internet Café
19. Paradox Bookshop & Hôtel des Quatre Dauphins
20. Electric Minibus Stop
21. Car Rental

towards the fountain that's splashing La Rotonde (the big traffic circle by the TI). If you get lost, ask "oo ay la roh-ton-duh?" for help finding La Rotonde.

By Car: Follow signs to *Centre-Ville*, then look for yellow signs to your hotel. If your hotel has parking, follow that sign; otherwise, park in the first pay lot you see once you've spotted your hotel sign (I've noted the closest parking facilities in my hotel descriptions under "Sleeping," below). Day-trippers should look for the La Rotonde parking area, near the TI. If you miss it, follow signs for *gare routière* (bus station), and park there (the 10-min walk to the TI is described above). Allow €13 for 24 hours of parking.

Helpful Hints

Markets: Aix-en-Provence bubbles over with photogenic open-air morning markets in several of its squares: Richelme (produce daily), Palace of Justice and cours Mirabeau (flea market Tue, Thu, and Sat), and L'Hôtel de Ville (flower market Tue, Thu, and Sat; book market on first Sun of each month). Most pack up at 13:00, except the book market, which runs all day. The markets so enliven the town, it's well worth planning your visit for a market day if at all possible.

Internet Access: Internet cafés are plentiful in this college town. Ask at your hotel, or try **ProGamers,** with the longest hours (Mon–Sat 10:00–24:00, Sun 14:00–22:00, 14 forum des Cardeurs, tel. 04 42 96 14 22).

English Bookstore: A modest collection of adult and children's books (and a small supply of American grocery staples, like peanut butter) are available at the helpful **Paradox bookshop,** located on the quiet side of Aix-en-Provence. The owner, Ms. Graillon, carries my guidebooks, speaks fluent English, and is a good source for information (Mon–Sat 10:00–12:30 & 14:00–18:30, closed Sun, 15 rue du 4 Septembre, tel. 04 42 26 47 99).

Laundry: There's a launderette at 11 rue des Bernadines, and another at 3 rue Fernand Dol (both daily 8:00–19:00).

Supermarket: Monoprix, on cours Mirabeau, has a grocery store in the basement (Mon–Sat 8:30–21:00, closed Sun).

Taxi: Call tel. 04 42 27 71 11 or 06 16 23 82 39.

Car Rental: Hertz is at 43 avenue Victor Hugo, across from the Centre-Ville train station, tel. 04 42 27 91 32.

Local Guide: Caroline Bernard speaks great English and enjoys teaching visitors about the wonders of her city (bernardcaro @aol.com, or contact her through the TI).

Electric Minibus Joyride: For a mere €0.50, take an orientation ride on a *Diabline*—a six-seater electric-powered minibus that operates two routes through the old town. It leaves every

Aix-en-Provence History

Aix-en-Provence was founded in about 120 B.C. as a Roman military camp on the site of a thermal hot spring. The Romans' mission: To defend the Greek merchants of Marseille against the local Celts. Strategically situated Aix-en-Provence was the first Roman base outside of Italy—the first foreign holding of what would become a vast empire. (The region's name—Provence—comes from its status as the first Roman province.) But Rome eventually fell, and the barbarians destroyed Aix-en-Provence in the fourth century. Through the Dark Ages, Aix-en-Provence's Roman buildings were nibbled to nothing by people needing the pre-cut stone. No buildings from Roman Aix-en-Provence survive.

Aix-en-Provence was of no importance through the Middle Ages. Because the area was once owned by Barcelona, Provence has the same colors as Catalunya: gold and red. In 1481, the Count of Provence died. He was hairless (according to my guide). Without a hair, Provence was gobbled up by France. When Aix-en-Provence was made the district's administrative center, noble French families moved in, kicking off the city's beautiful age (belle époque). They built about 200 *hôtels particuliers* (private mansions)—many of which survive today, giving Aix-en-Provence its classy appearance. As you wander around the town, look up, peek in, and notice the stately architecture with its grandiose extra touches.

Aix-en-Provence thrived thanks to its aristocratic population. But when the Revolution made being rich dangerous, Aix-en-Provence's aristocracy and clergy fled. Aix-en-Provence entered the next stage of its history as the "Sleeping Beauty city." Later in the 19th century, the town woke up and resumed its pretentious ways. In Aix-en-Provence, the custom of rich people being bobbed along in sedan chairs survived longer than anywhere else in France. After the Revolution, you couldn't have servants do it—but you could hire pallbearers in their off-hours to give you a lift. If ostentatiousness ever became the norm…it happened in Aix-en-Provence.

10 minutes from the La Rotonde fountain, opposite the TI (Mon–Sat 8:30–13:00 & 15:00–19:30, none on Sun, 40 min round-trip). You can also wave down the driver anywhere to let him know you want to get on. There are two minibus lines (A and B, ask the driver for a map when you get on); line A gives you a better overview of the city. Designed with local seniors in mind, the minibus provides a fun (and less glamorous) slice-of-life experience in Aix-en-Provence.

Petit Train: Rest your feet and discover Aix-en-Provence's historic center on a 50-minute tour on the little train, while listening to English commentary (€6, depart from La Rotonde fountain). Ask about the longer tours that cover Cézanne's steps.

Dark Sunglasses: You may want to pick up a pair of especially dark glasses to be more discreet when appreciating the beautiful people of Aix-en-Provence.

SELF-GUIDED WALK

Welcome to Aix-en-Provence

I've listed these streets, squares, and sights in the order of a handy, lazy orientation stroll. Start at the TI, on the big round square.

La Rotonde: In the 1600s, the roads from Paris and Marseille met just outside the Aix-en-Provence town wall at a huge roundabout called La Rotonde. From here, locals enjoyed a sweeping view of open countryside before entering the town. As time passed, Aix-en-Provence needed space more than fortifications. The wall was destroyed, and replaced by a grand boulevard (cours Mirabeau). A modern grid-plan town, the Mazarin Quarter, arose across the boulevard from the medieval town. In 1860, to give residents water and shade, the town graced La Rotonde with a fountain and the boulevard with trees. Voilà: The modern core of Aix-en-Provence was created.

Cours Mirabeau: This "Champs-Elysées of Provence" divides the higgledy-piggledy old town and the stately Mazarin Quarter. Designed for the rich and famous to strut their fancy stuff, cours Mirabeau survives much as it was: a single lane for traffic and a very wide pedestrian promenade, shaded by plane trees (see sidebar on page 222) and lined by 17th- and 18th-century mansions for the nobility.

The street follows a plan based on fours: 440 meters long, 44 meters wide, plane trees (originally

Plane Trees

Stately old plane trees line roads and provide canopies of shade for town squares all over southern France. These trees are a part of the local scene.

The plane tree is a hybrid of the Asian and American sycamores—created accidentally in a 16th-century Oxford botanical garden. The result was the perfect city tree: fast-growing, resistant to urban pollution, and hearty (it can survive with little water and lousy soil). The plane tree was imported to southern France in the 19th century to replace the traditional elm trees. Napoleon planted them along roads to give his soldiers shade for their long marches. Plane trees were used to leaf up grand boulevards as towns throughout France—including Aix-en-Provence—built their Champs-Elysées wannabes.

elms) four meters apart, and decorated by four fountains. The "mossy fountain"—its original little angels covered by 200 years of neglect—trickles with water from the thermal spa. At the end of the boulevard, a statue celebrates the last count of Provence, under whose rule this region joined France.

Cours Mirabeau was designed for showing off. Today, it remains a place for *tendance* (trendiness)—or even *hyper-tendance*. Show your stuff and strut the broad sidewalk. Grab a seat in an upscale café (such as Café le Grillon at #49) and observe.

• *From the mossy fountain, rue du 4 Septembre leads into Aix-en-Provence's quiet side, directly to the appealing little place des Quatre Dauphins. This marks the center of the...*

Mazarin Quarter (Quartier Mazarin): Built in a grid plan during the reign of King Louis XIV, the Mazarin Quarter remains an elegant residential neighborhood—although each of its mansions now houses several families rather than just one. Study the quarter's Baroque and Neoclassical architecture (from the 17th and 18th centuries). The square's Fountain of the Four Dolphins, inspired by Bernini's fountains in Rome, dates from an age when Italian culture set the Baroque standard across Europe.

• *After a quick nip through the Mazarin Quarter, return to the cours Mirabeau and pop into #53, the venerable...*

Aux Deux Garçons: This café, once frequented by Paul Cézanne, is now popular with the local mafia—don't take photos. Check out its beautiful circa 1790 interior. It's a fine place for a

Paul Cézanne in Aix-en-Provence

Post-Impressionist artist Paul Cézanne (1839–1906) loved Aix-en-Provence. He studied law at the university (opposite the cathedral), and produced most of his paintings in and around Aix-en-Provence—even though this conservative town didn't understand him or his art. Today the city fathers milk anything remotely related to his years here. But because the conservative curator of the town's leading art gallery, the Granet Museum, decreed "no Cézannes," you won't be able to see any of Cézanne's original paintings in Aix-en-Provence. Bad curator.

Instead, fans of the artist will want to pick up the *In the Footsteps of Cézanne* self-guided-tour flier at the TI, and follow the bronze pavement markers around town.

Cézanne's **last studio** (Atelier Cézanne)—preserved as it was when he died—is open to the public. While there is no art here, his tools and personal belongings make it interesting for enthusiasts (€6, daily July–Aug 10:00–18:00, April–June and Sept 10:00–12:00 & 14:00–18:00, Oct–March until 17:00, 2 miles from TI at 9 avenue Cézanne, tel. 04 42 21 06 53, www.atelier-cezanne.com).

pricey drink or meal (see "Eating," page 227). The Cézanne family hat shop was next door (#55). Cézanne's dad must have been some hatter. He parlayed that successful business into a bank, then into greater wealth, setting up his son to be free to enjoy his artistic pursuits.

• *From here, we venture into the lively Old Town, where peaceful pedestrian streets are alive with strolling beauties and romantic street musicians. This is the place in Aix-en-Provence for shopping. Leave cours Mirabeau down the tiny passage Agard, 10 steps past Aux Deux Garçons, and continue down the passage for 100 yards. It leads directly to the **Palace of Justice Square**, which hosts a bustling flea market (Tue, Thu, and Sat mornings). Leave this square heading left along the first street you crossed to enter it. Rue Marius*

Reinaud hosts the top designer shops in town. Pause at the peaceful courtyard square of...

Place d'Albertas: This sweet little square was created by the guy who lived across the street at #10. He hated the medieval mess of buildings facing his mansion, so he drew up a harmonious facade with a fountain, and hired an architect to build his ideal vision and mask the ugly neighborhood. The neighbors got a nice new facade, and the rich guy got the view of his dreams.

• *From here, turn right on rue Aude, the main street of medieval Aix-en-Provence (which leads ultimately to the cathedral). Notice how effectively the green bollards keep cars from parking in this virtual car-free zone. Notice also the side streets, with their traffic-barrier stumps that lower during delivery hours. Make your way to...*

Richelme Square (Place Richelme): This square hosts a lively market, as it has for centuries (daily 7:00–13:00). It's a quintessential Provençal scene—classic architecture, plane trees, farmers selling local produce, and a guy in the goat-cheese stall who looks just like Paul Cézanne—or Jerry Garcia, if that's more your style. (He's fully aware of his special good looks. Drop by for a sample and a photo if you like.)

• *One block uphill is the stately...*

L'Hôtel de Ville Square (Place de l'Hôtel de Ville): This square, also known as place de la Mairie, is marked by a Roman column. Stand with your back to the column and face the Hôtel de Ville. The center niche of this 17th-century city hall once featured a bust of Louis XIV. But since the Revolution, Marianne (the Lady of the Republic) has taken his place. As throughout Europe, the three flags represent the region (Provence), country (France), and

the European Union. Provence's flag carries the red and yellow of Catalunya (the region in Spain centered on Barcelona) because the counts of Provence originated there. The coat of arms combines the Catalan flag and the French fleur-de-lis.

The 18th-century building on your left was once the town's corn exchange. Its glorious pediment features figures representing the two rivers of Provence: old man Rhône and the Durance. While the Durance River floods frequently (here depicted overflowing its frame), it also brings fertility to the fields (hence the cornucopia). The 16th-century bell tower opposite the corn exchange was built in part with stones scavenged from ancient Roman buildings (the white ones at the tower's base). The niche above the arch once displayed the bust of the king. Since the Revolution, it has housed a funerary urn that symbolically honors all who gave their lives for French liberty. Below, you'll find a small plaque that honors those who liberated the town in 1944. (Aix-en-Provence got through WWII relatively unscathed.)

History aside, the square is a favorite part of the Aix-en-Provence experience for its colorful morning markets: flowers (Tue, Thu, and Sat) and old books (Sun). Each afternoon, café tables replace the market stalls.

• *Stroll under the bell tower and up rue Gaston de Saporta, to the...*

Museum of Old Aix-en-Provence (Musée du Vieil Aix): This museum fills a 17th-century mansion with a scant collection of artifacts. The building interior itself is of most interest. Pop in for a look at the grand staircase and fancy ceilings. The exhibits include lots of *santons*—painted clay figurines popular in old-time manger scenes (€4, pick up the English handout, April–Sept Tue–Sun 10:00–12:00 & 14:30–18:00, Oct–March until 17:00, closed Mon, 17 rue Gaston de Saporta, tel. 04 42 21 43 55).

• *A block farther uphill, facing the historic university building (where Cézanne studied) is the...*

Cathedral of the Holy Savior (Saint-Sauveur): This church was built atop the Roman forum—likely on the site of a pagan temple. As the cathedral grew with the city, its interior became a parade of architectural styles. The many-faceted interior is at once confusing and fascinating, with three distinct sections: Standing at the entrance, you face the Romanesque section; to the left are the Gothic and then the Baroque sections. We'll visit each in turn.

In the **Romanesque section,** branching off to the right is the baptistery, with its early Christian (fourth-century) Roman font. It's big enough for immersion, which was the baptismal style in Roman times. Also notice that it's eight-sided, symbolizing eternity: one side more than the seven days it took God to create everything. The font is surrounded by ancient columns with original fourth-century capitals below a Renaissance cupola. Farther down is the door to the 12th-century cloister (viewable free upon request to church attendant). Beyond that, find the architectural footprint of the tiny original Roman Christian chapel.

In the **Gothic section,** two organs flank the nave: One works, but the other is a prop, added for looks...an appropriately symmetrical Neoclassical touch, as was the style in the 18th century. The precious door (facing the street from this section) is carved of chestnut with a Gothic top (showing sibyls, or ancient female prophets) and Renaissance lower half (depicting prophets). Since it faces the street, it's covered by a second, protective door (also viewable on request).

In the **Baroque section,** don't miss the finely detailed three-paneled altar painting of the burning bush (15th century, by Nicolas Froment).

• *Your tour is over. Walking back through town, drop by a bakery to try a calisson, Aix-en-Provence's local pastry (popular all over France). It's made with almond paste—kind of like a marzipan cake. Or, for fewer calories and just as much fun, marvel at a town filled with people who seem to be living life very, very well.*

SLEEPING

(€1 = about $1.30, country code: 33)

Hotel rooms, starting at about €50, are surprisingly reasonable in this highbrow city. Reserve ahead for the first three hotels, particularly on weekends. Stars have little meaning in this town.

$$$ Hôtel Cézanne****, a block up from the Centre-Ville train station, has a safari-themed lobby and 55 plush rooms with every creature comfort (standard Db-€145, deluxe Db-€160, suite Db-€200, some king-size beds, air-con, free minibar, elevator, free Internet access and Wi-Fi, 40 avenue Victor Hugo, tel. 04 42 91 11 11, fax 04 42 91 11 10, www.hotelaix.com, hotelcezanne@hotelaix.com).

$$$ Hôtel Aquabella**** is a razzle-dazzle, resort-and-business-class hotel that tries to be all things to all people...and it seems to work. It's big, modern, and stylish, with an Olympic-size pool flanked by a snazzy café-restaurant. There's also an indoor pool, Jacuzzi, sauna, and exercise room. The 110 amply sized rooms are Holiday Inn–predictable, but tastefully appointed. Half come with decks and views over the old city (Db-€160, Db with deck and view-€180, suite Db-€200, air-con, bathrobes, elevators, parking garage, near the ring road at 2 rue des Etuves, tel. 04 42 99 15 00, fax 04 42 99 15 01, www.aquabella.fr, info@aquabella.fr).

$$$ Grand Hôtel Negre Coste*** occupies a privileged position at the center of cours Mirabeau. It's a faded, grand hotel where rooms are as traditional as the staff is formal (Db-€85–105, big Db-€130–145, air-con, Internet access and Wi-Fi, 33 cours Mirabeau, closest parking is La Rotonde, tel. 04 42 27 74 22, fax 04 42 26 80 93, www.hotelnegrecoste.com, contact@hotelnegrecoste.com).

$$ Hôtel le Manoir**** is a find—simple, peaceful, and central, built on the heavy arches of a medieval monastery. Most of its 40 smallish rooms hang over a large courtyard. The decor is strictly traditional, and the air is pin-drop quiet...but not conditioned (small Db-€60, standard Db-€78, big Db-€90, Tb-€90, Qb-€98, elevator, limited free parking, 8 rue d'Entrecasteaux, tel. 04 42 26 27 20, fax 04 42 27 17 97, www.hotelmanoir.com, infos@hotelmanoir.com).

$$ Hôtel Saint Christophe**, a business hotel with fair-enough rates, is located right behind the TI and above a swanky brasserie. It has 58 average-but-quiet rooms, some with small terraces (Db-€80–92, Tb-€105–115, mezzanine suite sleeps up to 4-€100–140, air-con, elevator, parking garage-€11, 2 avenue Victor Hugo, tel. 04 42 26 01 24, fax 04 42 38 53 17, www.hotel -saintchristophe.com, saintchristophe@francemarket.com).

$$ Hôtel Cardinale** is a solid value on Aix-en-Provence's classy side, across cours Mirabeau from the pedestrian zone. It's a shy, rose-colored hotel with 29 traditionally furnished rooms and a helpful owner, Madame Bernhard (Sb-€60, Db-€70, cavernous Db suite in nearby annex €105, elevator, Internet access, closest parking is Mignet, 24 rue Cardinale, tel. 04 42 38 32 30, fax 04 42 26 39 05, hotel.cardinale@wanadoo.fr).

$$ Hôtel des Quatre Dauphins** is a small, unassuming hotel in the quiet quarter with traditional decor, soft rooms, and fair prices (Db-€70–85, bigger Db with bath-€80–100, Tb-€120, air-con, closest parking is Mignet, 54 rue Roux Alphéran, tel. 04 42 38 16 19, fax 04 42 38 60 19).

$$ Hôtel de France** couldn't be more central, in the thick of the pedestrian zone near the TI. The place is frumpy, with some squishy beds, and it could use some upgrading—but that keeps the prices acceptable. Rooms on the noisier street side are bigger than on the quieter courtyard side (Db-€66, bigger Db-€72–82, air-con, elevator, 63 rue Espariat, use La Rotonde parking, tel. 04 42 27 90 15, fax 04 42 26 11 47, www.hoteldefrance-aix.com, hoteldefrance-aix @wanadoo.fr, Mr. Gaunet doesn't speak English).

EATING

In Aix-en-Provence, you can dine on squares, along a grand boulevard, or tucked into little restaurants on side streets. The squares are mostly for desserts and drinks (consider dining better elsewhere without the ambience, then heading to a square for dessert). Cours Mirabeau hosts the promenade scene, with plenty of eating options.

Along Cours Mirabeau

If you're interested in a delicious view more than delicious food, eat with style on cours Mirabeau. If you need to see and be seen, **Aux Deux Garçons** has always been the place: a vintage brasserie with door-to-door waiters in aprons, a magnificent interior, and well-positioned outdoor tables with properly placed silverware on white tablecloths (€18 *plats*, 2-course *menus* from €28, open daily, 53 cours Mirabeau, tel. 04 42 26 00 51). Even if you're not eating here, pop in to see the decor (see page 222).

Le Grillon, both a restaurant and a bar, is my choice on cours Mirabeau (white tablecloths, €15 *plats*). Its bar is a hit with locals for the prime seating: front and center on the boulevard's strolling fashion show. One key to its popularity is a generous happy hour featuring some cheaper drinks that come with tasty and free tapas (€4.50 cocktails, happy hour daily 18:00–21:00, open daily for lunch and dinner, corner of rue Clémenceau and cours Mirabeau, tel. 42 27 58 81).

On Aix-en-Provence's Squares

While Aix-en-Provence is blessed with many atmospheric squares, few come with real restaurants. To eat outdoors enjoying the ambience of a square, consider these options.

On Forum des Cardeurs: Just off L'Hôtel de Ville Square, the forum des Cardeurs is filled with a sea of tables. **Le Coquet Café/ Bar** works for basic café fare and serious people-watching (open daily, 2 forum des Cardeurs, tel. 04 42 23 46 21). The food is better farther on at **Le Papagayo,** which has a good selection of salads and a quiche of the day (big €14 salads, open daily for lunch and dinner, 22 forum des Cardeurs, tel. 04 42 23 98 35). **Juste en Face** features grilled specialties and Mediterranean cuisine prepared with ingredients fresh from the market (open daily, 6 rue Verrerie, tel. 04 42 96 47 70).

On Place Ramus: Both romantic and convivial, this square has a fun selection of restaurants (French, Vietnamese, and a very popular Italian) competing for its shady cobbles. **Restaurant Chez Maxime** is good for Provençal cuisine with jolly service—but double-check your bill (closed Sun, tel. 04 42 26 28 51).

On Place des Martyrs de la Resistance: A short block below the cathedral, this square is good for a light meal. **Café l'Archeveché** is reasonable and understandably proud of its pizzas (lunch only except June–mid-Sept, tel. 04 42 21 43 57).

Eateries Where You'll Pay for Food Rather than Location

Restaurant le Formal is the love child of Jean-Luc le Formal and Yvonne Kruithof, who cook and serve beautifully presented dishes in their comfortable and welcoming eatery. In romantic nooks, in-the-know locals enjoy their hosts' "inventive French nouveau cuisine" (€30 *menu*, lunch specials, reservations wise for dinner, Tue–Sat lunch from 12:00 and dinner from 19:30, closed Sun– Mon, 32 rue Espariat, tel. 04 42 27 08 31).

La Brochurie offers French rather than Provençal cuisine, and a stony, rustic ambience. This friendly, family-run bistro—run by Messieurs Soudain and Tourville—is in the Mazarin Quarter. Dig into the hearty self-service salad buffet (all you can eat, €12), meats grilled over a wood fire, and a good €18 *menu* that includes the salad bar (closed Sun, indoor seating only, 5 rue Fernand Dol, tel. 04 42 38 33 21).

Le Passage, a dazzling eatery without a tourist in sight, caters to locals by combining a simple, modern menu with a love of wine. Trendy yet inviting, the spacious atrium interior has several floors (each with a different ambience), a wine bar, and a breezy backyard terrace. Monday nights have live jazz from 20:00. Its slogan, *le goût du plaisir* ("the taste of pleasure"), says it all (ground floor limited to daily €20–35 *menus,* upstairs serves à la carte, great prices from extensive list of fine French wines, daily 10:00–24:00, hiding out a block off La Rotonde at 10 rue Villars, tel. 04 42 37 09 00).

TRANSPORTATION CONNECTIONS

Remember, Aix-en-Provence has both a TGV station and a Centre-Ville station (see "Arrival in Aix-en-Provence," page 217). In some cases, destinations are served from both stations; I've listed the station with the best connection.

From Aix-en-Provence's Centre-Ville Station by Train to: Marseille (18/day, 35 min), **Cassis** (12/day, 1.5 hrs, transfer in Marseille), **Arles** (10/day, 2 hrs, transfer in Marseille).

From Aix-en-Provence's TGV Station by Train to: Avignon TGV (10/day, 25 min), **Nice** (10/day, 3.5 hrs, usually change in Marseille), **Paris** (14/day, 3 hrs, may require transfer in Lyon).

From Aix-en-Provence by Bus to: Marseille (4/hr, 50 min), **Marseille airport** (2/hr, 30 min), **Lourmarin** (75 min total—bus to Pertuis leaves 2/hr, transfer there to Avignon-bound bus, 3/day).

THE FRENCH RIVIERA

La Côte d'Azur

A hundred years ago, celebrities from London to Moscow flocked to the French Riviera to socialize, gamble, and escape the dreary weather at home. Belle époque resorts now also cater to budget vacationers at France's most sought-after, fun-in-the-sun destination. This scenic strip is speckled with intriguing museums and countless sun-worshippers.

The region got its nickname from turn-of-the-20th-century vacationing Brits, who simply extended the Italian Riviera west to France. Their original definition of the French Riviera only went as far as Nice, though the Riviera label has been stretched west since these Victorian Brits strolled their promenade. Today, this summer fun zone—which, for our purposes, runs from St-Tropez to the Italian border—is *La Côte d'Azur* to the French. All of my French Riviera destinations are on the sea, except for a few hill towns and the Gorges du Verdon.

This sunny sliver of land has been inhabited for more than 3,000 years. Ligurians were first, then Greeks, then Romans—who, as usual, had the greatest impact. After the fall of Rome, Nice became an important city in the Kingdom of Provence (along with Marseille and Arles). In the 14th century, Nice's leaders voted to throw their beach towel in with the Duke of Savoy's mountainous kingdom (also including several regions of northern Italy), which would later evolve into the Kingdom of Sardinia. It was not until 1860 that Nice (and Savoy) became a part of France—the result of a citywide vote made possible by Napoleon III and the King of Sardinia.

Nice has world-class museums, a splendid beachfront promenade, a seductive old town, and all the drawbacks of a major city (traffic, crime, pollution, and so on). But the day-trip possibilities are easy and exciting: Monte Carlo welcomes everyone with its cash registers open; Antibes has a romantic port and silky sand

The French Riviera

beaches; and gentle Cannes is the Riviera's self-appointed queen, with an elegant veneer hiding...very little. Yacht-crazy St-Tropez swims alone an hour west (halfway to Cassis and Marseille). The Riviera's overlooked interior offers travelers a world apart, with cliff-hanging villages, impossibly steep canyons, and alpine scenery—a refreshing alternative to the beach scene.

Choose a Home Base

My favorite home bases are Nice, Antibes, and Villefranche-sur-Mer.

Nice is the region's capital and France's fifth-largest city. With convenient train and bus connections to most regional sights, this is the most practical base for train travelers. Urban Nice also has a full palette of museums, a beach scene that rocks, the best selection of hotels in all price ranges, and good nightlife options. A car is a headache in Nice, though it's easily stored at one of the many pricey parking garages.

Nearby **Antibes** is smaller, with a bustling center, terrific nightlife, great sandy beaches, grand vistas, and good walking trails. (Its much-admired Picasso Museum should reopen in early 2008 after renovation.) Antibes has frequent train service to Nice and Monaco, and it's easy for drivers.

Villefranche-sur-Mer is the romantic's choice, with a serene setting and small-town warmth. It has finely ground pebble beaches, quick public transportation to Nice and Monaco, easy parking, and hotels in most price ranges.

Planning Your Time

Ideally, allow a day and a half for Nice itself, an afternoon to explore inland hill towns, a day for Italian-esque Villefranche-sur-Mer and lovely Cap Ferrat, a day for Monaco and the Corniches, and—if time allows—a day for Antibes and Cannes. Consider using two different Riviera bases, and enjoy each for at least two nights—Villefranche-sur-Mer pairs well with Antibes or Nice. And if you must do St-Tropez, visit it while traveling to or from destinations farther west (such as Cassis, Aix-en-Provence, and Arles) and avoid it on weekend afternoons, as well as all summer.

Monaco has a unique energy at night, and Antibes is best during the day (good beaches and hiking). Hill town– and nature-lovers should add a night or two inland, to explore the charming, hill-capping hamlets near Vence and the Gorges du Verdon.

Priorities: Depending on the amount of time you have in the Riviera, spend it this way:

3 days:	Nice, Villefranche-sur-Mer with Cap Ferrat, and Monaco
5 days, add:	Antibes and maybe Cannes, and hill towns near Vence
7 days, add:	Gorges du Verdon and St-Tropez

Helpful Hints

Medical Help: Riviera Medical Services has a list of English-speaking physicians for anywhere along the Riviera. They can help you make an appointment or call an ambulance (tel. 04 93 26 12 70, www.rivieramedical.com).

Sightseeing Schedules: On Monday, the Modern and Contemporary Art Museum, Fine Arts Museum, and cours Saleya market in Nice, along with Antibes' Marché Provençal, are closed; on Tuesday, the Chagall, Matisse, and Archaeological museums in Nice are closed.

Events: The Riviera is famous for staging major events. Unless you're actually taking part in the festivities, these events give you only room shortages and traffic jams. Here are the three biggies in 2008: Nice Carnival (Feb 16–March 2), Grand Prix of Monaco (May 22–25), and Festival de Cannes, better known as the Cannes Film Festival (May 14–25).

Getting Around the Riviera

By Train and Bus: Trains and buses do a good job of connecting places along the coast (with views along many sections), and buses provide reasonable service to some inland hill towns. The high-speed TGV trains stop in Cannes and Antibes, as well as in Nice and Marseille. Nice is well-connected to most sights on the Riviera (for details on all the connections, see "Getting Around the Riviera" in the Nice chapter). While trains are usually faster, buses can be cheaper and more frequent to destinations near Nice. St-Tropez is remote, requiring a bus or boat connection. Details are provided under each destination's "Transportation Connections" section. For a scenic inland train ride, take the narrow-gauge train into the Alps (see page 253).

By Car: After Paris, this is France's second most challenging region to drive in. The dangerous combination of loads of Sunday-driving tourists and beautifully distracting vistas (natural and human), along with the sheer number of cars, means you need to pay extra attention down here. Parking can be tricky for the same reasons, so have patience and consider the bus or train. Have lots of coins ready for parking and for autoroute tolls.

The Riviera bubbles over with scenic roads. To sample some of the Riviera's best scenery, drivers should not miss the splendid coastal road between Cannes and Fréjus (D-98), which works well when connecting the Riviera with Provence—if it weren't for the Mediterranean sea below, you'd swear you were in Arizona (in Fréjus, follow signs to *Centre-Ville*, then *Cannes par la Bord de la Mer;* from Cannes, drive to the western end of town and follow *La Napoule* to reach the road). Drivers should also scour the three Corniches between Nice and Monaco (see page 294) and take my recommended inland hill-towns drive (on page 344). Farther inland, the Gorges du Verdon patiently awaits, with breathtaking canyons and alpine scenery. But even if you have a car, consider the convenience that trains and buses offer for basic sightseeing between Monaco and Cannes.

By Boat: Trans Côte d'Azur offers boat service from Nice to Monaco or to St-Tropez from June into September, as well as between Cannes and St-Tropez (tel. 04 92 00 42 30, www.trans-cote-azur.com). For details, see "Getting Around the Riviera" in the Nice chapter (page 240).

The Riviera's Art Scene

The list of artists who have painted the Riviera reads like a Who's Who of 20th-century art. Pierre-Auguste Renoir, Henri Matisse, Marc Chagall, Georges Braque, Raoul Dufy, Fernand Léger, and Pablo Picasso all lived and worked here—and raved about the region's wonderful light. Their simple, semi-abstract, and—most

Top Sights of the Riviera

Fondation Maeght (St-Paul-de-Vence)
Chagall Museum (Nice)
Picasso Museum (Antibes, reopens in early 2008)
Matisse Museum (Nice)
Museum of the Annonciade (St-Tropez)
Chapel of the Rosary (Vence)
Modern and Contemporary Art Museum (Nice)
Fine Arts Museum (Nice)
Renoir Museum (Cagnes-sur-Mer)

importantly—colorful works reflect the Riviera. You'll experience the same landscapes they painted in this bright, sun-drenched region, punctuated with views of the "azure sea." Try to imagine the Riviera with a fraction of the people and development you see today.

But the artists were mostly drawn to the uncomplicated lifestyle of fishermen and farmers that has reigned here since time began. As the artists grew older, they retired in the sun, turned their backs on modern art's "isms," and painted with the wide-eyed wonder of children, using bright primary colors, basic outlines, and simple subjects.

A dynamic concentration of well-organized modern- and contemporary-art museums (many described in this book) litter the Riviera, allowing art-lovers to appreciate these artists' works while immersed in the same sun and culture that inspired them. Many of the museums were designed to blend the art with the surrounding views, gardens, and fountains, thus highlighting that modern art is not only stimulating, but sometimes simply beautiful.

Entire books have been written about the modern-art galleries of the Riviera. If you're a modern-art fan, do some studying before your visit to be sure you know about that far-out museum of your dreams. Take the opportunity to experience the brilliant display of modern art, even if you aren't usually turned on by it, by visiting the Fondation Maeght in St-Paul-de-Vence, and the Chagall and Matisse museums in Nice.

The Riviera's Cuisine Scene

The Riviera adds a Mediterranean flair to the food of Provence. While many of the same dishes served in Provence are available throughout the Riviera (see "Provence's Cuisine Scene," page 37), celebrate the differences by looking for anything Italian or from the sea. The proximity to the water and historic ties to Italy are clear in this region's dishes.

La salade niçoise (nee-swahz) is where most Riviera meals start. A true specialty from Nice, this salad has many versions, though most include a base of green salad topped with green beans, boiled potatoes (sometimes rice), tomatoes (sometimes corn), anchovies, olives, hard-boiled eggs, and lots of tuna. Every café and restaurant adds its own twist to this filling dish that goes down well on sultry days.

For lunch on the go, look for a *pan bagnat* (like a *salade niçoise* stuffed into a hollowed-out soft roll). Other tasty bread treats include *pissaladière* (bread dough topped with onions, olives, and anchovies), *fougasse* (a spindly, lace-like bread sometimes flavored with nuts, herbs, olives, or ham), and *socca* (a thin chickpea crêpe, seasoned with pepper and olive oil and often served in a paper cone by street vendors).

Invented in Nice, ravioli and potato gnocchi can be found on menus everywhere (ravioli can be stuffed with a variety of fillings, but it's best with seafood). Thin-crust pizza and *pâtes fraîches* (fresh pasta) are generally a good value throughout the Riviera.

Bouillabaisse is the Riviera's most famous dish; look for it in any seafront village or city. It's a spicy fish stew based on recipes handed down from sailors in Marseille. It must contain at least four types of fresh fish, though most have five to twelve kinds. A true bouillabaisse never has shellfish. The fish—cooked in a tomato-based stock and flavored with saffron (and sometimes anise and orange)—is separated from the stock before serving. The cook then heightens the flavor of the stock by adding toasted croutons and a dollop of *rouille* sauce (a thickened reddish mayonnaise heady with garlic and spicy peppers). This dish often requires a minimum order of two to justify its considerable preparation time, so beware of sticker shock and allow €35–40.

Those on a budget can enjoy other seafood soups and stews. Less pricey but equally good is the local *soupe de poisson* (fish soup). It's flavored like bouillabaisse, with anise and orange, and served with croutons and *rouille* sauce. For a less colorful but still tasty soup, look for *bourride,* a creamy fish soup thickened with an aioli garlic sauce instead of the red *rouille* or *baudroie,* a fishy soup cooked with vegetables and garlic.

The Riviera specializes in all sorts of fish and shellfish. Other options include *"fruits de mer,"* or platters of seafood (including tiny shellfish, from which you get the edible part only by sucking really hard), herb-infused mussels, stuffed sardines, squid (slowly simmered with tomatoes and herbs), and tuna *(thon).* The popular *loup flambé au fenouil* is grilled sea bass, flavored with fennel and torched with *pastis* prior to serving.

Cheese and dessert dishes of the Riviera are indistinguishable from those in Provence. Refer to "Provence's Cuisine Scene" (page 37) for suggestions.

You're better off avoiding fixed-price *menus* at most places and just ordering a first course and a main course, or a main course and dessert. I prefer licking my dessert on an after-dinner waterfront stroll (works great in all three home bases I recommend).

Unfortunately, memorable restaurants that showcase the Riviera's cuisine are more difficult to find than in neighboring Provence. Because most visitors come more for the sun than the food, and because the clientele is predominantly international, many restaurants aim for the middle and are hard to tell apart. When dining on the Riviera, I look for views and ambience more than top-quality cuisine.

Wines of the Riviera

Do as everyone else does: Drink wines from Provence. *Bandol* (red) and *cassis* (white) are popular, and from a region nearly on the Riviera. The only wines made in the Riviera are Bellet rosé and white, the latter often found in fish-shaped bottles. For more on Provençal wine, see page 39.

NICE

Nice (sounds like "niece"), with its spectacular Alps-to-Mediterranean surroundings, eternally entertaining seafront promenade, and intriguing museums, is an enjoyable big-city highlight of the Riviera. In its traffic-free old city, Italian and French flavors mix to create a spicy Mediterranean dressing. Nice may be nice, but it's hot and jammed in July and August—reserve ahead and get a room with air-conditioning *(une chambre avec climatisation)*. Everything you'll want to see in Nice is walkable or a short bus or taxi ride away.

ORIENTATION

Most recommended sights and hotels are between the train station and the beach, near avenue Jean Médecin or boulevard Victor Hugo. It's a 20-minute walk (or a €10 taxi ride) from the train station to the beach, and a 20-minute walk along the promenade from the fancy Hôtel Negresco to the heart of Old Nice.

The first of three new tramway lines should be running in time for your visit in 2008 (see "Getting Around Nice" on page 240).

Tourist Information

Nice's helpful TI has three locations: at the **airport** (daily 8:00–21:00), next to the **train station** (usually busy, Mon–Sat 8:00–19:00, Sun 10:00–17:00, 1 hour later in summer), and facing the **beach** at 5 promenade des Anglais (often fairly quiet, daily 9:00–18:00, until 20:00 July–Aug, tel. 08 92 70 74 07 costs €0.34/min, www.nicetourisme.com). Pick up the thorough *Practical Guide to Nice*, information on day trips (such as city maps and details on boat excursions), and a free Nice map (or find a better one at your hotel).

Only art-lovers should consider buying the seven-day, Nice-only **museum pass,** called Carte Passe-Musées 7 Jours (€7, does not include Chagall Museum). A second museum pass, the Riviera Carte Musée, may be brought back for 2008—ask about it at any TI (this pass had been discontinued when many museums were undergoing extensive renovation, but most will be open again in 2008).

Arrival in Nice

By Train: All trains stop at Nice's main station, Nice-Ville (baggage check at the far right with your back to the tracks, lockers open daily 7:00–21:45, left luggage desk Mon–Sat 8:45–12:00 & 14:00–15:45, closed Sun). This is one busy station, and theft is a problem, so never leave your bags unattended.

Turn left out of the station to find a branch of the **TI** a few steps away. Continue a few more blocks for the **tram** to place Masséna, the **old city,** and **bus station** (board the tram on the near side of the street, going to the right down avenue Jean Médecin). Many of my recommended **hotels** are within walking distance down the same street (figure 15 minutes from the station; see "Sleeping—Between Nice Etoile and Old Nice" on page 257).

To find **car rental** offices and more recommended **hotels,** turn right out of the station. For more recommended **hotels,** cross avenue Thiers, then walk down the steps by Hôtel Interlaken (see "Sleeping—Between the Train Station and Nice Etoile," page 254). Continue past these hotels if you'd rather head straight to the beach—keep walking down avenue Durante as it turns into rue des Congrés to find yourself in the heart of Nice's beachfront promenade.

Walking straight out of the train station puts you right by **taxis** (in the first lane), express **bus #99** to the airport (in the second lane), and local **bus #23** (in the third lane).

By Bus: Nice's bus station *(gare routière)* is sandwiched between boulevard Jean Jaurès and avenue Félix Faure, next to the old city. The station has no bag check. Cross boulevard Jean Jaurès and enter teeming Old Nice, or cross avenue Félix Faure to get to my recommended hotels near Nice Etoile.

By Car: Driving into Nice on the autoroute from the west, take the first Nice exit (for the airport—called Côte d'Azur, Central) and follow signs for *Nice Centre* and *Promenade des Anglais.* (Be ready to cross three left lanes of traffic right after getting off the autoroute.) Try to avoid arriving at rush hour, when promenade des Anglais grinds to a halt (usually Mon–Fri 8:00–9:30 & 17:00–19:30). Hoteliers know where to park (allow €14–20/day). The parking garage at the Nice Etoile shopping center on avenue Jean Médecin is pricey but near many of my recommended hotels (ticket booth on third floor, about €20/day, €10–12 20:00–8:00).

All on-street parking is metered 9:00–18:00 or 19:00, but usually free all day on Sunday.

By Plane: For information on Nice's handy airport, see "Transportation Connections" at the end of this chapter.

Helpful Hints

Theft Alert: Nice has more than its share of pickpockets. Have nothing important on or around your waist, unless it's in a money belt tucked out of sight (thieves target fanny packs); don't leave anything visible in your car; be wary of scooters when standing at intersections; don't leave things unattended on the beach while swimming; and stick to main streets in Old Nice after dark.

US Consulate: You'll find it at 7 avenue Gustave V (tel. 04 93 88 89 55, fax 04 93 87 07 38).

Canadian Consulate: It's at 10 rue Lamartine (tel. 04 93 92 93 22, fax 04 93 92 55 51).

Medical Help: Riviera Medical Services has a list of English-speaking physicians. They can help you make an appointment or call an ambulance (tel. 04 93 26 12 70, www.rivieramedical.com).

Museums: Some Nice museums (Chagall, Matisse, Archaeological) are closed Tuesdays, while others (Modern and Contemporary Art, Fine Arts) close on Mondays. Most are free (and crowded) the first and third Sundays of the month. For information on Nice's museum pass, see "Tourist Information," above.

Internet Access: Places to get online are everywhere in Nice. Ask at your hotel, or just look up as you walk (keep your eye out for the @ symbol).

English Bookstore: The Cat's Whiskers has an eclectic selection of novels and regional travel books, including mine. Say *bonjour* to mellow owner Linda (Mon–Sat 9:30–12:00 & 14:00–19:00, closed Sun, 26–30 rue Lamartine, near recommended Hôtel du Petit Louvre, tel. 04 93 80 02 66).

Laundry: You'll find launderettes everywhere in Nice—ask your hotelier for the nearest one. The self-service Point Laverie at the corner of rue Alberti and rue Pastorelli, next to Hôtel Vendôme, is central (daily 8:00–20:00).

Grocery Store: The big **Monoprix** on avenue Jean Médecin and rue Biscarra has a wide selection and cold drinks (closed Sun). You'll also find many small grocery stores (some open Sun and/or until late hours) near my recommended hotels.

Renting a Bike (and Other Wheels): Roller Station rents bikes (*vélos*, €5/hr, €10/half-day, €15/day), rollerblades (*rollers*, €6/day), Razor-type scooters (*trotinettes*, €6/half-day, €9/day), and skateboards (€6/half-day, €9/day). You'll need to leave your ID as a deposit (daily 9:30–19:00, next to yellow awnings of Pailin's Asian restaurant at 49 quai des Etats-Unis—see map on page 259, another location at 10 rue Cassini near place Garibaldi, tel. 04 93 62 99 05).

Car Rental: Renting a car is easiest at Nice's airport, which has offices for all the major companies. You'll also find most companies represented at Nice's train station.

English Radio: Tune into Riviera-Radio at FM 106.5.

Views: For panoramic views, climb Castle Hill (see page 251), or take a one-hour boat trip (see page 243).

Rocky Beaches: To make life tolerable on the rocks, swimmers should buy a pair of the cheap plastic beach shoes sold at many shops (flip-flops fall off in the water). **Go Sport** at 13 place Masséna has them for cheap (daily 10:00–19:00).

Getting Around Nice

While you can easily walk to most attractions in Nice, you'll want to ride the **bus** to the Chagall and Matisse museums and maybe to the Russian Cathedral. A single ride costs €1.30 (ticket good for 74 min in one direction—can't be used for a round-trip or for express buses to airport). An all-day pass is €4 (not valid on TAM buses). Make sure to validate your ticket in the machine just behind the driver—watch to see how locals do it.

Taxis are even handier for getting to Nice's outlying sights, and worth it if you're nowhere near a bus stop (figure €10–12 from promenade des Anglais). They normally only pick up at taxi stands *(tête de station)*, or you can call 04 93 13 78 78.

The inaugural line of the brand-new **tramway** runs along avenue Jean Médecin and boulevard Jean Jaurès. This handy tram connects the main train station, bus station, Old Nice, place Masséna (a few blocks from the sea), the Modern and Contemporary Art Museum, and comes within a few blocks of the Gare du Sud station (where the scenic Chemins de Fer de Provence trains depart from; see page 253).

The hokey **tourist train** gets you up Castle Hill (see "Tours," below).

Getting Around the Riviera

Nice is perfectly situated for exploring the Riviera by public transport. Eze-le-Village, Villefranche-sur-Mer, Antibes, St-Paul-de-Vence, and Cannes are all within a one-hour bus or train ride of each other. Boats go from Nice to Monaco and St-Tropez.

By Bus: At Nice's efficient bus station on boulevard Jean Jaurès (Mon–Sat 8:00–18:00, closed Sun), you'll find a snack bar with sandwiches and drinks, WCs, and several bus companies (but no baggage

Nice

1/4 MILE
400 METERS

━━ TRAM
P PARKING

MEDITERRANEAN   SEA

DCH

1. To High Corniche (sky-high route to Monaco)
2. To Middle Corniche (middle route, best for Monaco & Èze-le-Village)
3. To Low Corniche (low route to Villefranche-sur-Mer)
4. Start of "Welcome to the Riviera" Walk
5. Start of "Old Nice" Walk
6. To Fine Arts Museum

7. Trans Côte d'Azur Cruises to Villefranche/Cap Ferrat, Monaco & St-Tropez
8. Le Grand Tour Bus Departure Point & Albert I Park
9. Bus #15 Stops
10. Bus #17 Stops
11. World War II Monument
12. US Embassy

Nice

Public Transportation in the Nice Region

Many key Riviera destinations are connected by direct service from Nice. As the fare for any bus ride is just €1.30, the pricier train is only a better choice when it saves you time. You make the call—both modes of transportation work well.

Destination	Bus from Nice	Train from Nice
Villefranche	4/hr, 20 min	2/hr, 10 min, €1.80
Cap Ferrat	every 40 min, 30 min (no service on Sun)	none
Monaco	4/hr, 45 min	2/hr, 20 min, €3.40
Menton	4/hr, 60 min	2/hr, 25 min, €3.60
Antibes	3/hr, 60 min	2/hr, 15–30 min, €3.90
Cannes	3/hr, 75 min	2/hr, 30–40 min, €6
St-Paul	every 40 min, 45 min	none
Vence	every 40 min, 50 min	none
Grasse	every 40 min, 65 min	1/hr, 75 min, €7
Eze-le-Village	16/day, 25 min	none
La Turbie	4/day, 45 min	none

Buses also run from Monaco to Eze-le-Village, allowing travelers to triangulate Nice, Monaco, and Eze-le-Village (then back to Nice) for a good all-day excursion (see page 319 for details).

check). I've listed general bus information below, but you can get specific timetables and prices from the English-speaking clerk at the information desk (tel. 04 93 85 61 81). Buy tickets from the driver. To make life easier for drivers and cheaper for travelers, all fares are €1.30—whether you're riding 20 minutes to Villefranche-sur-Mer, 45 minutes to Monaco, or 60 minutes to Antibes (but you'll need to pay another €1.30 for the return trip). This is an amazing deal.

Nice has two main private bus companies, Lignes d'Azur and TAM. Both charge €1.30 for rides anywhere on their systems, but you can't transfer between them on the same ticket. The €4 all-day ticket offered by Ligne d'Azur is good on Nice's city buses as well as on Ligne d'Azur's lines, but it only makes sense if you have very ambitious sightseeing plans and don't need to use a TAM bus (ask at the bus station to find out which company serves your destinations). The express buses to and from the airport, #98 and #99, require the €4 ticket—savvy riders use the ticket for other bus rides on the day of their flight.

By Minivan Excursion: The TI and most hotels have information on minivan excursions from Nice (€50–60/half-day, €80–110/day). **Med-Tour** is one of many (tel. 04 93 82 92 58, www .med-tour.com), **Tour Azur** is a bit pricier (tel. 04 93 44 88 77, www.tourazur.com), and **Revelation Tours** specializes in English tours (tel. 04 93 53 69 85, www.revelation-tours.com). All companies also offer private tours by the day or half-day (check with them for their outrageous prices, about €90/hr).

By Boat: From June to mid-September, Trans Côte d'Azur offers scenic trips from Nice to Monaco and to St-Tropez. Boats leave in the morning and return in the evening, giving you all day to explore your destination. Drinks and WCs are available on board. Boats to **Monaco** depart at 9:30 and return at 18:00 (€28 round-trip, 50 min each way, July–Aug daily; May, June, and Sept Tue, Thu, and Sat only). Boats to **St-Tropez** depart at 9:00 and return at 19:00 (€55 round-trip, 2.5 hrs each way; July–Aug Tue–Sun, no boats Mon; late June and early Sept Tue, Thu, and Sun only). Tickets for St-Tropez boats often sell out—book a few days ahead (tel. 04 92 00 42 30, fax 04 92 00 42 31, www.trans-cote-azur.com). The boats leave from Nice's port, bassin des Amiraux, just below Castle Hill, with a blue ticket booth *(billeterie)* on quai de Lunel (see map on page 241). The same company also runs one-hour round-trip cruises along the coast to Cap Ferrat (see "Tours," below).

TOURS

Bus Tour—Le Grand Tour Bus provides a hop-on, hop-off option on an open-deck bus with headphone commentary. The full route (about 90 min) includes promenade des Anglais, old port, Cap de Nice, and the Chagall and Matisse museums on Cimiez Hill (€19/1-day pass, €22/2-day pass, cheaper for seniors and students, €10 for last tour of the day at about 18:45, departures 2/hr, buy tickets on bus, main stop is near where promenade des Anglais and quai des Etats-Unis meet, across from plage Beau Rivage—look for signs, tel. 04 92 29 17 00). This tour is a pricey way to get to the Chagall and Matisse museums, but it's a good option if you also want a city overview tour.

Tourist Train—For €6.50, you can spend 40 embarrassing minutes on the tourist train tooting along the promenade, through the old city, and up to Castle Hill. This is a sweat-free way to get to Castle Hill...but so is the elevator, which is much cheaper (every 30 min, recorded English commentary, meet train near Le Grand Tour Bus stop on quai des Etats-Unis, tel. 04 93 62 85 48).

▲**Boat Cruise**—Here's your chance to join the boat parade and see Nice from the water. On this one-hour, star-studded tour, you'll cruise in a comfortable, yacht-size vessel to Cap Ferrat and

Nice at a Glance

▲▲▲**Chagall Museum** The world's largest collection of Chagall's work, popular even with people who don't like modern art. **Hours:** Wed–Mon 10:00–17:00, July–Sept until 18:00, closed Tue.

▲▲**Promenade des Anglais** Nice's four-mile, sunstruck seafront promenade. **Hours:** Always open.

▲▲**Old Nice** Charming old city offering enjoyable atmosphere and a look at Nice's French-Italian cultural blend. **Hours:** Always open.

▲**Matisse Museum** A worthwhile collection of Henri Matisse's paintings. **Hours:** Wed–Mon 10:00–18:00, closed Tue.

▲**Russian Cathedral** Finest Orthodox church outside Russia. **Hours:** Daily 9:00–12:00 & 14:30–18:00, until 17:00 off-season.

Modern and Contemporary Art Museum Ultramodern museum with enjoyable collection from the 1960s–1970s, including Warhol and Lichtenstein. **Hours:** Tue–Sun 10:00–18:00, closed Mon.

Molinard Perfume Museum Small museum tracing the history of perfume. **Hours:** Daily 10:00–19:00, sometimes closed Mon off-season.

Castle Hill Site of an ancient fort, and today boasting great views—especially in early mornings and evenings. **Hours:** Park closes at 20:00 in summer, earlier off-season. Elevator runs daily 10:00–19:00, until 20:00 in summer.

past Villefranche-sur-Mer, then return to Nice with a run along promenade des Anglais. It's a scenic trip, worthwhile if you won't be hiking along the Cap Ferrat trails that provide similar views. French (and sometimes English-speaking) guides play Robin Leach, pointing out mansions owned by some pretty famous people, including Elton John (just as you leave Nice, soft-yellow square-shaped place right on the water), Sean Connery (on the hill above Elton, with rounded arches and tower), Microsoft mogul Paul Allen (in saddle of Cap Ferrat hill, above yellow-umbrella beach with sloping red-tile roof), and Mick Jagger (between Cap Ferrat and Villefranche-sur-Mer, pink place hidden by trees).

I wonder if this gang ever hangs out together.... The best views are from the seats on top (€13, June–Oct 2/day, fewer departures in off-season, arrive 30 min early to get best seats, drinks and WCs available). For directions to the dock and contact information, see "Getting Around the Riviera—By Boat," above.

Walking Tours—The TI on promenade des Anglais organizes weekly walking tours of Old Nice (€12, May–Oct only, usually Sat morning, 2.5 hours, reservations necessary, depart from TI, tel. 08 92 70 74 07).

Nice's cultural association (Centre du Patrimoine) offers €3 on-demand walks on varying themes in English that are a great value. Call 04 92 00 41 90 a day ahead to make a reservation. Most tours start at their office at 75 quai des Etats-Unis; look for the red plaque next to Musée des Ponchettes.

Les Petits Farcis Cooking Tour and Classes—Canadian food-journalist-turned-Francophile Rosa Jackson is making a Mediterranean splash with her one-day or four-day cooking classes in Old Nice. Her single-day classes include a morning trip to the open-air market, where you'll pick up ingredients, and an afternoon session, where you'll learn what to do with your purchases. Her four-day courses focus exclusively on the art of cooking (1 day-€200, 4 days-€480, tel. 06 81 67 41 22, www.petitsfarcis.com).

Local Guide—Lovely Pascale Rucker tailors excellent tours to your interests in and around Nice. Book in advance or on short notice (€125/half-day, €200/day, tel. & fax 04 93 87 77 89, mobile 06 16 24 29 52).

SIGHTS

Remember that many Nice museums are free (and more crowded) the first and third Sundays of the month. The first two museums (Chagall and Matisse) are northeast of Nice's city center. Because they're both relatively difficult to reach and on the same bus line (in the same direction), it only makes sense to visit them at the same time. The Chagall Museum is much closer to the center, while the Matisse Museum is a 30-minute walk (or quick bus ride) farther out.

▲▲▲Chagall Museum (Musée National Marc Chagall)—Inspired by the Old Testament, modern artist Marc Chagall custom-painted works for this building, which he considered a "House of Brotherhood." In typical Chagall style, these paintings are lively, colorful, and simple (some might say simplistic). The museum is an

Nice

Henri Matisse
(1869–1954)

Here's an outline of Henri Matisse's busy life:

1880s and 1890s—At age 20, Matisse, a budding lawyer, is struck down with appendicitis. Bedridden for a year, he turns to painting as a healing escape from pain and boredom. After recovering, he studies art in Paris and produces dark-colored, realistic still lifes and landscapes. His work is exhibited at the Salons of 1896 and 1897.

1897–1905—Influenced by the Impressionists, he experiments with sunnier scenes and brighter colors. He travels to southern France, including Collioure (on the coast near Spain), and seeks still more light-filled scenes to paint. His experiments are influenced by Vincent van Gogh's bright, surrealistic colors and thick outlines, and by Paul Gauguin's primitive visions of a Tahitian paradise. From Paul Cézanne, he learns how to simplify objects into their basic geometric shapes. He also experiments (like Cézanne) with creating the illusion of 3-D not by traditional means, but by using contrasting colors for the foreground and background.

1905—Back in Paris, Matisse and his colleagues (André Derain and Maurice de Vlaminck) shock the art world with an exhibition of their experimental paintings. The thick outlines, simple forms, non-3-D scenes, and—most of all—bright, clashing, unrealistic colors seemed to be the work of "wild animals" *(fauves)*. Fauvism is hot, and Matisse is instantly famous. (Though notorious as a "wild animal," Matisse himself was a gentle, introspective man.)

1906–1910—After just a year, Fauvism is out, and African masks are in. This "primitive" art form inspires Matisse to simplify and distort his figures further, making them less realistic but more expressive.

1910–1917—Matisse creates his masterpiece paintings. Cubism is the rage, pioneered by Matisse's friend and rival for the World's Best Painter award, Pablo Picasso. Matisse dabbles in Cubism, simplifying forms, emphasizing outline, and muting his colors. But ultimately, it proves to be too austere and analytical for his

unmissable treat for Chagall fans, and a hit even for people who usually don't like modern art.

Cost, Hours, Location: €6.70, can cost a little more during special exhibits, Oct–June Wed–Mon 10:00–17:00, July–Sept until 18:00, closed Tue, avenue Docteur Ménard, tel. 04 93 53 87 20, www.musee-chagall.fr. ⊙ See Chagall Museum Tour on page 277 for directions and more information.

deeply sensory nature. The Cubist style is most evident in his sculpture.

1920s—Burned out from years of intense experimentation, Matisse moves to Nice (spending winters there from 1917, settling permanently in 1921). Luxuriating under the bright sun, he's reborn, and he paints colorful, sensual, highly decorative works. Harem concubines lounging in their sunny, flowery apartments epitomize the lush life.

1930s—A visit to Tahiti inspires more scenes of life as a sunny paradise. Increasingly, Matisse plays around with the lines of the figures he draws to create swirling arabesques and decorative patterns.

1940s—Duodenal cancer (in 1941), requiring two operations, confines Matisse to a wheelchair for the rest of his life. Working at an easel becomes a struggle for him, and he largely stops painting in 1941. But as World War II ends, Matisse emerges with renewed energy. Now in his 70s, he explores a new medium: paper cutouts pasted onto a watercolored surface (découpages on gouache-prepared surface). The medium plays to his strengths: The cutouts are essentially blocks of bright color (mostly blue) with a strong outline. Scissors in hand, Matisse says, "I draw straight into the color." (His doctor advises him to wear dark glasses to protect his weak eyes against the bright colors he chooses.) In 1947, Matisse's book *Jazz* is published, featuring the artist's joyful cutouts of simple figures. Like jazz music, the book is a celebration of artistic spontaneity. And like music in general, Matisse's works balance different tones and colors to create a mood.

1947–1951—Matisse's nurse becomes a Dominican nun in Vence. To thank her for her care, he spends his later years designing a chapel there. He oversees every aspect of the Chapel of the Rosary (Chapelle du Rosaire) at Vence, from the stained glass to the altar to the colors of the priest's robe (see page 348). Though Matisse is not a strong Christian, the church exudes his spirit of celebrating life and sums up his work.

1954—Matisse dies.

▲**Matisse Museum (Musée Matisse)**—This museum, worth ▲▲▲ for his fans, contains the world's largest collection of Henri Matisse paintings. It offers a painless introduction to the artist, whose style was shaped by Mediterranean light and by fellow Côte d'Azur artists Pablo Picasso and Pierre-Auguste Renoir. (For more on Matisse, see the sidebar above.) The collection is scattered through several rooms with a few worthwhile works, though it lacks a certain *je ne sais quoi* when compared to the Chagall Museum.

Henri Matisse, the master of leaving things out, could suggest a woman's body with a single curvy line—leaving it to the viewer's mind to fill in the rest. Ignoring traditional 3-D perspective, he used simple dark outlines saturated with bright blocks of color to create recognizable but simplified scenes composed into a decorative pattern to express nature's serene beauty. You don't look "through" a Matisse canvas, like a window; you look "at" it, like wallpaper.

Matisse understood how colors and shapes affect us emotionally. He could create either shocking, clashing works (Fauvism) or geometrical, balanced, harmonious ones (later works). While other modern artists reveled in purely abstract design, Matisse (almost) always kept the subject matter at least vaguely recognizable. He used unreal colors and distorted lines not just to portray what an object looks like, but to express the object's inner nature (even inanimate objects). Meditating on his paintings helps you connect with nature—or so Matisse hoped.

Touring the Museum: The museum has undergone a significant renovation, so some rooms may hold different works than those listed below. The entrance is on the middle floor. After entering (minuscule-print English handout available), go down one flight of stairs and continue straight ahead, where you'll find a timeline of Matisse's life (on a wall plaque, in English), a WC, and temporary exhibits of his work. An extremely colorful paper cutout *(Flowers and Fruits)*, hanging below, screams "Riviera."

Go back upstairs to the entry level and find the two rooms at the far right (Rooms 9 and 10) that house paintings from his formative years as a student. In Room 10, notice how his work evolves: from Impressionist to simpler and more abstract. Other rooms on this floor highlight Matisse's fascination with dance, and display pencil drawings and bronze busts. Look for the orange-bearded 1905 portrait of Matisse by André Derain. Head up one flight of stairs, following the smaller steps halfway up to the right, and see sketches and models of his famous Chapel of the Rosary in nearby Vence (see page 348) and related religious works. On the same floor, find paper cutouts from his *Jazz* series, more bronze sculptures, and linen embroideries inspired by his travels to Polynesia.

As you tour the museum, look for Matisse's favorite motifs, including fruit, flowers, wallpaper, and interiors of sunny rooms—often with a window opening onto a sunny landscape. Another favorite subject is the odalisque (harem concubine), usually shown sprawled in a seductive pose and with a simplified, masklike face. You'll also see a few souvenirs from his travels, which influenced much of his work.

Cost, Hours, Location: €4, Wed–Mon 10:00–18:00, closed Tue, tel. 04 93 81 08 08, www.musee-matisse-nice.org. The museum, at 164 avenue des Arènes de Cimiez, is set in an olive grove amid the ruins of the Roman city of Cemenelum. Part of the ancient Roman city of Nice, Cemenelum was a military camp that housed as many as 20,000 people.

Getting to the Matisse Museum: It's a long uphill walk from the city center. Take the bus (details below) or a cab (about €12 from promenade des Anglais). Once here, walk into the park to find the pink villa.

Buses #15 and **#17** offer frequent service to the Matisse Museum from just off place Masséna on rue Gioffredo, a block east of the Galeries Lafayette department store (€1.30). The bus stop for the museum is called Arènes–Matisse. When leaving the museum, find the stop for bus #15 (with the most frequent service downtown, stopping en route at the Chagall Museum) by exiting the park and crossing boulevard de Cimiez, where the two roads meet (the stop is on boulevard de Cimiez, not avenue des Arènes de Cimiez; see map on page 256). The stop for bus #17 (less frequent, no Chagall stop) also faces downhill, but it's on avenue des Arènes de Cimiez. Confusing, I know.

Modern and Contemporary Art Museum (Musée d'Art Moderne et d'Art Contemporain)—This ultramodern museum features an explosively colorful, far-out, yet manageable permanent collection (on the second floor) of mostly American and European art from the 1960s and 1970s. The exhibits include a few works by Andy Warhol, Roy Lichtenstein, and Jean Tinguely, and small models of Christo's famous wrappings. Several of Niki de Saint Phalle's works are almost huggable. The temporary exhibits can be as appealing to modern-art-lovers as the permanent collection—ask the TI what's playing.

Cost, Hours, Location: €4, Tue–Sun 10:00–18:00, closed Mon, about a 15-minute walk from place Masséna, near bus station on promenade des Arts, tel. 04 93 62 61 62, www.mamac-nice.org.

Molinard Perfume Museum—The Molinard family has been making perfume in Grasse (about an hour's drive from Nice) since 1849. Their Nice store has a small museum in the back that illustrates the story of their industry. Back when people believed water spread the plague (Louis XIV supposedly bathed less than once a year), doctors advised people to rub fragrances into their skin and then powder their body. Back then, perfume was a necessity of everyday life.

Room 1 shows photos of the local flowers used in perfume production. Room 2 shows the earliest (18th-century) production method. Petals would be laid on a bed of animal fat. After baking in the sun, the fat would absorb the essence of the flowers. Petals would be replaced daily for two months until the fat was saturated. Models and old photos show the later distillation process

(660 pounds of lavender would produce only a quarter-gallon of essence). Perfume is "distilled like cognac and then aged like wine." Room 3 shows the desk of a "nose" (top perfume creator). Of the 150 real "noses" in the world, more than 100 are French. You are welcome to enjoy the testing bottles before heading into the shop.

Cost, Hours, Location: Free, daily 10:00–19:00, sometimes closed Mon off-season, just between beach and place Masséna at 20 rue St. François de Paule, tel. 04 93 62 90 50, www.molinard.com.

Other Nice Museums—These museums are acceptable rainy-day options.

The **Fine Arts Museum** (Musée des Beaux-Arts), located in a sumptuous villa with lovely gardens, houses 6,000 works from the 17th to 20th centuries, and will satisfy your need for a fine-arts fix (€4, Tue–Sun 10:00–18:00, closed Mon, 3 avenue des Baumettes, western end of Nice, take bus #38 from the bus station, tel. 04 92 15 28 28).

The **Archaeological Museum** (Musée Archeologique) displays various objects from the Romans' occupation of this region. It's convenient—just below the Matisse Museum—but has little of interest to anyone but Ancient Rome aficionados. You also get access to the Roman bath ruins...which are, sadly, overgrown with weeds (€4, very limited information in English, Wed–Mon 10:00–18:00, closed Tue, near Matisse Museum at 160 avenue des Arènes de Cimiez, tel. 04 93 81 59 57).

Nice's city-history museum, **Masséna Museum** (Musée Masséna), is closed, probably through 2008 (but may re-open earlier than expected—check with the TI for the latest).

▲**Russian Cathedral (Cathédrale Russe)**—Nice's Russian Orthodox church—claimed to be the finest outside Russia—is worth a visit. Five hundred rich Russian families wintered in Nice in the late 19th century. Since they couldn't pray in a Catholic church, the community needed a worthy Orthodox house of worship. Czar Nicholas I's widow provided the land (which required tearing down her house), and Czar Nicholas II gave this church to the Russian community in 1912. (A few years later, Russian comrades—who didn't winter on the Riviera—assassinated him.) Here in the land of olives and anchovies,  these proud onion domes seem odd. But, I imagine, so did those old Russians.

Step inside (pick up English info sheet). The one-room interior is filled with icons and candles, and the old Russian music adds to the ambience. The wall of icons (iconostasis) divides things between the spiritual world and the temporal world of the worshippers. Only the priest can walk between the two worlds, by using the "Royal Door." Take a close look at items lining the front (starting in the left corner). The angel with red boots and wings—the protector of the Romanov family—stands over a symbolic tomb of Christ. The tall, black, hammered-copper cross commemorates the massacre of Nicholas II and his family in 1918. Notice the Jesus icon to the right of the Royal Door. According to a priest here, as the worshipper meditates, staring deep into the eyes of Jesus, he enters a lake where he finds his soul. Surrounded by incense, chanting, and your entire community...it could happen. Farther to the right, the icon of the unhappy-looking Virgin and Child is decorated with semiprecious stones from the Ural Mountains. Artists worked a triangle into each iconic face—symbolic of the Trinity.

Cost, Hours, Location: €3, daily 9:00–12:00 & 14:30–18:00, until 17:00 off-season, chanted services Sat at 17:30 or 18:00, Sun at 10:00, no tourist visits during services, no short shorts, tel. 04 93 96 88 02. The park around the church stays open at lunch and makes a fine setting for picnics.

Getting to the Russian Cathedral: From the train station, it's a 10-minute walk; exit the station to the right onto avenue Thiers, turn right on avenue Gambetta, and follow signs to the cathedral. Or, from the station, take any bus heading west on avenue Thiers and get off at avenue Gambetta (a few stops away). The cathedral is at 17 boulevard du Tzarewitch.

Castle Hill (Colline du Château)—Nice was first settled on this hill, which offers sweeping views over the city—best by far in the early morning or late in the day (park closes at 20:00 in summer, earlier off-season). You can get to the top by foot, by elevator (€0.70 one-way, €1.10 round-trip, runs daily 10:00–19:00, until 20:00 in summer, next to beachfront Hôtel Suisse), or by tourist train (described under "Tours" on page 243). Up top, you'll find cafés and an extensive play area for kids. For more on Castle Hill, see page 270.

ACTIVITIES

In Nice

▲▲**Wandering Old Nice (Vieux Nice)**—Offering an intriguing look at Nice's melding of French and Italian cultures, the old city is a fine place to meander with ice cream in hand. Enjoy its belle époque buildings, bustling market squares, tempting shops, and colorful people.

○ See Old Nice Walk on page 271.

▲▲**Strolling the Promenade des Anglais**—Sauntering along Nice's four-mile seafront promenade is a must. From the days when wealthy English tourists lined the seaside with grand hotels up to today, as a favorite spot for Europeans to enjoy some fun in the sun—this stretch is *the* place to be in Nice.

○ See Welcome to the Riviera Walk on page 267.

▲▲**Wheeling the Promenade**—Get a bike and ride along the coast in both directions (about 30 min each way). Roller Station

rents bikes, in-line skates, and mini-scooters (see "Helpful Hints" on page 239). Both of the following paths start along promenade des Anglais.

The path to the west stops just before the airport at perhaps the most scenic *boules* courts in France. Stop and watch the old-timers while away their afternoon tossing those shiny metal balls (see page 174).

Heading east, you'll round the hill—passing a scenic cape and the town's memorial to both world wars—to the harbor of Nice, with a chance to survey some fancy yachts. Pedal around the harbor and follow the coast past the Corsica ferry terminal (you'll need to carry your bike up a flight of steps). From there, the path leads to an appealing tree-lined residential district.

Relaxing at the Beaches—Nice is where the masses relax on the rocks. After settling into the smooth pebbles, you can play beach

volleyball, table tennis, or *boules* (see page 174); rent paddleboats, personal watercraft, or windsurfing equipment; explore ways to use your zoom lens as a telescope; or snooze on comfy beach beds with end tables. To rent a spot on the beach, compare rates, as prices vary—beaches on the east end of the bay are usually cheaper (mattress and chaise longue-€12–18, umbrella-€5, towel-€3). Many hotels have special deals with certain beaches for discounted rental (check with your hotel for details). Consider lunch in your bathing suit (€10–12 salads and pizzas in bars and restaurants all along the beach). For a peaceful cup of coffee on the beach, stop here first thing in the morning before the crowds hit. *Plage Publique* signs explain the 15 beach no-nos (translated in English).

While Nice's beaches are traditionally rocky, a few years ago a small sandy area appeared toward the Italy end of the bay.

Near Nice

Narrow-Gauge Train into the Alps (Chemins de Fer de Provence)—Leave the tourists behind and take your kids on the

scenic train-bus-train combination that runs between Nice and Digne through canyons, along whitewater rivers, and through many tempting villages (Nice to Digne: 4/day, 3 hours, about €18, 25 percent discount with railpass, departs Nice from the South Station—Gare du Sud—about 10 blocks behind the city's main train station, two blocks from the tramway, 4 rue Alfred Binet, tel. 04 97 03 80 80).

Start with a 8:50 departure and go as far as you want. Little **Entrevaux** is a good destination (about 2 scenic hours from Nice, about €9) and feels forgotten and still stuck in its medieval shell. Climb high to the citadel for great views. The train ends in **Digne-les-Bains,** where you can catch a main-line train (covered by railpasses) to other destinations—or better, take the bus (quick transfer if you take the 8:50 train from Nice, free with railpass) to **Veynes** (4/day, 90 min), where you can catch the most scenic two-car train to **Grenoble** (5/day, 2 hours), then catch a train to Annecy (arriving about 18:50).

To do the entire trip from Nice to Annecy in one day, you must start with the 8:50 departure, but I'd spend a night in one of the tiny villages en route. Clelles has a decent hotel: **Hôtel Ferrat****, a basic, family-run mountain hacienda at the base of Mont Aiguille, is a good place with a swimming pool and a good restaurant (Sb-€38, Db-€53, tel. 04 76 34 42 70, fax 04 76 34 47 47, hotel .ferrat@wanadoo.fr).

NIGHTLIFE

Promenade des Anglais, cours Saleya, and rue Masséna are all worth an evening walk. Nice's bars play host to one of the Riviera's most happening late-night scenes, full of jazz, rock, and heat-seeking singles. Most activity focuses on Old Nice, near place Rossetti and along rue Droite. *Distilleries Ideales* is a fine place to start or end your evening, with a lively, international crowd and a fun interior (where rues de la Poissonnerie and Barillerie meet, happy hour 18:00–20:00).

Plan on a cover charge or expensive drinks when music is

involved. If you're out very late, avoid walking alone. The plush bar at Hôtel Negresco is fancy-cigar old English. Nice is well-known for its lively after-dark action; for more relaxed and accessible nightlife, consider nearby Antibes (page 321).

SLEEPING

Don't look for charm in Nice. Go for modern and clean, with a central location and, in summer, air-conditioning. Reserve early for summer visits. The rates listed here are for April through October. Prices generally drop €10–20 from November through March, but go sky-high during the Nice Carnival (Feb 16–March 2 in 2008), Monaco's Grand Prix (May 22–25 in 2008), and the Cannes film festival (May 14–25 in 2008). June is convention month, and Nice is one of Europe's top convention cities—so book ahead and be ready for higher prices at some hotels. For parking, ask your hotelier (several have limited private parking), or see "Arrival in Nice—By Car" on page 238.

I've divided my sleeping recommendations into three areas: between the train station and Nice Etoile shopping center (with easy access to the train station and a 15-min walk to Old Nice, or a 20-min walk to promenade des Anglais); between Nice Etoile and Old Nice (east of avenue Jean Médecin, with better access to Old Nice and the sea at quai des Etats-Unis); and between boulevard Victor Hugo and promenade des Anglais (a somewhat classier area, offering better access to the promenade but longer walks to the train station and Old Nice). I've also listed a hotel near the airport.

Every hotel I list has Wi-Fi, and nearly all have Internet access.

Between the Train Station and Nice Etoile

Most hotels near the station ghetto are overrun, overpriced, and loud. These are the pleasant exceptions (most are near avenue Jean Médecin).

$$$ Hôtel Excelsior***, one block below the station, is an elegant place with turn-of-the-century decor, a pleasing garden courtyard, and 40 top-notch rooms. Rooms on the garden are best in the summer; streetside rooms have balconies and get winter sun (standard Db-€140, bigger Db-€160, Tb-€160–190, Qb with kitchenettes on the garden-€200–250, air-con, 19 avenue Durante, tel. 04 93 88 18 05, fax 04 93 88 38 69, www.excelsiornice.com, excelsior@wanadoo.fr).

$$ Hôtel le Laurier Blanc***, clean and homey, is run with pride by the hardworking owners, the Marets. The quite comfortable rooms come with real quilts and ceiling fans, but no air-

Sleep Code

(€1 = about $1.30, country code: 33)
S = Single, **D** = Double/Twin, **T** = Triple, **Q** = Quad, **b** = bathroom,
s = shower only, ***** = French hotel rating (0–4 stars). Hotels
speak English, have elevators, and accept credit cards unless
otherwise noted.

To help you sort easily through these listings, I've divided
the rooms into three categories based on the price for a standard double room with bath:

$$$ **Higher Priced**—Most rooms €100 or more.
$$ **Moderately Priced**—Most rooms between €70–100.
$ **Lower Priced**—Most rooms €70 or less.

Nice

conditioning (Db-€70–90, fine 2-room Tb-€95–150, on a quiet dead-end street, 18 avenue Durante, tel. 04 93 88 89 45, fax 04 93 88 16 11, www.hotel-laurier-blanc.fr, reservation@hotel-laurier -blanc.fr).

$$ Hôtel Durante**, run by smiling Nathalie, feels like a Mediterranean villa, with its way-orange facade, spacious central courtyard, and cool bathroom tiles. Rooms are good enough, and the price is right (Db-€71–79, bigger Db-€130–150, Tb-€130–150, air-con, 16 avenue Durante, tel. 04 93 88 84 40, fax 04 93 87 77 76, www.hotel-durante.com, info@hotel-durante.com).

$$ Hôtel St. Georges** is big and bright, with a backyard garden, reasonably clean and comfortable high-ceilinged rooms, orange tones, blue halls, fair rates, and happy Jacques at reception (Sb-€76, Db-€90, Tb with 3 separate beds-€106, extra bed-€19, air-con, 7 avenue Georges Clemenceau, tel. 04 93 88 79 21, fax 04 93 16 22 85, www.hotelsaintgeorges.fr, contact@hotelsaintgeorges .fr).

$ Hôtel Clemenceau**, run by the La Serre family, is an exceptional budget value with a humble, comfy feel. Rooms—some with balconies, some without closets, all air-conditioned—are mostly spacious, simple, and traditional (S-€31, Sb-€43, D-€46, Db-€58, Tb-€69, Qb-€84, kitchenette-€8 extra and only for stays of at least 3 nights, no elevator, 3 avenue Georges Clemenceau, 1 block west of avenue Jean Médecin, tel. 04 93 88 61 19, fax 04 93 16 88 96, hotel-clemenceau@wanadoo.fr, Marianne and Cedric speak English, Mama and Papa no speak).

$ Hôtel la Belle Meunière, in a fine old mansion built for Napoleon III's mistress, has cheap beds and private rooms just a block below the train station. Lively and hostel-esque, this place attracts budget-minded travelers of all ages with basic-but-adequate,

Nice Hotels

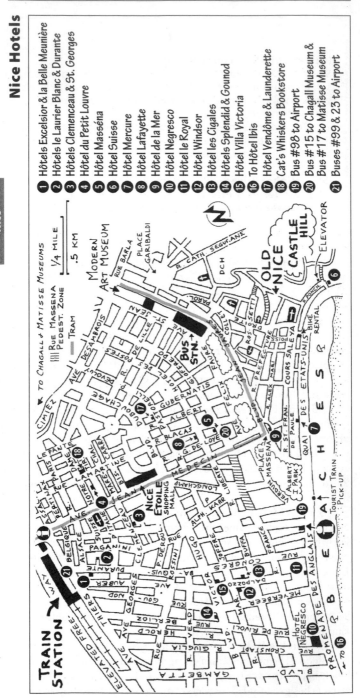

1. Hôtels Excelsior & la Belle Meunière
2. Hôtels le Laurier Blanc & Durante
3. Hôtels Clemenceau & St. Georges
4. Hôtel du Petit Louvre
5. Hôtel Masséna
6. Hôtel Suisse
7. Hôtel Mercure
8. Hôtel Lafayette
9. Hôtel de la Mer
10. Hôtel Negresco
11. Hôtel le Royal
12. Hôtel Windsor
13. Hôtels les Cigales
14. Hôtels Splendid & Gounod
15. Hôtel Villa Victoria
16. To Hôtel Ibis
17. Hôtel Vendôme & Launderette
18. Cat's Whiskers Bookstore
19. Bus #98 to Airport
20. Bus #15 to Chagall Museum & Bus #17 to Matisse Museum
21. Buses #99 & 23 to Airport

decent-value rooms and charismatic Madame Marie-Pierre presiding. Tables in the front yard greet guests and provide opportunities to meet other travelers (bed in 4-person dorm with private bathroom-€23, €18 *sans* private shower, Db-€60, includes breakfast, 21 avenue Durante, tel. 04 93 88 66 15, fax 04 93 82 51 76, www .bellemeuniere.com, hotel.belle.meuniere@cegetel.net).

$ **Hôtel du Petit Louvre*** offers an interesting concept at a good price, with clean, small rooms—all recently renovated with kitchenettes and air-conditioning—and beds that convert to couches to allow more space during the day (Db-€58, Tb-€68, no breakfast, 10 rue Emma Tiranty, tel. 04 93 80 15 54, fax 04 93 62 45 08, www.hotelgoodprice.com, petilouvr@wanadoo.com).

Between Nice Etoile and Old Nice

$$$ **Hôtel Masséna******, in a classy building a few blocks from place Masséna, is a stylish business hotel showcasing 100 rooms with every amenity at almost-reasonable rates (small Db-€130, larger Db-€165, still larger Db-€240, extra bed-€30, some non-smoking rooms, reserve parking ahead-€20/day, 58 rue Giofreddo, tel. 04 92 47 88 88, fax 04 92 47 88 89, www.hotel-massena-nice.com, info@hotel-massena-nice.com).

$$$ **Hôtel Suisse*****, below Castle Hill, has Nice's best ocean and city views for the money, and is surprisingly quiet given the busy street below. Rooms are quite comfortable and decorated with class. There's no reason to sleep here if you don't land a view, so I've listed prices only for view rooms—many of which have balconies (Db-€150–190, extra bed-€36, breakfast-€15, 15 quai Rauba Capeu, tel. 04 92 17 39 00, fax 04 93 85 30 70, www.hotels-ocre-azur .com, hotel.suisse@hotels-ocre-azur.com).

$$$ **Hôtel Mercure*****, a chain hotel ideally situated across from the sea and behind cours Saleya, offers smallish yet tastefully designed rooms (some with beds in a loft). The rates are decent, considering the sensational location (Sb-€105–125, Db-€115–130, Tb-€145–160, sea view-€30 extra, air-con, 91 quai des Etats-Unis, tel. 04 93 85 74 19, fax 04 93 13 90 94, h0962@accor.com).

$$$ **Hôtel Vendôme***** gives you a whiff of the belle époque, with pink pastels, high ceilings, and grand staircases in a mansion set off the street with limited parking (book ahead, €11/day). That whiff could be sharper (many tour groups stay here and the rooms seem a tad tired), but the location is good, prices are almost fair, and rooms are modern and come in all sizes. The best have balconies—request *une chambre avec balcon* (Sb-€95–110, Db-€144, Tb-€160, air-con, 26 rue Pastorelli, tel. 04 93 62 00 77, fax 04 93 13 40 78, www.vendome-hotel-nice.com, contact@vendome-hotel -nice.com).

$$ Hôtel Lafayette***, well-located a block behind the Galeries Lafayette department store, looks average from the outside. But inside it's homey and a good value, with 18 well-designed, mostly spacious rooms, all one floor up from the street. Sweet Sandrine and Christine take darned good care of you (standard Db-€90–110, spacious Db-€95–120 extra bed-€22, central air-con, no elevator, 32 rue de l'Hôtel des Postes, tel. 04 93 85 17 84, fax 04 93 80 47 56, www.hotellafayettenice.com, info@ hotellafayettenice .com).

$$ Hôtel de la Mer** sits in an enviable location between place Masséna and Old Nice. It's one of my closest listings to Old Nice and is a small, modest place run by gracious Madame Ferry (Db-€65–95, Tb-€78–120, air-con, 4 place Masséna, tel. 04 93 92 09 10, fax 04 93 85 00 64, www.hoteldelamernice.com, hotel .mer@wanadoo.fr).

Between Boulevard Victor Hugo and Promenade des Anglais

$$$$ Hôtel Negresco**** owns Nice's most prestigious address on promenade des Anglais and knows it. Still, it's the kind of place that, if you were to splurge just once in your life.... Rooms are opulent (see page 267 for further description), and tips are expected (viewless Db-€360, Db with sea view-€460–580, view suite-€770–1,900, breakfast-€35, cool bar, 37 promenade des Anglais, tel. 04 93 16 64 00, fax 04 93 88 35 68, www.hotel-negresco-nice.com, reservation@hotel-negresco.com).

$$$ Hôtel le Royal*** stands shoulder-to-shoulder on promenade des Anglais with the big boys (the Negresco, Concorde, and Westminster hotels). With 140 rooms, big lounges, and hallways that stretch forever, it feels a bit institutional. But considering the solid, air-conditioned comfort and terrific location, this is a good value—and they sometimes have rooms when others don't (viewless Db-€110, Db with sea view-€150–170, bigger view room-€180 and worth the extra euros, extra person-€25, 23 promenade des Anglais, tel. 04 93 16 43 00, fax 04 93 16 43 02, www.hotel-royal -nice.cote.azur.fr, royal@vacancesbleues.com).

$$$ Hôtel Windsor*** is a snazzy garden retreat that feels like a cross between a modern-art museum and a health spa. The contemporary rooms include some designed by modern artists that defy explanation. It has a full-service bar, a swimming pool and gym (both free for guests), an €11 sauna, €55 massages, and light, full meal service in the garden (standard Db-€120, bigger Db-€150, big Db with balcony-€175, extra bed-€20, rooms over garden worth the higher price, air-con, Internet access, 11 rue Dalpozzo, tel. 04 93 88 59 35, fax 04 93 88 94 57, www.hotelwindsornice.com, reservation@hotelwindsornice.com).

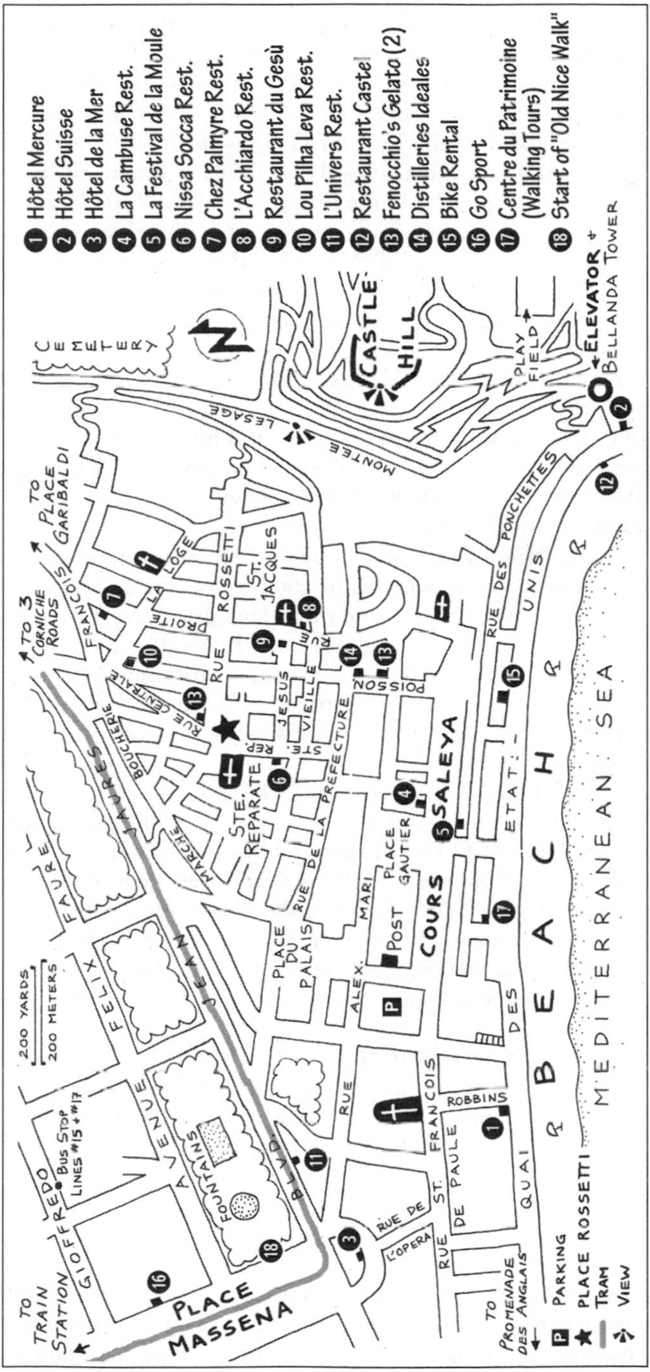

Old Nice Hotels and Restaurants
1 Hôtel Mercure
2 Hôtel Suisse
3 Hôtel de la Mer
4 La Cambuse Rest.
5 La Festival de la Moule
6 Nissa Socca Rest.
7 Chez Palmyre Rest.
8 L'Acchiardo Rest.
9 Restaurant du Gesù
10 Lou Pilha Leva Rest.
11 L'Univers Rest.
12 Restaurant Castel
13 Fenocchio's Gelato (2)
14 Distilleries Ideales
15 Bike Rental
16 Go Sport
17 Centre du Patrimoine (Walking Tours)
18 Start of "Old Nice Walk"
P Parking
Place Rossetti
Tram
View
200 Yards
200 Meters
To Train Station
Bus Stop Lines #15 + #17
To Place Garibaldi
To 3 Corniche Roads
To Promenade des Anglais
Place Massena
Cemetery
Castle Hill
Elevator + Bellanda Tower
Play Field
Montee Lesage
Cours Saleya
Place Gautier
Place du Palais
Post
Mediterranean Sea
Beach
Quai des Etats-Unis
Rue des Ponchettes
Blvd. Jean Jaures
Avenue Felix Faure
Rue Gioffredo
Fountains
Rue de l'Opera
Rue de St. François de Paule
Rue François
Rue Alex. Mari
Rue de la Prefecture
Rue Droite
Rue Rossetti
Rue de la Loge
Rue Centrale
Boucherie
Marché
Ste. Reparate
Rue Ste. Rep.
Jesus
Vieille
St. Jacques
Poisson
Robbins

$$$ Hôtel les Cigales*** is a smart little pastel place with tasteful decor, 19 plush rooms (most with tub-showers), air-conditioning, and a nifty upstairs terrace, all well-managed by friendly Mr. Valentino, with Veronique and Elaine. Book directly through the hotel and show this book for a surprise treat on arrival (standard Db-€90–120, big Db-€115–140, Tb-€150, €30 more during major events, extra bed-€20, 16 rue Dalpozzo, tel. 04 97 03 10 70, fax 04 97 03 10 71, www.hotel-lescigales.com, info@hotel-lescigales.com).

$$$ Hôtel Splendid**** is a worthwhile splurge if you miss your Marriott. The panoramic rooftop pool, Jacuzzi, bar, restaurant, and breakfast room alone almost justify the cost...but throw in good rooms (4 of 6 floors are non-smoking), a free gym, and air-conditioning, and you're as good as home. Check their website for deals (Db-€225, deluxe Db with terrace-€250, suites-€335–360, free breakfast if you stay at least 3 nights, 10 percent off for weeklong stays, parking-€20/day, 50 boulevard Victor Hugo, tel. 04 93 16 41 00, fax 04 93 16 42 70, www.splendid-nice.com, info @splendid-nice.com).

$$$ Hôtel Gounod*** is behind Hôtel Splendid and shares the same owners, who allow its clients free access to Hôtel Splendid's pool, Jacuzzi, and other amenities. Don't let the lackluster lobby fool you. Most rooms are richly decorated, with high ceilings and air-conditioning—though quality can vary (Db-€145, palatial 4-person suites-€225, parking-€14/day, 3 rue Gounod, tel. 04 93 16 42 00, fax 04 93 88 23 84, www.gounod-nice.com, info @gounod-nice.com).

$$$ Hôtel Villa Victoria*** is well-managed by cheery Marlena, who welcomes travelers in a classy old building with a green awning and an attractive lobby, which overlooks a generous garden. Rooms are traditional and well-kept, with space to stretch out (Db-€115–140, Tb-€128–153, suites-€160–180, pricier rooms face the garden, breakfast-€15, air-con, parking-€10–15, 33 boulevard Victor Hugo, tel. 04 93 88 39 60, fax 04 93 88 07 98, www.villa-victoria.com).

Closer to the Airport

$$ Hôtel Ibis** offers a handy port-in-the-storm outlet for those with early flights or single nights (Db-€80–120, 359 promenade des Anglais, tel. 04 89 88 30 30, fax 04 93 21 19 43, reception @ibisnice.com).

EATING

Remember, you're in a resort...go for ambience and fun, and lower your palate's standards. Italian is a low-risk and local cuisine. My recommended restaurants are concentrated in neighborhoods close to my favorite hotels, though you should focus your dining energy on Old Nice. Promenade des Anglais is ideal for picnic dinners on warm, languid evenings. Old Nice has the best and busiest dining atmosphere, while the Nice Etoile area is more convenient and offers a good range of choices. To eat cheaply, eat on rue Droite in Old Nice, or explore the area around the train station. For a more peaceful meal, dine in nearby Villefranche-sur-Mer (see page 293). For terribly touristy trolling, wander the wall-to-wall places lining rue Masséna. Yuck.

In Old Nice

Nice's dinner scene converges on cours Saleya (koor sah-lay-yuh)—entertaining enough in itself to make its restaurants' generally mediocre food a good value. It's a fun, festive place to compare tans and mussels. Even if you're eating elsewhere, wander through here in the evening. For locations, see the map on page 259.

La Cambuse, a small island of refinement for those who want to dine on cours Saleya, is the one place along here that doesn't try to reel in passersby. Owner Gregory is swimming upstream in his effort to provide quality cuisine with attentive service in this touristy area. Split a starter like the filling *petits farcis niçois* (stuffed vegetables), then order your own *plat* (€13 starters, €18–24 *plats*, open daily, 5 cours Saleya, tel. 04 93 80 82 40).

La Festival de la Moule is a fun place where it's all about the mussels. For just €11, you get all-you-can-eat mussels and fries (across the square from la Cambuse, 20 cours Saleya, tel. 04 93 62 02 12).

Nissa Socca offers good, cheap Italian cuisine and a lively atmosphere in a small room a few blocks from cours Saleya. Inside tables are usually steamy—arrive early to land a table outside (€9 pizza, €10 pastas, €15 *menus*, Mon–Sat from 19:00, closed Sun, a block off place Rossetti on rue Ste. Réparate, tel. 04 93 80 18 35).

L'Univers, a block off place Masséna, earned a Michelin star while maintaining a warm ambience. This elegant place is as relaxed as a "top" restaurant can be, from its casual decor to the tasteful dinnerware. When the artfully presented food arrives, you know this is high cuisine (*menus* from €42, closed Sun, 53 boulevard Jean Jaurès, tel. 04 93 62 32 22, plumailunivers@aol.com).

Restaurant Castel is your best eat-on-the-beach option. Eating here, you almost expect Don Ho to grab a mic. You're right on the beach below Castle Hill, perfectly positioned to watch evening swimmers get in their last laps as the sky turns pink and city lights flicker on. The views are unforgettable; you can even have lunch at your beach chair if you've rented one. Dinner here is best, so arrive before sunset and linger long enough to merit the few extra euros the place charges (open daily, €13–15 salads

Nice Restaurants

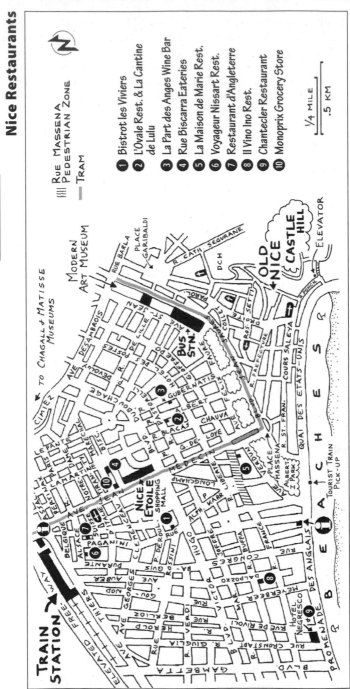

Nice

RUE MASSENA
PEDESTRIAN ZONE

TRAM

1 Bistrot les Viviers
2 L'Ovale Rest. & La Cantine de Lulu
3 La Part des Anges Wine Bar
4 Rue Biscarra Eateries
5 La Maison de Marie Rest.
6 Voyageur Nissart Rest.
7 Restaurant d'Angleterre
8 Il Vino Ino Rest.
9 Chantecler Restaurant
10 Monoprix Grocery Store

¼ MILE
.5 KM

and pastas, €20–24 main courses, 8 quai des Etats-Unis, tel. 04 93 85 22 66).

Dining Cheap *à la Niçoise*

Try at least one of these four places—not just because they're terrific budget options, but primarily because they offer authentic *niçoise* cuisine.

Chez Palmyre is as real as it gets, where your hostess Madame Palmyre shuffles between her small kitchen and the seven-table dining room. The four-course *menu* is only €13, and the cuisine could not be more homemade (closed Sun, cash only, 5 rue Droite, tel. 04 93 85 72 32).

L'Acchiardo, in the heart of Old Nice, does a good job mixing a loyal local and tourist clientele. Its simple, hearty, *niçoise* cuisine is served for fair prices in a homey setting overseen by gentle Monsieur Acchiardo (€13 dinner *plats,* cash only, closed Sat–Sun, 38 rue Droite, tel. 04 93 85 51 16).

Restaurant du Gesù, a happy-go-lucky budget eatery, squeezes plastic tables into a slanting square deep in the old city (sailors accustomed to dining at an angle will feel right at home). Arrive early or join the mobs waiting for an outside table, or, better, have fun in the soccer banner–draped interior (€8 pizzas, €10 pastas, closed Sun, 1 place du Jésus, tel. 04 943 62 26 46).

Lou Pilha Leva offers a fun, *très* cheap dinner option with *niçoise* specialties and outdoor-only benches. Order your food from one side and drinks from the other (open daily, located where rue de la Loge and Centrale meet in Old Nice).

And for Dessert...

Gelato-lovers should save room for the tempting ice cream stands in Old Nice—such as **Fenocchio,** which serves up 86 flavors, from tomato to lavender (daily until 23:30, 2 locations in Old Nice: on place Rossetti and on rue de la Poissonnerie).

Eating near Nice Etoile

On Rue Biscarra: Laid-back cafés line up along the broad sidewalk on rue Biscarra (just east of avenue Jean Médecin behind Nice Etoile, all closed Sun). **L'Authentic, Le Vin sur Vin, Marre'n,** and **Le Cenac** are all reasonable enough. **Le Vin sur Vin** seems most popular, though **L'Authentic** is also good, with memorable owners (burly Philippe and sleek Laurent), daily specials, €19 *menus,* and reasonable pasta dishes (closed Sun, 18 bis rue Biscarra, tel. 04 93 62 48 88).

Bistrot les Viviers appeals to those who require attentive service, silver warming covers, and authentic *niçoise* cuisine. At this cozy splurge, allow €65 per person for wine and three courses. It has two different settings: a formal restaurant and a more relaxed *bistrot* next door. Reserve for the atmospheric *bistrot;* the prices are the same. Fish is the chef's forte (closed Sun, 22 rue Alphonse Karr, 5-min walk west of avenue Jean Médecin, tel. 04 93 16 00 48).

L'Ovale is a find. How this ever-so-local and rugby-loving café survives in a tourist mecca, I'll never know. It's run by Nice's nicest couple, Jean-Marc and Jacqueline, who serve quality food at good prices. Join the lively local crowd and dine inside on big *plats* for €11. Consider their specialty, *cassoulet* (€36 for two people), or enjoy *la planche de charcuterie* as a meaty, filling first course (excellent €15 3-course *menu*, closed Sun, air-con, 29 rue Pastorelli, tel. 04 93 80 31 65).

La Maison de Marie is a surprisingly high-quality refuge off touristy rue Masséna, where most other places serve mediocre food to tired tourists. Enter through a deep-red arch to a bougainvillea-draped courtyard, and enjoy the fair prices and good food that draw locals and travelers alike. The interior tables are as appealing as those in the courtyard (*menus* from €20, open daily, look for the square red flag at 5 rue Masséna, tel. 04 93 82 15 93).

La Cantine de Lulu is small, charming, and Czech-owned, with homemade recipes from Nice and Prague (closed Sat–Mon, 26 rue Alberti, tel. 04 93 62 15 33).

La Part des Anges, an atmospheric wine shop with a few tables in the back, serves a limited, good menu with a large selection of wines (open daily for lunch, Fri–Sat only for dinner, reserve ahead, 17 rue Gubernatis, tel. 04 93 62 69 80).

Near Promenade des Anglais

Il Vino Ino, near several recommended hotels a block from promenade des Anglais, has street appeal. This lively, reasonably priced eatery serves only Italian food amid cheery decor inside or out (closed Sun, 33 rue de la Buffa, tel. 04 93 87 94 25).

Chantecler has Nice's most prestigious address—inside the Hôtel Negresco. This is everything a luxury restaurant should be: elegant, soft, and top-quality. If your trip is ending in Nice, call or email for reservations—you've earned this splurge (*menus* from €90, open daily, 37 promenade des Anglais, tel. 04 93 16 64 00, chantecler@hotel-negresco.com).

Near the Train Station

These two places are hardly undiscovered—they're listed in many other guidebooks—but they deserve their acclaim.

Restaurant d'Angleterre is ideal for hungry travelers on a tight budget. For €15 you get a filling three-course dinner with tasty choices and great service (indoor and outdoor tables, closed Sun–Mon, 25 rue d'Angleterre, tel. 04 03 88 64 48).

Voyageur Nissart blends budget cuisine with cool Mediterranean ambience and friendly service (€17 *menus*, closed Mon, 19 rue d'Alsace-Lorraine, tel. 04 93 82 19 60).

TRANSPORTATION CONNECTIONS

For rough train, bus, and boat schedules from Nice to nearby towns, see "Getting Around the Riviera," page 240. Note that most long-distance train connections to other French cities require a change in Marseille.

From Nice by Train to: Marseille (18/day, 2.5 hrs), **Cassis** (14/day, 3 hrs, transfer in Toulon or Marseille), **Arles** (11/day, 3.75–4.5 hrs, most change in Marseille or Avignon), **Avignon** (20/day, 13 of which are by TGV, 4 hrs, a few direct, most require transfer in Marseille), **Paris**' Gare de Lyon (10/day, 6 hrs, may require change; 11-hr night train goes to Paris' Gare d'Austerlitz), **Aix-en-Provence** TGV station (10/day, 3.5 hrs, may require transfer in Marseille or Toulon), **Chamonix** (4/day, 10 hrs, 3 transfers), **Beaune** (7/day, 7 hrs, 1–2 changes), **Munich** (4/day, 12–13 hrs with 2–4 transfers, night trains possible via Italy), **Interlaken** (6/day, 9–11 hrs, 2–5 transfers), **Florence** (6/day, 7–9 hrs, 1–3 transfers), **Milan** (7/day, 5–5.5 hrs, 4 with transfers), **Venice** (5/day, 2/night, 8–9 hrs, all require transfers except one direct night train), **Barcelona** (2/day, 11–12 hrs; 1 decent night train via Port Bou, 13 hrs).

Nice's Airport

Nice's easy-to-navigate airport (Aéroport de Nice Côte d'Azur) is on the Mediterranean, a 20–30-minute drive west of the city center. Planes leave about hourly to Paris (1-hour flight, about the same price as a train ticket). The two terminals (Terminal 1 and Terminal 2) are connected by frequent shuttle buses. Both terminals have TIs, banks, ATMs, taxis, and buses to Nice (www.nice.aeroport.fr, tel. 08 20 42 33 33 or 04 89 88 98 28).

Taxis into the center are expensive, charging €30 to Nice hotels and €50 to Villefranche-sur-Mer (10 percent more at night—that's 19:00–7:00—and all day Sunday). Taxis stop outside door *(Porte)* A-1 at Terminal 1 and outside *Porte* A-3 at Terminal 2. Nice taxis are not always so nice—and are notorious for overcharging. If your fare for a ride into Nice is much higher than €30 (or €33 at night or on Sun), refuse to pay more. If this doesn't work, tell the cabbie to call a *gendarme* (police officer).

Airport shuttle vans work with some of my recommended hotels. These only make sense when going *to* the airport, not when arriving. Unlike taxis, shuttle vans offer a fixed price that doesn't rise on Sundays, early mornings, or evenings. Prices are best for groups (figure €25 for one person, and only a little more for additional people—ask at your hotel).

Three bus lines connect the airport with the city center, offering good alternatives to high-priced taxis and shuttles. **Bus #99** runs from both terminals to Nice's main train station (€4, 2/hr, 8:00–21:00, 30 min, drops you within a 10-min walk of many recommended hotels). To take this bus *to* the airport, catch it right in front of the train station (departs on the half-hour). If you're sleeping within walking distance of the station, #99 is a €4 breeze. The **yellow "NICE" bus #98** serves both terminals, and runs along promenade des Anglais to Nice's main bus station *(gare routière)*, near Old Nice (€4, 3/hr, 30 min). The slower, cheaper local **bus #23** serves only Terminal 1, and makes every stop between the airport and train station (€1.30, 4/hr, 40 min, direction: St. Maurice). Buy tickets in the information office just outside either terminal, or from the driver. To reach the bus information office and stops at Terminal 1, turn left after passing customs and exit the doors at the far end. Buses serving Terminal 2 stop across the street from the exit. If you take **bus #98** or **#99,** keep your ticket, which is good all day on any public bus in Nice, and for Ligne d'Azur buses between Nice and nearby towns (see page 242 for details).

To get to **Villefranche-sur-Mer** from the airport, take the yellow "NICE" bus #98 to Nice's bus station *(gare routière)*, then transfer to the Villefranche-sur-Mer bus (bus #100, use same ticket).

To reach **Antibes** and **Cannes,** take line #200 from either terminal (€1.30, 2–3/hr, 45–70 min to Antibes depending on traffic, an additional 30 min to Cannes). Express buses (line #110) run directly to **Monaco** from the airport (€15, hourly, 50 min).

WELCOME TO THE RIVIERA WALK

*From the Promenade des Anglais
to Castle Hill*

This leisurely, level walk begins on the promenade des Anglais (near the landmark Hôtel Negresco) and ends on Castle Hill above Old Nice. While the entire walk works well anytime, the first half makes a fine pre- or post-dinner stroll. Allow one hour at a Mediterranean pace to reach the elevator up to Castle Hill.

THE WALK BEGINS

Promenade des Anglais

Welcome to the Riviera. There's something for everyone along this four-mile-long seafront circus. Watch the Europeans at play, admire the azure Mediterranean, anchor yourself on a blue bench, and prop your feet up on the made-to-order guardrail. Later in the day, come back to join the evening parade of tans along the promenade.

For now, stroll like the belle époque English aristocrats for whom the promenade was built. The broad sidewalks of the promenade des Anglais ("walkway of the English") were financed by wealthy English tourists who wanted a safe place to stroll and admire the view. The walk was paved in marble in 1822 for aristocrats who didn't want to dirty their shoes or smell the fishy gravel. This grand promenade leads to the old city and Castle Hill.

• *Start at the pink-domed...*

Hôtel Negresco

Nice's finest hotel (also a historic monument) offers the city's most expensive beds (€460 minimum for a sea view, see "Sleeping," page 258), and a free "museum" interior (always open—provided you're dressed decently, absolutely no beach attire). March straight through the lobby (as if you're staying there) into the exquisite Salon Royal, a cozy place for a drink (opens at 11:00) and a frequent host to art exhibits. The chandelier hanging from the Eiffel-built dome is made of 16,000 pieces of crystal. It was built in France for the Russian czar's Moscow palace...but because of the Bolshevik Revolution in 1917, he couldn't take delivery. Read the explanation of the dome and saunter around counterclockwise: The bucolic dome scene, painted in 1913 for the hotel, sets the tone. Nip into the toilets for either a turn-of-the-century powder room or a Battle of Waterloo experience. The chairs nearby were typical of the age (cones of silence for an afternoon nap sitting up).

The hotel's Chantecler restaurant is one of the Riviera's best (allow €120 per person with wine; described on page 264). Two years ago, it lost one of its Michelin stars, so you'll understand if the staff doesn't smile. In France, big-time chefs are like famous athletes: People know about them and talk about who's hot and who's not. (A few years ago, a famous Burgundian chef lost a star and committed suicide.) On your way out, pop into the Salon Louis XIV (right of entry lobby as you leave), where the embarrassingly short Sun King models his red platform boots (English descriptions explain the room).

Outside, turn left and walk past the bar entrance to the back to see the hotel's original entrance (grander than today's)—in the 19th century, classy people stayed out of the sun, and any posh hotel that cared about its clientele would design its entry on the shady north side.

• *Cross the promenade des Anglais, and—before you begin your seaside promenade—grab a blue seat and gaze out to the...*

Bay of Angels (Baie des Anges)

Face the water. The body of Nice's patron saint, Réparate, was supposedly escorted into this bay by angels in the fourth century. To your right is where you might have been escorted into France—Nice's airport, built on a massive landfill. On that tip of land way beyond the runway is Cap d'Antibes. Until 1860, Antibes and Nice were in different countries—Antibes was French, but Nice was a protectorate of the Italian kingdom of Savoy-Piedmont, a.k.a. the Kingdom of Sardinia. (During that period, the Var River—just west of Nice—was the geographic border between these two peoples.) In 1850, the people here spoke Italian and ate pasta. As Italy was uniting, the region was given a choice: join the new country of Italy or join France (which was enjoying good times under the rule of Napoleon III). The vast majority voted in 1860 to go French... and voilà!

The green hill to your left (Castle Hill) marks the end of this walk. Further left lies Villefranche-sur-Mer (marked by the tower at land's end, and home to lots of millionaires), then Monaco (which you can't see, with more millionaires), then Italy (with lots of pasta). Behind you are the foothills of the Alps (Alpes Maritimes), which gather threatening clouds, ensuring that the Côte d'Azur enjoys sunshine more than 300 days each year. While half a million people live here, pollution is carefully treated—the water is routinely tested and very clean.

· *With the sea on your right, begin...*

Strolling the Promenade

The block next to Hôtel Negresco has a lush park and the Masséna Museum (city history, eternally closed for renovation). Nearby sit two other belle époque establishments: the West End and Westminster hotels—English names to help those original guests feel at home. These hotels symbolize Nice's arrival as a tourist mecca a century ago, when the combination of leisure time and a stable economy allowed tourists to find the sun even in winter.

Even a hundred years ago, there was sufficient tourism in Nice to justify building its first casino (a leisure activity imported from Venice). Part of an elegant casino stood on those white pilings that you see in the sea, until the Germans destroyed it during World War II. While that's gone, you can see the striking 1930s Art Nouveau facade of the Palais de la Méditerranée, a grand casino, hotel, and theater.

As you walk, be careful to avoid the bike lane. You'll pass a number of separate beaches—some private, others public. In spite of the rocks, they're still a popular draw. You can rent your gear (mattress and chaise longue-€12–18, umbrella-€5, towel-€3) and kick back. You'll also pass several beach restaurants (a highly recommended experience—see page 261). Some of these eateries serve breakfast, all serve lunch, some offer dinner, and a few have cool bars...tailor-made for a break from this walk. A few promote package deals, including a lounge chair, umbrella, locker, and meal, all for about €26. Why all this beach-gear rental? In Europe, most beach-going families take planes or trains, since parking is pricey and traffic is awful. (So, unlike my family's beach trips, they can't stuff chairs, coolers, and the like in the trunk of their car and park right near the beach.)

The unappealing Casino Ruhl is farther along (just before the park). Anyone can drop in for some one-armed-bandit fun, but for the tables at night you'll need to dress up and bring your passport. Albert I Park is named for the Belgian king who enjoyed wintering here. While the English came first, the Belgians and Russians were also big fans of 19th-century Nice. That tall statue at the edge of the park commemorates Nice's being part of France for 100 years.

Continue along the promenade, past the park. You're now on quai des Etats-Unis (quay of the United States). This name was given as a tip-of-the-cap to the Americans for finally entering World War I in 1917. (US involvement was essential to French victory.) Five minutes past the Hôtel Suisse (brilliant views as you walk), there's a monumental war memorial sculpted out of the rock in honor of the thousands of local boys who died serving their country in World Wars I and II.

• *Take the elevator next to the Hôtel Suisse up to Castle Hill (elevator open daily 10:00–19:00, until 20:00 in summer, €0.70 one-way, €1.10 round-trip).*

Castle Hill (Colline du Château)

This hill—in an otherwise flat city center—offers sensational views over Nice, the port (to the east), the foothills of the Alps, and the Mediterranean. The views are best early or at sunset, or whenever the weather's really clear (park closes at 20:00 in summer, earlier off-season). Nice was founded on this hill. Its residents were crammed onto the hilltop until the 12th century, as it was too risky to live in the flatlands below, where marauders were on the rampage. Today, you'll find a waterfall, a playground, two cafés (fair prices), and a cemetery—but no castle—on Castle Hill.

• *Your tour is finished. Enjoy the vistas. To walk down to Old Nice, follow signs from just below the upper café to* Vieille Ville *(not* Le Port*), turn right at the cemetery, then look for the walkway down on your left. If you're planning a boat tour (2/day, 1 hour, see page 243), follow the* Le Port *signs to the bassin des Amiraux.*

OLD NICE WALK

From Place Masséna to Place Rossetti

This self-guided walking tour gives a helpful introduction to Nice's bicultural heritage and most interesting neighborhoods. It's best done early in the morning (while the outdoor market still thrives and the *socca*'s hot), and preferably not on a Sunday, when many shops are closed. Allow about an hour at a leisurely pace for this level walk, including a stop for coffee and *socca* (chickpea crêpe). Because this walk ends near the bus station, it works well on the way to an afternoon bus excursion (e.g., to Monaco, Villefranche-sur-Mer, Cap Ferrat, or the inland hill towns).

THE WALK BEGINS

• *Start on the edge of place Masséna facing the fountains with the Grand Hôtel Aston up ahead on your left.*

Place Masséna

This grand *place* is Nice's ground zero, where old Nice meets new, and where the recently built tramway bends between the bus and train stations. It's also a good spot to appreciate the Italian heri-

tage of the city. The rich color of the buildings that line this square reflect the taste of previous Italian rulers, back when Nice residents rooted for Italian soccer teams. Those fountains are the product of more recent tastes—to save money, they only have high pressure after 17:00. The hills you see in the distance separate Nice from Villefranche-sur-Mer, and that Italianesque clock tower is barely

Old Nice Walk

1. Place Masséna
2. Rue St. François de Paule
3. Cours Saleya
4. Café les Ponchettes
5. Rue de la Poissonnerie
6. Rue Droite
7. Place Rossetti

P PARKING
★ PLACE ROSSETTI
⚐ VIEW
▬ TRAM

200 YARDS
200 METERS

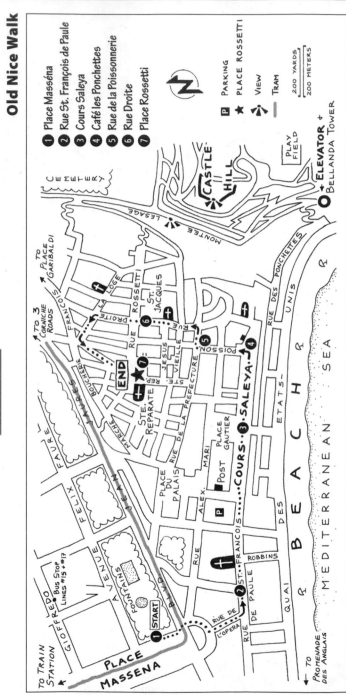

beyond Nice's bus station.

Turn around. You're standing on Nice's historic river, the Paillon. It runs under the greenbelt in front of you to the sea, and has been covered since the late 1800s. For centuries, this river was Nice's natural defense to the north and west (the sea protected the south, and Castle Hill defended the east). Imagine the fortified wall that once ran along its length from the hills behind you to the sea.

With the arrival of tourism in the 1800s, Nice spread beyond the river to your right (where your hotel is probably located). The modern, can't-miss-it sculpture in the parkway is meant to represent the "curve of the French Riviera"—whatever that means—but looks more like an answer to local skateboarders' prayers.

As you stand here, you may be dodging trams on its long-awaited tramway line (the first of three). The tramway system is Nice's attempt to curb its debilitating traffic problem. The city is also considering some controversial traffic-reduction techniques, such as charging drivers a fee to enter the city center during peak periods.

• Cross the square toward the Caisse d'Epargne Côte d'Azur bank, and walk between the curved buildings. Head down rue de l'Opéra, turning left on...

Rue St. François de Paule

You've entered Old Nice. Peer into the Alziari olive-oil shop at #14 (on the right, closed Sun). Dating from 1868, the shop produces top-quality, stone-ground olive oil. The proud owner, Gilles Piot, claims that stone wheels create less acidity (since metal grinding builds up heat). Locals fill their own containers from the huge vats (the cheapest one is peanut oil, not olive oil). Consider a gift for the olive-oil lover on your list.

A block down on the left (at #7), Pâtisserie Auer's grand old storefront has changed little since the pastry shop opened in 1820 (closed Sun). The writing on the window says, "Since 1820 from father to son." The royal medallions on the back wall remind shoppers that Queen Victoria fed her sweet tooth here.

Across the street is Nice's grand opera house, dating from the same era. Imagine this opulent jewel buried deep in the old town of Nice, back in the 19th century. With all the fancy big-city folks wintering here, the rough-edged town needed some high-class entertainment. The four statues on top represent theater, dance, music, and singing.

• Continue on, sifting your way through souvenirs to the cours Saleya (koor sah-lay-yuh).

Cours Saleya

Named for its broad exposure to the sun *(soleil)*, this commotion of color, sights, smells, and people has been Nice's main market square since the Middle Ages (produce market held Tue–Sun until 13:00—on Mon, an antique market takes center stage). Amazingly, part of this square was a parking lot until 1980, when the mayor of Nice had an underground garage built.

The first section of the market is devoted to the plants and flowers that grow effortlessly and everywhere in this climate. Carnations, roses, and jasmine are local favorites in this, the Riviera's largest flower market since the 19th century. Fresh flowers are perhaps the best value in this otherwise pricey city.

The boisterous produce section trumpets the season with mushrooms, strawberries, white asparagus, zucchini flowers—whatever's fresh gets top billing.

Place Pierre Gautier (also called Plassa dou Gouvernou—bilingual street signs include the old Niçoise language, an Italian dialect) is where the actual farmers set up stalls to sell their produce and herbs directly. For a great market overview, climb the steps (leading up on both sides; you'll have to step over the trash sacks) above the Côte and Grand Bleu restaurants.

From your perch, look up to the hill that dominates to the east. The city of Nice was first settled up there by Greeks (circa 400 B.C.). In the Middle Ages, a massive castle stood there, with turrets, high walls, and soldiers at the ready. Over time, the city grew at the base of the castle, where you are now. With the river guarding one side and the sea the other, this mountain fortress seemed strong—until Louis XIV leveled it in 1706. Nice's medieval seawall ran along the lineup of two-story buildings where you're standing.

Now, look across place Pierre Gautier to the large "palace." This Ducal Palace was where the kings of Sardinia (until 1860, the city's Italian rulers) would reside when in Nice. Today, it's police headquarters.

Resume your stroll down the center of cours Saleya, stopping when you see La Cambuse restaurant on your left. In front, hovering over the black barrel fire with the paella-like pan on top, is the self-proclaimed Queen of the Market, Thérèse (tehr-ehz). When she's not looking for a husband, Thérèse is cooking *socca*, Nice's chickpea crêpe specialty. Spend €2 for a wad of *socca* (careful—it's hot, but good). If she doesn't have a pan out, that means it's on its way (watch for the frequent scooter deliveries). Wait in line...or else it'll be all gone when you return.

• *Continue down cours Saleya. The fine golden building at the end is where Henri Matisse lived for 17 years. (The Café les Ponchettes is perfectly positioned for a people-watching break.) Turn left a block before the end of the square and head down...*

Rue de la Poissonnerie

Look up at the first building on your right. Adam and Eve are squaring off, each holding a zucchini-like gourd. This scene (post-apple) represents the annual rapprochement in Nice to make up for the sins of a too-much-fun Carnival (Mardi Gras). Nice residents have partied hard during Carnival for more than 700 years.

Now, walk a few doors down to #6 (right side). That filthy iron grill above the door allows air to enter the building, but keeps out uninvited guests. You'll see lots of these open grills in Old Nice. They were part of a clever system that sucked in cool air from the sea, through the homes, and out through vents in the roof.

A few steps away, check out the small Baroque church (Notre-Dame-de-l'Annonciation) dedicated to St. Rita, the patron saint of desperate causes. She holds a special place in locals' hearts, and this church is the most popular in Nice.

• *Turn right on the next street, where you'll pass Old Nice's most happening café/bar (Distilleries Ideales), with a lively happy hour (18:00–20:00) and a* Pirates of the Caribbean–*style interior. Now turn left on "Right" Street (rue Droite), and enter an area that feels like a Little Naples.*

Rue Droite

In the Middle Ages, this straight, skinny street provided the most direct route from wall to wall, or river to sea. Stop at Espuno's bakery (at place du Jésus) and say *bonjour* to the friendly folks. Thirty years ago, this baker was voted the best in France—the trophies you see were earned for bread making, not bowling. His son now runs the place. Notice the firewood stacked by the oven.

Farther along, at #28, Thérèse (whom you met earlier) cooks her *socca* in the wood-fired oven before she carts it to her barrel on cours Salcya. The balconies of the mansion in the next block mark the Palais Lascaris (1647, gorgeous at night), a rare souvenir from one of Nice's most prestigious families (free, Wed–Mon 10:00–18:00, closed Tue, worth touring for a peek at 1700s Baroque Italian high life, look up and make faces back at the guys under the balconies).

• *Turn left on the rue de la Loge, then left again on rue Centrale, to reach...*

Place Rossetti

The most Italian of Nice's piazzas, place Rossetti feels more like Rome than Nice. This square comes alive after dark. Fenocchio is popular for its many gelato flavors.

Walk to the fountain and stare back at the church. This is the Cathedral of St. Réparate—an unassuming building for a major city's cathedral. The cathedral was relocated here in the 1500s, when Castle Hill was temporarily converted to military-only. The name comes from Nice's patron saint, a teenage virgin named Réparate whose martyred body floated to Nice in the fourth century accompanied by angels (remember the Bay of Angels?). The interior of the cathedral gushes Baroque. Baroque was a response to the Protestant Reformation; with the Catholic Church's Counter-Reformation, the theatrical energy of churches was cranked up—with re-energized, high-powered saints and eye-popping decor.

• *Our tour is over. If you've got energy to burn, take a walk up Castle Hill. To get there, cross place Rossetti and follow the lane leading uphill (see Castle Hill description in the "Welcome to the Riviera Walk," page 267). If it's early enough and you're up for a day trip, take a left outside the church and you'll eventually arrive at the bus station.*

CHAGALL MUSEUM TOUR

Musée Chagall

Even if you're suspicious of modern art, this museum—with the largest collection of Marc Chagall's work in captivity anywhere—is a delight. After World War II, Chagall returned from the United States to settle in nearby Vence. Between 1954 and 1967, he painted a cycle of 17 large murals designed for, and donated to, this museum. These paintings, inspired by the biblical books of Genesis, Exodus, and the Song of Songs, make up the "nave," or core, of what Chagall called the "House of Brotherhood."

ORIENTATION

Cost: €6.70, free first Sunday of the month, sometimes a bit more during special exhibits.

Hours: Oct–June Wed–Mon 10:00–17:00, July–Sept until 18:00, closed Tue year-round.

Getting There: You can reach the museum, located on avenue Dr. Ménard, by bus or on foot.

Bus #15 serves the Chagall Museum from place Masséna (stop faces eastbound on rue Gioffredo, a block east of Galeries Lafayette; 5/hr Mon–Sat, 3/hr Sun, €1.30). The museum's bus stop (called Musée Chagall, shown on the bus shelter) is on boulevard de Cimiez (walk uphill from the stop to find the museum).

To **walk** from central Nice to the Chagall Museum, go to the train-station end of avenue Jean Médecin and turn right onto boulevard Raimbaldi. Walk four long blocks along the elevated road, then turn left onto avenue Raymond Comboul, and follow *Musée Chagall* signs.

Information: While Chagall would suggest that you explore his works without help, the €3 museum guidebook is useful

Chagall Museum

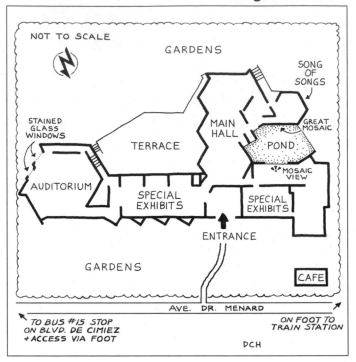

NOT TO SCALE

GARDENS

SONG OF SONGS

STAINED GLASS WINDOWS

MAIN HALL

GREAT MOSAIC

TERRACE

POND

MOSAIC VIEW

AUDITORIUM

SPECIAL EXHIBITS

SPECIAL EXHIBITS

ENTRANCE

GARDENS

CAFE

AVE. DR. MENARD

TO BUS #15 STOP ON BLVD. DE CIMIEZ + ACCESS VIA FOOT

ON FOOT TO TRAIN STATION

DCH

in explaining the symbolism. The free *Plan du Musée* helps locate the rooms, though you can probably do without, as the museum is pretty simple. Tel. 04 93 53 87 20, www.musee -chagall.fr.

Leaving the Museum: Taxis usually wait outside the museum.

To take bus #15 back to downtown Nice, turn right out of the museum, then make a left up boulevard de Cimiez, and catch the bus on the near side of the street. To continue on to the Matisse Museum, catch bus #15 using the uphill stop, located across the street.

To walk to the train station from the museum, turn left out of the museum, turn left on the street behind it, and then look for the staircase on your left (leading down). Cross under the freeway, then turn right to reach the station.

Length of This Tour: Allow one hour.

Cuisine Art and WCs: An idyllic garden café (open April–Oct) with fair prices awaits by the entrance to the museum grounds. A spick-and-span WC is to the far left in the garden as you face the museum (there's one inside, too).

THE TOUR BEGINS

This small museum consists of six rooms: two rooms with the 17 large murals, two rooms for special exhibits, an auditorium with stained-glass windows, and a mosaic-lined pond (viewed from inside). In the main hall, you'll find the core of the collection (Genesis and Exodus scenes). The adjacent octagonal room houses five paintings—the Song of Songs room.

• *Turn right after the ticket-taker and find...*

Old Testament Scenes

Each painting is a lighter-than air collage of images that draw from Chagall's Russian folk-village youth, his Jewish heritage, biblical themes, and his feeling that he existed somewhere between heaven and earth. He believed that the Bible was a synonym for nature, and that color and biblical themes were key ingredients for understanding God's love for his creation. Chagall's brilliant blues and reds celebrate nature, as do his spiritual and folk themes. Notice the focus on couples. To Chagall, humans loving each other mirrored God's love of creation.

The paintings are described below in the order you should see them, going counterclockwise around the room (some paintings might be on loan to other museums).

Abraham and the Three Angels

In the heat of the day, Abraham looked up and saw three men. He said, "Let a little food and water be brought, so you can be refreshed..." (Genesis 18:1–5)

Abraham refreshes God's angels on this red-hot day, and in return, they promise Abraham a son (in the bubble, at right), thus making him the father of the future Israelite nation.

The Sacrifice of Isaac

Abraham bound his son Isaac and laid him on the altar. Then he took the knife to slay his son. But the angel of the Lord called out to him from heaven, "Abraham!" (Genesis 22:9–11)

Tested by God, Abraham prepares to kill his only son, but the angel stops him in time. Notice that Isaac is posed exactly as Adam is in *The Creation* (described below). Abraham's sacrifice echoes three others: the sacrifice all men must make (i.e., Adam, the everyman), the sacrifice of atonement (the goat tied to a tree at left), and even God's sacrifice of his own son (Christ carrying the cross, upper right).

Chagall Mus'm

Chagall's Style

Chagall uses a deceptively simple, almost childlike style to paint a world that's hidden to the eye—the magical, mystical world below the surface. Here are some of his techniques:

- **Deep, radiant colors,** inspired by Expressionism and Fauvism (an art movement pioneered by Matisse and other French painters).
- **Personal imagery,** particularly from his childhood in Russia—smiling barnyard animals, fiddlers on the roof, flower bouquets, huts, and blissful sweethearts.
- **A Hasidic Jewish perspective,** the idea that God is everywhere, appearing in everyday things like nature, animals, and humdrum activities.
- **A fragmented Cubist style,** multifaceted and multidimensional, a perfect style to capture the multifaceted, multidimensional complexity of God's creation.
- **Overlapping images,** like double-exposure photography, with faint imagery that bleeds through, suggesting there's more to life under the surface.
- **Stained-glass-esque technique** of dark, deep, earthy, "potent" colors, and simplified, iconic, symbolic figures.
- **Gravity-defying compositions,** with lovers, animals, and angels twirling blissfully in midair.
- **Happy, not tragic mood,** that despite the violence and turmoil of world wars and revolution, he painted a world of personal joy.
- **Childlike simplicity,** drawn with simple, heavy outlines, filled in with Crayola colors that often spill over the lines. Major characters in a scene are bigger than the lesser characters. The grinning barnyard animals, the bright colors, the magical events presented as literal truth...Was Chagall a lightweight? Or a lighter-than-air-weight?

The Creation

God said, "Let us make man in our image, in our likeness..." (Genesis 1:26)

A pure-white angel descends through the blue sky and carries a still-sleeping Adam from radiant, red-yellow heaven to earth. Heaven is a whirling dervish of activity, spinning out all the events of future history, from the tablets of the Ten Commandments to the Crucifixion—an overture of many images that we'll see in later paintings. (Though not a Christian, Chagall saw the Crucifixion as a universal symbol of man's suffering.)

Moses Receives the Ten Commandments
The Lord gave him the two tablets of the Law, the tablets of stone inscribed by the finger of God... (Exodus 31:18)

An astonished Moses is tractor-beamed toward heaven, where God reaches out from a cloud to hand him the Ten Commandments. While Moses tilts one way, Mount Sinai slants the other, leading our eye up to the left, where a golden calf is being worshipped by the wayward Children of Israel. But down to the right, Aaron and the menorah assure us that Moses will set things right. In this radiant final panel, the Jewish tradition—after a long struggle—is finally established.

Driven from Paradise
So God banished him from the Garden of Eden...and placed cherubim and a flaming sword to guard the way... (Genesis 3:23–24)

An angel drives them out with a fire hose of blue (there's Adam still cradling his flaming-red *coq*), while a sparkling yellow sword prevents them from ever returning. Deep in the green colors, we get glimpses of the future—Eve giving birth (lower right corner) and the yellow sacrificial goat of atonement (top right).

Paradise
God put him in the Garden of Eden...and said, "You must not eat from the tree of the knowledge of good and evil..." (Genesis 2:15–17)

Paradise is a rich, earth-as-seen-from-space pool of blue, green, and white. Amoebic, still-evolving animals float around Adam (celibately practicing yoga) and Eve (with lusty-red hair). On the right, an angel guards the tempting tree, but Eve offers an apple, and Adam reaches around to sample the forbidden fruit.

The Rainbow
God said, "I have set my rainbow in the clouds as a sign of the covenant between me and the earth." (Genesis 9:13)

A flaming angel sets the rainbow in the sky, while Noah rests beneath it and his family offers a sacrifice of thanks. The pure-white rainbow's missing colors are found radiating from the features of the survivors.

Jacob's Ladder
He had a dream in which he saw a ladder resting on the earth with its top reaching to heaven, and the angels of God were ascending and descending on it... (Genesis 28:12)

In the left half, Jacob (Abraham's grandson) slumps asleep

Marc Chagall
(1887–1985)

1887–1910: Russia

Chagall is born in the small town of Vitebsk, Belarus. He's the oldest of nine children in a traditional Russian, Hasidic Jewish family. He studies realistic art in his hometown. In St. Petersburg, he is first exposed to the Modernist work of Paul Cézanne and the Fauves.

1910–1914: Paris

A patron finances a four-year stay in Paris. Chagall hobnobs with the avant-garde and learns technique from the Cubists, but he never abandons painting recognizable figures or his own personal fantasies. (Some say his relative poverty forced him to paint over used canvases, which gave him the idea of overlapping images that bleed through. Hmm.)

1914–1922: Russia

Returning to his hometown, Chagall marries Bella Rosenfeld (1915), whose love will inspire him for decades. He paints happy scenes despite the turmoil of wars and the Communist Revolution. Moving to Moscow (1920), he paints his first large-scale works, sets for the New Jewish Theatre. These would inspire many of his later large-scale works.

1923–1941: France and Palestine

Chagall returns to France. In 1931, he travels to Palestine, where the bright sun and his Jewish roots inspire a series of gouaches (opaque watercolor paintings). These gouaches would later inspire 105 etchings to illustrate the Bible (1931–1952), which would eventually inspire the 17 large canvases of biblical scenes in the Chagall Museum (1954–1967).

1941–1947: United States/World War II

Fearing persecution for his Jewish faith, Chagall emigrates to New York, where he spends the war years. The Crucifixion starts to appear in his paintings—not as a Christian symbol, but as a representation of the violence mankind perpetrates on itself. In 1947, his beloved Bella dies, and he stops painting for months.

1947–1985: South of France

After the war, Chagall returns to France, eventually settling in St-Paul-de-Vence. He remarries (Valentina Brodsky, in 1952). His new love, plus the southern sunshine, bring Chagall a revived creativity—he will be extremely prolific for the rest of his life. He experiments with new techniques and media—ceramics, sculpture, book illustrations, tapestry, and mosaic. In 1956, he's commissioned for his first stained-glass project. Eventually he'll do windows for cathedrals in Metz and Reims, and a synagogue of Jerusalem (1960). The Chagall Museum opens in 1973.

and dreams of a ladder between heaven and earth. On the right, a spinning angel with a menorah represents how heaven and earth are bridged by the rituals of the Jewish tradition.

Jacob Wrestles with an Angel

So Jacob wrestled with him till daybreak. Jacob said, "I will not let you go unless you bless me..." (Genesis 32: 24, 26)

Jacob holds on while the angel blesses him with descendants (the Children of Israel) and sends out rays from his hands, creating, among others, Joseph (stripped of his bright red coat and sold into slavery by his brothers).

Noah's Ark

Then he sent out a dove to see if the water had receded... (Genesis 8:8)

Adam and Eve's descendants have become so wicked that God destroys the earth with a flood, engulfing the sad crowd on the right. Only righteous Noah (center), his family (lower right), and the animals (including our yellow goat) were spared inside an ark. Here Noah opens the ark's window and sends out a dove to test the waters.

Moses Brings Water from the Rock

The Lord said, "Strike the rock, and water will come out of it for the people to drink..." (Exodus 17:5–6)

In the brown desert, Moses nourishes his thirsty people with water miraculously spouting from a rock. From the (red-yellow) divine source, it rains down actual (blue) water, but also a gush of spiritual yellow light.

Moses and the Burning Bush

The angel of the Lord appeared to him in flames of fire from within a bush... (Exodus 3:2)

Horned Moses—Chagall depicts him according to a medieval tradition—kneels awestruck before the burning bush, the event that calls him to God's service. On the left, we see Moses after the call, his face radiant, leading the Israelites out of captivity across the Red Sea, while Pharaoh's men drown (lower half of Moses' robe). The Ten Commandments loom ahead.

• *Pass Moses and walk past a stained-glass window on your way to the octagonal room.*

Song of Songs

Chagall wrote, "I've been fascinated by the Bible ever since my earliest childhood. I have always thought of it as the most extraordinary source of poetic inspiration imaginable. As far as I am

Song of Songs

Song of Solomon 7:11
*Come, my lover, let us go to the countryside,
let us spend the night in the villages.*
Song of Solomon 5:2
I slept but my heart was awake.
Song of Solomon 2:17
*Until the day breaks and the shadows flee, turn,
my lover, and be like a gazelle or like a young stag
on the rugged hills.*
Song of Solomon 3:4
I held him and would not let him go.
Song of Solomon 7:7
*Your stature is like that of the palm, and your
breasts like clusters of fruit.*

concerned, perfection in art and in life has its source in the Bible, and exercises in the mechanics of the merely rational are fruitless. In art as well as in life, anything is possible, provided there is love."

Chagall enjoyed the love of two women in his long life—his first wife Bella, then Valentina, who gave him a second wind as he was painting these late works. Chagall was one of the few "serious" 20th-century artists to portray unabashed love. Where the Bible uses the metaphor of earthly, physical, sexual love to describe God's love for humans, Chagall uses unearthly colors and a mystical ambience to celebrate human love. These red-toned canvases are hard to interpret on a literal level, but they capture the rosy spirit of a man in love with life.

• Head back toward the entry and turn left just before leaving the main hall and visit...

The Pond

The great mosaic reflected in the pond evokes the prophet Elijah in his chariot of fire (from the Second Book of Kings)—with Chagall's own addition of the 12 signs of the Zodiac, which he used to symbolize Time.

• Back at the entry, turn right at the ticket-taker and pass through the exhibition room with temporary displays. At the end, you'll find...

The Auditorium

This room is worth a peaceful moment to enjoy three Chagall stained-glass windows: the creation of light, elements, and planets (a visual big bang that's four "days" wide); the creation of animals, plants, man and woman, and the ordering of the solar system (two "days" wide, complete with fish and birds still figuring out where they belong); and the day of rest, with angels singing to the glory of God (the narrowest—only one "day" wide).

BETWEEN NICE AND MONACO

Villefranche-sur-Mer, Cap Ferrat, and the Three Corniches

The Riviera's richest stretch of real estate lies east of Nice. It's paved with famously scenic roads (called the Three Corniches), worthwhile stops, million-dollar vistas, and sea-splashed walking trails. Ten minutes from Nice, little Villefranche-sur-Mer stares across the bay to woodsy and exclusive Cap Ferrat. The eagle's-nest village of Eze-le-Village and the Corniche-topping village of La Turbie survey the scene from high above.

Villefranche-sur-Mer

Located halfway between the world-famous resorts of Nice and Monaco, Villefranche-sur-Mer offers travelers an easygoing slice of small-town Mediterranean life. In just 15 minutes, you can be gambling in style in Monaco or sauntering the promenade des Anglais in Nice. This town feels Italian, with soft-orange buildings, steep, narrow streets spilling into the sea, and pasta *con* pesto. Luxury sailing yachts glisten in the bay—an inspiration to those lazing along the harborfront to start saving when

their trips are over. Sand-pebble beaches, a handful of interesting sights, and quick access to Cap Ferrat keep visitors just busy enough.

Originally a Roman port, Villefranche-sur-Mer was overtaken by fifth-century barbarians. Villagers fled into the hills, where they stayed and farmed their olives. In 1295, the Duke of

Between Nice and Monaco

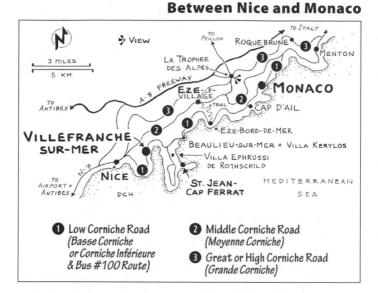

1 Low Corniche Road
(*Basse Corniche*
or Corniche Inférieure
& Bus #100 Route)

2 Middle Corniche Road
(*Moyenne Corniche*)

3 Great or High Corniche Road
(*Grande Corniche*)

Provence—like many in coastal Europe—was threatened by the Saracen Turks. He asked the hillside olive farmers to move down to the water and establish a front line against the invaders—denying them a base from which to attack Nice. In return for tax-free status, they stopped farming, took up fishing, and established *Ville-* (town) *franche* (without taxes). Since there were many such towns, this one was specifically "Tax-free town on the sea" *(sur Mer)*. In about 1560, the Duke of Savoy built the town an immense citadel (which you can still tour). Because two-thirds of its 8,000 people call this town their primary residence, Villefranche-sur-Mer today feels more like a real community than neighboring Riviera towns.

ORIENTATION

Tourist Information

The TI is in the park named jardin François Binon, below the main bus stop, labeled *Octroi* (July–Aug daily 9:00–19:00; Sept–June Mon–Sat 9:00–12:00 & 14:00–18:00, closed Sun; a 20-min walk or €10 taxi from train station, tel. 04 93 01 73 68, www.villefranche-sur-mer.org). Pick up the brochure detailing a self-guided walking tour of Villefranche-sur-Mer and information on boat rides (usually mid-June–Sept). If you plan to visit Cap Ferrat, ask for the simple brochure-map showing the walks around this peninsula and information on the Villa Ephrussi de Rothschild's gardens (see "The Three Corniches," page 294).

Arrival in Villefranche-sur-Mer

By Bus: Buses from Nice and Monaco drop you next to jardin François Binon, at the bus stop labeled *Octroi* just above the TI. The old town and most hotels are downhill. The stop for buses going back to Nice is across the street from where you were left off (buses run every 10–15 min). Bus #81 and #100 (see page 294) to and from Cap Ferrat uses the same Villefranche-sur-Mer stops.

By Train: Villefranche-sur-Mer's train station is a level 15-minute walk along the water from the old town and many of my listed hotels. Taxis to my recommended hotels cost €10, but they don't wait here and prefer longer rides; call instead, and pray the phone is working (tel. 06 09 33 36 12 or 06 39 32 54 09).

By Car: From Nice's port, follow signs for *Menton, Monaco,* and *Basse Corniche.* In Villefranche-sur-Mer, turn right at the TI (first signal after Hôtel la Flore) for parking and hotels. For a quick visit to the TI, park at the nearby pay lot. You'll find free parking in the moat areas within the boundaries of the citadel, a bit farther down—better for longer visits and well-signed from main road *(Parking Fossés).* There's a safer pay lot on the water across from the recommended Hôtel Welcome, and some hotels also have parking.

Helpful Hints

Market Day: An antiques market enlivens Villefranche-sur-Mer on Sundays (on place Amélie Pollonnais by Hôtel Welcome and in jardin François Binon by the TI). On Saturday mornings, a small food market sets up near the TI (only in jardin François Binon).

Internet Access: Chez Net, an "Australian International Sports Bar Internet Café," is a fun place to get a late-night drink or check your email (open daily, place du Marché).

Laundry: The town has two launderettes—both just below the main road on avenue Sadi Carnot. The upper *laverie* does your wash for you (next to Hôtel Riviera, Tue–Sun 8:00–12:00 & 14:00–18:30, closes Sat at 17:00, closed Mon, tel. 04 93 01 73 71), while the lower *laverie* is self-service (daily 7:00–20:00, opposite 6 avenue Sadi Carnot).

Taxi: Beware of taxi drivers who overcharge—the normal weekday, daytime rate to central Nice is about €35; to the airport, figure €50; one-way to Cap Ferrat is about €20 and to Eze-le-Village is about €30; and the five-minute trip up to the main street level (to bus stops on Low Corniche) from the waterfront should be less than €10 (tel. 06 09 33 36 12 or 06 39 32 54 09).

Minibus: Little electric bus #80 will save you the sweat from the harbor up the hill, but only runs once per hour (€1.30). It runs from the port to the top of the hill, stopping near my

Villefranche-sur-Mer

❶ Hôtel Welcome &
Souris Gourmande Rest.

❷ Hôtel Villa Vauban

❸ Hôtel la Flore

❹ To Hôtel la Fiancée du
Pirate & Minibus Stop

❺ Hôtel le Provençal

❻ Hôtel de la Darse

❼ Les Palmiers, Michel's
& Le Cosmo Rest.

❽ La Mère Germaine Rest.

❾ Le Roxy Rest.

❿ La Grignotière Rest.

⓫ Casino Grocery

⓬ Chez Net Bar & Internet

⓭ Boat Rides

⓮ Launderette

⓯ Octroi Bus Stop (from Nice; to
Monaco & Cap Ferrat)

⓰ Octroi Bus Stop (to Nice; from
Monaco & Cap Ferrat)

P PARKING

T TAXI STAND

STEPPED
STREETS

TO EZE + MONACO
VIA LOW CORNICHE ROAD

TRAIN STATION

BLVD. NAPOLEON III

FONCHARD

BEACH

TO CAP FERRAT ON FOOT

ALBERT 1er

AVE. GALLIENI

AVE. GEORGES CLEMENCEAU

QUAI AM. COURBET

R. VOLTI

R. BARON

POILU

RUE OBSCURE

AVE. SADI

POST

AVE. CH. JEUN.

AVE. JOFFRE

AVE. CARNOT

OLD TOWN

CHAPEL OF ST. PIERRE

+ ATM

AVE. VERDUN

ALLEE DUVAL

CITADEL

SCENIC WALKWAY

PLAY AREA

AVE. FOCH

AVE. AVENUE DE GAULLE

QUAI CORDERIE

TO NICE

PLAY AREA

PORT DE LA DARSE

MEDITERRANEAN SEA

200 YARDS
200 METERS

DCH

recommended hotel, La Fiancée du Pirate, before going over the hill to the outlying, suburban Nice Riquier train station (only convenient if you're already on minibus, must transfer to train to downtown Nice).

Sports Fans: Lively *boules* action takes place each evening just below the TI and the huge soccer field (see page 174).

SIGHTS

The Harbor—Browse Villefranche-sur-Mer's minuscule harbor. Only eight families still fish to make money. Gaze out to sea and marvel at the beautiful sailing yachts that call this bay home. (You might see well-coiffed captains being ferried in by dutiful mates to pick up their statuesque call girls.) Local guides keep a list of the world's 100 biggest yachts and talk about some of them like they're part of the neighborhood.

Parallel to the beach and about a block inland, you can walk the mysterious rue Obscura—a covered lane running 400 feet along the medieval rampart.

Chapel of St. Pierre (Chapelle Cocteau)—This chapel, decorated by artist, poet, and filmmaker Jean Cocteau, is the town's cultural highlight. A brooding fisherwoman collects a €2 donation for the fishermen's charity, and then sets you free to enjoy the chapel's small but intriguing interior. In 1955, Jean Cocteau covered the barrel-vaulted chapel with heavy black lines and pastels. Each of the Cocteau scenes—the Roma (Gypsies) of Stes-Maries-de-la-Mer who dance and sing to honor the Virgin, girls wearing traditional outfits, and three scenes from the life of St. Peter—are explained in English. Is that Villefranche-sur-Mer's citadel in the scene above the altar? (€2, Tue–Sun 9:30–12:00 & 15:00–19:00, closed Mon and when fisherwoman is tired, below Hôtel Welcome.)

Citadel—The town's immense castle was built in the 1500s by the Duke of Savoy to defend against the French. When the region joined France in 1860, it became just a barracks. In the 20th century, with no military use, the city started using the citadel to house its police station, City Hall, and two art galleries.

Church—The town church features a fine crucifix—carved, they say, from a fig tree by a galley slave in the 1600s.

Boat Rides (Promenades en Mer)—These little cruises, with English handouts, are offered two to three days a week (€11 for 1-hour cruise around Cap Ferrat, €16 for 2-hour cruise as far as Monaco—but doesn't stop there, boats depart from the harbor across from Hôtel Welcome, 4/day July–Aug, 2/day late June and Sept, none off-season, tel. 04 93 76 65 65).

Beachwalk—A seaside walkway leads under the citadel and connects the old town with the yacht harbor, where you'll find one hotel and a few cafés. This scenic walk turns downright romantic after dark. Even if you're sleeping elsewhere, consider an ice-cream-licking stroll here. You can also saunter Villefranche-sur-Mer's waterfront going the other direction, and continue beyond the train station for postcard-perfect views back to Villefranche-sur-Mer (ideal in the morning—go before breakfast). You'll come to a quieter beach with good picnic benches. You can even extend your walk to Cap Ferrat (see "Getting to Cap Ferrat," page 296).

SLEEPING

You have a handful of good hotels to choose from in Villefranche-sur-Mer. The ones I list have sea views from at least half of their rooms—well worth paying extra for.

$$$ Hôtel Welcome*, with easily the best location in Villefranche-sur-Mer, is anchored right on the water in the old town, with all 32 balconied rooms overlooking the harbor. You'll pay top price for all the comforts in this smart hotel. Skip the claustrophobic sixth-floor rooms ("comfort" Db-€182, bigger "superior" Db-€210, suites-€320–365, extra bed-€35, air-con, no Wi-Fi, elevator, parking garage-€20/day, 1 quai Amiral Courbet, tel. 04 93 76 27 62, fax 04 93 76 27 66, www.welcomehotel.com, resa@welcomehotel.com).

$$$ Hôtel Villa Vauban*** is an intimate villa two blocks below the TI, with nine freshly painted, handsome rooms—many with balconies and sea views, and most with Old World bathrooms. Amiable British expat Alan Powers adds a personal touch

---

Sleep Code

(€1 = about $1.30, country code: 33)
S = Single, **D** = Double/Twin, **T** = Triple, **Q** = Quad, **b** = bathroom, **s** = shower only, ***** = French hotel rating (0–4 stars). Unless otherwise noted, credit cards are accepted and English is spoken.

　　To help you sort easily through these listings, I've divided the rooms into three categories based on the price for a standard double room with bath:

　$$$ **Higher Priced**—Most rooms €100 or more.
　$$ **Moderately Priced**—Most rooms between €80–100.
　$ **Lower Priced**—Most rooms €80 or less.

that's rare in this area. He's happy to answer your questions (Db with small view-€90–120, Db with big sea view-€125–165, Db suite with sea view-€135–175, air-con, Wi-Fi, 11 avenue Général de Gaulle, tel. & fax 04 93 55 94 51, www.hotelvillavauban.com, info@hotelvillavauban.eu).

$$$ Hôtel la Flore*** is good if your idea of sightseeing is to enjoy the view from your spacious bedroom deck, or the pool. Most rooms have decks, there's a swimming pool, and the free parking couldn't be easier, but the staff is a tad formal and it's a 10-minute uphill walk from the old town (Db with no view-€85–125, Db with view and deck-€120–140, bigger Db that sleeps up to five and has a better view and bigger deck-€165–210, Db mini-suite-€220, Qb loft with huge terrace-€240, extra bed-€34, 10–15 percent cheaper Oct–March, air-con, elevator, restaurant open evenings only, just off main road high above harbor—near the bus stop to Nice and Monaco, 5 boulevard Princesse Grace de Monaco, 2 blocks from TI toward Nice, tel. 04 93 76 30 30, fax 04 93 76 99 99, www.hotel-la-flore.fr, hotel-la-flore@wanadoo.fr).

$$ Hôtel la Fiancée du Pirate is only for drivers, as it's high up in Villefranche-sur-Mer on the Middle Corniche (parking is no problem). Don't let the streetside appearance deter you. Friendly Eric and Laurence offer 15 bright and comfortable rooms with a pool, Jacuzzi, lush garden, roomy lounge area, and breakfast terrace with partial views of Cap Ferrat and the sea. Choose between rooms in the main building (Db-€88–108, Tb/Qb-€130–165), or view rooms on the garden patio (standard Db-€75–95, Tb/Qb-€100–125). From June to September, they require a three-night minimum stay and offer lunch, salads, and snacks by the pool (air-con, Wi-Fi, 8 boulevard de la Corne d'Or, Moyenne Corniche N7, tel. 04 93 76 67 40, fax 04 93 76 91 04, www.fianceedupirate.com, info@fianceedupirate.com).

$$ Hôtel le Provençal** is a well-situated, bare-bones place crying out for an owner who cares. The uninspired yet sleepable rooms are affordable, and some come with fine views and balconies (Db-€66–115, most about €90, Tb-€90–125, extra bed-€10, forget the cheaper non-view rooms, air-con, right below the main road, a block from TI at 4 avenue Maréchal Joffre, tel. 04 93 76 53 53, fax 04 93 76 96 00, www.hotelprovencal.com, provencal@riviera.fr).

$ Hôtel de la Darse**, a shy and unassuming little hotel burrowed in the shadow of its highbrow neighbors, offers a good value, low-profile alternative right on the water at Villefranche-sur-Mer's old port (a 10-min walk to the harbor). The sufficiently comfortable rooms facing the sea have million-dollar-view balconies and are worth the extra euros (view Db-€80, view Tb-€93, most with air-con, some noise on weekend nights, quieter garden view Db-€65, extra bed-€10, no elevator, from TI walk or drive down avenue

Nice-Monaco

Général de Gaulle to the old Port de la Darse, parking usually available nearby, tel. 04 93 01 72 54, fax 04 93 01 84 37, www.hotel -dela-darse-villefranche-sur-mer.cote.azur.fr, hoteldeladarse @wanadoo.fr).

EATING

Comparison-shopping is half the fun of dining in Villefranche-sur-Mer. Make an event out of a pre-dinner stroll through the old city. Check what looks good on the lively place Amélie Pollonnais (next to the Hôtel Welcome), saunter the string of candlelit places lining the waterfront, and consider the smaller, cheaper eateries embedded in the old city's walking streets. I prefer eating on place Amélie Pollonnais, where the whole village seems to converge at night.

Les Palmiers is a beachy place buzzing with cheery diners (€11–14 hearty salads and pizza, open daily, on place Amélie Pollonnais, tel. 04 93 01 71 63).

Le Cosmo Restaurant is next door. It's sharper, with great tables overlooking the harbor and the Cocteau chapel's facade (after some wine, Cocteau pops). It serves nicely presented and tasty meals. Ask for the daily suggestions and consider the €10 *omelet niçoise* (€10–14 fine salads and pastas, €13–21 *plats*, open daily, great Bandol red wine, place Amélie Pollonnais, tel. 04 93 01 84 05).

Michel's, on the other side of the fountain, is more romantic and stylish, and is the most reliable splurge restaurant in Villefranche-sur-Mer (allow €35 per person, closed Tue and in Nov, tel. 04 93 76 73 24).

La Mère Germaine, right on the harborfront, is the only place in town classy enough to lure a yachter ashore. It's dressy, with fine service and a harborside setting. The name comes from when the current owner's grandmother fed hungry GIs in World War II. Try the bouillabaisse, served with panache (€68 per person with 2-person minimum, ask about the less-expensive but ample mini-version, €39 *menu,* open daily, reserve harborfront table, tel. 04 93 01 71 39).

Le Roxy, on the main road just above the TI, is a *très* local, friendly, and cheap diner with hardworking Monique and chef hubbie Bebert. They make good pizza (€8.50), salads, and a killer *soup de poisson* that makes a meal for €11. Ask for seconds (closed Mon–Tue, 2 avenue de Grande Bretagne, tel. 04 93 76 71 80).

Disappear into Villefranche-sur-Mer's walking streets and find cute little **La Grignotière,** serving a €31 *gourmet menu,* an €18 couscous, and plenty of pizza and pasta options (May–Oct open daily, Nov–April closed Wed, cozy in bad weather, 3 rue Poilu, tel. 04 93 76 79 83).

Souris Gourmande ("Gourmet Mouse") is handy for a sandwich, either to take away or to eat there (daily 11:30–19:30, closed Fri in winter, at base of steps behind Hôtel Welcome, €5 made-to-order sandwiches...be patient and get to know your chef, Albert). Sandwich in hand, you'll find plenty of great places to enjoy a harborside sit.

There's a handy **Casino market/grocery store** a few blocks above the Hôtel Welcome at 12 rue Poilu (Thu–Tue 7:30–13:00 & 15:00–19:30, Wed 7:30–13:00 only).

For Drivers: If you have a car and are staying a few nights, consider the short drive up to Eze-le-Village or, better still, La Turbie. If it's summer (June–Sept), the best option of all is to go across to Cap Ferrat's plage de Passable for a before-dinner drink or a dinner you won't soon forget (recommendations listed under each destination below).

TRANSPORTATION CONNECTIONS

The last bus leaves Nice for Villefranche-sur-Mer at about 19:45; the last bus from Villefranche-sur-Mer to Nice leaves at about 20:50; and one train runs later (24:00).

To get to Cap Ferrat by bus, you have two choices: **#81,** which follows a circular route from Nice to Villefranche-sur-Mer to all the Cap Ferrat stops and back (runs Mon–Sat every 40 min until 19:00, no service on Sun) and the more-frequent Nice to Monaco bus **#100,** which connects the two cities and stops at the edge of Cap Ferrat (longer walk to Cap Ferrat sights than #81) and Villefranche-sur-Mer along the way (runs daily 6:00–20:00, 4/hr). All buses in this area cost €1.30 per ride (buy from driver); a ticket is good for 74 minutes (you can hop on and off within that time-frame). In Villefranche-sur-Mer, all buses use stops on the main drag; the most convenient is just above the TI (labeled *Octroi*).

It's a 50-minute walk to Cap Ferrat (see "Getting to Cap Ferrat," page 296).

From Villefranche-sur-Mer by Train to: Monaco (2/hr, 10 min), **Nice** (2/hr, 10 min), **Antibes** (2/hr, 40 min).

By Bus to: Cap Ferrat (#81, every 40 min, 10 min; #100, every 15 min, 10 min to edge of Cap Ferrat), **Beaulieu-sur-Mer** (#100, 10 min), **Monaco** (#100, 25 min), **Nice** (#100, 20 min).

The Three Corniches

Nice, Villefranche-sur-Mer, and Monaco are linked with three coastal routes: the Low, Middle, and High Corniches. The roads are nicknamed for the decorative frieze that runs along the top of a building (cornice). Each Corniche offers sensational views and a different perspective on this exotic strip of land. You can find the three routes from Nice by driving up boulevard Jean Jaurès past the bus station *(gare routière)*. For the Low Corniche, follow signs to N-98 *(Monaco par la Basse Corniche)*, which leads past Nice's port. Shortly after the turnoff to the Low Corniche, you'll see signs for the N-7 *(Moyenne Corniche)* leading to the Middle Corniche. Signs for the High *(Grande)* Corniche appear a bit after that; follow D-2564 to Col des 4 Chemins and the Grande Corniche.

Low Corniche: The Basse Corniche (also called "Corniche Inférieure") strings ports, beaches, and villages together for a traffic-filled ground-floor view. It was built in the 1860s (along with the train line) to bring people to the casino in Monte Carlo. When this Low Corniche was finished, many hill-town villagers descended to the shore and started the communities that line the sea today. Before 1860, the population of the coast between Villefranche-sur-Mer and Monte Carlo was zero. Think about that as you make the trip today.

Middle Corniche: The Moyenne Corniche is higher, quieter, and far more impressive. It runs through Eze-le-Village (described below) and provides breathtaking views over the Mediterranean, with several scenic pullouts. (The ones above Villefranche-sur-Mer are particularly stunning.)

High Corniche: Napoleon's crowning road-construction achievement, the Grande Corniche, caps the cliffs with staggering views from almost 1,600 feet above the sea. It is actually the Via Aurelia, used by the Romans to conquer the West.

Villas: Driving from Villefranche-sur-Mer to Monaco, you'll come upon impressive villas. A particularly grand entry leads to the sprawling estate built by King Leopold II of Belgium in the 1920s. Those driving up to the Middle Corniche from Villefranche-sur-Mer will look down on this yellow mansion that fills an entire hilltop with a lush garden. This estate was later owned by the Agnelli family (of Fiat fame and fortune), and then by the Safra family (American bankers).

The Best Route: For a ▲▲▲ route, **drivers** should take the Middle Corniche from Nice or Villefranche-sur-Mer to Eze-le-Village; from there, follow signs to the Grande Corniche and La Turbie, then finish by dropping down into Monaco. **Buses** travel each route; the higher the Corniche, the less frequent the buses (roughly 5–6/day on Middle and High, 4/hr on Low; get details at Nice's bus station). There are no buses between Eze-le-Village and La Turbie, though buses do connect Nice and Monaco with La Turbie.

Self-Guided Bus Tour: If traveling by bus, be sure to follow my self-guided bus tour commentary on page 305.

Nice-Monaco

The following villages and sights are listed from west to east, as you'll reach them when going from Villefranche-sur-Mer to Monaco.

Cap Ferrat

This peninsula, rated ▲▲, decorates Villefranche-sur-Mer's sea views. An exclusive, largely residential community, it's a peaceful eddy off the busy Nice–Monaco route (Low Corniche). You could spend a fine day on this peninsula, wandering the pleasing port village of St. Jean-Cap-Ferrat (a.k.a. St. Jean), touring the Villa Ephrussi de Rothschild mansion and gardens and the nearby Villa Kérylos, and walking on sections of the beautiful trails that follow the coast. If you have a house here, Microsoft mogul Paul Allen is your neighbor. The TI is between the port and Villa Ephrussi (at 59 avenue Denis Séméria, tel. 04 93 76 08 90).

Planning Your Time

Here's how I'd spend a day on the Cap: From Nice or Villefranche-sur-Mer, take the bus (#81 or #100—see below) to a stop near the Villa Ephrussi, then visit the villa. Walk 30 minutes, mostly downhill, to St. Jean-Cap-Ferrat for lunch (many options, including grocery shops for picnics) and poke about the village. After lunch, walk the beautiful 30-minute trail to Villa Kérylos in Beaulieu-sur-Mer and tour that villa. Return to Villefranche-sur-Mer, Nice, or points beyond by train or bus. Details for all aspects of this day are provided below. (Skip the drive on the loop road around Cap Ferrat's peninsula.)

Getting to Cap Ferrat

From Nice: From Nice, the **bus** (#81) runs to all key Cap Ferrat stops (Mon–Sat every 40 min until 19:00, no service on Sun, 25 min to Villa Ephrussi de Rothschild, schedules at bus station or at TI). The more frequent (4/hr) bus #100 to Monaco drops you at Cap Ferrat's edge (stops *Ange Gardien* or *Pont St. Jean*), and from there, you can walk 20 minutes to Villa Ephrussi de Rothschild (after crossing over main road from bus stop, look for the alleyway—chemin des Moulins—running straight up the Cap, turn left at the end, then keep right). By **car,** take the Low Corniche via Villefranche-sur-Mer.

From Villefranche: It's quick by **car** (Low Corniche) or **taxi** (allow €20 one-way), and easy by **bus** (#81 and #100). Both buses run from the main bus stop above Villefranche-sur-Mer's TI (marked *Octroi*). Bus #81 runs every day but Sunday (Mon–Sat every 40 min until 19:00, 10 min, get a schedule from the TI, times

Cap Ferrat

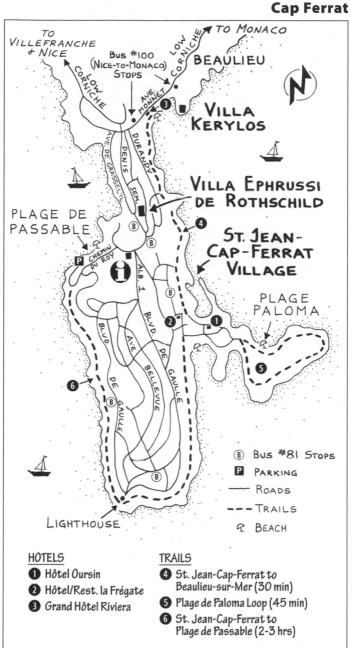

B Bus #81 Stops
P Parking
— Roads
- - - Trails
☙ Beach

HOTELS
1 Hôtel Oursin
2 Hôtel/Rest. la Frégate
3 Grand Hôtel Riviera

TRAILS
4 St. Jean-Cap-Ferrat to Beaulieu-sur-Mer (30 min)
5 Plage de Paloma Loop (45 min)
6 St. Jean-Cap-Ferrat to Plage de Passable (2-3 hrs)

listed for *Direction Le Port/Cap Ferrat* are when bus leaves Nice's *gare routière*—allow about 10 min after that for the bus to reach Villefranche-sur-Mer). The return bus (direction: Nice) begins at the port in St. Jean-Cap-Ferrat. Bus #100 to Monaco has more frequent service (daily 6:00–20:00, every 15 min), but drops you at the edge of Cap Ferrat (see "From Nice," above).

You can also **walk** 50 minutes to Cap Ferrat from Villefranche-sur-Mer. Go past the train station along the beach and climb the steps at the far end. Continue straight past the mansions (with ornate gates) and make the first right on avenue de Grasseuil. You'll see signs to the Villa Ephrussi de Rothschild, then to Cap Ferrat's port.

SIGHTS AND ACTIVITIES

Villa Ephrussi de Rothschild—In what seems like the ultimate in Riviera extravagance, Venice, Versailles, and the Côte d'Azur come together in the pastel-pink Villa Ephrussi. Rising above Cap Ferrat, this 1905 mansion has views west to Villefranche-sur-Mer and east to Beaulieu-sur-Mer.

Start with the well-furnished belle époque **interior** (helpful English handout provided). Upstairs, an 18-minute film (English subtitles) gives good background on the life of rich and eccentric Beatrice, Baroness de Rothschild, the French woman from an important banking family who built and furnished the place. As you stroll through the halls, you'll pass rooms of royal furnishings and personal possessions, including her bathroom case for cruises. A fancy tearoom serves drinks and lunch with a view (11:00–17:30).

But the gorgeous **gardens** are why most come here. Behind the mansion, stroll through the seven lush gardens re-created from other gardens all over the world. The sea views from here are amazing. Don't miss the Alhambra-like Spanish gardens, the rose garden at the far end, and the view back to the house from the "Temple of Love" gazebo.

Cost and Hours: Palace and gardens-€9.50, skippable tour of upstairs-€3 extra, combo-ticket with Villa Kérylos-€14.50—valid for one week; mid-Feb–Oct daily 10:00–18:00, July–Aug until 19:00; Nov–mid-Feb Mon–Fri 14:00–18:00, Sat–Sun 10:00–18:00; tel. 04 93 01 45 90, www.villa-ephrussi.com. Kids will enjoy the free treasure-hunt booklet. Parking is tricky; a small turnaround is at the top. The name of the nearest bus stop for bus #81 is Passable (a 10-min walk uphill to the villa).

Walks from Villa Ephrussi: It's a lovely 30-minute walk, mostly downhill, from Villa Ephrussi to the Villa Kérylos in Beaulieu-sur-Mer (described below) or to the port of St. Jean-Cap-Ferrat.

To get to both (see map on page 297), make a hard left at the stop sign below the Villa Ephrussi and follow signs along a small road toward the Grand Hôtel Riviera. When the road comes to a T, keep going straight, passing a green gate down a pedestrian path. This path ends at your trail—to the left, Villa Kérylos; to the right, St. Jean-Cap-Ferrat. It's about 15 minutes to either destination once you join the path. To get to plage de Passable, hike five minutes below the Villa Ephrussi (following signs).

Plage de Passable—This pleasant beach, located below Villa Ephrussi, comes with great views of Villefranche-sur-Mer and a rough, pebbly surface. It's a peaceful beach, popular with families. Half is public (free, with shower), and the other half is run by a small restaurant (€22 with changing locker, lounge chair, and shower; reserve ahead in summer or on weekends as this is a prime spot, kayak rental available, tel. 04 93 76 06 17).

To park near the beach, follow signs past it, and go around the bend to a surprise lot. If that lot is full, follow signs over the hill and around to Lido Parking, a few steps from plage de Passable (€6/day). If ever you were to do the French Riviera rent-a-beach ritual, this is the place.

For me, the best reason to come here is for dinner. Beg, borrow, or steal a way here and arrive before sunset, and then watch as darkness descends and lights flicker over Villefranche-sur-Mer's heavenly setting. At Restaurant de la Plage Passable, enjoy a surprisingly elegant dining experience to the sounds of children still at play on the beach. Notice the streetlights that show the path of the Low and Middle Corniches (€15 starters, €18–25 *plats*, open daily late June–Sept only; until 20:00 in good weather April–May and Oct, tel. 04 93 76 06 17).

St. Jean-Cap-Ferrat—This sophisticated village port lies in Cap Ferrat's center, yet off most tourist itineraries. It boasts yachts, boardwalks, views, and boutiques packaged in a "take your time, darling" atmosphere. It's a few miles off the busy Nice-to-Monaco road, convenient for drivers but so quiet that it feels overlooked. St. Jean-Cap-Ferrat is especially peaceful at night. A string of restaurants line the port, with just enough visitors to keep them in business.

The bus stop back to Villefranche-sur-Mer is a block above the port (right side of street) near the Hôtel Fregate. The hiking trail to Beaulieu-sur-Mer (with access to Villa Ephrussi) begins just after the beach, to the left of the port as you look out to the water (see below).

▲▲Walks Around Cap Ferrat—The Cap is perfect for a walk, as well-maintained foot trails follow most of its length. You have three easy, mostly level options (30 min, 45 min, or 2–3 hours). The TIs in Villefranche-sur-Mer and St. Jean-Cap-Ferrat have maps of

Nice-Monaco

Cap Ferrat with walking paths marked. On segments of all of the hikes, you can make out the three Corniche roads cut into the side of the massive cliffs. (For all hikes, see the map on page 297.)

Walk Between St. Jean-Cap-Ferrat and Beaulieu-sur-Mer: A level, 30-minute walk takes you past sumptuous villas, great views, and fun swimming opportunities. To reach the trail from St. Jean-Cap-Ferrat's port, walk along the harbor, with the water on your right, and work your way past the beach. Head up the steps to promenade Maurice Rouvier and continue; before long, you'll see smashing views of the whitewashed Villa Kérylos. To get to St. Jean-Cap-Ferrat from Beaulieu-sur-Mer, leave the Villa Kérylos in Beaulieu-sur-Mer, walk with the sea on your left to the Grand Hôtel Riviera, and find the trail. You can also reach this trail by walking 10 minutes downhill from the Villa Ephrussi (described above).

Plage de Paloma Loop Trail: Just east of St. Jean-Cap-Ferrat's port, a 45-minute, sea-soaked, view-loaded trail gives a terrific sampling of Cap Ferrat's beauty for relatively modest effort. From the port, walk or drive about a quarter-mile east (with the port to your left); you'll find the trailhead behind the phone booth where the road comes to a T. (Parking is available at the port or on streets near plage de Paloma.) Do this walk counterclockwise. The trail is level and paved, yet uneven enough that good shoes are helpful. Plunk your picnic on one of the benches along the trail, or eat at the café on plage de Paloma at the end of the walk (sandwiches and salads). If time is tight, walk clockwise a hundred yards along the trail for great views.

St. Jean-Cap-Ferrat to Plage de Passable: For a two- to three-hour hike, follow the signs below Villa Ephrussi to plage de Passable (10 min downhill on foot from the villa, parking available near the trailhead). Walk down to the beach (good café, ideal for lunch), turn left, and cross the beach. Go along a paved road behind a big apartment building, and after about 300 feet, take the steps down to a trail *(Sentier Littoral)* that circles the Cap. You'll pass by the port of St. Jean-Cap-Ferrat near the end of the trail, where you have three options: take bus #81 back to Villefranche-sur-Mer, walk back to the Villa Ephrussi and plage de Passable, or continue on to Beaulieu-sur-Mer and take a bus to Monaco or Nice.

SLEEPING

In St. Jean-Cap-Ferrat

This sleepy village offers surprisingly good values, probably because it's off the main route (and less convenient for non-drivers).

$ Hôtel Oursin** is central to the port, with 14 fine value rooms on one homey floor. It's a welcoming, humble place with white walls and surprisingly well-appointed rooms (Db-€60–80, air-con, 1 avenue Denis Séméria, tel. 04 93 76 04 65, fax 04 93 76 12 55, www.hoteloursin.com, reception@hoteloursin.com).

$ Hôtel/Restaurant la Frégate, run by a reserved family, overlooks the port. A very simple place with no email address or stylish touches, it offers 10 spotless rooms. Some have good views, while others overlook the garden courtyard (Db-€55–80, air-con, 11 avenue Denis Séméria, tel. 04 93 76 04 51, fax 04 93 76 14 93).

Beaulieu-sur-Mer

This town, right on the Low Corniche road (just after Cap Ferrat), is busy with traffic. It's a good place to pick up the hiking trail to St. Jean-Cap-Ferrat (see above), though the main point of interest is the remarkable **Villa Kérylos.** In 1902, an eccentric millionaire modeled his new mansion on a Greek villa from the island of Delos from about 200 B.C. No expense was spared—from floor mosaics to Carrara marble columns to exquisite wood furnishings—as he recreated his Greek fantasy. The rain-powered shower is fun, and the included audioguide will increase your Greek IQ (€8, combo-ticket with Villa Ephrussi de Rothschild-€14.50—valid for one week; mid-Feb–Oct daily 10:00–18:00, July–Aug until 19:00; Nov–mid-Feb Mon–Fri 14:00–18:00, Sat–Sun 10:00–18:00; tel. 04 93 01 01 44, www.villa-kerylos.com).

Getting to and from Villa Kérylos

Drivers should park near the casino in Beaulieu-sur-Mer, not on the villa's access road. The Monaco–Nice bus (4/hr, 20 min from Nice or Monaco) drops you at the Eglise stop at the Hôtel Metropole in Beaulieu, where signs direct you to the few blocks to the Villa Kérylos. Trains (2/hr, 10 min from Nice or Monaco) leave you a 10-minute walk away: Turn left out of the train station and left again down the main drag. Walk to the end, turn right, then follow signs. The walking trail to Cap Ferrat from Villa Kérylos begins on the other side of Beaulieu-sur-Mer, just below the Grand Hôtel Riviera.

Eze-le-Village

Floating high above the sea, flowery and flawless Eze-le-Village (don't confuse it with the seafront town of Eze-Bord-de-Mer) is entirely consumed by tourism. This *village d'art et de gastronomie* (as it calls itself) houses perfume outlets, upscale boutiques, steep cobbled lanes, and magnificent views. Touristy as this place

Nice-Monaco

certainly Eze, its stony state of preservation and magnificent hilltop setting over the Mediterranean justify a visit.

Bus stops and parking lots weld the town to the highway (Middle Corniche) that passes under its lowest wall. The helpful TI is in the far corner of the car park below the town; ask them about English-language tours of the village and gardens (May–Oct daily 9:00–18:00; Nov–April Mon–Sat 9:00–17:00, closed Sun; place de Gaulle, tel. 04 93 41 26 00, www.eze-riviera.com). Public WCs are located just behind the TI and in the village behind the church.

Getting to Eze-le-Village: There are two Ezes: Eze-le-Village (the spectacular hill town, your destination) and Eze-Bord-de-Mer (a modern beach resort far below Eze-le-Village). Eze-le-Village is about 20 minutes east of Villefranche-sur-Mer on the Middle Corniche. Two bus lines (#82 and #112, €1.30/ticket) provide 16 buses per day from Nice to Eze-le-Village (eight on Sun), and one less-frequent bus runs directly from Monaco to Eze-le-Village (none on Sun). You can also take the train or Nice–Monaco bus to Eze-Bord-de-Mer. From there, take the shuttle bus (#83, also €1.30) straight up to Eze-le-Village from the Gare SNCF stop (daily 9:30–18:30, 8/day). There are no direct buses from Villefranche-sur-Mer to Eze-le-Village or between La Turbie and Eze-le-Village.

You can also take a taxi between the two Ezes (allow €22 one-way, tel. 06 09 84 17 84).

SELF-GUIDED WALK

Welcome to Eze-le-Village

• *From the TI and parking lot, wander uphill into the town. You'll pass an exclusive hotel and the start of a steep trail down to the beach marked* Eze/Mer. *(For a panoramic view and ideal picnic perch, walk 60 steps down this path.) Continuing up, enter...*

Place du Centenaire: In this square, a monument celebrates the 100th anniversary of the 1860 plebiscite, the time when all 133 Eze residents voted to leave the Italian Duchy of Savoy and join France. A town map here helps you get oriented.

• *Now pass through the once-formidable town gate (designed to keep the Turks out) and climb into the 14th-century village. You'll find the odd English information plaque on walls in the old city. Wandering the narrow lanes—ever uphill—you'll come to the...*

Eze Château: This was the winter getaway of the Swedish royal family from 1923 until 1953; today, it's a hotel. The château's tearoom (Salon de Thé) offers the most scenic €6 coffee or beer break you'll ever enjoy, on a cliff overlooking the jagged Riviera and sea. The sensational view terrace is also home to an expensive-but-sensational restaurant. Reserve well ahead for dinner (dinner *menus* from €90, lunch for €35, open daily, tel. 04 93 41 12 24).

• *Eventually the town ends at its hilltop castle ruins—now blanketed by the...*

Jardins d'Eze: Here, you'll find a prickly festival of cactus. Since 1949, these ruins have been home to 400 different plants 1,300 feet above the sea (well-described in English, €5, open daily, hours change frequently but usually May–Sept 9:00–19:00, Oct–April until dusk, tel. 04 93 41 10 30). At the top, you'll be treated to a commanding 360-degree view, with a helpful *table d'orientation*. On a really clear day, you can see Corsica. The castle was demolished by Louis XIV in 1706. The French destroyed castles like this all over Europe (most notably along the Rhine), because they didn't want to risk having to do battle with them at some future date.

• *As you descend, drop by the...*

Eze Church: While built during Napoleonic times, it has an uncharacteristic Baroque fanciness—a reminder that 300 years of Savoy rule left the townsfolk with an Italian savoir faire and a sensibility for decor.

SIGHTS

Perfume Factory Fragonard—This factory, with its huge tour-bus parking lot, lies on the Middle Corniche, 350 feet below Eze-le-Village. Designed for tour groups, it cranks them through all day long. If you've never seen mass tourism in action, this place will open your eyes. (The gravel is littered with the color-coded *F* stickers that each tourist wears so that the salespeople know which guide gets the kickback.) Drop in for a free 20–40 minute tour—the tour's length depends on walking ability of the group (daily 8:30–18:00 but best Mon–Fri 9:00–11:00 & 14:00–15:30—when the "factory" actually has people working, tel. 04 93 41 05 05). You'll see how the perfume and scented soaps are made and bottled before you're herded into the gift shop.

For a more personal and intimate look at perfume, cross the main road in Eze-le-Village to visit the **Gallimard** shop. Take a perfume tour and let the lovely ladies show you their scents.

EATING

To enjoy Eze-le-Village in relative peace, visit at sunset and stay for dinner. You'll dine well at the stone-cozy **Le Troubador** (€33 *menu*, closed Sun–Mon, 4 rue du Brec, tel. 04 93 41 19 03), or for less, at the basic **Nid de l'Aigle** ("Eagle's Nest," open daily in summer, otherwise closed Wed, tel. 04 93 41 19 08).

La Trophée des Alpes

High above Monaco, on the Grande (High) Corniche in the overlooked village of La Turbie, lies one of this region's most evocative historic sights (with dramatic views over the entire country of Monaco as a bonus). This massive Roman monument, rated ▲▲, commemorates Augustus Caesar's conquest of the Alps and its 44 hostile tribes. It's exciting to think that, in a way, La Trophée des Alpes celebrates a victory that kicked off the Pax Romana—joining Gaul and Germania, freeing up the main artery of the Roman Empire, and lacing together Spain and Italy.

Walk around the monument and notice how the Romans built a fine, quarried-stone exterior, filled in with rubble and coarse concrete. Flanked by the vanquished in chains, the towering inscription tells the story: It was erected "by the senate and the people to honor the emperor." The monument was restored in the 1930s and 1940s with money from the Tuck family of New Hampshire.

The one-room museum shows a reconstruction and translation of the dramatic inscription, which lists all the feisty alpine tribes that put up such a fight (€5; mid-May–mid-Sept Tue–Sun 9:30–13:00 & 14:30–18:30, mid-Sept–mid-May Tue–Sun 10:00–13:30 & 14:30–17:00, closed Mon year-round; tel. 04 93 41 20 84). Escorts from the museum take people up to the monument, but it's not worth waiting for.

The sweet old village of **La Turbie** sees almost no tourists, but it has plenty of cafés and restaurants at its doorstep. To stroll the old village, park in the main lot on place Neuve (follow *Monaco* signs one block from the main road), then walk behind the post office and find brick footpaths—they lead through a village with nary a shop. To eat very well in the Riviera's most welcoming restaurant (I'm not kidding), try **La Terrasse,** where tables gather under sun shades, the sea lies miles below, and clients seem oblivious to the incredible setting. Let Helen and Jacques tempt you to return for dinner at sunset, and book ahead for a table with a view (closed Tue evening and all day Wed, near the PTT/post office at the main parking lot, 17 place Neuve, tel. 04 93 41 21 84).

Getting to and from La Trophée des Alpes (in La Turbie):

By **car,** take the High Corniche to La Turbie, ideally from Eze-le-Village (La Turbie is 10 min east of, and above, Eze-le-Village), then look for signs to *La Trophée des Alpes.* Once in La Turbie, you can park in the lot in the center of town (place Neuve, follow *Monaco* signs for a short block) and walk from there (walk 5 min around the old village, with the village on your right); or drive to the site by turning right in front of La Régence Café. Those coming from farther afield can take the efficient A-8 to the La Turbie exit. To reach Eze-le-Village from La Turbie, follow signs to Nice, and then look for signs to Eze-le-Village.

You can also get here by **bus** from Nice (4/day, 45 min, €1.30; last bus returns to Nice at about 18:00) or Monaco (6/day, 20 min, €1.30). The bus stop is across from the PTT/post office on place Neuve (the 5-min walk to La Trophée des Alpes is described earlier in this chapter).

Quickie Riviera Bus Tour from Nice to Monaco

Don't have a car? You can still enjoy the trip from Nice to Monaco (and on to Menton, described on page 319). While most travelers see the Riviera from their train window as they zoom along the coast, the public bus affords a far better view of the crags, dreamy villas, and much-loved beaches that make it Europe's coast with the most.

This tour works best if you take the bus from Nice, ride the entire Nice–Monaco–Menton route (60 scenic minutes), enjoy Menton, and hop on and off on the way back to Nice. If possible, time it so that you're in Monaco for late-afternoon sightseeing. Coming home, consider getting off the bus at Nice's harbor and taking the coastal walk back into town.

Riding the bus couldn't be easier. Bus #100 runs four times an hour along the Low Corniche (daily 6:00–20:00, departs Nice bus station). One simple €1.30 ticket (buy from the driver) is good for 74 minutes, no matter how far you go. Since bus fares are cheap, consider hopping on and off at great viewpoints (the next bus will be by soon). Riding from Nice toward Monaco, get a seat on the right-hand side. All stops have names (usually posted on the shelter or bus stop sign)—I'll identify the ones that matter along this route.

At the Nice bus station (see page 238), TV monitors list the platform, destination, and time for the next departure. You're looking for bus #100 to *destination: Monaco/Menton* (most likely from stall 17). Pay the driver as you get on, and be assertive with the crowds trying to board.

Nice–Monaco

SELF-GUIDED BUS TOUR

This Nice-to-Monaco route—which follows the Low Corniche, riding on bus #100—was inaugurated with the opening of the Monte Carlo Casino in 1863. It was designed to provide easy and safe access from Nice (and the rest of France) to the gambling fun in Monaco. Here's what you'll see along the way:

In Nice: Shortly after the bus pulls out, you'll pass under Nice's snazzy Museum of Modern Art before passing through place Garibaldi, with its statue of Giuseppe Garibaldi (one of the men credited with uniting Italy in the 1860s) marking the center.

Nice Harbor: This harbor was built in the 1700s. Before then, boats littered the Nice beach. You'll see fine yachts, an occasional cruise ship, and the daily ferry to Corsica. If you get on or off here, it's a pleasant 30-minute walk around the point to or from the promenade des Anglais.

From Nice to Villefranche-sur-Mer: As you scenically glide away from Nice, look back for views of the harbor, Castle Hill, and the sweeping Bay of Angels (consider hopping off here for photos). Imagine the views from the homes below. That soft, yellow, rounded tower ahead near the top of the hill is part of Sean Connery's property.

You'll soon come to the yacht-studded bay of Villefranche-sur-Mer and the peninsula called Cap Ferrat—playground of the rich and famous, marked by its lighthouse on the point just across the bay. This bay is a rare natural harbor along the Riviera. Since it's deeper than Nice's, it hosts the huge cruise ships.

Villefranche-sur-Mer and Cap Ferrat: To see Villefranche-sur-Mer, one of the most charming towns along the Riviera, get off at the stop labeled *Octroi* (for more on Villefranche, see page 286).

After passing through Villefranche-sur-Mer, keep an eye out as the road arcs to the right (Mick Jagger's home is somewhere below). You'll see sensational views over Villefranche-sur-Mer. At Cap Ferrat, the Baroness Rothschild's pink Villa Ephrussi, with its red-tiled roof, breaks the horizon. A little farther to the right is Baron Paul Allen's home.

Consider stopping off to take a picture along this stretch, and combining your photo op with a stroll to nearby Cap Ferrat. For a Cap Ferrat adventure, hop out at the stop marked *Pont St. Jean* (just after the Total station). Cross the main road and find the walkway that runs up the center of the Cap (see "Getting to Cap Ferrat," page 296, for details).

Beaulieu-sur-Mer: To visit the Villa Kérylos (see page 301), get off at the *Eglise* stop, in front of the Hôtel Metropole. Just after the town of Beaulieu-sur-Mer, the cliffs create a microclimate and a zone nicknamed "Little Africa." Exotic vegetation (including the only bananas on the Riviera) grows among private, elegant villas that made Beaulieu-sur-Mer the place to be in the 19th century.

Eze-Bord-de-Mer and Cap d'Ail: A few minutes after leaving Beaulieu-sur-Mer, be ready for scant, short-lived views way up to the fortified town of Eze-le-Village, which towers high above the little hamlet of Eze-Bord-de-Mer. If you want to get to Eze-le-Village, a shuttle bus (#83) makes the climb from the Gare SNCF stop in Eze-Bord-de-Mer, sharing the same eastbound stop used by bus #100 (8/day).

Passing through a tunnel, you emerge at Cap d'Ail. The huge, yellow, hospital-like building nearby was once a luxury hotel popular with the Russian aristocracy. Now it's occupied by private condos. At the first stop after the big yellow building, look up at the switchbacks halfway up the barren hillside. It was at the bend connecting these two switchbacks that Princess Grace Kelly (the former American movie star) was killed in a car crash in 1982.

Monaco (three bus stops): Cap d'Ail borders Monaco—you're now leaving France. On your right, just before the castle-topped hill (Monaco-Ville, a.k.a. Le Rocher), is Monaco's Fontvieille district—tall apartments all built on land reclaimed from the Mediterranean. The first Monaco stop (Place d'Armes) is the best one to use for the palace and other old-town sights in Monaco-Ville.

If you stay on the bus, you'll pass through the tunnel, then emerge to follow the road that Grand Prix drivers race along. In late May, you'll see the bleachers and barriers set up for the big race.

You'll pass the second Monaco stop (Stade Nautique), then enjoy the harbor and city views as you climb to the last Monaco stop (Casino). Get off here for a peek at the gambling action (a plush, terraced garden leads down to the casino) and an easy walk back into Monte Carlo. For information on Monaco, see the next chapter. If you stay on the bus for a few more minutes, you'll be back in France, and in 15 more minutes you'll reach the end of the line, **Menton** (described on page 319).

Bonne route!

MONACO

Despite overdevelopment, high prices, and wall-to-wall daytime tourists, Monaco is a Riviera must. Monaco is on the go. Since 1929, cars have raced around the port and in front of the casino in one of the world's most famous auto races, the Grand Prix de Monaco (May 22–25 in 2008; see page 316). The new breakwater—constructed elsewhere and towed in by sea—enables big cruise ships to dock here. The district of Fontvieille, reclaimed from the sea, bristles with luxury high-rise condos. But don't look for anything too deep in this glittering tax haven. Two-thirds of its 30,000 residents live here because there's no income tax—leaving fewer than 10,000 true Monegasques.

This minuscule principality (0.75 square mile) borders only France and the Mediterranean. The country has always been tiny, but it used to be...less tiny. In an 1860 plebiscite, Monaco lost two-thirds of its territory when the region of Menton voted to join France. To compensate, France suggested that Monaco build a fancy casino and promised to connect it to the world with a road (the Low Corniche) and a train line. This started a high-class tourist boom that has yet to let up.

While "independent," Monaco is run as a piece of France. A French civil servant appointed by the French president—with the blessing of Monaco's prince—serves as state minister and manages the place. Monaco's phone system, electricity, water, and so on, are all French.

The death of Prince Rainier in 2005 ended his 56-year career of enlightened rule. Today, Monaco is ruled by Prince Rainier's

Monaco

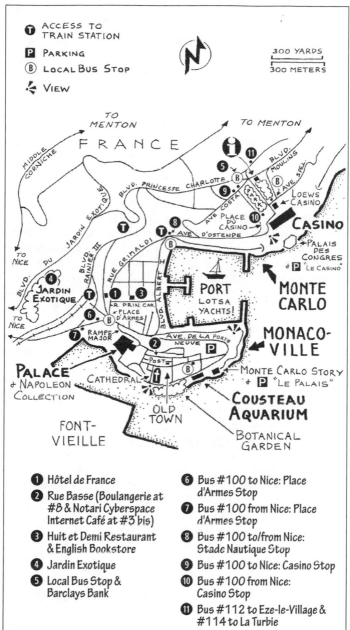

- **T** ACCESS TO TRAIN STATION
- **P** PARKING
- **B** LOCAL BUS STOP
- **☇** VIEW

300 YARDS
300 METERS

TO MENTON

TO MENTON

MIDDLE CORNICHE

F R A N C E

BLVD. PRINCESSE CHARLOTTE

BLVD. MOULINS

AVE. SPEL.

AVE. COSTA

LOEWS CASINO

PARK

JARDIN EXOTIQUE

AVE. PLACE DU CASINO

CASINO

TO NICE

BLVD. DU JARDIN EXOTIQUE

AVE. D'OSTENDE

PALAIS DES CONGRÈS

P "LE CASINO"

BLVD. RAINIER III

RUE GRIMALDI

PORT

LOTSA YACHTS!

MONTE CARLO

TO NICE

4 JARDIN EXOTIQUE

R. PRIN. CAR.

PLACE D'ARMES

BLVD. ALBERT I

MONACO-VILLE

TO NICE

7 RAMPE MAJOR

AVE. DE LA PORTE NEUVE

POST

P

MONTE CARLO STORY

P "LE PALAIS"

PALACE
& NAPOLEON COLLECTION

CATHEDRAL

COUSTEAU AQUARIUM

FONT-VIEILLE

OLD TOWN

BOTANICAL GARDEN

- **1** Hôtel de France
- **2** Rue Basse (Boulangerie at #8 & Notari Cyberspace Internet Café at #3 bis)
- **3** Huit et Demi Restaurant & English Bookstore
- **4** Jardin Exotique
- **5** Local Bus Stop & Barclays Bank
- **6** Bus #100 to Nice: Place d'Armes Stop
- **7** Bus #100 from Nice: Place d'Armes Stop
- **8** Bus #100 to/from Nice: Stade Nautique Stop
- **9** Bus #100 to Nice: Casino Stop
- **10** Bus #100 from Nice: Casino Stop
- **11** Bus #112 to Eze-le-Village & #114 to La Turbie

Monaco

unassuming son, Prince Albert Alexandre Louis Pierre, Marquis of Baux. Prince Albert is 47 and considered Europe's most eligible bachelor—though he has admitted to fathering two children out of wedlock. He's a bobsled enthusiast and avid environmentalist who seems determined to clean up Monaco's tarnished, tax-haven, money-laundering image. (Monaco is infamously known as a "sunny place for shady people.")

Monaco is big business, and Prince Albert is its CEO. While its famous casino provides only 5 percent of the state's revenue, its 43 banks—which offer an attractive way to hide your money—are hugely profitable. The prince also makes money with a value-added tax (19.6 percent, the same as in France), plus real estate and corporate taxes.

The glamorous romance and marriage of the American actress Grace Kelly to Prince Rainier added to Monaco's fairy-tale mystique. Grace Kelly (Prince Albert's mother) first came to Monaco to star in the 1955 Hitchcock film *To Catch a Thief*, in which she was filmed racing along the Corniches. Later, she married the prince and adopted the country. Tragically, Monaco's much-loved Princess Grace died in a car wreck on that same Corniche in 1982.

It's a special place...there are more people in Monaco's philharmonic orchestra (about 100) than in its army (about 80 guards). The princedom is well-guarded, with police and cameras on every corner. (They say you could win a million dollars at the casino and walk through the wee hours to the train station without a worry.) Stamps are so few that they increase in value almost as soon as they're printed. And collectors snapped up the rare Monaco versions of euro coins (with Prince Rainier's portrait) so quickly that many locals have never even seen one.

ORIENTATION

The principality of Monaco consists of three distinct tourist areas: Monaco-Ville, Monte Carlo, and La Condamine. Monaco-Ville fills the rock high above everything else and is referred to by locals as Le Rocher ("The Rock"). This is the oldest section, home to the Prince's palace and all the sights except the casino. Monte Carlo is the area around the casino; La Condamine is the port (which divides Monaco-Ville and Monte Carlo). You'll look  down over a fourth, less-interesting area, Fontvieille, reclaimed from the sea by Prince Rainier in the 1970s.

The port is the center of Monaco. From here, it's a 15-minute walk up to the Prince's Palace or to the casino (40 min from palace to casino). Local buses shave time off this commute (see "Getting Around Monaco," below).

Tourist Information

The main TI is near the casino (Mon–Sat 9:00–19:00, Sun 10:00–12:00, 2 boulevard des Moulins). You'll run across TI annexes in other parts of Monaco, including one at the train station (Mon–Sat 9:00–19:00, Sun 10:00–12:00, tel. 00-377/92 16 61 16 or 00-377/92 16 61 66, www.visitmonaco.com). From June to September, you might find information kiosks in the Monaco-Ville parking garage and on the port.

Arrival in Monaco

By Bus from Nice and Villefranche-sur-Mer: See my "Quickie Riviera Bus Tour from Nice to Monaco" on page 305 to plan your route and for bus- riding tips. Bus riders need to pay attention, since stops are not announced. Cap d'Ail is the town before Monaco, so be on the lookout after it. You'll enter Monaco by passing the modern high-rises of the Fontvieille district. When you see the rocky outcrop of old Monaco, be ready to get off.

There are three stops in Monaco. Listed in order from Nice, they are: Place d'Armes (in front of a tunnel at the base of Monaco-Ville's rock), Stade Nautique (on the port, though this stop may change in 2008), and Casino (below the casino, on avenue d'Ostende). The Place d'Armes stop is the best starting point. From there, you can walk up to Monaco-Ville and the palace (10 min straight up), or catch a local bus (line #1 or #2, details below). To reach the bus stop and steps up to Monaco-Ville, cross the street right in front of the tunnel and walk with the rock on your right for about 200 feet. If you prefer starting at the casino, turn left off the bus at the Casino stop, then turn right and walk past Häagen-Dazs to find the casino.

For directions on returning to Nice by bus, see "Transportation Connections" near the end of this chapter.

By Train from Nice: This loooooong underground train station is in central Monaco, about a 15-minute walk to the casino in Monte Carlo or to the port, and about 25 minutes to the palace in Monaco-Ville.

The TI and ticket windows are up the escalator at the Italy end of the station. There are three exits: two from the train platform level (one at each end) and one from above the platforms (up the escalator, past the TI). To walk to the casino, use this upper exit (go past the TI, then up the elevator, then up the escalator, exit station, turn left on boulevard de la Princesse Charlotte, and turn right after about 5 blocks when you see the pedestrian *Casino* sign; allow 10 min).

To reach Monaco-Ville and the palace from the station, take one of the two platform-level exits. The exit near the Italy end of the platform leads to the port and right to the bus stop for city buses #1 and #2, serving Monaco-Ville and the casino (follow *Sortie la Condamine* and go down 2 escalators, then go left following *Accès Port* signs). The port is across the street from this exit, from which you can walk another 25 minutes to the palace (to your right) or to the casino in 15 minutes (up the road to your left).

The other platform-level exit is at the Nice end of the tracks (signed *Sortie Fontvieille/Monaco Ville*), which takes you through a long tunnel (TI annex at end) to the foot of Monaco-Ville; turn left at the end of the walkway and walk 15 minutes up to the palace, or take the bus (#1 or #2).

To take the short-but-sweet coastal **walking path** into Monaco's Fontvieille district, get off the train one station before Monaco, in Cap d'Ail. Turn left out of the little station and walk 50 yards up the road, then turn left, going downstairs and under the tracks. Turn left onto the coastal trail, and hike the 20 minutes to Fontvieille. Once you reach Fontvieille, it's a 20-minute uphill hike to Monaco's sights.

By Car: Follow *Centre-Ville* signs into Monaco, then follow the red-letter signs to parking garages at *Le Casino* (for Monte Carlo) or *Le Palais* (for Monaco-Ville). The first hour of parking is free (€4 next hr, €7/3 hrs).

Helpful Hints

Telephone Tip: To call Monaco from France, dial 00, then 377 (Monaco's country code) and the eight-digit number. Within Monaco, simply dial the eight-digit number.

Internet Access: Notari Cyberspace is just a block off Palace Square in Monaco-Ville (daily 10:00–19:00, 3 bis rue Basse).

English Bookstore: Scruples Bookstore has plenty of English offerings (Mon–Fri 10:00–12:30 & 14:30–19:00, Sat 10:00–12:30 & 14:30–18:30, closed Sun, at 7 rue de la Princesse Caroline, just below the recommended Huit et Demi restaurant).

Minivan Tours from Nice: Several companies offer day and nighttime tours of Monaco, allowing you freedom to gamble without worrying about the last train or bus home (see "Getting Around the Riviera," page 240).

Loop Trip by Bus: From Nice or Villefranche-sur-Mer you can visit Monaco by bus, then return via Eze-le-Village or La Turbie (no Sun bus). See "Transportation Connections" on page 319 for details.

Monaco

Monaco at a Glance

▲**Casino of Monte Carlo**—Classy casino that saved Monaco's economy. **Hours:** Slots and some gaming rooms—open Mon–Fri at 14:00 and Sat–Sun at 12:00; elegant game rooms—open Mon–Fri at 16:00 and Sat–Sun at 15:00, some at 21:00–22:00.

Prince's Palace—Prince Albert's extravagant palace. **Hours:** Daily May–Sept 9:30–18:30, April and Oct 10:30–17:30, closed Nov–March.

Napoleon Collection—The prince's private collection of Napoleonic stuff, from medals, swords, and guns, to his cool *chapeau*. **Hours:** Daily May–Sept 9:30–18:30; April and Oct 10:00–17:00, closed Nov–March.

Changing of the Guard—Big ceremony for a tiny nation. **Hours:** Daily at 11:55 on the palace square.

Cathedral of Monaco—Final resting place for Princess Grace and Prince Rainier. **Hours:** Daily 8:30–18:45, until 18:00 in winter.

Cousteau Aquarium—Jacques Cousteau's cliff-hugging aquarium. **Hours:** Daily April–Sept 9:30–19:30, Oct–March 10:00–18:00.

Monte Carlo Story Film—Informative 35-minute film describing Monaco's sexy history. **Hours:** Daily 10:00–17:00, July–Aug until 18:00, closed Nov–Dec.

Jardin Exotique—Cliffside botanical garden mixing thousands of cacti and fantastic views. **Hours:** Daily mid-May–mid-Sept 9:00–19:00, mid-Sept–mid-May 9:00–18:00 or dusk.

Getting Around Monaco

By Local Bus: Buses #1 and #2 link all areas (single ticket-€1, 10 tickets-€6, pay driver, 10/hr, buses run until 21:00, less on Sun). You can split a 10-ride ticket with your travel partners. For most, two rides in Monaco does it.

By Tourist Train: "Monaco Tour" tourist trains begin at the aquarium and pass by the port, casino, and palace (€7, 2/hr, 10:30–18:00 in summer, 11:00–17:00 in winter depending on weather, 30 min, recorded English commentary).

By Taxi: If you've lost track of time at the casino, you can call

Monaco

the 24-hour taxi service (tel. 08 20 20 98 98)...provided you still have enough money to pay for the cab home.

SELF-GUIDED WALK

Welcome to Monaco-Ville

All of Monaco's sights (except the casino) are in Monaco-Ville, packed within a few Disney-esque blocks. This walk makes a tidy loop around Monaco-Ville.

• *To get from anywhere in Monaco to the palace square (place du Palais, Monaco-Ville's sightseeing center, home of the palace and the Napoleon Collection), take bus #1 or #2 to place de la Visitation. Turn right as you step off the bus and walk straight for five minutes, passing a fountain and continuing down either street. If you're walking up from the port, the well-marked lane leads directly to the Palais.*

Palace Square (Place du Palais): This square is the best place to get oriented to Monaco, as it offers views on both sides of the rock. Facing the palace, go to the right and look out over the city (err...principality). This rock gave birth to the little pastel Hong Kong look-alike in 1215, and it's managed to remain an independent country for most of its nearly 800 years. Looking beyond the glitzy port, notice the faded green roof above and to the right: the casino that put Monaco on the map. The famous Grand Prix runs along the port, and

then up the ramp to the casino. And Italy is so close, you can almost smell the pesto. Just beyond the casino is France again—you could walk one way from France to France, passing through Monaco in about 50 minutes.

The curious statue of a woman with a fishing net is dedicated to Prince Albert I's glorious reign (1889–1922). Albert was a Renaissance man with many skills and interests. He possessed a Jacques Cousteau–like fascination with the sea (and built Monaco's famous aquarium), and was a determined pacifist who made many attempts to dissuade Germany's Kaiser Wilhelm II from becoming involved in World War I.

• *Now walk to the statue of the monk grasping a sword near the palace.*

Meet **François Grimaldi,** a renegade Italian dressed as a monk, who captured Monaco in 1297 and began the dynasty that still rules the principality. Prince Albert is his great-great-great...grandson, which makes Monaco's royal family Europe's longest-lasting dynasty.

• *Walk to the opposite side of the square.*

Monaco

At the Louis XIV cannonballs, look down below to Monaco's newest area, the reclaimed-from-the-sea **Fontvieille** district, which has seen much of Monaco's post-WWII growth (residential and commercial—notice the lushly-planted building tops). Prince Rainier continued (some say, was obsessed with) Monaco's economic growth, creating landfills (topped with homes, such as Fontvieille), flashy ports, new beaches, and the new rail station. Today, thanks to Prince Rainier's efforts, tiny Monaco is a member of the United Nations.

You can buy Monaco stamps (popular collectibles, or mail from here) at the post office (PTT) a few blocks down rue Comte Félix Gastaldi.

• *Make your way to the...*

Prince's Palace (Palais Princier): A medieval castle sat where Monaco's palace is today. Its strategic setting has had a lot to do with Monaco's ability to resist attackers. Today, Prince Albert lives in the palace; princesses Stephanie and Caroline live just down the main street. The palace guards protect the prince 24/7 and still stage a Changing of the Guard ceremony with all the pageantry of an important nation (daily at 11:55, fun to watch but jam-packed). Audioguided tours take you through part of the prince's lavish palace in 30 minutes. The rooms are well-furnished and impressive, but interesting only if you haven't seen a château lately (€7 includes audioguide, €9 with Napoleon Collection, daily May–Sept 9:30–18:30, April and Oct 10:30–17:30, closed Nov–March, tel. 00-377/93 25 18 31).

• *Next to the palace entry is the...*

Napoleon Collection: Napoleon occupied Monaco after the French Revolution. This is the prince's private collection of what Napoleon left behind: military medals, swords, guns, letters, and, most interesting, his hat. I found this collection more appealing than the palace (€4 includes audioguide, €9 with Prince's Palace, daily May–Sept 9:30–18:30, April and Oct 10:00–17:00, closed Nov–March).

• *With your back to the palace, leave the square through the arch to the right and you'll find the...*

Cathedral of Monaco (Cathédrale de Monaco): The somber cathedral, rebuilt in 1878 to show that Monaco cared for more than just its new casino, is where centuries of Grimaldis are buried. Circle slowly behind the altar (counterclockwise). The second-to-last tomb—inscribed *"Gratia Patricia, MCMLXXXII"*—is where Princess Grace was buried in 1982. The last tomb is Prince Rainier's (daily 8:30–18:45, until 18:00 in winter).

• *As you leave the cathedral, walk left through the immaculately maintained Jardin Botanique, with more fine views and good places to picnic. Find the...*

Le Grand Prix Automobile de Monaco

Each May (May 22–25 in 2008), the Grand Prix de Monaco focuses the world's attention on this little country. The car race started as an enthusiasts' car rally by the Automobile Club  of Monaco (and is still run by the same group, 90 years later). Racers still consider this one of the most important races on their circuits. By Grand Prix standards, it's an unusual course, running through the streets of this tiny principality, sardined between mountains and sea. The hilly landscape makes the streets of Monaco narrow, with tight curves, steep climbs, and extremely short straightaways.

Each lap is about two miles, beginning and ending at the port. Cars climb along the sea from the port, pass in front of the casino, race through the commercial district, and do a few dandy turns back to the port. The race lasts 78 laps, and whoever is still rolling at the end wins (most don't finish). The Formula 1 cars look like overgrown toys that kids might pedal up and down their neighborhood street (if you're here a week or so before the race, look in the parking structure below Monaco-Ville where many race cars are kept—you're free to browse). Time trials to establish pole position begin three days before race day, which is always a Sunday. In 2008, the time trials take place on May 22, 23, and 24, and the race itself is on May 25. More than 150,000 people attend the gala event;

Cousteau Aquarium (Musée Océanographique): Prince Albert I built this impressive cliff-hanging aquarium in 1910 as a monument to his enthusiasm for things from the sea. One wing features Mediterranean fish; tropical species swim around in the other (all well-described in English). Overall, the aquarium has 2,000 different specimens and 250 species. Jacques Cousteau directed the aquarium for 17 years. The fancy Albert I Hall upstairs houses the museum (included in entry, little English information), featuring models of Albert and his beachcombers hard at work (€12.50, kids-€7, daily April–Sept 9:30–19:30, Oct–March 10:00–18:00; at opposite end of Monaco-Ville from palace, down the steps from Monaco-Ville bus stop; tel. 00-377/93 15 36 00, www.oceano.mc). Don't miss the rooftop terrace (with WCs and a café).

• *The redbrick steps across from the aquarium lead up to buses #1 and #2, both of which run to the port, the casino, and the train station. To walk back to the palace and through the old city, turn left at the top of the brick steps. For a brief movie break, take the escalator to the right of the aquarium; as you leave it into the parking garage, you'll find the...*

Monte Carlo Story: This informative 35-minute film gives a helpful account of Monaco's history and offers a comfortable, soft-chair break from all that walking (€7, headphone commentary in English, usually shows on the hour, daily 10:00–17:00, July–Aug until 18:00, closed Nov–Dec, you can join frequent extra showings for groups on summer mornings, tel. 00-377/93 25 32 33).

SIGHTS

Above Monaco-Ville

Jardin Exotique—This cliffside municipal garden, located above Monaco-Ville, has eye-popping views from France to Italy. It's a fascinating home to more than a thousand species of cacti (some giant) and other succulent plants, but probably worth the entry only for view-loving botanists (some posted English explanations provided). Your ticket includes entry to a skippable natural cave and an anthropological museum, as well as a not-to-be-missed view snack bar/café (€7, daily mid-May–mid-Sept 9:00–19:00, mid-Sept–mid-May 9:00–18:00 or dusk, tel. 00-377/93 15 29 80). Bus #2 runs here from any stop in Monaco and makes a worthwhile mini tour of Monaco, even if you don't visit the gardens. You can get similar views over Monaco for free from behind the souvenir stand at the Jardin's bus stop, or cross the street and hike toward La Turbie for even grander views.

In Monte Carlo

▲**Casino**—Monte Carlo, which means "Charles' Hill" in Spanish, is named for the local prince who presided over Monaco's 19th-century makeover. Begin your visit to Europe's most famous casino in the park above the traffic circle. In the mid-1800s, olive groves stood here. Then, with the construction of this casino, spas, and easy road and train access, one of Europe's poorest countries was on the Grand Tour map—*the* place for the vacationing aristocracy to play. Today, Monaco has the world's highest per-capita income.

The casino is designed to make the wealthy feel comfortable while losing money. Charles Garnier designed this casino (with an opera house inside) in 1878, in part to thank the prince for his financial help in completing Paris'

Opéra Garnier (which Garnier also designed). The central doors provide access to slot machines, private gaming rooms, and the opera house. The private gaming rooms occupy the left wing of the building.

Count the counts and Rolls-Royces in front of Hôtel de Paris (built at the same time, visitors allowed but not with shorts on, www.montecarloresort.com), then strut inside past the slots to the sumptuous atrium. This is the lobby for the opera house (open only for performances). There's a model of the opera at the end of the room, and marble WCs on the right. Anyone over 21 (even in shorts, if before 20:00) can get as far as the one-armed bandits (push button on slot machines to claim your winnings), though you'll need decent attire to go any further. After 20:00, shorts are off-limits everywhere.

The scene, flooded with camera-toting tourists during the day, is great at night—and downright James Bond–like in the private rooms. The park behind the casino offers a peaceful café and a good view of the casino's rear facade and of Monaco-Ville.

If paying an entrance fee to lose money is not your idea of fun, access to all games in the new, plebeian, American-style Loews Casino, adjacent to the old casino, is free.

Cost and Hours: The slot machines and the first gaming rooms *(salons européens)* open Mon–Fri at 14:00 and Sat–Sun at 12:00. Slots are free, but you'll pay €10 to enter *les salons européens*. The glamorous private game rooms—where you can rub elbows with high rollers—open Mon–Fri at 16:00 and Sat–Sun at 15:00, others not until 21:00–22:00, and cost an additional €10 (you must be 18 and have your passport). Men can rent a tie and jacket (necessary in the evening) at the bag check for €30, plus a €40 deposit. Dress standards for women are far more relaxed (only tennis shoes are a definite no-no, tel. 00-377/92 16 20 00, www.casino-monte-carlo.com).

Take the Money and Run: The return bus stop to Nice is at the top of the park, above the casino on avenue de la Costa (under the arcade to the left). To return to the train station from the casino, walk up the parkway in front of the casino, turn left on boulevard des Moulins, turn right on impasse de la Fontaine, climb the steps, and turn left on boulevard de la Princesse Charlotte (the entrance to the train station is next to Parking de la Gare; look for *Gare SNCF* sign).

SLEEPING AND EATING

(€1 = about $1.30, country code: 377)
Hôtel de France** is a perfectly pleasant, central, spotless, and reasonable place, run by friendly Sylvie (Sb-€84, Db-€103, Tb-€135, includes breakfast, no air-con, Wi-Fi, 6 rue de la Turbie,

near west exit from train station, tel. 00-377/93 30 24 64, fax 00-377/92 16 13 34, www.monte-carlo.mc/france, hotel-france @monte-carlo.mc).

Several cafés serve basic, inexpensive fare (day and night) on the port. I prefer the places that line the flowery and traffic-free rue de la Princesse Caroline, which runs between rue Grimaldi and the port. The best on this street is **Huit et Demi,** with most of its tables outside. It has a white-tablecloth-meets-director's-chair ambience, and cuisine worth returning for (€11–13 salads, €12–15 pizzas, €18–24 *plats*, closed Sat for lunch and all day Sun, rue de la Princesse Caroline, tel. 00-377/93 50 97 02). In Monaco-Ville, you'll find incredible *pan bagnat*, quiche, and sandwiches at the *boulangerie* at 8 rue Basse, a block off Palace Square.

TRANSPORTATION CONNECTIONS

From Monaco by Train to: Nice (2/hr, 20 min, €3.40), **Villefranche-sur-Mer** (2/hr, 10 min), **Antibes** (2/hr, 45–60 min).

By Bus to: Nice (#100, 4/hr, 45 min, €1.30), **Nice Airport** (line #110 express on the freeway, hourly, 50 min, €15), **Villefranche-sur-Mer** (#100, 4/hr, 25 min, €1.30), **La Turbie** (#114, 6/day Mon–Fri, 3/day Sat morning only, none on Sun, 20 min), Eze-le-Village (#112, 3/day Mon–Sat, none on Sun, 20 min).

The Monaco-to-Nice bus (#100) is not identified at every stop—verify with a local by asking, *"Direction Nice?"* One stop is across from the Place d'Armes stop in front of the Brasserie Monte Carlo. Another is a few blocks above the casino, under the arcade to the left of Barclays Bank.

Bus #112 departs Monaco for Eze-le-Village and La Turbie from place de la Cremaillière, one block above the main TI and casino park. Walk up rue Iris with Barclays Bank to your left, curve right, and find the bus shelter across the street by the Costa à la Crémaillière café. Bus numbers for these routes are not posted, but this is the stop.

The last bus leaves Monaco for Villefranche-sur-Mer and Nice at about 20:00; the last train leaves Monaco for Villefranche-sur-Mer and Nice at about 23:30.

Near Monaco: Menton

If you wish the Riviera were less glitzy and just a place where humble locals take their families to lick ice cream and make sand castles, consider a visit to Menton (15 minutes by bus beyond Monaco). Menton feels like a poor man's Nice. It's unrefined and unpretentious, with lower prices, fewer rentable umbrellas, and lots of Italians day-tripping in from just over the border (5 miles away). There's not an American in sight.

The Menton beach, while a bit rough, is a joy. An inviting promenade lines the beach, and beachfront cafés serve light meals and salads (much cheaper than in Nice). A snooze or stroll here is a fine Riviera experience. From the promenade, a pedestrian street leads through town. Small squares are alive with jazz bands playing crowd-pleasers under palm trees.

Stepping into the old town—which blankets a hill capped by a fascinating cemetery—you're immersed in a pastel-painted, yet dark and tangled Old World scene with (strangely) almost no commerce. A few elegant restaurants dig in at the base of the towering, centuries-old apartment flats. The richly decorated Baroque St. Michael's Church (midway up the hill) is a reminder that, until 1860, Menton was a thriving part of the larger state of Monaco. Climbing past sun-grabbing flower boxes and people who don't get out much anymore, the steep stepped lanes finally deposit you at the ornate gate of a grand cemetery that fills the old castle walls. Explore the cemetery, which is the final resting place of many aristocratic Russians (buried here in the early 1900s) and offers breathtaking Mediterranean views.

Getting to Menton: While trains serve Menton regularly, the station is a 15-minute walk from the action. Buses (which drop visitors right on the beach promenade) are your best bet (#100, 4/hr, 60 min from Nice, 15 min past Monaco, €1.30; see my self-guided bus tour on page 305).

ANTIBES, CANNES, AND ST-TROPEZ

The Riviera opens up west of Nice with bigger, sandier beaches and cheap high-rise development. Ancient Antibes and superficial Cannes buck the blue-collar, high-rise trend, each with thriving centers jammed with pedestrians and yachts. Trendy St-Tropez, a scenic 90-minute drive from Antibes, marks the western edge of the French Riviera.

Antibes

Antibes has a down-to-earth, easygoing ambience that's rare in this area. Its old town is a maze of narrow streets and red-tile roofs rising above the blue Mediterranean, watched over by twin medieval lookout towers and wrapped in extensive ramparts. Visitors making the short trip from Nice browse Europe's biggest yacht harbor, snooze on a sandy beach, loiter through an enjoyable old town, and hike along a sea-swept trail. The town's cultural claim to fame, the Picasso Museum, will likely reopen in the spring of 2008 after renovation.

Though it's much smaller than Nice, Antibes has a history that goes back just as far. Both towns were founded by Greek traders in the fifth century B.C. To the Greeks, Antibes was "Antipolis"—the town *(polis)* opposite *(anti)* Nice. For the next several centuries, Antibes remained in the shadow of its neighbor. By the turn of the 20th century, the town was a military base—so the rich and famous partied elsewhere. But when the army checked out after World War I, Antibes was "discovered" and enjoyed a particularly roaring '20s—with the help of party animals like Rudolph Valentino and the rowdy-yet-very-silent Charlie Chaplin. Fun-seekers even invented water-skiing right here in the 1920s.

ORIENTATION

Antibes' old town lies between the port and boulevard Albert 1er and avenue Robert Soleau. Place Nationale is the old town's hub of activity. The restaurant-lined rue Aubernon connects the port and the old town. Stroll along the sea between the old port and place Albert 1er (where boulevard Albert 1er meets the water). The best beaches lie just beyond place Albert 1er, and the path is beautiful. Good play areas for children are on place des Martyrs de la Résistance (close to recommended Hôtel Relais du Postillon).

Tourist Information

Antibes has two TIs. The most convenient is in the old town, just inside the walls at 21 boulevard d'Aguillon (Mon–Sat 10:00–12:00 & 13:30–18:00, closed Sun, tel. 04 93 34 65 65, www.antibes-ville .com). The *Maison de Tourisme* is in the newer city, where the fountains squirt at 11 place Général de Gaulle (where boulevard Albert 1er and rue de la République meet, July–Aug daily 9:00–18:00; Sept–June Mon–Sat 9:00–12:30 & 13:30–18:00, closed Sun; tel. 04 92 90 53 00, www.antibesjuanlespins.com). At either TI, pick up the excellent city map and the *Strolling Through the Heart of Old Antibes* brochure, and get details on the hikes described below. The Nice TI has Antibes maps; plan ahead.

Arrival in Antibes

By Train: To get to the port and the old town (10-min walk), cross the street in front of the station, skirting left of the Piranha Café, and follow avenue de la Libération downhill. As you come to the end of the street, the port will be on the left and the old town to the right. To reach the main TI in the modern city (10-min walk), exit right from the station on avenue Robert Soleau; follow *Maison du Tourisme* signs to place Général de Gaulle. Or hop on the free minibus (see "Getting Around Antibes," later in this chapter; exit station to the right and cross the street to the park). The last train back to Nice leaves at about 21:00.

By Bus: Bus #200 from Nice and to Cannes stops on avenue Dugommier, around the corner from the main TI; buses going to Nice and coming from Cannes stop on Aristide Briand (a block below the stop on avenue Dugommier, also near the TI). Buses from other destinations use the bus station at the edge of the old town on place Guynemer, a block below the old town TI (info desk open Mon–Sat 8:30–12:00 & 14:30–17:30, closed Sun).

By Car: Day-trippers should follow signs to *Centre-Ville*, then *Vieux Port*, and park near the old town walls (first 30 min free, then about €2/hr). Enter the old town through the last arch on

Antibes Area

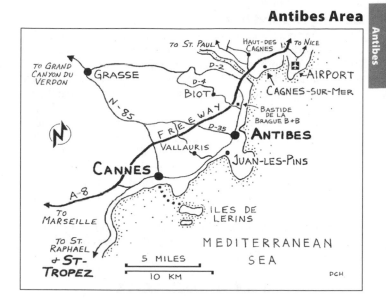

the right. If you're sleeping here, hotels are signed; get advice from your hotelier on where to park.

Helpful Hints

Internet Access: Get online at **Exlankaa Cyber Café,** near the main TI (24 avenue Gambetta, tel. 04 93 74 70 40), or **The Office,** in the old town (Galerie du Port, 8 boulevard d'Aguillon, tel. 04 93 34 09 96). The TI keeps an updated list of Internet cafés.

English Bookstore: Heidi's English Bookshop has a great selection of new and used books (daily 10:00–19:00, 24 rue Aubernon).

Laundry: Smiling Madame Hallepau will do your laundry while you swim. Her launderette is near the market hall on rue de la Pompe (Mon–Fri 8:30–12:00 & 15:00–19:00, closed Sat–Sun).

Grocery Store: Picnickers will appreciate Epicerie de la Place (daily until 22:00 in summer, until 21:00 off-season, where rue Sade meets place Nationale).

Taxi: Call 08 25 56 07 07 or 04 93 67 67 67.

Car Rental: The big-name agencies have offices in Antibes—Avis (32 avenue Albert 1er, tel. 04 93 34 65 15), Europcar (26 boulevard Foch, tel. 08 25 35 83 58), or Hertz (129 boulevard Wilson, tel. 04 93 61 18 15).

Airport Bus: Bus #200 runs from avenue Dugommier, near the main TI (at the second shelter when coming from the TI), to Nice's airport (2–3/hr, 45–70 min depending on traffic).

Getting Around Antibes

Antibes' most appealing hotels require a car to reach. Luckily, Antibes works well for drivers and most hotels have free parking. Compared to Nice, it's a breeze to navigate and a convenient springboard for the Inland Riviera. Pay parking is usually available at Antibes' train station, so drivers can ditch their cars and day-trip by train.

Several free **minibuses** *(Navettes Gratuites)* circle Antibes, serving the train station, the beaches, and Juan-les-Pins (Mon–Sat 7:30–19:30, not on Sun). There are four different circuits, making it hopelessly confusing for tourists—look for *Envibus* signs and ask if they are going near your destination (stops are tricky to find—look for bus stop signs around town; the TI has a small map).

A **tourist train** offers several circuits around old Antibes, the port, the ramparts, and to Juan-les-Pins (€7, departs from place de la Poste, tel. 06 03 35 61 35).

SELF-GUIDED WALK

Welcome to Antibes

This 40-minute amble will help you get your bearings, and works well day or night. Begin at the old port (Vieux Port) along avenue de Verdun (below the train station—parking right there). This is among the oldest of Europe's yachting harbors and was the model for many to come. Locals claim that this is Europe's first and biggest pleasure-boat harbor, with 1,600 stalls. That four-pointed structure crowning the opposite end of the port is **Fort Carré**—it

protected Antibes from foreigners for more than 500 years. At the end of the yachts, opposite the arch that leads into the old town, you'll see the pathetic remains of a once-hearty fishing fleet. The Mediterranean is pretty much fished out. Most of the seafood you'll eat here comes from fish farms or the Atlantic. Pass the sad fleet and keep walking along the harbor, then find the entry—through the wall on your right—to the shell-shaped **plage de la Gravette,** a normally quiet public beach tucked right in the middle of old Antibes. Wander up the ramp to the round lookout to better appreciate the scale of the ramparts that protected this town. Because Antibes was the last fort before the Italian border, the French king made sure the ramparts were strong and well-defended.

Backtrack and enter Antibes' **old town** through the arch under the rampart. Today, the town is the haunt of a large community of English, Irish, and Aussie boaters who help crew the giant yachts of the rich and famous. (That helps explain the Irish pubs and English bookstores.)

Continue straight and uphill, and you'll arrive at Antibes' **market hall** (Tue–Sun until 13:00, closed Mon except June–Aug). Like many other places in Antibes, this hall does double duty...it's filled with café tables at night.

If you take a left where the market starts, you'll find Antibes' pretty pastel **Church of Immaculate Conception,** built on the site of a Greek temple (worth a peek inside). The little church served as the area's cathedral until the mid-1200s.

Looming above the church on prime real estate is the white-stone **Château Grimaldi,** home to the **Picasso Museum** (should reopen in the spring of 2008 and is described below). This site has been home to the acropolis of the Greek city of Antipolis, a Roman fort, and a medieval bishop's palace (once connected to the cathedral below). The château was the home of the Grimaldi family (who still rule Monaco). Its proximity to the cathedral symbolized the sometimes too-cozy relationship between society's two dominant landowning classes: the Church and the nobility. (In 1789, the French Revolution changed all that.)

Find your way to the water and, heading right, follow the ramparts and views to the **History and Archaeology Museum.** From the terrace above the museum, you'll get a clear view of the forested **Cap d'Antibes,** crowned by its lighthouse and studded with mansions (see "Cap d'Antibes Hike," later in this chapter). The Cap was long the refuge of Antibes' rich and famous, and a favorite haunt of F. Scott Fitzgerald and Ernest Hemingway. After a quick tour of the museum (described below), continue hugging the coast past place Albert 1er until you see the terrific views back to old Antibes. Benches and soft sand await. You're on your own from here—strong walkers can continue to the fantastic view from the Phare de la Garoupe (see below); others can return to old Antibes and poke around in its peaceful back lanes.

SIGHTS AND ACTIVITIES

▲▲**Picasso Museum (Musée Picasso)**—Sitting serenely where the old town meets the sea, this small, three-floor museum will offer a remarkable collection of Picasso's paintings, sketches, and ceramics when it re-opens (with luck, by the spring of 2008). Picasso lived in the castle for four months in 1946, when he cranked out an amazing amount of art. The resulting collection (donated by Picasso) put Antibes on the tourist map. You'll see many of his

Antibes Hotels and Restaurants

B MINIBUS STOP
P PARKING
→ ONE-WAY STREET

1 To Hôtel Pension le Mas Djoliba
2 To Hôtels La Jabotte, Beau Site & Beach-Front Dining
3 Bastide de la Brague
4 Modern Hôtel
5 Hôtel Relais du Postillon
6 Hôtel le Cameo
7 Le Jardin Restaurant
8 Le Comptoir de la Tourraque
9 Le Brulot & Le Brulot Pasta
10 Auberge Provençale

11 Les Vieux Murs Rest.
12 Epicerie de la Place Grocery
13 Exlankaa Cyber Café
14 Heidi's English Bookshop
15 The Office Internet Café
16 Launderette
17 Bus to Nice Airport
18 Bus from Nice & to Cannes
19 Avis Car Rental
20 Hertz Car Rental
21 Europcar Car Rental

ceramics: plates with faces, bird-shaped vases, woman-shaped bottles, bull-shaped statues, and colorful tiles. But the highlight is his lively, frolicking *La Joie de Vivre* painting. This large (4 feet by 8 feet) Greek bacchanal sums up the newfound freedom in a newly liberated France (1946) and sets the tone for the rest of the collection. You'll also see several Cubist-style nudes *(nus couchés)*, plus the *Antipolis Suite*—a series of 25 (mostly reclining) nudes, very simplified and stripped-down in style, and works that demonstrate his cartoonist and caricaturist skills (details not yet available at press time, but possibly €5, covered by Riviera Carte Musées Pass, probably open Tue–Sun 10:00–18:00, maybe until 20:00 some evenings in summer, likely closed 12:00–14:00 off-season and Mon year-round; confirm these details—and be sure the museum is open—at Antibes' TI).

History and Archaeology Museum (Musée d'Histoire et d'Archéologie)—More than 2,000 years ago, Antibes was the center of a thriving maritime culture. It was also an important Roman city, featuring many of the hallmarks of Roman civilization—aqueducts, theaters, baths, and so on. This museum—the only place to get a sense of the city's ancient roots—displays Greek, Roman, and Etruscan odds and ends in two easy-to-visit rooms (no English descriptions). Your visit starts at an 1894 model of Antibes and continues past displays of Roman coins, cups, plates, and scads of amphorae. The curious, long lead pipe connected to a center box was used as a bilge pump; nearby is a good display of Roman anchors (€3, daily 10:00–18:00, on the water between Picasso Museum and place Albert 1er).

▲Market Hall (Marché Provençal)—The daily market bustles under a 19th-century canopy, with flowers, produce, Provençal products, and beach accessories (in old town behind Picasso Museum on cours Masséna). The market wears many appealing hats: produce daily until 13:00, handicrafts Thursday through Sunday in the afternoon, and fun outdoor dining in the evenings (market closed Mon in Sept–May).

Other Markets—Antibes' lively antique/flea market fills place Nationale and place Audiberti (next to the port) on Saturdays (7:00–18:00). Its clothing market winds through the streets around the post office (rue Lacan) on Thursdays (9:00–18:00).

Fort Carré—This impressively situated citadel, dating from 1487, was the last fort inside France. It protected Antibes from Nice, which until 1860 was part of Italy. You can tour this unusual four-pointed fort, but there's little to see inside. People visit for the fantastic views (€3, includes tour, daily June–Sept 10:00–18:00, Oct–May until 16:30).

Scenic footpaths link the fort and port along the sea. It's a 30-minute portside walk from the old town to the fort (or taxi there

Antibes

and walk back). By foot or car, follow avenue du 11 Novembre around the port, stay on the main road (walkers can follow the path by sports fields), then park for free just after the soccer field. A signed dirt path leads to Fort Carré. Keep following the green-lettered *Le Fort/Sens de la Visite* signs.

Beaches (*Plages*)—The best beaches stretch between Antibes' port and Cap d'Antibes, and the very best (plage de la Salis and plage du Ponteil) are just south of place Albert 1er. All are groomed and beautifully sandy. Plage de la Salis is busy but manageable in summer and on weekends, with snack stands  and views of the old town. The closest beach to the old town is at the port (plage de la Gravette), which seems calm in any season.

Walks and Hikes

From place Albert 1er (where boulevard Albert 1er meets the beach), you get a good view of plage de la Salis and Cap d'Antibes. That tower on the hill is your destination for the first walk described below. The longer "Cap d'Antibes Hike" begins on the next beach, just over that hill.

▲▲**Chapelle et Phare de la Garoupe**—The territorial views—good at sunset, best at sunrise, skippable if hazy—from this viewpoint more than make up for the 25-minute uphill climb from the plage de la Salis (a few blocks after Maupassant Apartments, follow the rough, cobbled chemin du Calvaire up to lighthouse tower). An orientation table explains that you can see from Nice to Cannes and up to the Alps. By car, follow signs for *Cap d'Antibes*, then look for *Chapelle et Phare de la Garoupe* signs.

▲**Cap d'Antibes Hike (Sentier Touristique Piétonnier de Tirepoil)**—At the end of the mattress-ridden plage de la Garoupe (over the hill from lighthouse) is a well-maintained trail around Cap d'Antibes. The beautiful path follows a rocky coastline below exclusive mansions for about two miles, then heads inland along small streets, ending at the recommended Hôtel Beau-Site (and bus stop). You can walk as far as you'd like and then double back, or do the whole loop (allow 2 hours, use the TI Antibes map). Locals call this the "Bay of Millionaires."

To get to the trail from Antibes, take **bus #2** from the bus station for about 15 minutes to the La Fontaine stop at the Hôtel Beau-Site (almost hourly Mon–Sat, 8/day Sun, return stop is 50 yards down on opposite side, get return times at station). Walk 10 minutes down to plage de la Garoupe and start from there. By **car,** follow signs to Cap d'Antibes, then plage de la Garoupe, and park there. The trail begins at the far-right end of plage de la Garoupe.

Near Antibes

Juan-les-Pins—This village, across the Cap d'Antibes isthmus from Antibes, is where the action is in the evenings. It's a modern beach resort with good beaches, plenty of lively bars and restaurants, and a popular jazz festival in July. Buses, trains, and even a tourist train (see "Getting Around Antibes," above) make the 10-minute trip to and from Antibes constantly.

Marineland and Parc de la Mer—A few backstrokes from Antibes, Parc de la Mer is a massive waterworld of waterslides, miniature golf, exhibits, and more. Marineland anchors this sea-park extravaganza with shows featuring dolphins, sea lions, and killer whales (Marineland only—€36, kids-€26, €2 more in July–Aug and €6 less in winter; Aquasplash waterslide park—€22, kids-€18, closed in winter; the whole shebang—€42, kids-€33; various combo-tickets available for Aquasplash waterslides, miniature golf, and other attractions; daily 10:00–19:00, until 22:00 July–Aug, tel. 04 93 33 49 49, www.marineland.fr). The park is five minutes on foot from the train station in Biot (between Nice and Antibes); exit Biot's station and walk toward Nice, following the signs. By car, the park is signed from RN-7, several miles from Antibes toward Nice.

Renoir Museum—Halfway between Antibes and Nice in Haut-des-Cagnes, the old city, above the unappealing seaside town of Cagnes-sur-Mer, is Pierre-Auguste Renoir's "Giverny." It's the home where the artist spent the last 12 years of his life (1907–1919), tending to his lush gardens, painting, and even dabbling in sculpture in spite of suffering from rheumatoid arthritis. His home has been converted into a small museum, where visitors can see his studio and art tools, stroll in his gardens, and enjoy 11 of his paintings of people and places around Cagnes-sur-Mer. It's a pleasant place—particularly for his fans—and makes a worthwhile excursion, thanks to the peaceful medieval village of Haut-des-Cagnes where it's located (€3, May–Sept Wed–Mon 10:00–12:00 & 14:00–18:00, closed Tue, Oct–April closes at 17:00, tel. 04 93 20 61 64). Take the Antibes–Nice bus (#200, 2–3/hr, about 30 min) to Cagnes-sur-Mer and walk uphill 15 minutes to the museum or drive to Cagnes-sur-Mer, then follow signs to *Haut-des-Cagnes* and look for *Musée Renoir* signs. For driving directions, see the Inland Riviera Self-Guided Driving Tour, page 344.

More Day Trips from Antibes—Antibes is halfway between Nice and Cannes (easy train service to both), and close to the artsy pottery and glassblowing village of Biot, home of the Fernand Léger Museum (frequent buses), and another pottery town, Vallauris, where Picasso fans will enjoy his murals in the Chapel of War and Peace (bus and train connections, get details at TI).

SLEEPING

My favorite Antibes hotels require a car or taxi—central pickings are slim in the city, where many hoteliers seem more interested in their restaurants.

Outside the Town Center

$$$ Hôtel Pension le Mas Djoliba*** is a good splurge, best for drivers (since it's a 15–20-min walk from the beach and old Antibes, and a 25-min walk from the train station). Reserve early for this tranquil, bird-chirping, flower-filled manor house where no two rooms are the same. From May to September, they definitely prefer (but won't insist) that you dine here. It's hard to pass up once you see the setting—after a busy day of sightseeing, dinner by the pool is a treat. The bigger rooms are well worth the small additional cost (Db with breakfast and dinner-€85–100 per person, Db only-€100–150, several excellent family rooms-€162–190, big suite-€240, breakfast-€11, air-con, Wi-Fi, cool *boules* court and loaner balls, 29 avenue de Provence; from boulevard Albert 1er, look for blue signs and turn right up avenue Gaston Bourgeois; tel. 04 93 34 02 48, fax 04 93 34 05 81, www.hotel-djoliba.com, hotel .djoliba@wanadoo.fr).

$$$ Hôtel La Jabotte** defies the rules. Hiding down an ignored alley just a block from the famous beaches and a 20-minute walk from the old town, this small, cozy place is run by owners who care. Yves, Claude, and dog Tommy have turned a small beach villa into a boutique hotel with personality: The colors are rich, the decor shows a personal touch, and most rooms have individual terraces that face a small, central garden (Db-€105–115, includes good breakfast and a few parking spots, no air-con, 13 avenue Max Maurey, take the third right after passing the big

---

Sleep Code

(€1 = about $1.30, country code: 33)
S = Single, **D** = Double/Twin, **T** = Triple, **Q** = Quad, **b** = bathroom, **s** = shower only, ***** = French hotel rating (0–4 stars). Unless otherwise noted, credit cards are accepted and English is spoken.

To help you sort easily through these listings, I've divided the rooms into three categories based on the price for a standard double room with bath:

$$$ **Higher Priced**—Most rooms €100 or more.
$$ **Moderately Priced**—Most rooms between €70–100.
$ **Lower Priced**—Most rooms €70 or less.

Hôtel Josse, tel. 04 93 61 45 89, fax 04 93 61 07 04, www.jabotte .com, info@jabotte.com).

$$ Hôtel Beau Site*** is my only listing on Cap d'Antibes, a 10-minute drive from the old town. It's a terrific value if you want to get away...but not *too* far away. This place is a sanctuary, with delightful owners (sweet Nathalie and papa Jean-Louis), a pool, a comfy patio garden, and easy parking. Eleven rooms have balconies (standard Db-€82–90, bigger Db-€100–115, even bigger Db-€134–148, family rooms-€160–210, extra bed-€25; incredible boaty-breakfast-€11.50, continental breakfast-€6.50, air-con, Wi-Fi, bikes available, 141 boulevard Kennedy, tel. 04 93 61 53 43, fax 04 93 67 78 16, www .hotelbeausite.net, hbeausit@club-internet.fr). From the hotel, it's a 10-minute walk down to the crowded plage de la Garoupe and a nearby hiking trail (see "Walks and Hikes," above).

$$ Bastide de la Brague is a six-room bed-and-breakfast hacienda in no-man's-land, up a dirt road above Marineland (10-min drive east of Antibes). But the place is a find as it's central to Riviera sights and run by Antibes' sweetest family (les Sanchis: wife Isabelle, hubby Frank, and Mama). Rooms are new, quite comfortable, air-conditioned, and affordable; several are made for families. Request the €20 home-cooked dinner and you'll get the works—from apéritif to coffee and everything in-between (costs less for kids). There's more than enough space to stretch out, and they love families (Db-€70–90, Tb/Qb-€90–110, includes breakfast, 55 avenue No. 6, Antibes 06600, tel. 04 93 65 73 78, www .bbchambreantibes.com, bb06@wanadoo.fr). From Antibes, drive toward Nice par Bord de la Mer, turn left at Marineland, then right at the roundabout (to Groules) and follow signs.

In the Town Center

$$ Modern Hôtel**, in the pedestrian zone near the bus station, is modest and spick-and-span. The 17 standard-size rooms, each with air-conditioning and bright decor, are an excellent value (Sb-€58–69, Db-€65–84, 1 rue Fourmillière, tel. 04 92 90 59 05, fax 04 92 90 59 06, www.modernhotel06.com, modern-hotel@wanadoo .fr, helpful Laurence).

$$ Hôtel Relais du Postillon**, on a thriving square, offers 15 mostly small but well-designed rooms. Each room has a name instead of a number, and they could all use a little TLC... which is promised for 2008 (Db-€46–84, price depends on size and whether you're facing courtyard or park, tight bathrooms, 8 rue Championnet, tel. 04 93 34 20 77, fax 04 93 34 61 24, www .relaisdupostillon.com, postillon@atsat.com). Owner Yves-Jean speaks flawless English.

$ Hôtel le Cameo** is a rambling old place above a bustling bar (where you'll find what reception there is). The public areas are dark, and the nine simple, linoleum-lined rooms are almost cute. All open onto the boisterous place Nationale, which means you don't sleep until the restaurant sleeps (Ds-€55, Db-€66, Tb-€74, Qb-€82, 5 place Nationale, tel. 04 93 34 24 17, fax 04 93 34 35 80, no English spoken).

EATING

Antibes is a fun place to dine out. You can eat on a budget, enjoy a fine meal at an acceptable price, or join the party just inside the walls on boulevard d'Aguillon, under the festive Marché Provençal, or on place Nationale (all filled with tables and tourists—I prefer the Marché Provençal). The options are endless. Take a walk and judge for yourself, and be tempted by these good suggestions. Romantics should picnic at the beach. Everyone should stroll along the ramparts after dinner.

Le Jardin is reliable and reasonable, with tables filling a pretty and peaceful garden courtyard. Arrive early to secure a table outside and enjoy good regional cooking (€19–27 *menus* and good €17 *plats,* closed Tue, 5 rue Sade, tel. 04 93 34 64 74).

Le Comptoir de la Tourraque bucks Antibes' showy trend. It has an intimate interior, caring service, fair prices, and top-notch cuisine mixing traditional French and Italian flavors (€34 *menu,* closed Mon, 1 rue de la Tourraque, tel. 04 93 95 24 86).

Le Brulot runs two restaurants—Le Brulot and Le Brulot Pasta—that sit almost side-by-side a short block below Marché Provençal on rue Frédéric Isnard. Join locals at the very popular and inexpensive **Le Brulot,** known for its Provençal cuisine and meats cooked on an open fire. It's a small place, overflowing onto the street, with a few outside tables and a dining room below. Try the aioli (€15 *menus,* €12 *plats,* closed Sun, at #2, tel. 04 93 34 17 76). **Le Brulot Pasta** is family-friendly and goes Italian with excellent pizza (the €11 Printanière is tasty and huge) and big portions of pasta, served in air-conditioned comfort under stone arches (open daily, at #3, tel. 04 93 34 19 19).

Auberge Provençale entertains discerning diners in a vine-covered courtyard. This is where the locals go for seafood specialties (*menus* from €34, open daily, 61 place Nationale, tel. 04 93 34 13 24).

Les Vieux Murs is *the* place to splurge in Antibes for regional specialties. Its candlelit, red-tone, *très romantique* interior overlooks the sea, and the outside tables are worth booking ahead for—pass on the upstairs room (€43 *menu,* open daily June–mid-Sept, closed Tue off-season, valet parking available, along ramparts beyond Picasso Museum at 25 promenade Amiral de Grasse, tel. 04 93 34 06 73).

Beachfront Dining: You'll find two restaurants on pretty plage de la Garoupe, below the recommended Hôtel Beau Site. **Le César/Plage Keller** makes for an elegant seaside meal (same owner as Les Vieux Murs above, allow €60 per person with wine, open daily, tel. 04 93 61 33 74). **Plage Joseph Restaurant** next door features basic fare at lower prices with the same view (open daily).

TRANSPORTATION CONNECTIONS

TGV and local trains serve Antibes' little station.

From Antibes by Train to: Cannes (2/hr, 15 min), **Nice** (2/hr, 15–30 min, €3.90), **Villefranche-sur-Mer** (2/hr, 40 min), **Monaco** (2/hr, 45–60 min), **Marseille** (16/day, 2.5 hrs).

By Bus to: Cannes (2–3/hr, 25 min), **Nice Airport** (bus #200, 2–3/hr, 40–70 min depending on traffic), **Biot** (2/hr, 20 min).

Cannes

Cannes (pronounced "can") is famous for its film festival. Its sister city is Beverly Hills. That says it all. When I asked the TI for a list of museums and sights, they simply smiled. Cannes—with big, exclusive hotels lining mostly private stretches of perfect, sandy beach—is for strolling, shopping, dreaming of meeting a movie star, and lounging on the seafront. Cannes has nothing unique to offer the traveler...except a mostly off-limits film festival. You can buy an ice cream cone at the train station and see everything before you've had your last lick. Money is what Cannes has always been about—wealthy people come here to make the scene, so there's always enough *scandale* to go around. The king of Saudi Arabia purchased a serious slice of waterfront just east of town and built his compound with no regard to local zoning regulations. Money talks on the Riviera...always has.

ORIENTATION

Don't sleep or drive in Cannes. Day-trip in by train. It's a breeze, as trains run frequently along the Riviera, and they all stop in Cannes (2/hr, 15 min from Antibes, 30–40 min from Nice, €6).

Turn left out of the train station (bag check available 8:30–20:30), find the busy **TI** next door, and pick up the nifty little city map (Mon–Sat 9:00–19:00, closed Sun, tel. 04 93 99 19 77, www.cannes.fr). On Sundays, when the train station TI is closed, drop by the glamorously quiet main TI, in the film festival building at 1 avenue de la Croisette.

SELF-GUIDED WALK

Do the Cannes Cancan

This self-guided walking tour will take you to Cannes' sights in a level, one-hour walk at, of course, a movie-star pace.

• *From the train station TI, cross the street (veering slightly left) and walk for five unimpressive minutes down rue des Serbes to the beach-front. Cross the busy boulevard de la Croisette and make your way past snack stands to the sea. Find the round lookout and get familiar with...*

The Lay of the Land: Cannes looks different from Nice. It was never part of Italy, so its architecture (and cuisine) is more French-Provençal. Face inland. You won't find the pastel oranges and reds that so define Old Nice and Villefranche-sur-Mer. On the left, look for the modern, rust-colored building that's home to the famous film festival (we'll visit there soon). The hill in the distance with the medieval tower caps Cannes' old town (Le Suquet). This hilltop offers grand views, but little else. Below the old town, the port welcomes yachts of all sizes...provided they're big. Look way to the left. The impressive mountains that sweep down to the sea are the Massif de l'Esterel, which preside over spectacular car and train routes. Back the other way, gaze up the boulevard. That classy building with twin black-domed roofs is the Hôtel Carlton, our eventual target and as far as we'll go in that direction.

• *Continue with the sea on your right and stroll the...*

Promenade (La Croisette): You're walking along boulevard de la Croisette—Cannes' famed two-mile-long promenade. First

popular with kings who wintered here after Napoleon fell, the elite parade was later joined by British aristocracy. Today, boulevard de la Croisette is fronted by some of the most expensive (and garish) apartments and hotels in Europe. Even if you lack a poodle, stroll here to people-watch and wonder what architect would design such awful buildings in such a glorious setting. Notice the blue boxes that help keep La Croisette poodle-poop-free.

• *Stop when you get to the...*

Hôtel Carlton: This is the most famous address on boulevard de la Croisette (allow €700–5,100 for a night). Face the beach. The iconic Cannes experience is to slip out of your luxury hotel (preferably this one), into a robe (ideally monogrammed with your initials), and onto the beach—or better yet, onto the pier (this avoids getting irritating sand on your carefully oiled skin). While you may not be doing the "fancy hotel and monogrammed robe" ritual on this Cannes excursion, you can—for about €15—rent a chair and umbrella and pretend you're tanning for a red-carpet premiere. Cannes does have a few token public beaches, but most are private and run by hotels like the Carlton. You could save money by sunning among the common folk, but the real Cannes way to flee the rabble and paparazzi is to rent a spot on a private beach (best to reserve ahead in July–Aug).

Cross over and wander into the elegant hotel—you're welcome to visit. Ask for a hotel brochure, verify room rates, then find the swanky Bar des Célébrités. Imagine the scene here during the film festival (see anyone famous?). A surprisingly affordable café (considering room rates) lies just beyond.

• *Time to turn around and double back to the dull orange building that is Cannes'...*

Film Festival Hall: Cannes' film festival (Festival de Cannes), staged since 1939, completes the "Big Three" of Riviera events (with Monaco's Grand Prix and Nice's Carnival). The hall where the festival takes place—a busy-but-nondescript convention center—sits like a plump movie star on the beach. You'll recognize the formal grand entryway—but the red carpet won't be draped for your visit. Find the famous (Hollywood-style) handprints in the sidewalk all around. To get inside during the festival, you have to be a star (or a photographer—some 3,000 paparazzi attend the gala event). Even though it's off-limits to us, it's still a big deal around here. Locals claim that it's the world's third-biggest media event, after the Olympics and the World Cup (soccer). The festival prize is the Palme d'Or (like the Oscar for Best Picture). The French press can't cover the event enough, and the average Jean in France follows it as Joe would the World Series in the States. The French won it in 2005 with *L'Enfant,* by Luc and Jean-Pierre Dardenne. The Brits grabbed it in 2006 with Ken Loach's Irish war flick, *The Wind that Shakes the Barley.* In 2007, the prize went to Romania for the first time, for *4 Months, 3 Weeks & 2 Days.* (The 2008 festival runs May 14–25.)

• *Around the other side of the festival hall is the gare Maritime port, with a vast open square and mega-yachts.*

The Port and Old Town (Le Suquet): The big-boy yachts line up closest to the Film Festival Hall. After seeing this yacht frenzy, everything else looks like a dinghy. Boats to St-Tropez (see below) depart from the far side of the port (at quai Laubeuf). Cannes' oldest neighborhood, Le Suquet—which we saw from afar earlier—is a 15-minute walk above the port, with little of interest except the panoramic views from its ancient church, Notre-Dame-de-l'Espérance (Our Lady of Hope).

Handy Cannes and St-Tropez Phrases

Where is a movie star?	*Où est une vedette?*
I am a movie star.	*Je suis une vedette.*
I am rich and single.	*Je suis riche et célibataire.*
Are you rich and single?	*Etes-vous riche et célibataire?*
How long is your yacht?	*Quelle est la longeur de votre yacht?*
How much did that cost?	*Combien coûtait-il?*
You can always dream...	*Vous pouvez toujours rêver...*

ACTIVITIES

Shopping—Cannes is made for window-shopping (the best streets are between the station and the waterfront). Stroll down rue d'Antibes for the trendiest boutiques. Rue Meynadier anchors a pedestrian zone with more affordable shops closer to the port. To bring home a real surprise, consider cosmetic surgery. Cannes is well-known as the place on the Riviera to have your face (or other parts) realigned.

Yachters' Itinerary—If you're visiting Cannes on your private yacht, here's a suggested itinerary:

1. Take in the Festival de Cannes and the accompanying social scene. Organize an evening party on your boat.

2. Motor over to Monte Carlo for the Grand Prix, now scheduled—conveniently for yachters—just after the film festival.

3. Drop by Porto Chervo on Sardinia, one of the few places in the world where your yacht is "just average."

4. Head west to Ibiza and Marbella in Spain, where your friends are moored for the big party scene.

EATING

For a tasty, easy lunch in Cannes, consider **Fournil St. Nicholas.** You'll get mouthwatering quiche and sandwiches and exquisite salads at affordable prices (leaving the train station, turn right and walk a few blocks to 5 rue Venizelos, tel. 04 93 38 81 12).

TRANSPORTATION CONNECTIONS

TGV and local trains serve Cannes' station.

From Cannes by Train to: Antibes (2/hr, 15 min), **Nice** (2/hr, 30 min, €6), **Grasse** (1/hr, 30 min).

By Bus to: Nice Airport (2–3/hr, 60–90 min depending on traffic), **Antibes** (2–3/hr, 25 min).

By Boat: Trans Côte d'Azur runs boat excursions from Cannes to **St-Tropez** (€38 round-trip, 75 min each way; July–mid-Sept daily 2/day; mid-Sept–June Tue, Thu, and Sat–Sun only 1/day; tel. 04 92 00 42 30, fax 04 92 00 42 31, www.trans-cote-azur.com). This boat trip is popular—book a few days ahead from June to September.

St-Tropez

St-Tropez is a busy, charming, and traffic-free port town smothered with fashion boutiques, elegant restaurants, and luxury boats. If you came here for history or quaintness, you caught the wrong yacht.

But if you have more money than you know what to do with, you're home. There are 5,700 year-round residents...and more than 100,000 visitors daily in the summer. Come in the winter if you can.

As with many seaside villages in southern France, the pastel beauty of St-Tropez was first discovered by artists. Paul Signac introduced several of his friends to St-Tropez in the late 1800s, giving the village its first notoriety. But it wasn't until Brigitte Bardot made the scene here in the 1956 film ...*And God Created Woman* that St-Tropez became synonymous with Riviera glamour. Since then, it's the first place that comes to mind when people think of the jet set luxuriating on Mediterranean beaches. For many, the Riviera begins here and runs east to Menton, on the Italian border.

In St-Tropez, the village itself is the attraction, as the nearest big beach is miles away. Wander the harborfront, where fancy yachts moor stern-in, their carefully coiffed captains and first mates enjoying *pu-pus* (snacks) for happy hour—they're seeing and being seen. Take time to stroll the back streets while nibbling a chocolate-and–Grand Marnier crêpe.

ORIENTATION

St-Tropez lies between its famous port and the hilltop Citadelle (with great views). The network of lanes between the port and Citadelle are strollable in a Carmel-by-the-Sea sort of way.

Tourist Information

The TI is starboard on the port (to you landlubbers, that's to the right as you face the sea), where quai Suffren and quai Jean Jaurès meet (daily April–Oct 9:30–12:30 & 14:00–19:00, July–Aug until 20:00, Nov–March until 18:00, tel. 08 92 68 48 28, www.ot-saint -tropez.com). Pick up their good, free walking-tour brochure in English (included in the *St-Tropez Culture & Loisirs* brochure), ask about events in town, and get maps and bus information if you plan to hike along the coast.

Arrival in St-Tropez

For bus and boat details, see "Transportation Connections," page 342.

By Bus: Buses leave you a few minutes' walk to the port, near the parking lot—Parking du Vieux Port—on avenue Général de Gaulle.

By Boat: Boats from St. Raphael deposit you by the Parking du Vieux Port, a five-minute walk to the port.

By Car: Prepare for traffic in any season—worse on weekends (forget driving on Sun afternoons), ugly during summer, and downright impossible between St-Tropez and St. Maxime on weekends. You can avoid this bottleneck by taking the autoroute to Le Luc, and following the windy D-558 to St-Tropez from here (via La Garde Freinet and Port Grimaud).

The last few miles to St-Tropez are along a too-long, two-lane road with one way in, one way out, and too many people going exactly where you're going. There are two main parking lots (both about €2.50/hr): Parking des Lices (near all recommended hotels) and Parking du Vieux Port (best for day-trippers).

SELF-GUIDED WALK

Welcome to St-Tropez

This quick, scenic walk is best done with the TI's walking-tour brochure.

• *Begin at the round tower (Bureau du Port) at the port's vessel entry, by the Parking du Vieux Port.*

Climb the steps for a fine view. Check out the massive crane—it's used to pull yachts that are bigger than my house out of the water for off-season maintenance. Moorage fees for the bigger yachts run €2,000 per day.

Walk along the port, and notice the busy deckhands (hustling before their captains arrive) and the artists competing for room to showcase their work. Saunter around to the opposite corner of the port, and work your way to the TI.

The red-tabled café (Le Sénéquier) by the TI is one of the

town's most venerated, and has long attracted celebrities, including Jean-Paul Sartre. High-end cafés and restaurants line the port from here to the jetty—it doesn't seem to matter that you can't see the sea for the big yachts. See if you recognize anyone famous, and by all means, stop to wiggle your toes in the gleaming white sandy floor of Joseph l'Escale's restaurant.

Find the bulky round tower at the port's end with views across the bay—to St. Maxime and out to sea. A plaque honors the American, British, and French troops who liberated Provence on August 15, 1944.

Climb the jetty for great views over St-Tropez's port, then wander past the round tower to a walking path that leads to small beaches and swimming opportunities. Notice how clear the water is, and how the homes seem at one with the sea. From here, you can continue along the shore, or walk up to the Citadelle for more views (see below). The small lanes below the Citadelle are St-Tropez's most appealing. Work your way to the big place des Lices (good cafés) and see if anyone is playing *pétanque*.

SIGHTS AND ACTIVITIES

In St-Tropez

Window-shopping, people-watching, tan maintenance, and enjoying slow meals fill people's days, weeks, and in some cases, lives. Here, one dresses up, sizes up one another's yachts, and trolls for a partner. While the only models you'll see are in the shop windows, Brigitte Bardot—who turns 74 in 2008—still hangs out on a bench in front of the TI signing autographs (Thu 15:00–17:30).

Museum of the Annonciade (Musée de l'Annonciade)—Though generally ignored, this museum houses an enchanting collection of Post-Impressionist and Fauvist artists who were here before Brigitte. Almost all canvases feature St-Tropez. You'll see colorful paintings by Paul Signac, Henri Matisse, Georges Braque, Pierre Bonnard, Maurice de Vlaminck, and more. Gaze out the windows and notice how the port has changed since they were here (€5.50, daily 10:00–12:00 & 14:00–18:00, longer hours during special exhibits, closed in Nov, may be closed Tue in off-season, place Grammont, tel. 04 94 17 84 10).

La Citadelle—This old fortress offers little but peacocks, occasional special exhibits (inquire at TI), and views over St-Tropez from its high walls (€4, daily 10:00–12:00 & 13:00–17:30, closed in Nov, longer hours and more expensive during special exhibits, tel. 04 94 97 59 43).

Coastal Hike—The scenic Sentier du Littoral path runs past the Citadelle for 20 miles along the coast and is marked with yellow dashes on the pavement, walls, and trees. Leave St-Tropez along the road below the Citadelle, pass the "Sailors cemetery," and you'll join the path before long. If you're really into this, take the 20-minute bus *(La Navette)* from place des Lices in St-Tropez to the Capon/Pinet stop and walk three hours back to St-Tropez (bus only runs 2/day, get details at TI).

Boat Excursions—Several companies offer mildly interesting tours of the bay (paralleling the Sentier du Littoral described above). Le Brigantin has reliable outings in comfortable wooden vessels with personalized English commentary. You'll learn a smidgen about St-Tropez's history and a lot about villas of the rich and famous (Conrad Hilton and John Grisham both have little bungalows, and you'll sail right past Brigitte Bardot's surprisingly modest-looking home). Redhead Victoria (from Britain) staffs the information desk on the quai Suffren and can explain the trip (€8, kids age 5–10-€4, 4/day, tel. 04 94 54 40 61).

Boules—The vast *pétanque (boules)* court on place des Lices is worth your attention. Have a drink at the recommended Le Café and take in the action. Study up on the sport (see page 174) and root for your hero. The cafés on quai Bouchard offer fine port views and quieter confines.

Near St-Tropez

Port Grimaud—While more modern than St-Tropez, Port Grimaud (located a few miles toward St. Maxime) is no less attractive or upscale. This "Venice of Provence" was reclaimed from a murky lagoon about 40 years ago, and is now lined with four miles of canals, lovely homes, and moorage for thousands of yachts. It's actually a fascinating look at what clever minds can produce from a swamp. Park at the lot across from the town entry (TI next to the parking, tel. 04 94 56 02 01), and cross the barrier and bridge into a beautiful world of privilege. Climb the church bell tower for a good panorama.

SLEEPING

(€1 = about $1.30, country code: 33)

Though everything seems pricey in this golden town, I've uncovered a few jewels. Sleep only in the town center, as traffic makes coming and going a royal headache. High season in St-Tropez runs from June through September, and weekends are busy year-round.

$$$ Hôtel La Ponche**** offers a warm welcome and the most central, luxurious beds I could find (Db-€190–370, Db with top floor deck and sea view-€380–570, breakfast-€20, parking-€21, near the sea, several blocks behind the TI at 3 rue des Remparts, tel. 04 94 97 02 53, fax 04 94 97 78 61, www.laponche.com, hotel @laponche.com).

$$$ Hôtel les Plamiers*** is relaxed place with a lush garden, a bar-lounge and good rooms at normal three-star rates. It's on place des Lices so parking is easy (standard Db-€85–106, bigger Db-€115–140, air-con, place des Lices, tel. 04 94 97 01 61, www .hotel-les-palmiers.com, info@ hotel-les-palmiers.com).

$$ Hôtel le Colombier**, little and adorable, is on a quiet street. Its 11 soft and comfortable rooms enclose a small, sweet garden-patio. This is a terrific value (Db-€64–86, bigger Db with air-con-€115–130, T/Qb-€170–190, easy parking nearby, follow *Parking des Lices* and look for signs on left, impasse des Conquêtes, tel. 04 94 97 05 31, fax 04 94 97 32 57).

$$ Hôtel Lou Cagnard** looks average from the outside. But enter the courtyard garden and you'll find a pretty, well-managed, and shockingly reasonable hotel (Ds-€50–64, bigger Db-€80–120, higher prices are for garden-side and larger rooms, 1-week minimum June–Sept, air-con, free parking, follow signs to *parking des Lices* and you'll pass hotel, 18 avenue Paul Roussel, tel. 04 94 97 04 24, fax 04 94 97 09 44, www.hotel-lou-cagnard.com, no reservations by email).

EATING

There are several grocery stores in the old city. The Casino market is a block off the port, up rue V. Laugier.

Start or end your evening with St-Tropez's best port-view seats on the small deck at **Hôtel Sube's** bar on quai Suffren, near the TI (drinks only, fine interior).

Dining on place des Lices is a great opportunity to watch *pétanque* matches, with several appealing eateries to choose from. **Le Café** has long been the place to hang one's beret on this square, and serves surprisingly good cuisine. Stroll inside past the soft chairs and old wooden floor, and find one of the best zinc counters in France, complete with an atmospheric bar (open daily, €30 *menus*, €18 *plats*, tel. 04 94 97 44 69). **Café des Arts,** at the end of the square, has good ambience inside and out, and serves pizza, salads, and *plats* for €10–15 (open daily, tel. 04 94 97 02 25).

Christophe Leroy's **La Table du Marché,** just off the place des Lices, is an inviting pastry shop/deli/restaurant with *menus* from €26 that include a glass of wine (open daily, 38 rue Georges Clemenceau, tel. 04 94 97 85 20).

Elsewhere in St-Tropez, **L'Auberge des Maures** has a rich, lively decor, indoor and outdoor tables, and a welcoming staff. It's a good place to go for quality Provençal cuisine (€48 *menu,* open daily, 4 rue du Docteur Boutin, tel. 04 94 97 01 50).

TRANSPORTATION CONNECTIONS

From St-Tropez by Public Transportation: With no trains to St-Tropez, buses and boats are your only options. **Buses** serve St-Tropez from St-Raphaël's train station to the east (almost hourly, 80 min) and from Toulon to the west (7/day, 2 hrs). **Boats** make the one-hour trip from St-Raphaël to St-Tropez twice daily (€12 one-way, €22 round-trip, departs St-Raphaël at 9:30 and 14:30, departs St-Tropez at 10:30 and 17:15, tel. 04 94 95 17 46, or call the TI). For boats connecting St-Tropez with Nice, see page 243; with Cannes, page 337.

INLAND RIVIERA

For a verdant, rocky, fresh escape from the beaches, head inland and upward. Some of France's most perfectly perched hill towns and splendid scenery hang overlooked in this region that's more famous for beaches and bikinis. A short car or bus ride away from the Mediterranean reaps big rewards: lush forests, deep canyons, and swirling hilltop villages. A longer drive (though still doable as a day trip) brings you to Europe's greatest canyon, the Grand Canyon du Verdon.

Getting Around the Inland Riviera

By Car: Driving is the most flexible way to tour this area (particularly in the off-season)—though summer and weekend traffic and parking challenges will test your patience. A one-day car rental is worth considering (see the "Helpful Hints" sections in the Nice and Antibes chapters). I describe the best route below.

By Bus: Buses get you to many of the places in this chapter. Vence, St-Paul-de-Vence, and Grasse are well-served by bus from Nice about every 30 minutes, and Grasse has train service from Nice, Antibes, and Cannes (see "Getting Around the Riviera" on page 240). Buses to Tourrettes-sur-Loup, Le Bar-sur-Loup, and Grasse leave from Vence daily except Sunday (7/day, 15 min to Tourrettes-sur-Loup, 35 min to Le Bar-sur-Loup, 50 min to Grasse, tel. 04 93 42 40 79). Buses do not serve the Gorges du Loup, the village of Gourdon, or the Gorges du Verdon.

SELF-GUIDED DRIVING TOUR

The Inland Riviera:
From St-Paul-de-Vence to Grasse

This splendid loop drive connects St-Paul-de-Vence, Vence, Tourrettes-sur-Loup, and Grasse (all described below, in that order). It's best done by car as a day trip from the Nice/Antibes area (allow all day), though it could be done en route to the Gorges du Verdon (also described below—see page 354). Most of the villages described can be linked by bus (but note that there's no bus service on Sunday from Vence to Tourrettes-sur-Loup, Le Bar-sur-Loup, or Grasse); Grasse is also accessible by train. Each of the stops is only minutes away from the next by car or bus, but allow 45 minutes to drive from Nice to the first stop, St-Paul-de-Vence. Start early if you want to see St-Paul-de-Vence without the mobs (have breakfast at St-Paul-de-Vence's recommended Café de la Place, listed on page 346).

Begin your day by leaving Nice along the promenade des Anglais. Follow *Grasse* signs until you see *Vence* and *St-Paul-de-Vence* signs. You'll pass by the Renoir Museum in Cagnes-sur-Mer by following this route (described on page 329 of the Antibes chapter). Continue following *St-Paul-de-Vence* signs into the village, and park as close to the center as you can. After sampling too-beautiful-for-its-own-good **St-Paul-de-Vence,** visit the **Fondation Maeght** just above the town (page 346; park at the museum for free, or walk 20 min up from St-Paul-de-Vence, following blue signs).

After completing your course in contemporary art, find artsy **Vence,** a few miles away, with many good lunch options (see page 350). From Vence, visit Matisse's famous **Chapel of the Rosary** (limited opening hours—see page 348; best views of Vence are a mile beyond the chapel, where there's a turnaround).

Next, head for slippery-sloped **Tourrettes-sur-Loup** (poorly signed from Vence, follow D-2210). From there, follow signs for *Pont-du-Loup* (fine views of Tourrettes-sur-Loup a mile after leaving). Before long, you'll see views of **Le Bar-sur-Loup,** clinging to its hillside in the distance. When you arrive at the junction of Gourdon and Le Bar-sur-Loup, look way up to your destination— the tiny soaring village of Gourdon. Candy addicts can detour quickly down to **Pont-du-Loup** and visit the small candied-fruit factory of **Confiseries Florian** (page 351). Follow *Gourdon* and *Gorges du Loup* signs to the right and climb into the teeth of a rocky canyon, the **Gorges du Loup** (page 351). It's a mostly second-gear road that winds between intimidating rock faces above a surging stream. (Buses can not enter the Gorges du Loup, so non-drivers must continue directly on to Grasse.)

Inland Riviera

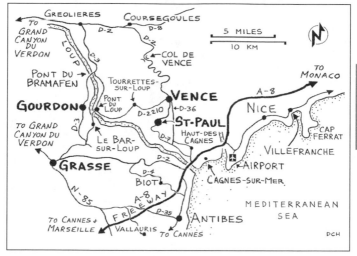

The drive passes all too quickly to the pont de Bramafen bridge, where the road hooks back and up toward Gourdon. Climb above the canyon you just drove through and watch the world below miniaturize. At the top, the sky-high (2,400 feet) village of **Gourdon** waits for tourists with shops, good lunch options, and grand panoramas (see page 351).

From Gourdon, slide downhill to **Grasse** with views down to (literally) overlooked Le Bar-sur-Loup. Follow signs to *Grasse,* then *Centre-Ville,* and park at the first underground lot you come to (by the Grasse bus station—see page 352). After improving your body odor in Grasse, return to your Riviera home base (allow 45 minutes to Nice, via Cannes and the autoroute), or continue to the Gorges du Verdon.

Alternate Route: If you won't be visiting the Gorges du Verdon, consider a more rugged loop drive that skips Grasse (and is ideal if staying in Vence). Follow the route described above until Vence, then find D-2 just before the bridge that leads to St-Jeannet, and follow signs for *Col de Vence* (the Vence pass). This road switches up and up beyond the tree line into a stone-filled landscape to the pass in about 15 minutes. Great views over Vence begin a few minutes after leaving the town. From the pass, continue on D-2 to the pretty villages of Coursegoules and Grélolières (each a tempting stop). In Grélolières, find D-3, which leads to Gorges du Loup and Gourdon. At the pont de Bramafen, you can continue through the Gorges du Loup, then join D-2210 to Tourrettes-sur-Loup and return to Nice or Vence, or follow signs to *Gourdon* and end your day there before returning home.

Inland Riviera

St-Paul-de-Vence

The most famous of Riviera hill towns, and the most-visited village in France, feels that way—like an overrun and over-restored artist-shopping-mall. Its attraction is understandable, as every cobble and flower seems *just-so,* and the setting is remarkable.

Still, wall-to-wall galleries and ice cream shops, and hordes of day-trippers strangle the appeal for many. Avoid visiting between 11:00 and 18:00, particularly on weekends. If you must go, arrive early and have *café et croissant* (a.k.a. breakfast) at the picture-perfect **Café de la Place.** The TI, just through the gate into the old city on rue Grande, has maps with minimal explanations of key buildings (daily 10:00–18:00, tel. 04 93 32 86 95, www.saint-pauldevence .com). If the entrance to the old city is jammed, take the road that veers left just before the entrance, and enter the town through its side door. Meander deep into St-Paul-de-Vence's quieter streets to find the panoramic views. See if you can find the hill town of Vence at the foot of an impressive mountain.

Fondation Maeght

This inviting, pricey, far-out, private museum is situated a steep walk or short drive above St-Paul-de-Vence. Fondation Maeght (fohn-dah-shown mahg) offers an excellent introduction to modern Mediterranean art by gathering many of the Riviera's most famous artists under one roof. The founder, Aimé Maeght, long envisioned the perfect exhibition space for the artists he supported and befriended as an art dealer. He purchased a dry piece of hilltop land, planted more than 35,000 plants, and hired an architect (José Luis Sert) with the same vision.

A sweeping lawn laced with amusing sculptures and bending pine trees greets visitors. On the right, a chapel designed by Georges Braque—in memory of the Maeghts' young son, who died of leukemia—features a moving, purple stained-glass work over the altar. The unusual museum building is purposefully low-profile, to let its world-class modern-art collection take center stage. Works by Fernand Léger, Joan Miró, Alexander Calder, Georges Braque, and Marc Chagall are thoughtfully arranged in well-lit rooms. The backyard of the museum has views, a Gaudí-esque sculpture labyrinth by Miró, and a courtyard filled with the wispy works of Alberto Giacometti. The only permanent collection in the museum consists of the sculptures, though the museum tries to keep a good selection of paintings by the famous artists here year-round. For a review of modern art, see "The Riviera's Art Scene" on page 233. There's also a great gift shop and cafeteria.

Cost and Hours: €11, €2.50 to take photos, daily July–Sept 10:00–19:00, Oct–June 10:00–12:30 & 14:30–18:00, tel. 04 93 32 81 63, www.fondation-maeght.com.

Getting There: The museum is a steep, uphill-but-doable, 20-minute walk from St-Paul-de-Vence and the bus stop. Blue signs indicate the way (parking is available at the top, though the lot can be full).

Vence

Vence is a well-discovered yet appealing town set well above the Riviera. While growth has sprawled well beyond Vence's old walls, and cars jam its roundabouts, the mountains are front and center and the breeze is fresh in this engaging town that bubbles with workaday life and ample tourist activity. Vence is peaceful at night and makes a handy base for travelers wanting the best of both worlds: a hill-town refuge near the sea. Many enjoy the Gorges du Verdon as a day trip from Vence (see the route described under "Les Gorges du Verdon," later in this chapter).

ORIENTATION

Tourist Information
Vence's fully loaded and eager-to-help TI faces the main square at 8 place du Grand Jardin. They have bus schedules, brochures on the cathedral, and a city map with a well-devised self-guided walking tour (25 stops, incorporates informative wall plaques). They also publish a list of Vence art galleries with English descriptions of the collections. To properly engage you in French culture, the TI also has information on French-language classes, and—even better—*pétanque* instruction with loaner *boules* (TI open June–Sept Mon–Sat 9:00–19:00, Sun 10:00–17:00; Oct–May Mon–Sat 9:00–18:00, closed Sun; tel. 04 93 58 06 38, www.ville-vence.fr).

Market day in the Cité Historique is on Tuesday and Friday mornings on place Clemenceau. There's a big, all-day antique market on place du Grand Jardin every Wednesday.

Arrival in Vence

By Bus: The bus stop is on place du Grand Jardin, next to the TI (schedules are posted in the window).

By Car: Follow signs to *cité historique*, and park where you can. A central pay lot is under place du Grand Jardin, across from the TI. Park here if you're spending the night somewhere other than Hôtel Miramar (which has its own parking).

SIGHTS

Stroll the narrow lanes of the old town *(cité historique)* using the TI's self-guided tour map. Connect the picturesque streets, enjoy a drink on a quiet square, inspect an art gallery, and find the small, 11th-century cathedral with its colorful Chagall mosaic of Moses (for background, see the Chagall Museum Tour on page 277). If you're here later in the day, enjoy the *boules* action across from the TI (and ask at the TI to borrow a set).

Château de Villeneuve—This 17th-century mansion, adjoining an imposing 12th-century watchtower, bills itself as "one of the Riviera's high temples of modern art," with a rotating collection. Check with the TI to see what's playing in the temple (€5, Tue–Sun 10:00–12:30 & 14:00–18:00, closed Mon, tel. 04 93 58 15 78).

▲**Chapel of the Rosary (Chapelle du Rosaire)**—The chapel, a 20-minute walk from town, was designed by an elderly and ailing Henri Matisse in thanks to the Dominican sister who had taken care of him (he was 81 when the chapel was completed—see the timeline of Matisse's life in the Nice chapter, page 246). The modest chapel is a simple collection of white walls laced with yellow, green, and blue stained-glass windows and charcoal black-on-white tile sketches. The sunlight filtered through glass does a cheery dance across the sketches.

The experience may underwhelm all but his fans, for whom this is the ultimate pilgrimage (€2.80, Mon, Wed, and Sat 14:00–17:30, Tue and Thu 10:00–11:30 & 14:00–17:30, Sun only open for Mass at 10:00 followed by tour of chapel, closed Fri and Nov, tel. 04 93 58 03 26). To reach the chapel from the Vence TI, turn right out of the TI and walk down avenue Henri Isnard, then right on avenue de Provence, following signs to

St. Jeannet. Or take the little white train that runs to the chapel from in front of the TI (1/hr).

SLEEPING

$$$ Hôtel Miramar*** is a fine refuge about a 10-minute walk from the old center. Friendly owner Daniel welcomes you into his 18-room Mediterranean villa, perched on a ledge with grand panoramas. The place is filled with personal touches, and every soothing room feels well cared for. The pool and view terrace could make you late for dinner, or seduce you into skipping it altogether—picnics are allowed (Sb-€80–92, standard Db-90–105, Db with balcony-€100–135, Db with great view and balcony-€148, family suite-€130–185, some rooms have air-con, most don't need it, bar, table tennis, parking, turn left out of the TI and follow the brown signs to 167 avenue Bougearel, tel. 04 93 58 01 32, fax 04 93 58 20 22, www.hotel-miramar-vence.com, resa@hotel-miramar -vence.com).

$$$ La Maison du Frêne is an art-packed B&B with four sumptuous rooms located behind the TI. Energetic Thierry combines his passion for contemporary art and hosting travelers in his lovingly restored manor house (Db-€140, includes breakfast, air-con, 1 place du Frêne, tel. 04 93 24 37 83, www.lamaisondufrene .com, lamaisondufrene@wanadoo.fr).

$$ L'Auberge des Seigneurs** is an overlooked throwback just inside the old town. Its six character-filled rooms—above a cozy restaurant—have wood furnishings, red-tile floors, and good-enough bathrooms (spacious Sb-€65, Db-€85–95, place du Frêne, tel. 04 93 58 04 24, fax 04 93 24 08 01). It's a short walk from the TI, next to the Château de Villeneuve: Turn right out of the TI, then right again, then left.

Sleep Code

(€1 = about $1.30, country code: 33)
S=Single, **D**=Double/Twin, **T**=Triple, **Q**=Quad, **b**=bathroom, **s** = shower only, ***** = French hotel rating (0–4 stars). Credit cards are accepted and English is spoken unless otherwise noted.

To help you sort easily through these listings, I've divided the rooms into three categories based on the price for a standard double room with bath:

$$$ **Higher Priced**—Most rooms €95 or more.
  $$ **Moderately Priced**—Most rooms between €65–95.
   $ **Lower Priced**—Most rooms €65 or less.

EATING

Tempting outdoor eateries litter the old town; they all look good to me.

On Place Clemenceau: These two restaurants serve delectable Provençal cuisine a few doors apart on the charming place Clemenceau: **La Cassolette,** at #10, is an intimate place with reasonable prices and a pleasant terrace across from the floodlit church (€16 and €25 *menus,* daily, tel. 04 93 58 84 15). **Le P'tit Provençal,** at #4, is the romantic's choice, with a lovely upstairs dining room (€24 and €30 *menus,* closed Mon all year, also closed Tue off-season, tel. 04 93 58 50 64).

At nearby **La Peyra,** enjoy an elegant dinner salad or pasta dish outdoors to the sound of the town's main fountain (closed Tue–Wed, 13 place du Peyra, tel. 04 93 58 67 63).

L'Auberge des Seigneurs is good for a cooler day, when you can sit by the fire and watch your meat being cooked (*menus* from €35, closed Sun–Mon; also recommended under "Sleeping," on page 349).

Hill Towns and Sights Between Vence and Grasse

The sights listed below are connected by the Inland Riviera self-guided driving tour on page 344.

Shortcut from Vence to the Gorges du Verdon—To save time and add scenery, skip the town of Grasse and take D-2 from Vence following Col de Vence (Vence pass), and climb above the tree line. Follow D-2 past Coursegoules and Gréolières, and continue west to where the road eventually meets N-85. From here, follow signs to *Draguignan* and *Gorges du Verdon*, and join the route described below under "Le Grand Canyon du Verdon."

Tourrettes-sur-Loup—This picturesque town, hemmed in by forests, looks ready to skid down its abrupt hill. Tourrettes-sur-Loup is small, with no sprawl. Known as the "Cité des Violettes," the village produces more violets than anywhere else in France, most of which get shipped off to end up in bottles that make you smell nice.

Park in the lot at the village center and stroll the lanes. You'll still find a smattering of arts and crafts, though much less than in the "Vence towns." Plunge deep to find good views, as well as **Tom's Ice Cream** (afternoons only, closed Mon) and a few places to eat. Wednesday is market day (on place de la Libération). Fabulous views of Tourrettes-sur-Loup await a minute away on the drive to Pont-du-Loup.

Le Bar-sur-Loup—This town is the yin to St-Paul-de-Vence's yang: It has almost no tourist shops and little to do except wander the peaceful, brick-lined lanes and enjoy the view. Park at the lot by the Hôtel de Ville and Syndicat d'Initiative (TI).

Confiseries Florian—The candied-fruit factory hides between trees down in Pont-du-Loup (though their big, bright sign is hard to miss). Ten-minute tours of their factory leave regularly, covering the candied-fruit process and explaining the use of flower petals (like violets and jasmine) in their products. Everything they make is fruit-filled—even their chocolate (with oranges). The tour ends with a tasting of the *confiture* in the dazzling gift shop (tours are free, request a tour with English commentary, daily 9:00–12:00 & 14:00–18:00, gift shop stays open during lunch, tel. 04 93 59 32 91).

Gorges du Loup—The inland Riviera is crawling with spectacular canyons only miles from the sea. Slotted between Grasse and Vence, the Gorges du Loup is the easiest gorge to reach and works in well with a day trip from the Nice area. You can drive about five miles right up into the canyon (on D-6), passing waterfalls and sheer rock walls, then return on the gorge's rooftop (on D-3) to the "eagle's nest" village of Gourdon for magnificent vistas and a complete change of scenery.

Gourdon—This 2,400-foot-high, cliff-topping hamlet features grassy picnic areas, a short lineup of tourist shops, and a few good lunch options. The village's most famous building is its château, which is best enjoyed from the outside (as its interior can be visited only with periodic French-only tours). The far side of the village features grand views and two fine lunch options. **La Taverne Provençale** boasts a popular spread of outdoor tables overlooking the grandeur (€10 omelets and pasta dishes, €18 *menu*, lunch only, closed Wed, place de l'Eglise, tel. 04 93 09 68 22). Just below is the most appropriately named restaurant in France—**Le Nid de l'Aigle** (The Eagle's Nest)—which tempts travelers with fine cuisine and an equally remarkable setting with interior and exterior seating (€20 lunch *menu*, €29 dinner *menu*, daily July–mid-Sept, otherwise closed Mon–Tue, tel. 04 93 77 52 02).

Grasse

Both the historic and contemporary capital of perfume, Grasse offers a contrast to the dolled-up hill towns above the Riviera. While famous for its pricey product, Grasse's urban center is a gritty yet appealing collection of walking lanes and vertical staircases. The place feels both in need of a facelift and refreshingly real. Its historic alliance with Genoa explains the Italian-esque look of the old city. Still, the only good reasons to visit Grasse are if you care about perfume, or if you're heading to or from the Grand Canyon du Verdon.

ORIENTATION

Tourist Information

All sights in Grasse cluster near the main TI in the Palais du Congrès on cours Honoré Cresp, sometimes referred to as place du Cours (July–Sept Mon–Sat 9:00–19:00, Sun 9:00–12:30 & 14:00–18:00; Oct–June Mon–Sat 9:00–12:30 & 14:00–18:00, closed Sun; tel. 04 93 36 66 66, free cold water fountain). There's a branch TI (Grasse Espace Accueil) on place de la Foux near the bus station. At either TI, pick up an English map with a self-guided tour of the old city (handy information plaques). If heading to the Grand Canyon du Verdon, get specifics here.

Arrival in Grasse

By Train: Fifteen trains a day connect Grasse with Nice, Antibes, and Cannes. Free *navette* shuttle buses (3/hour) take you from the train station up and up to the bus station (see below).

By Bus: Buses run directly to Cannes in 40 minutes and to Nice in 75 minutes. From the bus station on place de la Buanderie, it's a five-minute walk to the sights (walk one block up to boulevard du Jeu de Ballon, turn left, and take the pleasant stroll downhill to cours Honoré Cresp).

By Car: Grasse's size and hilly terrain make it terribly confusing for drivers. Those coming from Nice (via A-8), Antibes, and Cannes should follow signs to *Centre-Ville* and *Office du Tourisme*. Soon after passing the golden Fragonard perfume boutique, turn left around a fountain-centered roundabout into the Parking Honoré Cresp. The parking lot's *Sortie Parfumerie* leads directly to the Fragonard perfume tour. Those arriving from Vence, Gourdon, and the Gorges du Verdon should follow signs to *Centre-Ville*, then *Gare SNCF* (make a hard left around the Hôtel le Napoleon, then a quick right), and park at the lot next to the bus station *(gare routière)*.

SIGHTS

Fragonard Perfume—This well-run, functioning factory, located dead-center in Grasse, provides frequent, fragrant, informative 20-minute tours and an interesting "museum" to explore while you wait. Pick up the English brochure describing what's in the museum cases, then drop down to where the tour begins. On your tour, you'll learn that the difference between perfume, eau de toilette, and cologne is only a matter of perfume-percentages. You'll

Fragrant Grasse

Grasse has been at the center of the fragrance industry since the 1500s, when it was known for its scented leather gloves. The cultivation of aromatic plants around Grasse slowly evolved to produce ingredients for soaps and perfumes, and by the 1800s, Grasse was recognized as the center for perfume (thanks largely to its flower-friendly climate), making it a wealthy city.

It can take a ton (roughly 10,000 flowers) of carefully picked petals (like jasmine) to make about two pounds of essence. A damaged flower petal is bad news. Today, perfumes are made from as many as 500 different scents; most are imported to Grasse from countries around the world. The "blender" of these scents and the perfume mastermind is called the "nose" (who knows best). The five master "noses" who work here have studied their profession longer than a medical student (seven years). They had to show that they had the gift before entering "nose school" (in Versailles), and they cannot drink alcohol, ever.

Skip the outlying perfumeries with French-only tours. Only three factories out of 40 open their doors to visitors, and only one is worth visiting: Fragonard Perfume in Grasse.

also learn how the product is made today, as well as how they used to do it (I like the old way of pressing flowers in animal fat). The tour ends with a whiff in the elegant gift shop (daily 9:00–18:00, last tour at 17:00, just off cours Honoré Cresp at 20 boulevard Fragonard, tel. 04 93 36 44 65).

The same company runs a two-room **museum** (Musée Provençal du Costume et du Bijou) displaying traditional dresses and jewelry (free, daily 10:00–13:00 & 14:00–18:00, a block above the *parfumerie* on the pedestrian street at 2 rue Jean Ossola). Upon leaving, you'll be given a card to be exchanged for a free gift at a shop next door.

Villa Jean-Honoré Fragonard—The home of the 18th-century Baroque painter of swirling big bodies (whose father started the smelly business) houses a good collection of his paintings and reproductions (€3, excellent English handout; June–Sept daily 10:00–18:30; Oct–May Wed–Mon 10:00–12:30 & 14:00–18:30, closed Tue; turn left out of Fragonard Perfume and walk downhill to 23 boulevard Fragonard).

International Museum of Perfume (Musée International de la Parfumerie)—This city museum, between the main TI and the Fragonard factory should reopen in 2008 after renovation. When completed, it should be the pride of Grasse, offering a complete explanation of the history and production of perfume in a dazzling new home (get details at the TI).

Old Grasse—The rue Jean Ossola leads into the labyrinth of ancient streets that form an intriguing if unpolished pedestrian area. Follow the TI's self-guided tour with your map (takes an hour at a speedy pace), or just read the information plaques when you see them. At a minimum, walk down rue Jean Ossola to the Romanesque cathedral (worth peering into for its tree-trunk-like columns and austere decor). An unusual WWI monument sits below the cathedral entry, and the nearby *Pointe de Vue* gives a nice view over Grasse from the mountains to the sea.

Le Grand Canyon du Verdon

▲▲▲Parc Natural Grand Canyon du Verdon

Two hours north of Nice and three hours east of Avignon lies the Parc Naturel Grand Canyon du Verdon (a.k.a. les Gorges du Verdon), an immense area of natural beauty...even to Arizonans.

Planning Your Time

The Grand Canyon du Verdon, Europe's greatest canyon, offers a dilly of a detour between Provence and the Riviera. If you start

early in the day, you can reach the canyon on a long round-trip drive from the Nice area (easier if staying in Vence or Antibes; see my self-guided driving tour of the Inland Riviera, page 344). Or, better yet, connect your home bases in the Riviera and Provence (figure 7 hours with modest canyon time between Nice and Roussillon or Aix-en-Provence; allow 8 hours to Avignon). But many visitors prefer to stop and smell the canyon, overnighting en route (suggestions below).

Here are some very rough driving times: Riviera to Grasse (1 hour); Grasse to Balcon de la Mescla (1 hour); Balcon de la Mescla to Aiguines (1 hour); Aiguines to Manosque (en route to Provence, 1 hour).

ORIENTATION

The Park Naturel du Grand Canyon du Verdon, far more than just its famous canyon, is an extensive area combining alpine scenery with misty villages, poster-child lakes, meandering streams, and

Le Grand Canyon du Verdon

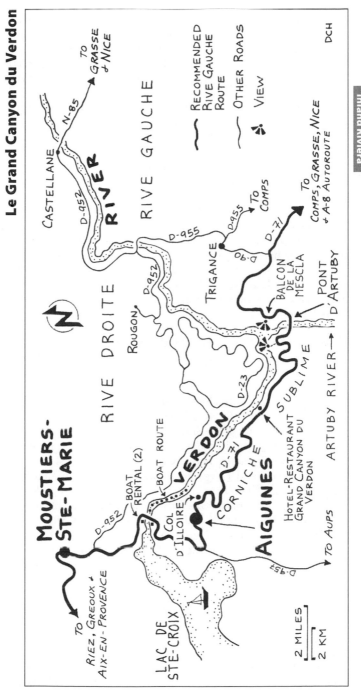

MOUSTIERS-STE-MARIE

RIVER

RIVE GAUCHE

RIVE DROITE

VERDON

AIGUINES

CORNICHE SUBLIME

ARTUBY RIVER →

LAC DE STE-CROIX

CASTELLANE

TRIGANCE

ROUGON

BALCON DE LA MESCLA

PONT D'ARTUBY

COL D'ILLOIRE

BOAT RENTAL (2)

BOAT ROUTE

HOTEL-RESTAURANT GRAND CANYON DU VERDON

N-85

D-952

D-955

D-90

D-71

D-23

D-952

D-957

TO GRASSE & NICE

TO COMPS

TO COMPS, GRASSE, NICE & A-8 AUTOROUTE

TO AUPS

RIEZ, GREOUX & AIX-EN-PROVENCE

RECOMMENDED RIVE GAUCHE ROUTE

OTHER ROADS

VIEW

N

2 MILES

2 KM

DCH

seas of gentle meadows. The canyon is the heart of the park, where overpowering slabs of white limestone plunge impossible distances to a snaking turquoise river below. You need a car, patience, and a lack of vertigo to explore this area. If traveling in summer, go really early or skip it. Fill your tank before leaving Grasse or Moustiers-Ste-Marie, as gas is scarce. Due to the steepness of the canyon, reasonable hiking options are limited—the best way to explore the canyon is by short walks from your car.

The drive alone between the Riviera or Provence and the park merits the detour; the canyon is the icing on *le gâteau*. Roads crawl along the length of the canyon on both sides (*Rive Gauche* and *Rive Droite*); the *Rive Gauche* (left bank) works best for most, though both are spectacular.

The Grand Canyon du Verdon is located between the villages of Moustiers-Ste-Marie and Aiguines to the west and Castellane to the east. The most scenic driving segments are along the right (north) bank between Moustiers-Ste-Marie and the Point Sublime overlook, and along the left (south) bank between Aiguines and the Balcon de la Mescla. (Thrill-seekers head for the Castellane area, where the whitewater rafting, climbing, and serious hiking trails are best.)

The Rive Gauche (Left Bank) Route

For drivers connecting the canyon with Provence or the Riviera, the left bank offers the most accessible and most scenic tour of the gorges.

Approaching from the Riviera: The most direct route from the Riviera follows N-85, which starts near Cannes (A-8 autoroute from Nice to Cannes saves time) and passes through Grasse, then continues north toward Digne and Castellane. You'll turn left off N-85 about 30 kilometers before Castellane, following signs to the *Gorges du Verdon* and *Draguignan* (see also my self-guided driving tour on page 344). Turn right at Comps-sur-Artuby, following signs to *Gorges du Verdon, Rive Gauche*. You'll reach the canyon rim at the Balcon de la Mescla and follow it for about 60 windy minutes (with stops) to the village of Aiguines (good overnight stop, described in the following pages). Those continuing to Provençal destinations will go on to Moustiers-Ste-Marie (described later in this chapter), then Riez, then Gréoux-les-Bains. From Gréoux-les-Bains, follow signs for *Manosque,* then *Apt* for Luberon and Avignon; or use A-51 to reach Aix-en-Provence, Cassis, Marseille, and Arles. Those making a day trip from Nice should return from Aiguines, following signs indicating *Aups,* then *Draguignan,* then *Nice* via A-8.

Approaching from Provence: All roads pass through Gréoux-les-Bains, which is about an hour northeast of Aix-en-

Provence. Those coming from Cassis, Aix-en-Provence, and Arles will find A-51 from Aix-en-Provence the fastest path; those coming from the Luberon and Avignon should take N-100 via Apt, then follow signs for *Manosque*. From Gréoux-les-Bains, follow the *Riez*, *Moustiers-Ste-Marie*, and *Aiguines* signs before entering the Grand Canyon du Verdon *(Rive Gauche)*. Leave the canyon after the Balcon de la Mescla, following signs for *Comps-sur-Artuby* (and *Draguignan* for a short distance), then *Grasse* and *Nice* for the Riviera. The fastest way from Grasse to Nice is via Cannes and A-8.

SELF-GUIDED DRIVING TOUR

Le Grand Canyon du Verdon Left Bank
(Rive Gauche)

At their deepest points, the gorges drop 2,200 feet to the river that carved them. At the bottom, the canyons can narrow to 26 feet across, while at the top, the canyon walls can be as far as 4,700 feet apart.

You'll drive at an escargot's pace, navigating hairpin turns along the Corniche Sublime with constant views of rocky masses and vanishing-point views up the canyon. Hikes into the canyon are too long and too steep for most. You're better off walking along the road for a bit, or better, walking along sections of two-track dirt roads that lead away from the asphalt (several to choose from). There are many small pullouts along the route, so stop frequently and get out of that car to allow the driver a look at the views. Here are the highlights along the route from east to west:

The **Balcon de la Mescla** is the first pullout that drivers reach as they approach from Nice. Crawl all over this viewpoint—the lookout below the gift shop/café is best. Just beyond, you can amble across Europe's highest bridge (pont d'Artuby) and imagine working on its construction crew *(non, merci)*. About a five-minute drive west of the bridge, you'll find a grassy pullout (north side) with a two-track dirt road that allows walkers to get away from the noise of the road and experience the gorges more peacefully (follow the dirt path to the rocky edge of the canyon).

About halfway through the canyon perches the **$$ Hôtel-Restaurant Grand Canyon du Verdon****, which must have been grandfathered-in to own its unbelievable location 2,500 feet high on the Corniche Sublime. This concrete, funky place looks slapped together, but the café terrace has a table for you with stupendous views (drinks, snacks, and meals available). The hotel rents 15 modern and basic rooms, half on the canyon and a few with view decks. Call ahead for Wednesdays, as the restaurant may be closed—B.Y.O. (open mid-April–mid-Oct, canyon-side

Db-€65, non-canyon-side Db-€60, prices are per person and include dinner and breakfast, tel. 04 94 76 91 31, fax 04 94 76 92 29, hotel.gd.canyon.verdon@wanadoo.fr).

The **Col d'Illioure,** the last pass before leaving the canyon, provides sensational views from the western portal. A large pullout allows parking. You'll find a few picnic tables just above the pullout and some good rock-scampering just below.

Just west of the canyon, the small village of **Aiguines** sits below waves of limestone and overlooks the long, turquoise Lac de Ste-Croix. This unspoiled village has a handful of hotels and cafés, and a 15th-century château (closed to the public). It's an outdoors-oriented place (popular with hikers) that most canyon visitors cruise right through.

Stop for a drink by the central fountain and consider a night at the town's most characteristic hotel, **$ Hôtel du Vieux-Château****, which has been in business for 200 years and is run by smiling Frédéric and his energetic mama. Its 10 simple rooms are clean and pleasant—and no two are alike. You'll likely be quoted prices including breakfast and dinner—half-pension (Db-€62–72, or €58 per person for half-pension including room, extra bed-€14, cozy restaurant with simple, hearty fare, place de la Fontaine, tel. 04 94 70 22 95, fax 04 94 84 22 36, www.hotelvieuxchateau.fr, contact @hotelvieuxchateau.fr).

Just below, **$ Hôtel Altitude 823**** offers more predictable comfort with a bit less character (Db-€72 includes breakfast, or €58 per person for half-pension, air-con, tel. 04 98 10 22 17, fax 04 98 10 22 16, altitude823@aol.com, Patrick). Both hotels want you to dine at their restaurants.

For fine views over Aiguines and the lake, stroll up to the small **Chapelle St. Pierre** at the northern edge of town and find the orientation table (and look for Mont Ventoux's white limestone peak). From here, you can walk along the road five minutes to the campground café with nice view tables on its broad terrace (ideal for a before-dinner drink or morning coffee), then join the main road (D-71) and walk back into Aiguines past the château (worth detouring to for views over Aiguines). A small play area and grassy field lie below the château.

Barely more than 30 years old, man-made **Lac de Ste-Croix** is about six miles long and is the last stop for water flowing out of the Gorges du Verdon. Since the rocky shore makes swimming unappealing, consider renting a canoe or pedal boat at the rental places on either side of the bridge halfway between Moustiers and Aiguines. For a sensational cruise, paddle or pedal under the bridge, then follow the brilliant turquoise inlet upstream as far as 2.5 miles, tracing the river's route up the gorge on its final journey to the lake (€8/hour for pedal boat or canoe, figure 2 hours for a good trip).

Moustiers-Ste-Marie is another pretty Provençal face lined with boutiques—though this one comes with an impressive setting

straddling a small stream at the base of the limestone cliffs of the Grand Canyon du Verdon. The town is popular with tourists who enjoy shopping for the locally famous china and the usual Provençal kitsch. The **TI** is in the center, next to the church (daily 10:00–12:30 & 14:00–18:00, place de l'Eglise, tel. 04 92 74 67 84).

You can escape some of the crowds by climbing 30 minutes on a steep, ankle-twisting path to the **Chapelle Notre-Dame de Beauvoir**—a simple chapel that has attracted pilgrims for centuries. A notebook in the chapel allows travelers to pen a request for a miracle for a loved one. For most, the chapel does not warrant the effort, though you'll get fine views over the village by walking a short way up the path.

If you decide to bed down in Moustiers-Ste-Marie, consider the **$ Restaurant/Chambres Clerissy,** where Sophie offers a great value and a warm welcome with four spacious and spotless rooms. It's good for families (Db-€45, Tb-€55, place du Chevalier de Blacas, in the village center to the left of the church as you face it from below, tel. & fax 04 92 74 62 67, www.clerissy.fr).

There is no shortage of dining options in Moustiers-Ste-Marie. The simple **Restaurant Clerissy** (whose rooms are listed above) offers inexpensive and simple meals and appealing indoor and outdoor tables. For a special occasion, enjoy **Les Santons de Moustiers**, with its carefully crafted setting (inside or out) and well-respected regional cuisine (*menus* from €25, closed Mon–Tue, next to the church and TI at place de l'Eglise, tel. 04 92 74 66 48).

TRAVELING WITH CHILDREN

With relatively few must-see museums, plenty of outdoor activities, and cooperative weather, Provence and the French Riviera are practically made for kids. This part of France has beaches, Roman ruins to scramble over, abundant sunshine, and swimming pools everywhere. Teenagers love the seaside resorts (Cassis is best), and they tend to prefer the hustle and bustle of cities like Avignon, Arles, Aix-en-Provence, and Nice. Younger kids tend to prefer the rural areas, which offer more swimming pools, open spaces, and parks.

To make your trip fun for everyone in the family, mix heavy-duty sights with kids' activities, like playing miniature golf or *boules*, renting bikes or canoes, and riding the little tourist trains popular in many towns. Kids also like audioguides, available at important sights in many cities. And if you're in France near Bastille Day, remember that firecracker stands pop up everywhere on the days leading up to July 14. Putting on their own fireworks show can be a highlight for teenagers.

Minimize hotel changes by planning three-day stops. Aim for hotels with restaurants, so kids can go back to the room and play while you finish a pleasant dinner.

We've listed swimming pools in many places, but be warned: Public pools in France commonly require a small, Speedo-like bathing suit for boys and men (American-style swim trunks won't do)—though they usually have these little suits to loan. At hotel pools, any type of swimsuit will do.

For breakfast, croissants are a hit, though a good *pain au chocolat* (croissant with chocolate bits) will be appreciated even more. Feel free to bring your own supplements, like fruit and yogurt. Hot chocolate is usually available. For lunch and dinner, it's easy to find fast-food places and restaurants with kids' menus, but it's more fun to find *crêperies,* which have a wide variety of fillings for both savory and dessert crêpes. For food emergencies, we travel with a plastic container of peanut butter brought from home and smuggle small amounts of jam from breakfast.

Kids homesick for friends can keep in touch with cheap international phone cards (see page 388). Hotel Internet stations and cybercafés are a godsend for parents with teenagers. Some parents find buying a French mobile phone—or roaming with an American mobile phone—a worthwhile investment; adults can stay connected to teenagers while allowing them maximum independence (see page 387). If you and your teenager both have mobile phones that work in Europe, sending each other text messages can be a relatively inexpensive way to keep in touch (much cheaper than actual phone calls).

Kids like the French adventure comics Astérix and Tintin (both available in English, sold in bigger bookstores with English sections).

It's fun to take kids to movies (even if not in English) just to see how theaters work elsewhere. Movies shown in their original language—usually with subtitles—are listed as *v.o.* at the box office. (One showing could be *v.o.* and the next could be dubbed in French, labeled *v.f.*) *Dessin animé* means "cartoon." While many live-action movies can be found in their original language with French subtitles, cartoons and kids' movies (intended for an audience that doesn't read so well yet) are almost always dubbed.

You'll find old-style merry-go-rounds in many cities, perfect for younger travelers (my daughter's goal was to ride a merry-go-round in every town...she came close).

The best thing we did on a recent trip was buy a set of *boules* (a.k.a. *pétanque,* a form of outdoor bowling—for the rules, see sidebar on page 174). We'd play *boules* before dinner, side-by-side with real players on the village court. Get your *boules de pétanque* at sporting-goods stores or larger department stores. Since they're quite heavy, buy a set only if you'll be driving. The *boules* also make great—if weighty—souvenirs, and are fun to play back at home.

Swap babysitting duties with your partner if one of you wants to take in an extra sight. And for memories that will last long after the trip, keep a family journal. Pack a small diary and a glue stick. While relaxing at a café over a *citron pressé* (lemonade), take turns writing the day's events and include mementos such as ticket stubs from museums, postcards, or stalks of lavender.

Before You Go

Get your kids into the spirit ahead of time using these tips:

- Pick up books at the library and rent videos. Watch or read the Madeline stories by Ludwig Bemelmans, *The Hunchback of*

Notre-Dame by Victor Hugo, *The Three Musketeers* by Alexandre Dumas, or Dumas' *The Man in the Iron Mask. Anni's Diary of France,* by Anni Axworthy, is a fun, picture-filled book about a young girl's trip; it could inspire your children. *How Would You Survive in the Middle Ages?,* by Fiona MacDonald, is an appealing "guide" for kids. Serious kid-historians will devour *The Kingfisher History Encyclopedia.* If your children are interested in art, get your hands on *The History of Art for Young People* by Anthony Janson and *Discovering Great Artists: Hands-On Art for Children in the Styles of the Great Masters* by MaryAnn Kohl. (Also see the recommended books and movies list, which includes some good choices for teenagers, in this book's appendix.)

- Involve your kids in trip planning. Have them read about the places that you may include in your itinerary (even the hotels you're considering) and let them help in your decisions.
- Hotel selection is critical. In my recommendations, I've identified hotels that seem particularly kid-friendly (pools, ping-pong, grassy areas, easygoing owners, etc.). If you're staying for a week or more in one place, rent a *gîte* (see "*Gîtes* and Apartments," page 22).

What to Bring

- Children's books are scarce and expensive in France. Our children read much more when traveling in Europe than while at home, so don't skimp here (see list above).
- Bring peanut butter (hard to find in France)...or help your kids acquire a taste for Nutella, the tasty hazelnut-chocolate spread available everywhere.
- Choose items that are small and convenient for use on planes, trains, and in your hotel room: compact travel games, a deck of cards, a handheld video game, and drawing and coloring supplies. Consider bringing your own drawing paper, which is surprisingly expensive in Europe.
- For younger kids, Legos are easily packed and practical (it's also fun to purchase kits in Europe, where the Legos are sometimes different than those in the US).
- If your child likes listening to music, an MP3 player (such as an iPod) is smaller and more convenient for travel than a CD player.
- Budding fashionistas might enjoy traveling with—and buying new outfits for—a Corelle doll or another 16-inch doll. The French have wonderful doll clothes, with a much wider selection than typically found in the US.
- Benadryl does miracles in keeping ears and noses open during flights—with the added benefit of sleepiness for most children.

We give our kids Benadryl before bed for the first two nights in Europe, and they rarely have serious jet-lag issues.

- For traveling with infants, car-rental agencies usually have car seats for a small price, though you must reserve one ahead of time. And while most hotels have some sort of crib, we brought a portable crib and did not regret it.
- Cameras (even disposable ones) are a great investment to get your kids involved.
- For longer drives, books on tape or CD can be fun for the whole family (if carefully chosen). I recommend Peter Mayle's *A Year in Provence,* available on CD (or put it on your MP3 player/iPod).

Planning Your Time

- Lower your sightseeing ambitions and prepare to savor fewer places for longer periods. Plan longer stays at fewer stops—you won't regret it.
- Don't overdo it. Tackle one key sight each day and mix in a healthy dose of fun activities.
- Follow this book's crowd-beating tips to a T. Kids despise long lines more than you do.
- Eat dinner early (19:00–19:30 at restaurants, earlier at cafés). Skip romantic eateries. Try relaxed cafés (or fast-food restaurants) where kids can move around without bothering others. Picnics work well.
- The best and cheapest toy selections are in the department stores, like Monoprix and Galeries Lafayette.
- Let kids help choose daily activities, lead you through ancient sights, and so on.
- Keep an eye out for *mini-golfs* (miniature golf).

Sights and Activities

These are listed in no particular order:

- Pont du Gard. An entire wing of the museum is dedicated to kids, who can also swim or take a canoe trip on the river. See page 125.
- Cassis: Boat trip to the *calanques* or the port and beaches for teenagers. See page 212.
- Changing of the Guard in Monaco (11:55 daily). See page 315.
- Cousteau Aquarium in Monaco. See page 316.
- Pedal boats on the Mediterranean. See page 252.
- Biking through vineyards to small villages, from Vaison la Romaine. See page 141.
- Les Baux's castle ruins, with medieval weaponry and great walls to climb. See page 71.

Children

- Canoeing on the Ardèche River (page 144), the Sorgue River (page 168), or into the Gorges du Verdon (page 358).
- Boat trips from Nice (page 243), Villefranche-sur-Mer (page 290), or St-Tropez (page 338).
- Biking or in-line skating on the promenade des Anglais in Nice. See page 239.
- Marineland near Antibes. See page 329.
- Little white tourist trains (in nearly every city).

Honorable mention goes to Arles' Ancient History Museum (see page 49), horseback riding in the Camargue (page 85), Roman arenas in Nîmes (page 114) and Arles (page 54), Cathédrale d'Images near Les Baux (page 74), the beaches of Antibes (page 327), and the narrow-gauge train ride from Nice (see page 253).

SHOPPING

Provence and the Riviera offer France's best shopping outside of Paris, with a great range of reasonably priced items ideal for souvenirs and gifts. If approached thoughtfully, shopping in the south of France can be a culturally enlightening experience. There's no better way to mix serious shopping business with travel pleasure than at the weekly markets in towns and villages throughout the region. These traditional market days are far more than fresh produce and fish; in many cases, at least half the market is devoted to durable goods (like baskets, tablecloths, pottery, and local fabrics), ideal for gift-scavenging travelers. If you miss market day, most Provençal towns have more than enough small shops that sell local products—and more than enough kitschy souvenirs. (They're often selling the same items you can find more cheaply at weekly markets.) The cities described in this book have unlimited boutique shopping for clothing. In this chapter, you'll find information on shopping for souvenirs, navigating market days, and browsing boutiques.

For information on VAT refunds and customs regulations, see page 385 in the appendix.

What to Buy

If you need ideas, here are some locally made goods to shop for in Provence and the Riviera. You'll find most of these items in tourist-oriented boutiques, though many of them can be had for less on market days. If you buy more expensive, nonperishable goods, most stores will work with you to send them home.

- **Jams** *(confiture)* containing lush and often exotic fruits, such as *fruits de passion* (passion fruit), *figues* (figs), and *pastèque* or *citre* (different types of watermelon).

- **Honey** *(miel)*, particularly lavender- or thyme-infused. Stronger palates should try the chestnut *(châtaigne)* or even oak-flavored *(chêne)* honey.
- Tins of **tapenade** (olive paste) and all kinds of olives: black, green, and pricked with garlic or anchovies.
- **Olive-wood products** such as utensils and bowls. Olives are not just for nibbling; in Provence, the entire tree is used.
- Canned **pâtés,** including the buttery, rich *foie gras* (its "home" is Périgord, but you'll also find it in the markets of Provence).
- Packets of **herbs** (including the famous *herbes de Provence*), **salt** from the Camargue (look for *Fleur de Sel* for the best, and use sparingly), and bottles or tins of **olive oil** from local trees (Nyons is France's olive capital). Most of these items can be found in attractive packaging that can be saved and enjoyed long after the product itself is gone.
- Sweets, including the famous *nougat de Montélimar* (a rich, chewy confection made with nuts and honey and sometimes flavored with lavender or other fragrances), *calissons* (orange-and-almond-flavored candy, shaped like the nut and originally from Aix-en-Provence), and **chocolates** from the Provençal producer Puyricard.
- **Soaps and lotions,** particularly those "perfumed" with local plants such as lavender, rosemary *(romarin)*, or linden *(tilleul)*. You'll also find colorful **sachets** containing the same fragrances.
- **Table linens,** brightly colored. Souleiado and Les Olivades are the most famous local manufacturers, but good-quality knockoffs can be found in most any market or store.
- Local **pottery** (*poterie*; *faïence* is hand-painted *poterie*). Terre Provence is a well-known (and pricey) brand, but many other producers offer excellent quality, usually for less.
- *Santons,* the tiny, brightly adorned clay or wood Provençal figurines. Originally designed for traditional Christmas crèche scenes, today's *santons* represent all walks of life—from the local *boulanger* to the woman sewing bright Provençal cloth to the village doctor. The most famous *santon* makers are in Séguret and Aubagne. All *santon* makers belong to the *santon*-maker guild (think medieval stonecutters or woodworkers), and each *santon* is handmade and signed.

Market Day *(Jour du Marché)*

Market days are a big deal throughout France, and in no other region are they more celebrated than in Provence and the Riviera. Markets have been a central feature of life in rural areas since the Middle Ages. No single event better symbolizes the French preoccupation with fresh products, and their strong ties to the small farmer, than the weekly market. Many locals mark their calendars with the arrival of the new season's produce.

Provence is France's melting pot, where Italy, Spain, and North Africa intersect with France to do business. Notice the ethnic mix of the vendors (and the products they sell). Spices from Morocco and Tunisia, fresh pasta from Italy, saffron from Spain, and tapenade from Provence compete for your attention at Provence's *marchés*.

There are two kinds of weekly, open-air markets: *les marchés* and *les marchés brocantes*. *Les marchés* are more general in scope, more common, and more colorful, featuring products of local farmers and artisans. *Les marchés brocantes* specialize in quasi-antiques and flea-market bric-a-brac. *Brocantes* markets began in the Middle Ages, when middlemen would gather to set up small stalls and sell old, flea-infested clothes and discarded possessions of the wealthy at bargain prices to eager peasants. Buyers were allowed to *rummage* through piles of aristocratic garbage.

Several general *marchés* have good selections of both produce and *brocantes*. The best of all market worlds may rest in the picturesque town of Isle-sur-la-Sorgue, where, on Sunday mornings, a brilliant food *marché* merges with an active flea market and a polished antiques enterprise.

I've listed days and locations for both market types throughout this book. Notice the signs as you enter towns indicating the *jours du marché* (essential information to any civilized soul, and a reminder not to park on the streets the night before). Most *marchés* take place once a week in the town's main square, and, if large enough, they spill into nearby streets. Markets can offer a mind-boggling array of products, from the perishable (produce, meats, cheeses, breads, and pastries) to the nonperishable (kitchen wares, inexpensive clothing, brightly colored linens, and pottery).

The bigger the market, the greater the overall selection, particularly for nonperishable goods. Bigger towns (like Arles) may have two weekly markets, one a bit larger than the other, with more nonperishable goods; in other towns (including Isle-sur-la-Sorgue), the second weekly market may simply be a smaller version of the main market day. The biggest market days are usually on weekends, so that everyone can go. In the largest cities (such as Avignon and Nîmes), market halls have been established with produce stands and meat counters selling fresh goods daily.

Market day is as important socially as commercially—it's a

weekly chance for locals to resume friendships and get the current gossip. Here, neighbors can catch up on Henri's barn renovation, see photos of Jacqueline's new grandchild, and relax over *un café*. Dogs are tethered to café tables while friends exchange kisses. Tether yourself to a café table and observe: three cheek-kisses for good friends (left-right-left), a fourth for friends you haven't seen in a while. (The appropriate number of kisses varies by region—Paris, Lyon, and Provence each have separate standards.)

Markets begin at about 8:00, with setup commencing in the predawn hours (for some, a reason not to stay in a main-square hotel the night before market day). They usually end by 13:00. Most perishable items are sold directly from the producers—no middlemen, no Visa cards, just really fresh produce (*du pays* means "grown locally"). Sometimes you'll meet a widow selling a dozen eggs, two rabbits, and a wad of herbs tied with string. But most vendors follow a weekly circuit of markets they feel works best for them, showing up in the same spot every week, year in and year out. At a favorite market, my family has done business with the same olive vendor and "cookie man" for 16 years.

It's bad form to be in a hurry on market day. Allow the crowd to set your pace. Observe the interaction between vendor and client. Notice the joy they can find in chatting each other up. Wares are displayed with pride. Generally the rule is "don't touch"—instead, point and let them serve you. If self-serve is the norm, the seller will hand you a bag. Remember, they use metric weight. Ask for *un kilo* (about 2 pounds), *un demi-kilo* (about 1 pound—also called *une livre*), or *un quart-kilo* (pronounced "car-kilo," about half a pound). Many vendors speak enough English to assist you in your selection. Your total price will be hand-tallied on small scraps of paper and given to you. Vendors are normally honest. If you're struggling to find the correct change, just hold out your hand and they will take only what is needed. (Still, you're wise to double-check the amount you just paid for that olive tree.)

At the root of a good market experience is a sturdy shopping basket or bag. Find the vendor selling baskets and other wicker items and go local (*osier* is the French name for wicker, *cade* is the Provençal name—from the basket-making Luberon village of Cadenet); you can also find plastic and nylon versions. Most baskets are inexpensive, make for fun and colorful souvenirs, and can come in handy for odd-shaped or breakable carry-ons for the plane trip home. With basket in hand, shop for your heaviest items first. (You don't want to put a kilo of fresh apples on top of the bread you bought for your picnic.)

Markets change seasonally. In April and May, look for asparagus (green, purple, or the prized white—after being cooked, these are dipped in vinegar or homemade mayonnaise and eaten

Key Shopping Phrases

English	French	Pronounced
Just looking.	*Je regarde.*	zhuh ruh-garde
How much is it?	*Combien?*	kohm-bee-ehn
Too big/small/ expensive	*Trop grand/ petit/cher*	troh grahn/ puh-tee/sher
May I try it on?	*Je peux l'essayer?*	zhuh puh luh-say-yay
Can I see more?	*Puis-je en voir d'autres?*	pweezh'en vwahr doh-truh
I'll think about it.	*Je vais y penser.*	zhuh vayz-ee pahn-say
I'd like this.	*Je voudrais ça.*	zhuh voo-dray sah
On sale	*Solde*	sold-ay
Discounted price	*Prix réduit*	pree ray-dwee
Big discounts	*Prix choc*	pree shock

by hand). In early summer, shop for strawberries, including the best: *fraises des bois* (wild strawberries). Almost equally prized are the *gariguettes* and *maras des bois*. Soon after, you'll see cherries and other stone fruits, plus the famously sweet Cavaillon melons (resembling tiny cantaloupes, often served cut in half with a spoonful or two of the sweet Rhône white wine Beaumes de Venise). Don't worry if these are split open—the abundance of sugar and sunshine are the cause, and the *fendus* are considered the sweetest. In late June and early September, watch for figs *(figues)*. From July through September, critical vegetables for the Provençal dish ratatouille—including eggplant, tomatoes, zucchinis, and peppers—will all come straight from the open fields. In the fall, you'll see stands selling game birds, other beasts of the hunt, and a glorious array of wild mushrooms.

After November and throughout the winter, look for little (or big, depending on your wallet size) black truffles. Truffles, preserved and sealed in jars, can safely be brought back to the United States. The Luberon is one of Provence's largest truffle-producing areas. The town of Carpentras hosts a truffles-only market on Friday mornings in winter, off the main roundabout in front of a café. Listen carefully and you'll hear the Provençal language being spoken between vendors and buyers. Richerenches, Northern Provence's truffle capital, holds its own winter truffle market; during its annual truffle-themed Mass, many parishioners would give a truffle as a small offering, instead of money.

For more immediate consumption, look for local cheeses

(cow; sheep or ewe, called *brebis*; or the Provençal favorite: goat cheese, or *chèvre*, named *picodons*). Cheeses range from very fresh (aged one day) to aged for weeks. The older the cheese, the more dried and shrunken. Some may even be speckled with edible mold. Cheeses come in many shapes (round, logs, pyramids) and various sizes (from single-bite mouthfuls to wheels that will feed you for several meals). Some are sprinkled with herbs or spices. Others are more adorned, such as those rolled in ash *(à la cendre)* or wrapped in leaves *(banon)*. Watch for the locally produced *banon de banon*, a goat cheese soaked in *eau-de-vie* (the highly alcoholic "water of life"), then wrapped in chestnut leaves and tied with string.

Next, move on to the sausages (many also rolled in herbs or spices). Samples are usually freely offered—try the *sanglier* (boar). Usually you can also taste locally produced wines or ciders. Look also for samples of *foie gras* (available in take-it-home tins), good with the sweet white wine of Beaumes de Venise. These items make perfect picnic fare when teamed with a crusty baguette.

Throughout Provence, you'll see vendors selling paella made *sur place* (on the spot) in huge, traditional round pans. Paella varies by area and by chef, but most recipes include the traditional ingredients of fresh shellfish, chicken, and sausages mixed into saffron-infused rice. And throughout France, you'll see vans selling sizzling, spit-roasted chicken (perfectly bagged for carrying-out) or pizza (made to your liking on the spot). *Bon appétit!*

Clothing Boutiques

Those preferring fashion to food will be pleased to learn that they don't have to go to Paris to enjoy the latest trends. The stylish boutiques lining the shopping streets of Avignon, Nîmes, Aix-en-Provence, and Nice offer more than sufficient selection and style for the fashion-conscious. The expression for window-shopping in French is *faire du lèche-vitrines* (literally, "window-licking"). While hardly as freewheeling and relaxed as *les marchés,* you're a long way from the intimidating clerks of Paris. Still, they play by a different set of rules in France, and the better knowledge you have of the rules, the better player you'll be. Consider these tips to get you off on the right track:

- In small stores, always say *"Bonjour, Madame/Mademoiselle/Monsieur"* when entering and *"Au revoir, Madame/Mademoiselle/Monsieur"* when leaving.
- Except in department stores, it's not normal for the customer to handle clothing. Ask first if you can look at an item.
- For clothing-size comparisons between the US and France, see page 387 of the appendix.
- Forget returns (and don't count on exchanges).

- The customer is not always right; in fact, some clerks figure they're doing you a favor by waiting on you.
- Saturdays are busiest.
- Observe French shoppers, then imitate.

FRENCH HISTORY AND CONTEMPORARY POLITICS

French History in an Escargot Shell

About the time of Christ, Romans "Latinized" the land of the Gauls. With the fifth-century A.D. fall of Rome, the barbarian Franks and Burgundians invaded. Today's France evolved from this unique mix of Latin and Celtic cultures.

While France wallowed with the rest of Europe in medieval darkness, it got a head start in its development as a nation-state. In 507, Clovis established Paris as the capital of his Christian Merovingian dynasty. Clovis and the Franks would eventually become Louis and the French. Charles Martel stopped the spread of Islam by beating the Spanish Moors at the Battle of Poitiers. And Charlemagne, the most important of the "Dark Age" Frankish kings, was crowned Holy Roman Emperor by the pope in 800. Charles the Great presided over the "Carolingian Renaissance" and effectively ruled an empire that was vast for its time.

The Treaty of Verdun (843), which divided Charlemagne's empire among his grandsons, marks what could be considered the birth of Europe. For the first time, a treaty was signed in vernacular languages (French and German), rather than in Latin. This split established a Franco-Germanic divide and heralded an age of fragmentation. While petty princes took the reigns, the Frankish king ruled only Ile de France, a small region around Paris.

Vikings, or Norsemen, settled in what became Normandy. Later, in 1066, these "Normans" invaded England. The Norman king, William the Conqueror, consolidated his English domain, accelerating the formation of modern England. But his rule also muddied the political waters between England and France, kicking off a centuries-long struggle between the two nations.

In the 12th century, Eleanor of Aquitaine (a separate country in southwest France) married Louis VII, king of France, bringing

Aquitaine under French rule. They divorced, and she married Henry of Normandy, soon to be Henry II of England. This marital union gave England control of a huge swath of land, from the English Channel to the Pyrénées. For 300 years, France and England would struggle over control of Aquitaine. Any enemy of the French king would find a natural ally in the English king.

In 1328, a French king (Charles IV) died without a son. The English king (Edward III), his nephew, was interested in the throne, but the French resisted. This quandary pitted France, the biggest and richest country in Europe, against England, which had the biggest army. They fought from 1337 to 1453 in what was modestly called the Hundred Years' War.

Regional powers from within France actually sided with England. Burgundy took Paris, captured the royal family, and recognized the English king as heir to the French throne. England controlled France from the Loire north, and things looked bleak for the French king.

Enter Joan of Arc, a 16-year-old peasant girl driven by religious voices. France's national heroine left home to support Charles VII, the dauphin (boy prince, heir to the throne but too young to rule). Joan rallied the French, ultimately inspiring them to throw out the English. In 1430, Joan was captured by the Burgundians, who sold her to the English, who convicted her of heresy and burned her at the stake in Rouen. But the inspiration of Joan of Arc lived on, and by 1453, English holdings on the Continent had dwindled to the port of Calais.

By 1500, a strong, centralized France had emerged, with borders similar to today's. Its kings (from the Renaissance François I through the Henrys and all those Louises) were model divine monarchs, setting the standard for absolute rule in Europe.

Outrage over the power plays and spending sprees of the kings, coupled with the modern thinking of the Enlightenment—whose leaders were the French *philosophes*—led to the French Revolution (1789). In France, it was the end of the *ancien régime*, as well as its notion that some are born to rule, while others are born to be ruled.

The excesses of the Revolution in turn led to the rise of Napoleon, who ruled the French empire as a dictator. Eventually, *his* excesses ushered him into a South Atlantic exile, and the French settled on a compromise role for their leader. The modern French king was himself ruled by a constitution. Rather than dress in leotards and powdered wigs, he went to work in a suit with a briefcase.

The 20th century spelled the end of France's reign as a military and political superpower. Devastating wars with Germany in 1870, 1914, and 1940—and the loss of her colonial holdings—left France

Top French Notables in History

Madame and Monsieur Cro-Magnon: Prehistoric hunter-gatherers who moved to France (c. 30,000 B.C.), painted cave walls at Lascaux and Font-de-Gaume, and eventually settled down as farmers (c. 10,000 B.C.).

Vercingétorix (72 B.C.–46 B.C.): This long-haired warrior rallied the Gauls against Julius Caesar's invading Roman legions (52 B.C.). Defeated by Caesar, France fell under Roman domination, enduring 500 years of peace, prosperity, the establishment of cities, building of roads, education in Latin, and conversion to Christianity.

Charlemagne (A.D. 742–814): For Christmas in A.D. 800, the pope gave King Charlemagne the title of Emperor, thus uniting much of Europe under the leadership of the Franks ("France"). Charlemagne stabilized France amid centuries of barbarian invasions. After his death, the empire was split, carving the outlines of modern France and Germany.

Eleanor of Aquitaine (c. 1122–1204): The beautiful, sophisticated ex-wife of the King of France married the King of England, creating an uneasy union between the two countries. During her lifetime, French culture was spread across Europe by roving troubadours, theological scholars, and skilled architects pioneering "the French style"—Gothic.

Joan of Arc (1412–1431): When France and England fought the Hundred Years' War to settle who would rule (1337–1453), teenager Joan of Arc—guided by voices in her head—rallied the French troops. Though Joan was captured and burned as a heretic, the French eventually drove England out of France for good, establishing the current borders. Over the centuries, the church upgraded Joan's status from heretic to saint (canonized 1920).

François I (1494–1547): This Renaissance king ruled a united, modern nation, making it a cultural center that hosted the Italian Leonardo da Vinci. François set the tone for future absolute monarchs, punctuating his commands with the phrase, "For such is our pleasure."

Louis XIV (1638–1715): Charismatic and cunning, the "Sun King" ruled Europe's richest, most populous, most powerful nation-state. Every educated European spoke French, dressed in Louis-style leotards and powdered wigs, and built

Versailles-like palaces. Though Louis ruled as an absolute monarch (distracting the nobility with courtly games), his reign also fostered the arts and philosophy, sowing the seeds of democracy and revolution.

Marie Antoinette (1755–1793): As the wife of Louis XVI, she came to symbolize (probably unfairly) the decadence of France's ruling class. When Revolution broke out (1789), she was arrested, imprisoned, and executed—one of thousands who were guillotined on Paris' place de la Concorde as an enemy of the people.

Napoleon Bonaparte (1769–1821): This daring young military man became a hero during the Revolution, fighting Europe's royalty. He went on to conquer much of the Continent, became leader of France, and eventually ruled as a dictator with the title of Emperor. In 1815, an allied Europe defeated and exiled Napoleon, reinstating the French monarchy—though future kings (including Napoleon's nephew, who ruled as Napoleon III) were subject to democratic constraints.

Claude Monet (1840–1926): Monet's Impressionist paintings capture the soft-focus beauty of the belle époque—middle-class men and women enjoying drinks in cafés, walks in gardens, and picnics along the Seine. At the turn of the 20th century, French culture reigned supreme while its economic and political clout was fading, soon to be shattered by the violence of World War I.

Charles de Gaulle (1890–1970): A career-military man, de Gaulle helped France survive occupation by Nazi Germany during World War II with his rousing radio broadcasts and unbending faith in France. As president, he led the country through its postwar rebuilding, through divisive wars in Vietnam and Algeria (trying to preserve France's colonial empire), and through turbulent student riots in the 1960s.

Contemporary French: Which recent French people will history remember? President François Mitterand (1916–1996), the driving force behind La Grande Arche and Opéra Bastille? Marcel Marceau (b. 1923), white-faced mime? Chef Paul Bocuse (b. 1926), inventor of *nouvelle cuisine?* Or Brigitte Bardot (b. 1934), film actress, crusader for animal rights, and popularizer of the bikini?

History

with not quite enough land, people, or production to be a top player on a global scale. But the 21st century may see France rise again: Paris is again the cultural capital of Europe, and France—under the EU banner—is leading the push to integrate Europe as one unified economic power. And when Europe is a superpower, Paris may yet be its capital.

Contemporary Politics in France

The five key political issues in France today are high unemployment (about 10 percent), high taxes (about 44 percent of the gross domestic product), a steadily increasing percentage of ethnic minorities (almost 10 percent of France's population is Muslim), what to do about the European Union (the EU), and the balancing act between maintaining cushy workers' benefits with the need to compete in a global marketplace. The nation's challenge is to address these issues while maintaining the social benefits that the French expect from their government.

The unification of Europe has been powered by France and Germany. The EU's constitution—still in limbo—was negotiated by former French president Valéry Giscard d'Estaing, and represents a serious step in European unification. The constitution was designed to simplify decision-making and provide a more consistent and coordinated foreign policy for member states. The 25-member EU was well on its way to becoming a "United States of Europe" (having successfully dissolved borders and implemented a single currency, the euro)—until French citizens voted resoundingly against ratification in 2005. While France's major political parties supported the treaty, voters felt it gave too many concessions to other countries (such as Britain), and would ultimately result in a loss of job security and social benefits (a huge issue in France). Because of France's important role in establishing the EU, progress on the constitution and further unification has stalled.

French national politics are complex but fascinating. While only two parties dominate American politics, France has seven major parties and several smaller ones. From left to right, the major parties include: the Ligue Communiste Révolutionnaire (LCR), which is as far left as you get in France; the more moderate reformed Communists (PCF, or Parti Communiste Français); the environmental party (Les Verts, a.k.a. "The Greens"); the middle-of-the-road Socialists (PS, or Parti Socialiste); the aristocratically conservative UDF (Union pour la Démocratie Française); the center right UMP (Union pour la Majorité Présidentielle); and the racist, isolationist Front National party. In general, the UDF and UMP split the conservative middle ground, and the Socialists dominate the liberal middle ground. But in France, unlike in the US, informal coalitions are generally necessary for any party to "rule."

You've likely read about the Front National party, led by Jean-Marie Le Pen. His infamous "France for the French" platform calls for the expulsion of ethnic minorities and broader police powers. The situation was especially tense in fall 2005, when Muslim youths rioted in Parisian suburbs, protesting discrimination. Although the Front National has a staunch voter base of about 15 percent, the recent rise in unemployment and globalization worries have increased its following, allowing Le Pen to nudge the political agenda to the right. On the far left, the once powerful Communists (PCF) draw only about 5 percent of the popular vote, forcing them to work more flexibly with the less radical Socialists and the environmental party (Les Verts). The left end of the political spectrum in France has seen its fortunes rise when the economy is strong, and fall when it's weak.

In 2006, Parisian students took to the streets to protest threats to job security. Guaranteed "tenure" for life is important to French workers, and makes it extremely difficult for businesses to fire employees. Any changes that could weaken job security do not sit well with the public.

While the French president is elected by popular vote every five years, he is more of a figurehead than his American counterpart. The more-powerful prime minister is chosen by the president, then confirmed by the parliament (Assemblée Nationale). With five major parties, a single majority is rare, so it takes a coalition to elect a prime minister. Over the past 15 years, the right has been more successful in marshaling its supporters than the left. Previous President Jacques Chirac and current President Nicolas Sarkozy (elected in 2007) are both conservatives.

Sarkozy is pro-US (though he doesn't speak English) and pro-EU. To address a sluggish economy, he proposes a tough-love, carrot-and-stick approach—limiting the power of unions and cutting workers' benefits, while offering tax incentives to workers who put in overtime (above the current 35–39-hour work week). Sarkozy is tough on crime and on unchecked immigration. It remains to be seen how his hard-line approach will play to France's feisty workers and disenfranchised immigrants. As the French say: *On verra* (we'll see).

History

APPENDIX

CONTENTS

RESOURCES

Tourist Offices

In the US

France has a national tourist information office (abbreviated **TI** in this book) that is a wealth of information. Before you go, you can contact the TI to briefly describe your trip and request any information (such as city maps and schedules of upcoming festivals).

To ask questions and request tourist materials, call 514/288-1904 or email info.us@franceguide.com. One brochure and the *France Guide* magazine are free; additional brochures are $0.50 each, with a handling fee of $2 per order. Orders will arrive in 2–3 weeks; rush delivery is an extra $4. You can download many brochures free of charge at www.franceguide.com.

In Provence and the French Riviera

The local TI is your best first stop in most places. Throughout Provence and the French Riviera, you'll find TIs are usually well organized with English-speaking staff. If you're arriving in town after the office closes, try calling ahead or picking up a map in a neighboring town. Most TIs will help you find a room by calling hotels (for free or for a small fee) or by giving you a complete listing of available bed-and-breakfasts. Towns with a lot of tourism generally have English-speaking guides available for private hire (about $120 for a 2-hour guided town walk).

The French call TIs by different names. *Office de Tourisme* and *Bureau de Tourisme* are used in cities, while *Syndicat d'Initiative* or *Information Touristique* are used in small towns. Also look for *Accueil* signs in airports and at popular sights. These are information booths staffed with seasonal helpers who provide tourists with limited, though generally sufficient, information. Smaller TIs are often closed from 12:00 to 14:00.

More Resources from Rick Steves

Guidebooks and Online Updates

This book is updated every year in person. The telephone numbers and hours of sights listed are accurate as of mid-2007—but

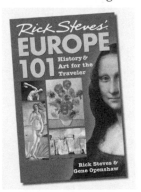

even with annual updates, things change. For the very latest, visit www .ricksteves.com/update. Also at my website, you'll find a valuable list of reports and experiences—good and bad—from fellow travelers (www .ricksteves.com/feedback).

This book is one of more than 30 titles in my series on European travel, which includes country guidebooks (including France), city and regional guidebooks (including Paris), and my budget-travel skills handbook,

Rick Steves' Europe Through the Back Door. My phrase books—for French, Italian, German, Spanish, and Portuguese—are practical and budget-oriented. My other books are *Europe 101* (a crash course on art and history, newly expanded and in full color), *European Christmas* (on traditional and modern-day celebrations), and *Postcards from Europe* (a fun memoir of my travels over 25 years, offering an insight into French culture that you won't find in guidebooks). For a complete list of my books, see the inside of the last page of this book.

Public Television and Radio Shows

My TV series, *Rick Steves' Europe,* covers European destinations in 70 shows, with six episodes on France. My weekly public radio show, *Travel with Rick Steves,* features interviews with travel

Begin Your Trip at www.ricksteves.com

At our travel website, you'll find a wealth of free information on European destinations, including fresh monthly news and helpful tips from thousands of fellow travelers.

Our **online Travel Store** offers travel bags and accessories specially designed by Rick Steves to help you travel smarter and lighter. These include Rick's popular carry-on bags (wheeled and rucksack versions), money belts, totes, toiletries kits, adapters, other accessories, and a wide selection of guidebooks, planning maps, and DVDs.

Choosing the right **railpass** for your trip—amidst hundreds of options—can drive you nutty. We'll help you choose the best pass for your needs, plus give you a bunch of free extras.

Rick Steves' Europe Through the Back Door travel company offers **tours** with more than two dozen itineraries and 450 departures reaching the best destinations in this book... and beyond. Our France tours include Paris and the South of France in 15 days, Paris and the Heart of France in 11 days (focusing on the best of the north; a kid-friendly version of this tour is also available), the Best of Paris and London in eight days, and the one-week Paris city tour. You'll enjoy great guides, a fun bunch of travel partners (with small groups of generally about 25), and plenty of room to spread out in a big, comfy bus. You'll find European adventures to fit every vacation length. For all the details, and to get our Tour Catalog and a free Rick Steves Tour Experience DVD (filmed on location during an actual tour), visit www.ricksteves.com or call the Tour Department at 425-608-4217.

experts from around the world, including several hours on France and French culture. All the TV scripts and radio shows (which are easy and free to download to an MP3 player) are at www.ricksteves .com.

Free Audio Tours

Rick Steves and Gene Openshaw (the co-author of seven books in the Rick Steves series) have produced free, self-guided audio tours of Paris—for the Louvre, Musée d'Orsay, Versailles, and Historic Paris—as well as Florence, Rome, and Venice. Created for users of iPods and other MP3 players, the tours allow you to focus on what you're seeing rather than what you're reading.

The Paris tours are available through iTunes and at www.ricksteves.com (Italy tours available after January 2008). Simply download them onto your computer and transfer them to your iPod or MP3 player. (Remember to bring a Y-jack and extra set of ear buds for your travel partner.)

Maps

The black-and-white maps in this book, drawn by Dave Hoerlein, are concise and simple. Dave, who is well-traveled in France, designed the maps to help you locate recommended places and reach TIs, where you'll find more in-depth (and often free) maps of cities or regions. Better maps are sold at newsstands—take a look before you buy to be sure the map has the level of detail that you want.

Michelin maps are available throughout France at bookstores, newsstands, and gas stations (about €5 each, half the US price). The Michelin #528 map (1:1,000,000 scale) covers this book's destinations with good detail for drivers. Train travelers do fine with Michelin's #721 map. Drivers going beyond Provence and the Riviera should consider the soft-cover Michelin France atlas (the entire country at 1:200,000, well-organized in a €20 book with an index and maps of major cities). Spend a few minutes learning the Michelin key to get the most sightseeing value out of these maps.

Other Guidebooks

If you're like most travelers, this book is all you need. But if you're heading beyond my recommended destinations, you might want some supplemental information. Considering the improvements they'll make in your $3,000 vacation, $30 for extra maps and books is money well spent.

Of the several guidebooks on Provence and the Riviera, many are high on facts and low on opinion, guts, or personality. For well-researched (though not updated annually) background information, try the Cadogan guide to Southern France. Serious learners prefer the Knopf guides to the Eyewitness guides' pretty pictures. The popular, skinny, green Michelin guides are dry but informative, especially for drivers. They're known for their city and sightseeing maps, and for their succinct, helpful information on all major sights. English editions, covering most of the regions you'll want to visit, are sold in France for about €14 (or $20 in the US).

Recommended Books and Movies

To get a feel for France in general, and specifically for Provence and the French Riviera, consider reading some of these books or seeing these films:

Non-Fiction

For a good introduction to French culture and people, read *French or Foe* (Polly Platt) and *Sixty Million Frenchmen Can't Be Wrong* (Jean-Benoit Nadeau and Julie Barlow). The latter is a must-read for anyone serious about understanding French culture, contemporary politics, and what makes the French tick.

In *A Distant Mirror,* respected historian Barbara Tuchman takes readers back to medieval France. *The Course of French History* (Pierre Goubert) is a concise and readable summary. Ina Caro's *The Road from the Past* is filled with enjoyable essays on her travels through France, with an accent on history. And *The Yellow House* (Martin Gayford) vividly recounts van Gogh and Gauguin's tumultuous stay in Arles.

Peter Mayle's bestselling memoirs, *A Year in Provence* and *Toujours Provence*, offer an evocative view of life in southern France. The travelogue *Portraits of France* (Robert Daley) includes chapters on Provence. In *At Home in France* (Ann Barry), an American author describes her visits to her country house. *Postcards from France* (Megan McNeill Libby) was written by an observant foreign exchange student. A mix of writers explore French culture in *Travelers Tales: Provence* (edited by Tara Austen Weaver and James O'Reilly).

A Goose in Toulouse (Mort Rosenblum) provides keen insights on rural France through its focus on cuisine. Foodies may also enjoy *From Here, You Can't See Paris* (Michael S. Sanders), about a local restaurant where foie gras is always on the menu.

Da Vinci Code fans will enjoy reading that book's inspiration, *Holy Blood, Holy Grail* (Michael Baigent, Richard Leigh, and Henry Lincoln), which takes place mostly in southern France.

If you'll be staying in France for a while, consider picking up *Adapter Kit France: A Traveler's Tools for Living Like a Local* (Terry Link) and/or *Culture Shock: France* (Sally Adamson Taylor).

Fiction

Written in the 1930s, *Joy of Man's Desiring* captures the charm of rural France. (The author, Jean Giono, also wrote the Johnny-Appleseed eco-fable set in Provence, *The Man Who Planted Trees*.) *The Fly-Truffler* (Gustaf Sobin) features a character who studies the Provençal dialect. Peter Mayle, whose non-fiction books are recommended above, also writes fiction set in Provence, including *Hotel Pastis* and *A Good Year*. For a list of recommended books for children, see page 361.

Films

To Catch a Thief (1955) features both the French Riviera and crackling performances by Grace Kelly and Cary Grant. In *La Grande Vadrouille* (1966), set during World War II, two French civilians aid the crew of a downed Allied bomber in crossing the demarcation line into southern France. *The Return of Martin Guerre* (1982) takes place during the Middle Ages.

Jean de Florette (1986), a marvelous tale of greed and intolerance, is about a city hunchback who inherits a valuable piece of property in rural France, only to have his efforts thwarted by his villainous neighbor. Its sequel, *Manon des Sources* (1986), continues the story, focusing on the hunchback's beautiful daughter.

Two films, based on the memoirs of writer/filmmaker Marcel Pagnol, show his early life in Provence: *My Father's Glory* (1991) and *My Mother's Castle* (1991).

Cyrano de Bergerac (1990), about a romantic poet with a large nose, has scenes filmed at the Abbaye de Fontenay. *French Kiss* (1995) includes scenes in the French countryside and Cannes, as well as Paris. *Chocolat* (2000), which was filmed in the Dordogne region, shows Juliette Binoche opening a chocolate shop and stirring up a tiny town. (*The Horseman on the Roof*, from 1995, is also set in southern France and features the beautiful Binoche.) *The Chorus* (2004), filled with angelic choir music, tells the story of a schoolteacher and the boys he brings together.

MONEY MATTERS

Damage Control for Lost Cards

If you lose your credit, debit, or ATM card, you can stop people from using it by reporting the loss immediately to the respective global customer-assistance centers. Call these 24-hour US numbers collect: Visa (410/581-9994), MasterCard (636/722-7111), and American Express (623/492-8427). For another option (with the same results), you can call these toll-free numbers in France: Visa (08 00 90 11 79), MasterCard (08 00 90 13 87), and American Express (08 00 89 00 11). Diners Club has offices in the US (702/797-5532, call collect) and Britain (from France, dial 00-44-1695-53760).

At a minimum, you'll need to know the name of the financial institution that issued you the card, along with the type of card (classic, platinum, or whatever). Providing the following information will allow for a quicker cancellation of your missing card: full card number, whether you are the primary or secondary cardholder, the cardholder's name exactly as printed on the card, billing address, home phone number, circumstances of the loss or theft, and identification verification (your birth date, your mother's maiden name, or your Social Security number—memorize this, don't carry a copy). If you are the secondary cardholder, you'll also need to provide the primary cardholder's identification-verification details. You can generally receive a temporary card within two or three business days in Europe.

If you promptly report your card lost or stolen, you typically won't be responsible for any unauthorized transactions on your account, although many banks charge a liability fee of $50.

Tipping

Tipping *(donner un pourboire)* in France isn't as automatic and generous as it is in the US, but for special service, tips are appreciated, if not expected. As in the US, the proper amount depends on your resources, tipping philosophy, and the circumstances, but some general guidelines apply.

Restaurants: At cafés and restaurants, a 15 percent service charge is generally included in the bill *(service compris)*, though it's customary to tip 5 percent extra for good service. When you hand your payment plus a tip to your waiter, you can say, "*C'est bon*" (say bohn), meaning, "It's good" (and you don't want any change back). If you order a meal at a counter, don't tip.

Taxis: To tip the cabbie, round up. For a typical ride, round up to the next euro on the fare (to pay a €13 fare, give €14); for a long ride, round to the nearest €10 (for a €75 fare, give €80). If the cabbie hauls your bags and zips you to the airport to help you catch your flight, you might want to toss in a little more. But if you feel like you're being driven in circles or otherwise ripped off, skip the tip.

Special Services: It's thoughtful to tip a couple of euros to someone who shows you a special sight and who is paid in no other way. Tour guides at public sites sometimes hold out their hands for tips after they give their spiel; if I've already paid for the tour, I don't tip extra, though some tourists do give a euro or two, particularly for a job well done. I don't tip at hotels, but if you do, give the porter a euro for carrying bags and leave a couple of euros in your room at the end of your stay for the maid if the room was kept clean. In general, if someone in the service industry does a super job for you, a tip of a couple of euros is appropriate...but not required.

When in doubt, ask. If you're not sure whether (or how much) to tip for a service, ask your hotelier or the tourist information office; they'll fill you in on how it's done on their turf.

Getting a VAT Refund

As is the case throughout the European Union, wrapped into the purchase price of your French souvenirs is a Value Added Tax (VAT) of about 19.6 percent. If you purchase more than €175 (about $225) worth of goods at a store that participates in the

VAT-refund scheme, you're entitled to get most of that tax back. Getting your refund is usually straightforward and, if you buy a substantial amount of souvenirs, well worth the hassle. If you're lucky, the merchant will subtract the tax when you make your purchase. (This is more likely to occur if the store ships the goods to your home.) Otherwise, you'll need to:

Get the paperwork. Have the merchant completely fill out the necessary refund document, *Bordereau de Vente a l'Exportation*, also called a "cheque." You'll have to present your passport at the store.

Get your stamp at the border or airport. Process your cheque(s) at your last stop in the EU (e.g., at the airport) with the customs agent who deals with VAT refunds. It's best to keep your purchases in your carry-on for viewing, but if they're too large or dangerous (such as knives) to carry on, track down the proper customs agent to inspect them before you check your bag. You're not supposed to use your purchased goods before you leave. If you show up at customs wearing your chic new French ensemble, officials might look the other way—or deny you a refund.

Collect your refund. You'll need to return your stamped document to the retailer or its representative. Many merchants work with a service, such as Global Refund (www.globalrefund.com) or Premier Tax Free (www.premiertaxfree.com), which have offices at major airports, ports, or border crossings. These services, which extract a 4 percent fee, can refund your money immediately in your currency of choice or credit your card (within two billing cycles). If the retailer handles VAT refunds directly, it's up to you to contact the merchant for your refund. You can mail the documents from home, or quicker, from your point of departure (using a stamped, addressed envelope you've prepared or one that's been provided by the merchant)—and then wait. It could take months.

Customs for American Shoppers

You are allowed to take home $800 worth of items per person duty-free, once every 30 days. The next $1,000 is taxed at a flat 3 percent. After that, you pay the individual item's duty rate. You can also bring in duty-free a liter of alcohol (slightly more than a standard-size bottle of wine; you must be at least 21), 200 cigarettes, and up to 100 non-Cuban cigars. As for food, if it's in cans or sealed jars, it's permissible (as long as no meat is included). Fresh fruits and vegetables are prohibited. Some, but not all, types of cheese are allowed. Note that you'll need to carefully pack any bottles of wine and other liquid-containing items (jars of olives, etc.) in your checked luggage due to limits on liquids in carry-ons. To check customs rules and duty rates before you go, visit www.cbp.gov, and click on "Travel," then "Know Before You Go."

Clothing Size Comparisons for Shoppers

When shopping for clothing, use these US-to-France comparisons as general guidelines (but note that no conversion is perfect).

- Women's dresses and blouses: Add 30 (US women's size 10 is about French size 40)
- Men's suits and jackets: Add 10 (US men's size 40 regular is about French size 50)
- Men's shirts: Multiply by 2 and add about 8 (US men's size 15 collar is close to French size 38)
- Women's shoes: Add about 31 (US women's size 8 is about French size 39)
- Men's shoes: Add 32–34 (US men's size 9 US is about French size 43; US size 11 is French size 45)

TELEPHONES, EMAIL, AND MAIL

Telephones

Smart travelers learn the phone system and use it daily to reserve or reconfirm rooms, get tourist information, reserve restaurants, confirm tour times, or phone home. When spelling out your name on the phone, you'll find that some letters are pronounced differently in French: *a* is pronounced "ah," *e* is pronounced "eh," and *i* is pronounced "ee." To avoid confusion, say "*a*, Anne," "*e*, euro," and "*i*, Isabelle."

Types of Phones

You'll encounter various kinds of phones on your trip:

Card-operated phones—where you insert a locally bought phone card into a public pay phone—are common in Europe.

Coin-operated phones, the original kind of pay phone, are rare in France. You might see them at gas stations and in big hotel lobbies.

Hotel room phones are sometimes cheap for local calls (confirm at the front desk first), but can be a rip-off for long-distance calls unless you use an international phone card (described below). But incoming calls are free, making this a cheap way for friends and family to stay in touch, provided they have a good long-distance plan for calls to Europe.

American mobile phones work in Europe if they're GSM-enabled, tri-band or quad-band, and on a calling plan that includes international calls. They're convenient, but pricey. For example, with a T-Mobile phone, you'll pay $1 per minute for calls.

European mobile phones run about $75 (for the most basic models) and come without contracts. These phones are loaded with prepaid calling time that you can recharge as you use up the minutes. As long as you're not "roaming" outside the phone's home country, incoming calls are free. If you're traveling to multiple countries within Europe, make sure the phone is electronically "unlocked," so that you can swap out its SIM card (a fingernail-size chip that holds the phone's information) for a new one in other countries.

Using Phone Cards

Get a phone card for your calls. Prepaid phone cards come in two types: international and insertable (both described below). Look for these cards at any post office and most newsstands and tobacco shops *(tabacs),* which you'll find everywhere, including at train stations and airports.

Either type of phone card works only in France. While traveling in France, you can share either type of card with your companions (and, in the case of an international phone card, your buddy doesn't even need the actual card—just the numbers on it). If you have time left on a card when you leave the country (as you likely will), simply give it to another traveler—anyone can use it.

For international calls, you'll get the best deal with an **international phone card,** called *carte à code* (cart ah code). It comes with a dial-up code that can be used from nearly any phone, including the one in your hotel room (if it's set on "pulse," switch it to "tone"). Cards are marked as national (for France) or international. All cards work for domestic or international calls, but you get better rates if you use the card for the purpose it was intended—so if you plan to use your card mostly for calls home, ask for an international card (denominations in €7 and €15 amounts). They're all good values—my €15 international card lasted for four weeks of regular calls home (about 5 cents a minute).

These *carte à code* cards all work the same way and are simple to use (English instructions provided). Scratch to get your code (begins with 08). Dial the free number. A voice (in French, but sometimes followed by English) tells you to enter your code. After entering your code, you may need to press (or *"touche,"* pronounced toosh) either the pound key (#, *dièse*, dee-ehz) or the star key (*, *étoile*, eh-twahl). At the next message, dial the number you're calling, again followed by pound or star (you don't have to listen through the entire sales pitch).

An **insertable phone card,** called a *télécarte* (tay-lay-kart), can only be used at pay phones. While per-minute rates are much cheaper with an international phone card than with an insertable phone card, the international cards are slower to use (more numbers to dial). Use a *télécarte* for quick local calls from a phone booth. There are two denominations: *une petite* costs about €7.50; *une grande* about €15. While you can use a *télécarte* to call anywhere in the world, it's only a good deal for making local calls.

Using Hotel-Room Phones, VoIP, or US Calling Cards

The best way to call home is using an international phone card, but here are some other alternatives.

The phone in your **hotel room** is convenient...but expensive. While incoming calls (made by folks back home) can be an affordable way to keep in touch, charges for *outgoing* calls can be a very unpleasant surprise. Make sure you understand all the charges and fees associated with outgoing calls before you pick up that receiver.

Dialing direct from your hotel room—without using an international phone card (described above)—is usually quite expensive for international calls. Always ask first how much you'll be charged, even for local and (supposedly) toll-free calls.

If your family has an inexpensive way to call Europe, either through a long-distance plan or prepaid calling card, have them call you in your hotel room. Give them a list of your hotels' phone numbers before you go. Then, as you travel, send them an email or make a quick pay-phone call to set up a time for them to give you a ring.

If you're traveling with a laptop, consider trying **VoIP (Voice over Internet Protocol).** With VoIP, two computers act as the phones, allowing for a free Internet-based call. The major providers are Skype (www.skype.com) and Google Talk (www.google .com/talk).

US Calling Cards (such as the ones offered by AT&T, MCI, or Sprint) are the worst option. You'll nearly always save a lot of money by paying with a phone card (see above).

How to Dial

Calling from the US to Europe, or vice versa, is simple—once you break the code. The European calling chart on page 390 will walk you through it.

Dialing Within France

France has a direct-dial 10-digit phone system (no area codes). To call anywhere within France, just dial the number. For example, the number of one of my recommended hotels in Arles is 04 90 96 11 89. That's the number you dial whether you're calling it from the Arles train station or from Paris.

France's toll-free numbers start with 0800 (like US 800 numbers, though in France you don't dial a 1 first). In France, these 0800 numbers—called *numéro vert* (green number)—can be dialed free from any phone without using a phone card. Note that you can't call France's toll-free numbers from America, nor can you

European Calling Chart

Just smile and dial, using this key:
AC = Area Code, LN = Local Number.

European Country	Calling long distance within ...	Calling from the US or Canada to ...	Calling from a European country to ...
Austria	AC + LN	011 + 43 + AC (without the initial zero) + LN	00 + 43 + AC (without the initial zero) + LN
Belgium	LN	011 + 32 + LN (without initial zero)	00 + 32 + LN (without initial zero)
Bosnia-Herzegovina	AC + LN	011 + 387 + AC (without initial zero) + LN	00 + 387 + AC (without initial zero) + LN
Britain	AC + LN	011 + 44 + AC (without initial zero) + LN	00 + 44 + AC (without initial zero) + LN
Croatia	AC + LN	011 + 385 + AC (without initial zero) + LN	00 + 385 + AC (without initial zero) + LN
Czech Republic	LN	011 + 420 + LN	00 + 420 + LN
Denmark	LN	011 + 45 + LN	00 + 45 + LN
Estonia	LN	011 + 372 + LN	00 + 372 + LN
Finland	AC + LN	011 + 358 + AC (without initial zero) + LN	999 + 358 + AC (without initial zero) + LN
France	LN	011 + 33 + LN (without initial zero)	00 + 33 + LN (without initial zero)
Germany	AC + LN	011 + 49 + AC (without initial zero) + LN	00 + 49 + AC (without initial zero) + LN
Greece	LN	011 + 30 + LN	00 + 30 + LN
Hungary	06 + AC + LN	011 + 36 + AC + LN	00 + 36 + AC + LN
Ireland	AC + LN	011 + 353 + AC (without initial zero) + LN	00 + 353 + AC (without initial zero) + LN

European Country	Calling long distance within ...	Calling from the US or Canada to ...	Calling from a European country to ...
Italy	LN	011 + 39 + LN	00 + 39 + LN
Montenegro	AC + LN	011 + 382 + AC (without initial zero) + LN	00 + 382 + AC (without initial zero) + LN
Netherlands	AC + LN	011 + 31 + AC (without initial zero) + LN	00 + 31 + AC (without initial zero) + LN
Norway	LN	011 + 47 + LN	00 + 47 + LN
Poland	LN	011 + 48 + LN (without initial zero)	00 + 48 + LN (without initial zero)
Portugal	LN	011 + 351 + LN	00 + 351 + LN
Slovakia	AC + LN	011 + 421 + AC (without initial zero) + LN	00 + 421 + AC (without initial zero) + LN
Slovenia	AC + LN	011 + 386 + AC (without initial zero) + LN	00 + 386 + AC (without initial zero) + LN
Spain	LN	011 + 34 + LN	00 + 34 + LN
Sweden	AC + LN	011 + 46 + AC (without initial zero) + LN	00 + 46 + AC (without initial zero) + LN
Switzerland	LN	011 + 41 + LN (without initial zero)	00 + 41 + LN (without initial zero)
Turkey	AC (if no initial zero is included, add one) + LN	011 + 90 + AC (without initial zero) + LN	00 + 90 + AC (without initial zero) + LN

- The instructions above apply whether you're calling a land line or mobile phone.
- The international access codes (the first numbers you dial when making an international call) are 011 if you're calling from the US or Canada, or 00 if you're calling from virtually anywhere in Europe (except Finland, where it's 999).
- To call the US or Canada from Europe, dial 00, then 1 (the country code for the US and Canada), then the area code and number. In short, 00 + 1 + AC + LN = Hi, Mom!

count on reaching America's toll-free numbers from France.

Note that any 08 number that does not have a 00 directly following is a toll call, generally costing €0.10 to €0.50 per minute. Many private companies and public services are changing to 08 numbers—expect some changes in telephone numbers.

Dialing Internationally
If you want to make an international call, follow these three steps:

1) Dial the international access code (00 if you're calling from Europe, 011 from the US or Canada).

2) Dial the country code of the country you're calling (33 for France, or 1 for the US or Canada).

3) Drop the initial zero of the 10-digit local number and dial the remaining nine digits.

For example, to call the recommended Arles hotel from the US, dial 011 (the US international access code), 33 (France's country code), then 4 90 96 11 89.

To call my office in Edmonds, Washington, from France, I dial 00 (Europe's international access code), 1 (the US country code), 425 (Edmonds' area code), and 771-8303.

Useful Phone Numbers
Consulates/Embassies
US Consulate in Nice: tel. 04 93 88 89 55, fax 04 93 87 07 38 (7 avenue Gustave V, does *not* provide visa services—Paris is the nearest office for these services)

Canadian Consulate in Nice: tel. 04 93 92 93 22, fax 04 93 92 55 51 (10 rue Lamartine)

US Consulate in Marseille: tel. 04 91 54 92 00, fax 04 91 55 09 47 (place Varian Fry)

US Consulate in Paris: tel. 01 43 12 22 22, passport services open Mon–Fri 9:00–12:00, closed Sat–Sun (2 rue St. Florentin, Métro: Concorde, www.amb-usa.fr)

US Embassy in Paris: tel. 01 43 12 22 22 (2 avenue Gabriel, to the left as you face Hôtel Crillon, Métro: Concorde)

Canadian Consulate and Embassy in Paris: tel. 01 44 43 29 00, open Mon–Fri 14:30–16:00, closed Sat–Sun (35 avenue Montaigne, Métro: Franklin D. Roosevelt, www.amb -canada.fr)

Emergency/Medical Needs
Police: tel. 17

Emergency Medical Assistance: tel. 15

Riviera Medical Services: tel. 04 93 26 12 70. They have a list of English-speaking physicians and can help you make an appointment or call an ambulance.

Travel Advisories

US Department of State: tel. 202/647-5225, www.travel.state.gov
Canadian Department of Foreign Affairs: Canadian tel. 800-
    267-6788, www.dfait-maeci.gc.ca
US Centers for Disease Control and Prevention: tel. 877-FYI-
    TRIP, www.cdc.gov/travel

Directory Assistance

Directory Assistance for Paris and France (some English
    spoken): tel. 12
Tourist Information Offices: To call any TI in France, dial
    3265 and say the name of the city in your best French accent
    (€0.34/min).
Collect Calls to the US: tel. 00 00 11

Trains

Train (SNCF) Reservations and Information: tel. 3635

Airports

Nice: Aéroport de Nice—tel. 08 20 42 33 33,
    www.nice.aeroport.fr
Marseille: Aéroport Marseille–Provence—tel. 04 42 14 14 14,
    www.marseille.aeroport.fr
Paris: Aéroports Charles de Gaulle and Orly share the same
    numbers—tel. 3950 (€.34/min), www.adp.fr
Lyon: Saint-Exupéry Airport—€0.15/min toll tel. 08 26 80 08 26,
    www.lyon.aeroport.fr

Airlines

The following 08 numbers are toll calls; the per-minute fee gener-
ally ranges from €0.10 to €0.50.
Aer Lingus: tel. 08 21 23 02 67
Air Canada: tel. 08 25 88 08 81
Air France: tel. 08 20 82 08 20 or 08 20 82 36 54
Alitalia: tel. 08 02 31 53 15
American Airlines: tel. 08 10 87 28 72
Austrian Airlines: tel. 08 02 81 68 16
BMI British Midlands: tel. 01 41 91 87 04
British Airways: tel. 08 25 82 54 00
Continental: tel. 01 71 23 03 35
Delta: tel. 08 11 64 00 05
EasyJet: tel. 08 99 70 00 41
Iberia: tel. 08 25 80 09 65
Icelandair: tel. 01 44 51 60 51
KLM: tel. 08 90 71 07 10
Lufthansa: tel. 08 26 10 33 34

The Language Barrier and that French Attitude

You've no doubt heard that the French are "mean and cold and refuse to speak English." This is an out-of-date preconception left over from the days of Charles de Gaulle—and it's especially incorrect in this region. In these southern lands kissed by the sun and sea, you'll find your hosts more jovial and easygoing (like their Italian neighbors just over the border) than in the comparatively serious north. Still, be reasonable in your expectations: Waiters are paid to be efficient, not chatty. And Provençal postal clerks are every bit as speedy, cheery, and multilingual as ours are back home.

The biggest mistake most Americans make when traveling to France is trying to do too much with limited time. This approach is a mistake in the bustling north, and a virtual sin in the relaxed south. Hurried, impatient travelers who miss the subtle pleasures of people-watching from a sun-dappled café often misinterpret French attitudes. By slowing your pace and making an effort to understand French culture by living it, you're much more likely to have a richer experience. With the five weeks of paid vacation and 35-hour work week that many French workers get as non-negotiable rights, your hosts can't comprehend why anyone would rush through their vacation.

The French take great pride in their customs, clinging to their belief in cultural superiority despite the fact that they're no longer a world superpower. Let's face it: It's tough to keep on smiling when you've been crushed by a Big Mac, Mickey Moused by Disney, and drowned in instant coffee. Your hosts are cold only

Northwest: tel. 08 90 71 07 10
Olympic: tel. 01 44 94 58 58
Royal Air Maroc: tel. 08 20 82 18 21
SAS: tel. 08 25 32 53 35
Swiss: tel. 08 20 04 05 06
United: tel. 08 10 72 72 72
US Airways: tel. 08 10 63 22 22

Car Leasing in France
Europe by Car: US tel. 800-223-1516, US fax 212/246 1458, www.europebycar.com
Auto France: US tel. 800-572-9655, US fax 201/729 1917, www.autofrance.net

if you decide to see them that way. Polite and formal, the French respect the fine points of culture and tradition. Here, strolling down the street with a big grin on your face and saying hello to strangers is a sign of senility, not friendliness (seriously). They think that Americans, while friendly, are hesitant to pursue more serious friendships. Recognize sincerity and look for kindness. Give them the benefit of the doubt.

French communication difficulties are exaggerated. To hurdle the language barrier, bring a small English/French dictionary, a phrase book (look for mine, which contains a dictionary and menu decoder), a menu reader (if you're a gourmet eater), and a good supply of patience. In transactions, a small notepad and pen minimize misunderstandings about prices; have vendors write the price down. If you learn only five phrases, learn and use these: *bonjour* (good day), *pardon* (pardon me), *s'il vous plaît* (please), *merci* (thank you), and *au revoir* (goodbye). The French place great importance on politeness. Begin every encounter with *"Bonjour (or S'il vous plaît), madame/monsieur"* and end every encounter with *"Au revoir, madame/monsieur."*

The French are language perfectionists—they take their language (and other languages) seriously. Often they speak more English than they let on. This isn't a tourist-baiting tactic, but timidity on their part about speaking another language less than fluently. Start any conversation with, *"Bonjour, madame/monsieur. Parlez-vous anglais?"* and hope they speak more English than you speak French.

Hotel Chains

Huge Chain of Hotels: www.accorhotels.com (handles Ibis, Mercure, and Novotel hotels); US tel. 800-515-5679

Ibis Hotels: www.ibishotel.com, tel. 08 92 68 66 86; from US, dial 011 33 8 92 68 66 86

Mercure Hotels: www.mercure.com, toll tel. 08 25 88 33 33; US tel. 800-221-4542

Kyriad Hotels: www.kyriad.com, tel. 08 25 00 30 03; from US, dial 011 33 1 64 62 46 46

Best Western Hotels: www.bestwestern.com, tel. 08 00 90 44 90; US tel. 800-428-2627

Country Home Rental: www.gites-de-france.fr/eng or www.gite.com

Youth Hostels

Hostelling International, US Office: www.hiayh.org
Hostelling International, Canada Office:
   www.hostellingintl.ca

Reliable Tours

Wine Safari: Mike Rijken, Provence only, tel. 04 90 35 59 21, mobile 06 19 29 50 81, www.winesafari.net, mikeswinesafari@wanadoo.fr

Taxi des Oliviers: Roland Vanove, Provence and Riviera, tel. 06 80 75 40 90, taxidesoliviers@wanadoo.fr, best to contact by phone

Visit Provence: Cheaper big-bus excursions, Provence only, tel. 04 90 14 70 00, www.provence-reservation.com

Cooking Schools

Maison d'Hôtes de Provence: In central Arles, you can take educational and convivial courses, either for several days or for a full week, offered by a Franco-American team (see listing under "Sleeping" in the Arles chapter, page 62).

Jardin de Bacchus: Northwest of Avignon, in their Tavel bed and breakfast, Christine and Erik offer relaxing cooking classes (tel. 04 66 90 28 62, www.provence-escapade.fr, jardindebacchus@free.fr).

Les Petits Farcis: In Old Nice, Rosa Jackson takes you to the open-air market, then helps you prepare the food (www.petitsfarcis.com, see listing on page 245).

Email and Mail

Email: Many travelers set up a free email account with Yahoo, Microsoft (Hotmail), or Google (Gmail). Email use among European hoteliers is quite common.

In France's key cities—Paris, Nice, Lyon, and Avignon—you'll find plenty of coffee shops that offer wireless connections (Wi-Fi, pronounced "wee-fee" by the French) to travelers with laptop computers. Little hole-in-the-wall Internet-access shops, while common in the rest of Europe, are not prevalent in France. Post offices are a good solution in smaller towns offering Internet access *(cyberposte)*; buy a chip-card (for about same prices as phone cards, rechargeable for €4 per hour) and you're in business.

More and more hotels now offer their guests (slow) Internet access in their lobbies from a terminal (which may be free or operated with coins or a telephone card). Every year, more hotels offer Wi-Fi (sometimes free, sometimes for a charge). And some even have laptop loaners. Ask if your hotel has access. If it doesn't, your hotelier will direct you to the nearest place to get online.

Mail: French post offices are sometimes called PTT, for "Post, Telegraph, and Telephone"—look for signs for *La Poste*. Hours vary, though most are open weekdays 8:00–19:00 and Saturday morning 8:00–12:00. Stamps and phone cards are also sold at *tabac* (tobacco) shops. It costs about €0.90 to mail a postcard to the US. While you can arrange for mail delivery to your hotel (allow 10 days for a letter to arrive), phoning and emailing are so easy that I've dispensed with mail stops altogether. Federal Express makes pricey two-day deliveries.

One convenient, if pricey, way to send packages home is by using the PTT's Colissimo XL postage-paid mailing box. It costs about €33 for the International version, which allows you to send home all the goodies you can stuff into an 18" × 12" × 8" box (no weight limit).

TRANSPORTATION

By Car or Train?

Cars are best for three or more traveling together (especially families with small kids), those packing heavy, and those scouring the countryside in search of the perfect hill town—a tempting plan for this region. Trains and buses are best for solo travelers, blitz tourists, and city-to-city travelers. If you intend to focus on Arles, Avignon, Aix-en-Provence, and seaside destinations along the Riviera, go by train. Stations are centrally located in each city, which makes hotel-hunting and sightseeing easy. Buses and taxis pick up where trains leave off. While bus service can be sparse, taxis are generally available and reasonable. If relying on public transportation, seriously evaluate the value of train or bus detours and focus on fewer destinations, or hire one of the excellent minivan tour guides I recommend (see "Tours of Provence," page 36).

Trains

France's rail system (SNCF) sets the pace in Europe. Its super TGV (*train à grande vitesse;* tay zhay vay) system has inspired bullet trains throughout the world. The TGV runs at 170–220 mph. Its rails are fused into one long, continuous track for a faster and smoother ride. The TGV has changed commuting patterns in much of France and put most of the country within day-trip distance of Paris. A lightning fast TGV line opened in 2001, with trains screaming from Paris' city center to Avignon in 2.5 hours and to Marseille in three hours. TGV trains serve these cities in Provence and the Riviera: Avignon, Arles (very few trains), Nîmes, Marseille, Orange, Aix-en-Provence, Antibes, Cannes, and Nice. Avignon and Aix-en-Provence have separate TGV stations on the edge of town (with handy bus connections into the center)—note

Best Two-Week Trip of Provence & the French Riviera by Train and Bus

Note that fewer buses and trains run on Sunday.

Day Plan

1 Fly into Nice. Settle in at your hotel, then take my Welcome to the Riviera Walk along the promenade des Anglais (page 267). Sleep in or near Nice.

2 Take my self-guided Old Nice Walk (page 271) in the morning, allowing time to smell the *fougasse* and sample *un café*. Spend your afternoon at one or more of Nice's fine museums (see Chagall Museum Tour on page 277). Have dinner on the beach. Sleep in or near Nice.

3 Take the bus to nearby Villefranche-sur-Mer, explore, and have lunch. Consider my recommended seaside walks in Cap Ferrat, or take the one-hour boat cruise from Nice's port. Everyone should spend the afternoon or evening in almost-neighboring Monaco. Sleep in or near Nice.

4 Take a bus north to Vence and St-Paul-de-Vence. Stop for a stroll and visit the Fondation Maeght and/or Matisse's Chapel of the Rosary. Sleep in Vence or back in Nice.

5 Take a train from Nice to Isle-sur-la-Sorgue via Marseille (best to arrive on Sat or Wed and awake to tomorrow's market day). Wander and explore the town. Consider a canoe ride down the crystal-clear Sorgue River. Sleep in Isle-sur-la-Sorgue.

6 Enjoy market day this morning, then take a train to Avignon. Take my self-guided Avignon walk this afternoon and enjoy dinner on one of Avignon's many atmospheric squares. Sleep in Avignon.

7 Relax in Avignon this morning, and divide the rest of your day between Nîmes and the Pont du Gard. If the weather's good, bring your swimsuit and float on your back below the 2,000-year-old Pont du Gard. Sleep in Avignon.

carefully which station your train serves (either "Centre-Ville" or "TGV"; if it's not specified, then it's the central station).

At any train station, you can get schedule information, make reservations, and buy tickets for any destination.

Schedules

Schedules change by season, weekday, and weekend. Verify train schedules shown in this book—on the Web, check Germany's excellent all-Europe schedule site, http://bahn.hafas.de/bin/query .exe/en). You can also book and print tickets and reservations online at www.sncf.com (click on British flag for English)—where you may also find some cheaper tickets.

8 Take a train to Orange, visit its Roman theater, then take a bus to Vaison la Romaine (market day is Tue, so a Mon arrival is ideal). Set up in Vaison la Romaine for two nights. This requires careful planning, as few buses run to Vaison la Romaine.

9 Explore Vaison la Romaine's upper medieval village and lower Roman city, then bike to Séguret and Gigondas, or hike to Le Crestet for lunch (taxi back). Check out Vaison la Romaine's wine cooperative. Wine and hill-town buffs should hire a local minivan guide to show them the ropes and villages (see "Tours of Provence," page 36). Sleep in Vaison la Romaine.

10 Take a bus to Orange, and then a train to Arles (big market day on Sat). Check into Arles for the next two days. Sleep in Arles.

11 Take a taxi (or, in summer, a rare public bus) to Les Baux and have breakfast with a view. Take a taxi to St. Rémy-de-Provence, explore there, then catch a bus back to Arles; or take a taxi from Les Baux back to Arles and spend your afternoon there. Sleep in Arles.

12 Take a train to Cassis. Take a boat trip to the *calanques*, watch the *pétanque* balls roll, and end your day with a taxi ride up Cap Canaille. Sleep in Cassis.

13 Take a train to Aix-en-Provence. Have lunch and take my self-guided walking tour of the city, then return home to Cassis and watch the sunset from the old port, while you savor a bouillabaisse dinner. Sleep in Cassis.

14 Take the short train ride into Marseille (check your bag at the station), explore the city, then take a train back to Nice. Sleep in Nice.

15 Trip over.

Bigger stations have helpful information agents (often in red vests) roaming the station and at *Accueil* offices or booths. They can answer rail questions more quickly than the information or ticket windows. The nationwide information line for train schedules and reservations is 3635. Dial this four-digit number, then press 3, then press 1 (trust me) for reservations or ticket purchase (you may be sent to a French-only phone tree as SNCF tries to automate its services; if so, hang up and ask your hotelier for help). Press 321 for Eurostar information, or 322 for Thalys. This incredibly helpful, time-saving service costs €0.34 per minute from anywhere in France. Ask for an English-speaking agent and hope for the best (allow 5 min per call). The time and energy you save easily justifies

French Railpasses

Prices listed are for 2007 and are subject to change. For the latest prices, details, and train schedules (and easy online ordering), see my comprehensive *Guide to Eurail Passes* at www.ricksteves.com/rail.

"Saver" prices are per person for two or more people traveling together. "Youth" means under age 26. The fare for children 4–11 is half the adult individual fare or Saver fare. Kids under age 4 travel free.

FRANCE PASS

	Adult 1st Class	Adult 2nd Class	Senior 1st Class	Youth 1st Class	Youth 2nd Class
3 days in 1 month	$278	$237	$254	$206	$175
Extra rail days (max 6)	41	35	36	29	26

Senior = 60 and up.

FRANCE SAVERPASS

	1st Class	2nd Class
3 days in 1 month	$238	$204
Extra rail days (max 6)	35	29

FRANCE RAIL & DRIVE PASS

Any 2 rail days and 2 car days in 1 month.

Car Category	1st Class	Extra Car Day
Economy	$271	$55
Compact	286	70
Intermediate	293	77
Full-size	335	119
Minivan	396	180

Prices are per person, two traveling together. Solo travelers pay about $100 extra; third and fourth adults pay $207 per person. Extra rail days (3 max) cost $36 per day. To order a Rail & Drive pass, call your travel agent or Rail Europe at 800-438-7245. *This pass is not sold by Europe Through the Back Door.*

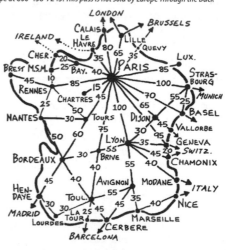

Map key:
Approximate point-to-point one-way second-class rail fares in US dollars. First class costs 50 percent more. Add up fares for your itinerary to see if a railpass will save you money.

Appendix

France Train Terms and Abbreviations

SNCF (*Société Nationale Chemins de Fer*): This is the Amtrak of France, operating all national train lines that link cities and towns.

TGV (*Train à Grande Vitesse*): SNCF's network of high-speed trains (twice as fast as regular trains) that connect major cities in France. These trains always require a reservation.

CORAIL: These trains are the next best compared to the TGV in terms of speed and comfort.

TER (*Trains Express Régionale*): These trains serve smaller stops within a region. For example, you'll find trains called TER de Bourgogne (trains operating only in Burgundy) and TER Provence (Provence-only trains).

the telephone torture, particularly when making seat reservations (note that phoned-in reservations must be picked up at least 30 minutes prior to departure).

Railpasses

Long-distance travelers can save big money with a France Railpass, sold only outside France (through travel agents or Europe Through the Back Door; see Railpass sidebar on page 400). For roughly the cost of a Paris–Avignon–Paris ticket, the France Railpass offers three days of travel (within a month) anywhere in France. You can add up to seven additional days for the cost of a two-hour ride each. Save money by getting the second-class instead of the first-class version and/or travel with a companion (the Flexi Saverpass gives 2 people traveling together a 20 percent discount). Each day of use allows you to take as many trips as you want on one calendar day (you could go from Paris to Beaune in Burgundy, enjoy wine-tasting, then continue to Avignon, stay a few hours, and end in Nice—though I don't recommend it). Buy second-class tickets in France for shorter trips and spend your valuable railpass days wisely.

If traveling *sans* railpass, inquire about the many point-to-point discount fares possible (for youths, those over 60, married couples, families, travel during off-peak hours, and more). Remember that second-class tickets provide the same transportation for up to 33 percent less (and many regional trains to less-trafficked places often have only second-class cars).

Reservations

Reservations, while generally unnecessary for non-TGV trains, are advisable during busy times (e.g., Fri and Sun afternoons, weekday rush hours, and particularly holiday weekends; see "Major Holidays and Weekends," page 8). Reservations are required for any TGV train (usually about €3, more during peak periods), for selected other routes, and for *couchettes* (berths, €15) on night trains. Even railpass-holders need reservations for the TGV trains, and only a limited number of reservations are available for passholders. To avoid the more expensive fares, avoid traveling at peak times; ask at the station. You are required to validate (*composter*, kohm-poh-stay) all train tickets and reservations. Before boarding any SNCF train, look for a machine nearby to stamp your ticket or reservation. (Do not *composter* your railpass, but do validate it at a ticket window before the first time you use it.) Watch others and imitate.

Baggage check *(consigne)* is available only at the biggest train stations (about €4–8 per bag depending on size), and is noted where available in this book (depends on security concerns, so be prepared to keep your bag). For security reasons, all luggage must carry a tag with the traveler's first and last name and current address. This applies to hand luggage, as well as bigger bags that are stowed. Free tags are available at all train stations in France.

For mixing train and bike travel, ask at stations for information booklets *(Train + Vélo)*.

Automatic Train Ticket Machines

The ticket machines available at most stations are great time-savers when ticket window lines are long (your American credit card won't work, so you'll need euro coins). Some have English instructions, but for those that don't, here is what you are prompted to do. (The default is usually what you want; turn the dial or move the cursor to your choice, and press *Validez* to agree to each step.)

1. *Quelle est votre destination?* (What's your destination?)
2. *Billet Plein Tarif* (Full-fare ticket—yes for most.)
3. *1ère ou 2ème* (First or second class; normally second is fine.)
4. *Aller simple ou aller-retour?* (One-way or round-trip?)
5. *Prix en Euro* (The price should be shown if you get this far.)

Train Tips

- Arrive at the station with plenty of time before your departure to find the right platform, confirm connections, and so on. In small towns, your train may depart before the station opens; if so, go directly to the tracks and find the overhead sign that confirms your train stops at that track. *Remember that Avignon and Aix-en-Provence have separate TGV stations that are outside the town center.*
- Larger stations have platforms with monitors showing each car's layout (numbered forward or backward) and where to board each car. Notice the low baggage area placed every two

Key Travel Phrases

Bonjour, monsieur/madame, parlez-vous anglais?
Pron: bohn-zhoor, muhs-yur/mah-dahm, par-lay-voo ahn-glay?
Meaning: Hello, sir/madam, do you speak English?

Je voudrais un départ pour (destination), *pour le* (date), *vers* (general time of day), *la plus direct possible.*
Pron: zhuh voo-dray uhn day-par poor (destination), poor luh (date), vehr (time), lah ploo dee-rehk poh-see-bluh.
Meaning/Example: I would like a departure for Avignon, on 23 May, about 9:00, the most direct way possible.

cars—people use it to avoid hoisting their suitcases to the high overhead rack.

- Check schedules in advance. Upon arrival at a station, find out your departure possibilities. Large stations have a separate information window or office; at small stations, the regular ticket office gives information.
- If you have a rail flexipass, write the date on your pass each day you travel (before you board your first train).
- Validate tickets (not passes) and reservations in yellow machines before boarding. If you're traveling with a pass and have a reservation for a specific trip, you must validate the reservation.
- Reservations for all TGV trains are required, and often sell out. You can reserve any train at any station, by telephone (dial 3635), or through SNCF Boutiques (small offices in city centers). A limited number of reservations are allocated for rail-pass users during peak times—reserve as far ahead as you can for Friday and Sunday afternoons and Saturday mornings.
- Before getting on a train, confirm that it's going where you think it is. For example, if you want to go to Antibes, ask the conductor or any local passenger, *"À Antibes?"* (ah ahn-teeb; meaning, "To Antibes?").
- Some trains split cars en route. Make sure your train car is continuing to your destination by asking, for example, *"Cette voiture va à Avignon?"* (seht vwah-tewr vah ah ah-veen-yohn; meaning, "This car goes to Avignon?").
- If a non-TGV train seat is reserved, it will usually be labeled *réservé*, with the cities to and from which it is reserved.
- Verify with the conductor all transfers you must make: *"Correspondance à?"* (kor-rehs-pohn-dahns ah; meaning, "Transfer to where?").

- To guard against theft, it's best to keep your bags right overhead. If you store them at the end of the car, make sure you can see them from your seat (they're most vulnerable to theft when the train stops).
- Note your arrival time so you'll be ready to get off.
- Use the train's free WCs before you get off (but not while the train is stopped).

Buses

Regional bus service is relatively good in Provence and the Riviera. Buses take over where the trains stop. You can get nearly anywhere in Provence and the Riviera by rail and bus...if you're well-organized, patient, and allow enough time. Review my bus schedule information and always verify times at the local tourist office or bus station; call ahead when possible. A handful of bus lines are run by SNCF (France's rail system) and are included with your railpass (show railpass at station to get free bus ticket), but most bus lines are independent of the rail system and are not covered by railpasses. Train stations often have bus information where train-to-bus connections are important—and vice versa for bus companies. On Sunday, regional bus service virtually disappears.

Bus Tips

- Read the train tips above and use those that apply.
- Use TIs often to help plan your trip; they have regional bus schedules and are happy to assist you.
- Remember that service is sparse to nonexistent on Sunday. Wednesday bus schedules are often different during the school year, since school is out this day.
- Be at bus stops at least five minutes early.
- On schedules, *en semaine* means Monday through Saturday.

Renting a Car

To rent a car in France, you must be at least 18 years old and have held your license for one year. Although an International Driving Permit is not required if your driver's license has been renewed within the last year, play it safe and get one anyway ($15 through AAA, plus two passport photos, www.aaa.com).

Drivers under the age of 25 may incur a young-driver surcharge, and some rental companies do not rent to anyone 75 and over. If you're considered too young or old, look into leasing, which has less-stringent age restrictions (see "Leasing," below).

Research car rentals before you go. It's cheaper to arrange most car rentals from the US. Call several companies and look online to compare rates or arrange a rental through your hometown travel agent. Two reputable companies among many are Auto Europe

(www.autoeurope.com) and Europe by Car (www.europebycar
.com). Rent by the week with unlimited mileage. I normally rent
the smallest, least expensive model with a stick-shift (cheaper than
an automatic). For a three-week rental, allow $800 per person
(based on two people sharing a car), including insurance, tolls, gas,
and parking. For a longer rental time, consider leasing (see page
408); you'll save money on insurance and taxes. Compare pickup costs (downtown can be cheaper than the airport) and explore
drop-off options. Returning a car at a big-city train station can be
tricky; get precise details on the car drop-off location and hours.

When picking up the car, check it thoroughly and make sure
any damage is noted on your rental agreement. Find out how your
car's lights, turn signals, wipers, and gas cap function. When you
return the car, make sure the agent verifies its condition with you.

If you want a car for only a day or two (e.g., for the Côtes du
Rhône wine route or Luberon villages), you'll likely find it cheaper
to rent it in France—most US-arranged rentals make financial
sense only for three days or more. You can rent a car on the spot just
about anywhere. In many cases, this is a worthwhile splurge. All
you need is your American driver's license and a major credit card
(figure €65–80/day, including 100 kilometers, or 60 miles, per day).

A **rail-and-drive pass** (such as a EurailDrive, Selectpass Drive,
or France Rail and Drive) allows you to mix car and train travel
economically (sold only outside France, from your travel agent).
Generally big-city connections are best done by train, and rural
regions are best by car. With a rail-and-drive pass, you can take
advantage of the speed and comfort of the TGV trains for longer
trips, and rent a car for as little as one day at a time for day trips that
can't be done without one.

The basic France Rail and Drive Pass comes with two days
of car rental and three days of rail in two months. You can pick
up a car in one city and drop it off in another. Though you're only
required to reserve the first car day, it's safer to reserve all days, as
cars are not always available on short notice.

Car Insurance Options

When you rent a car, you are liable for a very high deductible,
sometimes equal to the entire value of the car. There are various
ways you can limit your financial risk in case of an accident. For
France, you have three options: buy Collision Damage Waiver
(CDW) coverage from the car-rental company (figure roughly 25
percent extra), a travel insurance company, or get coverage through
your credit card (free, if your card automatically includes zero-
deductible coverage).

CDW includes a very high deductible (typically $1,000–
1,500). When you pick up the car, you'll be offered the chance to

Best Two-Week Trip of Provence & the French Riviera by Car

Day Plan

1 Fly into Nice. Settle in at your hotel, then take my Welcome to the Riviera Walk along the promenade des Anglais (page 267). Sleep in or near Nice.

2 Take my self-guided Old Nice Walk (page 271) in the morning, allowing time to smell the *fougasse* and sample a café. Spend your afternoon at one or more of Nice's fine museums (see Chagall Museum Tour on page 277). Have dinner on the beach. Sleep in or near Nice.

3 Take the bus to nearby Villefranche-sur-Mer, explore, and have lunch. Consider my recommended seaside walks in Cap Ferrat, or the one-hour boat cruise from Nice's port. Everyone should spend the afternoon or evening in almost-neighboring Monaco. Sleep in or near Nice.

4 First thing in the morning, pick up your rental car in Nice. Drive north to Vence or Grasse (you choose), then continue on to the Gorges du Verdon and sleep in tiny Aiguines or Moustiers-Ste-Marie.

5 Continue west into the Luberon and explore the villages of La Provence Profonde. Stay in or near Roussillon.

6 Spend your day sampling hill towns in the Luberon. Taste a village market, then drive over the hills to the valley of the Côtes du Rhône. Sleep in or near Vaison la Romaine (Monday arrival is ideal since market day is Tuesday). If you're here from mid-June to late-July when the lavender blooms, the drive to Vaison la Romaine via Sault is a must.

7 Explore Vaison la Romaine's upper medieval village and lower Roman city. Set sail along the Côtes du Rhône wine road (following my self-guided driving tour) and visit a winery or wine cooperative. Tour little Le Crestet and take a walk above Gigondas. Sleep in or near Vaison la Romaine.

8 Start your day touring the Roman Theater in Orange and consider a quick stop in Châteauneuf-du-Pape. Continue south and set up in Avignon. In the afternoon, take my self-guided Avignon walking tour and enjoy dinner on one of the town's many atmospheric squares. Sleep in Avignon.

Appendix

"buy down" the deductible to zero (for $10–30/day; this is often called "super CDW").

If you opt for credit-card coverage, there's a catch. You'll technically have to decline all coverage offered by the car-rental company, which means they can place a hold on your card for the full deductible amount. In case of damage, it can be time-consuming to resolve the charges with your credit-card company. Before you

Best Two-Week Trip by Car

9 Relax in Avignon this morning, then divide the rest of your day between Nîmes and the Pont du Gard. If the weather's good, bring your swimsuit and float on your back below the 2,000-year-old Pont du Gard. Sleep in Avignon.

10 Drive through the Camargue, consider lunch in Stes-Maries-de-la-Mer, and wind up in Arles (big market day on Saturday). Sleep in Arles.

11 Spend your day in Arles. Drive to Les Baux for dinner. Sleep in Arles.

12 Drive to Cassis and stop for lunch and a midday visit to Aix-en-Provence or Marseille (Marseille is dicier by car). Set up in Cassis and watch the sun set from the old port while you savor a bouillabaisse dinner. Sleep in Cassis.

13 Spend all day in Cassis enjoying *la vie douce*. Take a boat trip to the *calanques*, watch the *pétanque* balls roll, and end your day with a drive up Cap Canaille. Sleep in Cassis.

14 Drive to St-Tropez and spend your morning carousing along its old port (searching for Brigitte Bardot). In the afternoon, drive to Nice, by taking the eye-popping scenic detour from Fréjus to Cannes. Sleep in Nice.

15 Trip over.

decide on this option, quiz your credit-card company about how it works and ask them to explain the worst-case scenario.

Buying CDW insurance (plus "super CDW") is the easier but pricier option. Using the coverage that comes with your credit card saves money, but can involve more hassle. For longer trips, leasing—which includes taxes and insurance—is worthwhile.

Finally, you can buy CDW insurance from Travel Guard ($9/day plus a one-time $3 service fee covers you up to $35,000, $250 deductible, tel. 800-826-4919, www.travelguard.com). It's valid throughout Europe, but some car-rental companies refuse to honor it (especially in Italy and the Republic of Ireland). Oddly, residents of Washington State aren't allowed to buy this coverage.

For more fine print about car-rental insurance, see www.ricksteves.com/cdw.

Leasing

For trips of two and a half weeks or more, leasing (which automatically includes CDW-like insurance) is the best way to go. By technically buying and then selling back the car, you save lots of money on tax and insurance. Leasing provides you a brand-new car with unlimited mileage and a 24-hour emergency assistance program. You can lease for little as 17 days to as long as 6 months. Car leases must be arranged from the US. Two reliable companies offering 17-day lease packages from about $950 for a small car ($1,300 for a midsize) are Auto France (US tel. 800-572-9655, fax 201/729-1917, www.autofrance.net) and Europe by Car (US tel. 800-223-1516, www.europebycar.com). Anyone age 18 or over with a driver's license is eligible, and you can pick up and/or drop off at several cities in France and throughout Europe.

Driving in Provence and the French Riviera

An International Driving Permit is not necessary in France, though I recommend one (see "Renting a Car," above). Seat belts are mandatory for all, and children under age 10 must be in the back seat. Almost all rentals are manual by default, so you must request an automatic transmission when renting. Gas *(essence)* is expensive—about $6 per gallon. Diesel *(gazole)* is less—about $5 per gallon—so rent a diesel car if you can. Gas is most expensive on autoroutes and cheapest at big supermarkets (closed at night and on Sun). Many gas stations close on Sunday. Most drivers will spend about $125 per week in gas to prowl the roads in Provence and the French Riviera.

Four hours on the autoroute costs about €25 in tolls, but the alternative to these super "feeways" usually means being marooned in countryside traffic—especially near the Riviera. Autoroutes usually save enough time, gas, and nausea to justify the splurge. Mix high-speed "autorouting" with scenic country-road rambling (be careful of sluggish tractors on country roads). You'll usually take a ticket when entering an autoroute and pay when you leave. Shorter autoroute sections (including along the Riviera) have periodic unmanned toll booths, where you can pay by dropping coins into a basket (change given, but keep a good supply of coins

Quick-and-Dirty Road Sign Translation

Instructional Signs that You Must Obey:

Cédez le Passage	Yield
Priorité à Droite	Right-of-way is for cars coming from the right
Vous n'avez pas la priorité	You don't have the right of way (when merging)
Rappel	Remember to obey the sign
Déviation	Detour
Allumez vos feux	Turn on your lights
Doublage Interdit	No passing
Parking Interdit/ Stationnement Interdit	No parking

Signs for Your Information:

Route Barrée	Road blocked
Centre Commercial	Grouping of large, suburban stores (not city center)
Centre-Ville	City center
Feux	Traffic signals
Horadateur	Remote parking meter, usually at the end of the block
Parc de Stationnement	Parking lot
Rue Piétonne	Pedestrian-only street
Sauf Riverains	Local access only
Sortie des Camions	Work truck exit

Signs Unique to Autoroutes:

Aire	Rest stop with WCs, telephones, and sometimes gas stations
Bouchon	Traffic jam ahead
Fluide	No slowing ahead ("fluid conditions")
Péage	Toll
Télépéage	Toll booths—automatic toll payment only
Toutes Directions	All directions (leaving city)
Autres Directions	Other directions (leaving city)
Par temps de Pluie	When raining (modifies speed-limit signs)

Driving in Provence and the French Riviera: Distance and Time

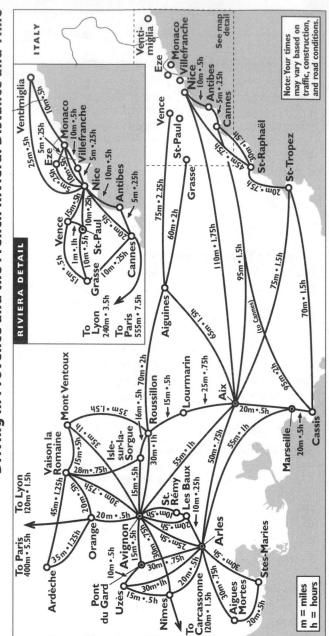

m = miles
h = hours

Note: Your times may vary based on traffic, construction, and road conditions.

RIVIERA DETAIL

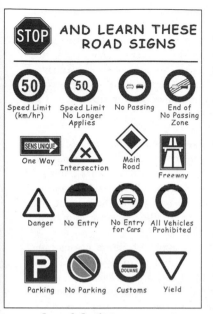

AND LEARN THESE ROAD SIGNS

STOP

50 Speed Limit (km/hr)

50 Speed Limit No Longer Applies

No Passing

End of No Passing Zone

SENS UNIQUE One Way

X Intersection

Main Road

Freeway

! Danger

No Entry

No Entry for Cars

All Vehicles Prohibited

P Parking

No Parking

DOUANE Customs

Yield

handy to avoid waiting) or by inserting a credit card (for even very small amounts). Autoroute gas stations usually come with well-stocked mini-marts, clean restrooms, sandwiches, maps, local products, and cheap vending-machine coffee (€1). Many have small cafés or more elaborate cafeterias with reasonable prices.

Roads are classified into departmental (D), national (N), and autoroutes (A). D routes (usually yellow lines on maps) are slow and often the most scenic. N routes (usually red lines) are the fastest after autoroutes (orange lines). Green road signs are for national routes; blue are for autoroutes. There are plenty of good facilities, gas stations, and rest stops along most French roads.

Because speed limits are by road type, they typically aren't posted, so it's best to memorize them:

- Two-lane D and N routes outside cities and towns: 90 km/hour
- Divided highways outside cities and towns: 110 km/hour
- Autoroutes: 130 km/hour

If it's raining, subtract 10 km/hour on D and N routes and 20 km/hour on divided highways and autoroutes. Speed-limit signs are a red circle around a number; when you see that same number again in gray with a broken line diagonally across it, this means that limit no longer applies. Speed limits drop to 30–50 km/hour in villages (always posted) and must be respected. France has a new system of photo ticketing, where movable cameras are carefully placed to trap the unsuspecting driver. They seem most common in 30–50 km/hour zones and will nail you even for going a few kilometers over the limit (believe me).

Parking is a headache in the larger cities, and theft is a problem throughout southern France. Ask your hotelier for ideas, and pay to park at well-patrolled lots (blue *P* signs direct you to parking lots in French cities). Parking structures often require that you take a ticket with you and prepay at a machine (called a *caisse*, credit cards usually accepted) on your way back to the car. Overnight parking (usually 19:00–8:00) is generally very reasonable (except in Nice).

Curbside metered parking also works (usually free 12:00–14:00 & 19:00–9:00, and all of Aug). Look for a small machine selling time (called *horadateur,* usually one per block), plug in a few coins (€1.50 buys about an hour, though this varies by city), push the green button, get a receipt showing the amount of time you have, and display it inside your windshield. Keep a pile of coins in your ashtray for parking meters and short stints on autoroutes.

Driving Tips

- Be aware that in city and town centers, traffic merging from the right normally has the right-of-way *(priorité à droite),* even when merging on to a major road. In contrast, cars entering the many suburban roundabouts must yield *(cédez le passage).*
- Be ready for many roundabouts—navigating them is an art. The key is to know your direction and be ready for your turn-off. If you miss it, just do another lap.
- When navigating through cities, approach intersections cautiously, stow the map, and follow the signs to *Centre-Ville* (city center). From there, head to the TI *(Office de Tourisme).*
- When leaving or just passing through cities, follow the signs for *Toutes Directions* or *Autres Directions* (meaning "anywhere else") until you see a sign for your specific destination.
- Driving on any roads but autoroutes will take longer than you anticipate, so allow yourself plenty of time (tractors, trucks, traffic, and hard-to-follow signs require patience). First-timers should estimate how long they think a drive will take...then double it. I pretend that kilometers are miles (for distances) and base my time estimates accordingly. While locals are eating lunch (12:00–14:00), many sights (and gas stations) are closed, so you can make great time driving—but keep it slow when passing through villages.
- U-turns are illegal throughout France, and you cannot turn right on red lights.
- Be very careful when driving on smaller roads—many are narrow, with little ditches alongside that are easy to slide into. I've met several readers who "ditched" their cars (and were successfully pulled out by local farmers).
- On autoroutes, keep to the right lanes to let fast drivers by, and be careful when merging into a left lane, as cars can be coming at very high speeds. Cars and trucks commonly keep their left blinker on while in a passing lane, indicating that they plan to get back over to the right.
- Motorcycles will scream between cars in traffic. Be ready—they expect you to keep to the right in your lane to let them pass.

- Gas can be tricky to find in rural areas on Sunday, so fill up on Saturday. Autoroute filling stations are always open.
- Keep a stash of coins in your ashtray for parking and small autoroute tolls.

Biking

You'll find areas in Provence and the Riviera where public transportation is limited and bicycle touring might be a good idea. For many, biking is a romantic notion whose novelty wears off after the first hill or headwind—realistically evaluate your physical condition and be clear on the limitations bikes present. Start with an easy pedal to a nearby village or through the vineyards, then decide how ambitious you feel. Most find that two hours on a narrow, hard seat is enough. I've listed bike-rental shops where appropriate and suggested a few of my favorite rides. Local TIs always have addresses for bike-rental places. For a good touring bike, figure about €10 for a half-day and €16 for a full day. You'll pay more for better equipment; generally the best is available through bike shops, not at train stations or other outlets. French bikers often do not wear helmets, though most rental outfits have them (for a small fee).

Cheap Flights

If you're visiting one or more French cities on a longer European trip—or linking up far-flung French cities (such as Paris and Nice)—you might want to look into the affordable intra-European airlines. While trains are still the best way to connect places that are close together, a flight can save both time and money on long journeys.

One of the best websites for comparing inexpensive flights is www.skyscanner.net. Other comparison search engines include www.kayak.com, www.mobissimo.com, www.sidestep.com, and www.wegolo.com.

Airlines offering inexpensive flights to Provence and the Riviera include easyJet (www.easyjet.com), Ryanair (www.ryanair.com), and Vueling (www.vueling.com). Be aware of the potential drawbacks of flying on the cheap: nonrefundable and nonchangeable tickets, rigid baggage restrictions (and fees if you have more than what's officially allowed), use of airports far outside town, tight schedules that can mean more delays, little in the way of customer assistance if problems arise, and, of course, no frills. To avoid unpleasant surprises, read the small print—especially baggage policies—before you book.

Appendix

2008

JANUARY						
S	M	T	W	T	F	S
		1	2	3	4	5
6	7	8	9	10	11	12
13	14	15	16	17	18	19
20	21	22	23	24	25	26
27	28	29	30	31		

FEBRUARY						
S	M	T	W	T	F	S
					1	2
3	4	5	6	7	8	9
10	11	12	13	14	15	16
17	18	19	20	21	22	23
24	25	26	27	28	29	

MARCH						
S	M	T	W	T	F	S
						1
2	3	4	5	6	7	8
9	10	11	12	13	14	15
16	17	18	19	20	21	22
23/30	24/31	25	26	27	28	29

APRIL						
S	M	T	W	T	F	S
		1	2	3	4	5
6	7	8	9	10	11	12
13	14	15	16	17	18	19
20	21	22	23	24	25	26
27	28	29	30			

MAY						
S	M	T	W	T	F	S
				1	2	3
4	5	6	7	8	9	10
11	12	13	14	15	16	17
18	19	20	21	22	23	24
25	26	27	28	29	30	31

JUNE						
S	M	T	W	T	F	S
1	2	3	4	5	6	7
8	9	10	11	12	13	14
15	16	17	18	19	20	21
22	23	24	25	26	27	28
29	30					

JULY						
S	M	T	W	T	F	S
		1	2	3	4	5
6	7	8	9	10	11	12
13	14	15	16	17	18	19
20	21	22	23	24	25	26
27	28	29	30	31		

AUGUST						
S	M	T	W	T	F	S
					1	2
3	4	5	6	7	8	9
10	11	12	13	14	15	16
17	18	19	20	21	22	23
24/31	25	26	27	28	29	30

SEPTEMBER						
S	M	T	W	T	F	S
	1	2	3	4	5	6
7	8	9	10	11	12	13
14	15	16	17	18	19	20
21	22	23	24	25	26	27
28	29	30				

OCTOBER						
S	M	T	W	T	F	S
			1	2	3	4
5	6	7	8	9	10	11
12	13	14	15	16	17	18
19	20	21	22	23	24	25
26	27	28	29	30	31	

NOVEMBER						
S	M	T	W	T	F	S
						1
2	3	4	5	6	7	8
9	10	11	12	13	14	15
16	17	18	19	20	21	22
23/30	24	25	26	27	28	29

DECEMBER						
S	M	T	W	T	F	S
	1	2	3	4	5	6
7	8	9	10	11	12	13
14	15	16	17	18	19	20
21	22	23	24	25	26	27
28	29	30	31			

HOLIDAYS AND FESTIVALS

This list includes major festivals in the Provence and French Riviera region, plus national holidays observed throughout France. Many sights close down on national holidays, and weekends around those holidays are often wildly crowded with vacationers (book your hotel room for the entire holiday weekend well in advance). Note that this isn't a complete list; holidays often strike without warning. For more information, contact the France TI (listed at the beginning of the appendix).

Jan 1: New Year's Day

Jan 6: Epiphany

Feb 16–March 2: Nice Carnival (Mardi Gras, parades, fireworks, www.nicecarnaval.com)

March 23: Easter Sunday

May 1: Labor Day and Ascension

May 8:	V-E Day
May 11:	Pentecost
May 14–25:	Cannes Film Festival, in Cannes (www.festival-cannes.fr)
May 22–25:	Monaco Grand Prix (auto race), in Monaco
June 21:	Music festival (Fête de la Musique), concerts and dancing in the streets throughout France
July 5–27:	Tour de France, the national bicycle race (www.letour.fr)
July 14:	Bastille Day (fireworks, dancing, and revelry)
July:	International Music and Opera Festival (www.festival-aix.com), Aix-en-Provence
July:	Avignon Festival (theater, dance, music, www.festival-avignon.com), Avignon
Early July:	Classical Music Festival, Cannes
Mid-July:	Chorégies d'Orange Music and Opera Festival (performed in a Roman theater, www.choregies.asso.fr), Orange
Mid-July:	"Jazz at Juan" International Jazz Festival, Antibes/Juan-les-Pins
Late July:	Jazz Festival (www.nicejazzfest.com), Nice
August:	International Fireworks Festival, Cannes
Aug 15:	Assumption of Mary
Nov 1:	All Saints' Day
Nov 11:	Armistice Day
Dec 20–Jan 4:	Winter holidays
Dec 25:	Christmas Day

CONVERSIONS AND CLIMATE

Numbers and Stumblers

- Europeans write a few of their numbers differently than we do. 1 = 1, 4 = 4, 7 = 7.
- In Europe, dates appear as day/month/year, so Christmas is 25/12/08.
- Commas are decimal points and decimals commas. A dollar and a half is 1,50, and there are 5,280 feet in a mile.
- When pointing, use your whole hand, palm down.
- When counting with fingers, start with your thumb. If you hold up your first finger to request one item, you'll probably get two.
- What Americans call the second floor of a building is the first floor in Europe.
- On escalators and moving sidewalks, Europeans keep the left "lane" open for passing. Keep to the right.

Metric Conversions (approximate)

1 foot = 0.3 meter   1 square yard = 0.8 square meter
1 yard = 0.9 meter   1 square mile = 2.6 square kilometers
1 mile = 1.6 kilometers   1 ounce = 28 grams
1 centimeter = 0.4 inch   1 quart = 0.95 liter
1 meter = 39.4 inches   1 kilogram = 2.2 pounds
1 kilometer = 0.62 mile   32°F = 0°C

Nice's Climate

First line, average daily high; second line, average daily low; third line, days of no rain.

J	F	M	A	M	J	J	A	S	O	N	D
50°	53°	59°	64°	71°	79°	84°	83°	77°	68°	58°	52°
35°	36°	41°	46°	52°	58°	63°	63°	58°	51°	43°	37°
23	22	24	23	23	26	29	26	24	23	21	21

Temperature Conversion: Fahrenheit and Celsius

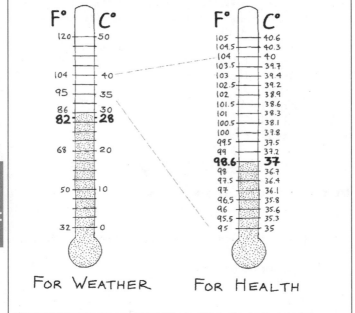

Europe takes its temperature using the Celsius scale, while we opt for Fahrenheit. For a rough conversion from Celsius to Fahrenheit, double the number and add 30. For weather, remember that 28°C is 82°F—perfect. For health, 37°C is just right.

Essential Packing Checklist

Whether you're traveling for five days or five weeks, here's what you'll need to bring. Remember to pack light to enjoy the sweet freedom of true mobility. Happy travels!

- ❏ 5 shirts
- ❏ 1 sweater or lightweight fleece jacket
- ❏ 2 pairs pants
- ❏ 1 pair shorts
- ❏ 1 swimsuit (women only—men can use shorts)
- ❏ 5 pairs underwear and socks
- ❏ 1 pair shoes
- ❏ 1 rainproof jacket
- ❏ Tie or scarf
- ❏ Money belt
- ❏ Money—your mix of:
  - ❏ Debit card for ATM withdrawals
  - ❏ Credit card
  - ❏ Hard cash in US dollars
- ❏ Documents (and backup photocopies)
- ❏ Passport
- ❏ Airplane ticket
- ❏ Driver's license
- ❏ Student ID and hostel card
- ❏ Railpass/car-rental voucher
- ❏ Insurance details
- ❏ Daypack
- ❏ Sealable plastic baggies
- ❏ Camera and related gear
- ❏ Empty water bottle
- ❏ Wristwatch and alarm clock
- ❏ Earplugs
- ❏ First-aid kit
- ❏ Medicine (labeled)
- ❏ Extra glasses/contacts and prescriptions
- ❏ Sunscreen and sunglasses
- ❏ Toiletries kit
- ❏ Soap
- ❏ Laundry soap (if liquid and carry-on, limit to 3 oz.)
- ❏ Clothesline
- ❏ Small towel
- ❏ Sewing kit
- ❏ Travel information
- ❏ Necessary map(s)
- ❏ Address list (email and mailing addresses)
- ❏ Postcards and photos from home
- ❏ Notepad and pen
- ❏ Journal

Appendix

Hotel Reservation

To: _____   _____
        hotel   *email or fax*

From: _____   _____
         name   *email or fax*

Today's date: _____ /_____ /_____
              day   *month*   *year*

Dear Hotel _____ ,
Please make this reservation for me:

Name: _____

Total # of people: _____   # of rooms: _____   # of nights: _____

Arriving: _____ /_____ /_____   My time of arrival (24-hr clock): _____
          day *month* *year*   (I will telephone if I will be late)

Departing: ____ /____ /_____
           day *month* *year*

Room(s): Single___   Double ___   Twin ___   Triple ___   Quad___

With: Toilet ____   Shower____   Bath ____   Sink only ___

Special needs: View___   Quiet___   Cheapest ___   Ground Floor___

Please email or fax confirmation of my reservation, along with the type of room reserved and the price. Please also inform me of your cancellation policy. After I hear from you, I will quickly send my credit-card information as a deposit to hold the room. Thank you.

_____
Name

_____
Address

_____
City   *State*   *Zip Code*   *Country*

Before hoteliers can make your reservation, they want to know the information listed above. You can use this form as the basis for your email, or you can photocopy this page, fill in the information, and send it as a fax (also available online at www.ricksteves.com/reservation).

French Survival Phrases

When using the phonetics, try to nasalize the <u>n</u> sound.

Good day.	**Bonjour.**	boh<u>n</u>-zhoor
Mrs. / Mr.	**Madame / Monsieur**	mah-dahm / muhs-yur
Do you speak English?	**Parlez-vous anglais?**	par-lay-voo ah<u>n</u>-glay
Yes. / No.	**Oui. / Non.**	wee / noh<u>n</u>
I understand.	**Je comprends.**	zhuh koh<u>n</u>-prah<u>n</u>
I don't understand.	**Je ne comprends pas.**	zhuh nuh koh<u>n</u>-prah<u>n</u> pah
Please.	**S'il vous plaît.**	see voo play
Thank you.	**Merci.**	mehr-see
I'm sorry.	**Désolé.**	day-zoh-lay
Excuse me.	**Pardon.**	par-doh<u>n</u>
(No) problem.	**(Pas de) problème.**	(pah duh) proh-blehm
It's good.	**C'est bon.**	say boh<u>n</u>
Goodbye.	**Au revoir.**	oh vwahr
one / two	**un / deux**	uh<u>n</u> / duh
three / four	**trois / quatre**	twah / kah-truh
five / six	**cinq / six**	sa<u>nk</u> / sees
seven / eight	**sept / huit**	seht / weet
nine / ten	**neuf / dix**	nuhf / dees
How much is it?	**Combien?**	koh<u>n</u>-bee-a<u>n</u>
Write it?	**Ecrivez?**	ay-kree-vay
Is it free?	**C'est gratuit?**	say grah-twee
Included?	**Inclus?**	a<u>n</u>-klew
Where can I buy / find...?	**Où puis-je acheter / trouver...?**	oo pwee-zhuh ah-shuh-tay / troo-vay
I'd like / We'd like...	**Je voudrais / Nous voudrions...**	zhuh voo-dray / noo voo-dree-oh<u>n</u>
...a room.	**...une chambre.**	ewn shah<u>n</u>-bruh
...a ticket to ___.	**...un billet pour ___.**	uh<u>n</u> bee-yay poor
Is it possible?	**C'est possible?**	say poh-see-bluh
Where is...?	**Où est...?**	oo ay
...the train station	**...la gare**	lah gar
...the bus station	**...la gare routière**	lah gar root-yehr
...tourist information	**...l'office du tourisme**	loh-fees dew too-reez-muh
Where are the toilets?	**Où sont les toilettes?**	oo soh<u>n</u> lay twah-leht
men	**hommes**	ohm
women	**dames**	dahm
left / right	**à gauche / à droite**	ah gohsh / ah dwaht
straight	**tout droit**	too dwah
When does this open / close?	**Ça ouvre / ferme à quelle heure?**	sah oo-vruh / fehrm ah kehl ur
At what time?	**À quelle heure?**	ah kehl ur
Just a moment.	**Un moment.**	uh<u>n</u> moh-mah<u>n</u>
now / soon / later	**maintenant / bientôt / plus tard**	ma<u>n</u>-tuh-nah<u>n</u> / bee-a<u>n</u>-toh / plew tar
today / tomorrow	**aujourd'hui / demain**	oh-zhoor-dwee / duh-ma<u>n</u>

In the Restaurant

I'd like / We'd like...	**Je voudrais / Nous voudrions...**	zhuh voo-dray / noo voo-dree-ohn
...to reserve...	**...réserver...**	ray-zehr-vay
...a table for one / two.	**...une table pour un / deux.**	ewn tah-bluh poor uhn / duh
Non-smoking.	**Non fumeur.**	nohn few-mur
Is this seat free?	**C'est libre?**	say lee-bruh
The menu (in English), please.	**La carte (en anglais), s'il vous plaît.**	lah kart (ahn ahn-glay) see voo play
service (not) included	**service (non) compris**	sehr-vees (nohn) kohn-pree
to go	**à emporter**	ah ahn-por-tay
with / without	**avec / sans**	ah-vehk / sahn
and / or	**et / ou**	ay / oo
special of the day	**plat du jour**	plah dew zhoor
specialty of the house	**spécialité de la maison**	spay-see-ah-lee-tay duh lah may-zohn
appetizers	**hors-d'oeuvre**	or-duh-vruh
first course (soup, salad)	**entrée**	ahn-tray
main course (meat, fish)	**plat principal**	plah pran-see-pahl
bread	**pain**	pan
cheese	**fromage**	froh-mahzh
sandwich	**sandwich**	sahnd-weech
soup	**soupe**	soop
salad	**salade**	sah-lahd
meat	**viande**	vee-ahnd
chicken	**poulet**	poo-lay
fish	**poisson**	pwah-sohn
seafood	**fruits de mer**	frwee duh mehr
fruit	**fruit**	frwee
vegetables	**légumes**	lay-gewm
dessert	**dessert**	duh-sehr
mineral water	**eau minérale**	oh mee-nay-rahl
tap water	**l'eau du robinet**	loh dew roh-bee-nay
milk	**lait**	lay
(orange) juice	**jus (d'orange)**	zhew (doh-rahnzh)
coffee	**café**	kah-fay
tea	**thé**	tay
wine	**vin**	van
red / white	**rouge / blanc**	roozh / blahn
glass / bottle	**verre / bouteille**	vehr / boo-teh-ee
beer	**bière**	bee-ehr
Cheers!	**Santé!**	sahn-tay
More. / Another.	**Plus. / Un autre.**	plew / uhn oh-truh
The same.	**La même chose.**	lah mehm shohz
The bill, please.	**L'addition, s'il vous plaît.**	lah-dee-see-ohn see voo play
tip	**pourboire**	poor-bwar
Delicious!	**Délicieux!**	day-lee-see-uh

For more user-friendly French phrases, check out *Rick Steves' French Phrase Book and Dictionary* or *Rick Steves' French, Italian & German Phrase Book*.

INDEX

Travel smart...carry on!

The latest generation of Rick Steves' carry-on travel bags is easily the best—benefiting from two decades of on-the-road attention to what really matters: maximum quality and strength; practical, flexible features; and no unnecessary frills. You won't find a better value anywhere!

Rick Steves' Convertible Carry-On $99.⁹⁵

Our roomy, versatile 9" x 21" x 14" carry-on has a large 2600 cubic-inch main compartment, plus four outside pockets (small, medium and huge) that are perfect for often-used items. Wish you had even more room to bring home souvenirs? Pull open the full-perimeter expando-zipper and its capacity jumps from 2600 to 3000 cubic inches. When you want to use it as a suitcase or check it as luggage (required when "expanded"), the straps and belt hide away in a zippered compartment in the back. It weighs just 3 lbs.

Rick Steves' Classic Back Door Bag $79.⁹⁵

This ultra-light (1½ lbs.) version of our Convertible Carry-On features the same 9" x 21" x 14" dimensions and hideaway straps, but does not include a waistbelt or expandability. This is the bag that Rick lives out of for three months a year!

Rick Steves' 21" Roll-Aboard $139.⁹⁵

Our sturdy 21" Roll-Aboard is rucksack-soft in front, but the rest is lined with a hard ABS-lexan shell to give maximum protection to your belongings. We've spared no expense on moving parts, splurging on an extra-long button-release handle and big, tough inline skate wheels for easy rolling on rough surfaces. It features the same 9" x 21" x 14" carry-on dimensions, pocket configuration and expandability as our Convertible Carry-On—and at 7 lbs. it's the lightest roll-aboard in its class.

Prices and features are subject to change.

For great deals on a wide selection of travel goodies, begin your next trip at the Rick Steves Travel Store!

Visit the Rick Steves Travel Store at
www.ricksteves.com

FREE-SPIRITED TOURS FROM
Rick Steves

Small Groups
Great Guides
No Grumps

Best of Europe ■ Family Europe
Italy ■ Village Italy ■ South Italy
Sicily ■ France ■ Eastern Europe
Adriatic ■ Prague ■ Scotland
Britain ■ Ireland ■ Scandinavia
Germany-Austria-Switzerland ■ Spain ■ Turkey ■ Greece
London-Paris ■ Paris ■ Rome ■ Venice-Florence-Rome…and more!

Looking for a one, two, or three-week tour that's run in the Rick Steves style? Check out Rick Steves' educational, experiential tours of Europe.

Rick's tours are an excellent value compared to "mainstream" tours. Here's a taste of what you'll get...

- **Small groups:** With just 24-28 travelers, you'll go where typical groups of 40-50 can only dream.

- **Big buses:** You'll travel in a full-size 40-50 seat bus, with plenty of empty seats for you to spread out and be comfortable.

- **Great guides:** Our guides are hand-picked by Rick Steves for their wealth of knowledge and giddy enthusiasm for Europe.

- **No tips or kickbacks:** To keep your guide and driver 100% focused on giving you the best travel experience, we pay them well—and prohibit them from accepting tips and merchant kickbacks.

- **All sightseeing:** Your tour price includes all group sightseeing, with no hidden extra charges.

- **Central hotels:** You'll stay in Rick's favorite small, characteristic, locally-run hotels in the center of each city, within walking distance of the sights you came to see.

- **Visit www.ricksteves.com:** You'll find all our latest itineraries, dates and prices, be able to reserve online, and request a free copy of our Rick Steves Tour Experience DVD!

Rick Steves' Europe Through the Back Door, Inc.
130 Fourth Avenue North, PO Box 2009, Edmonds, WA 98020 USA
Phone: (425) 771-8303 ■ Fax: (425) 771-0833 ■ www.ricksteves.com

Start your trip at
www.ricksteves.com

Rick Steves' website is packed with over 3,000 pages of timely travel information. It's also your gateway to getting FREE monthly travel news from Rick—and more!

Free Monthly Travel News

Fresh articles on Europe's most interesting destinations and happenings. Rick will even send you an email every month (often direct from Europe) with his latest discoveries!

Timely Travel Tips

Rick Steves' best money-and-stress-saving tips on trip planning, packing, transportation, hotels, health, safety, finances, hurdling the language barrier...and more.

Travelers' Graffiti Wall

Candid advice and opinions from thousands of travelers on everything listed above, plus whatever topics are hot at the moment (discount flights, politics, nude beaches, scams...you name it).

Rick's Guide to Eurail Passes

The clearest, most comprehensive guide to the confusing array of railpass options out there, and how to choo-choose the railpass that best fits your itinerary and budget.

Great Gear at Our Travel Store

In the past year alone, more than 50,000 travelers have enjoyed great online deals on Rick's guidebooks, maps, DVDs—and his custom-designed carry-on bags, day packs, and light-packing accessories.

Rick Steves Tours

This year, 12,000 lucky travelers will explore Europe on a Rick Steves tour. Learn about our 28 different one- to three-week itineraries, read uncensored feedback from our tour alums, and get our free Tour Experience DVD.

Rick on TV, Radio and Podcasts

Read the scripts from the popular Rick Steves' Europe TV series, and listen to or download your choice of over 100 hours of our Travel with Rick Steves radio show.

Respect for Your Privacy

Whether you buy something from us or subscribe to Rick's monthly Travel News emails, we'll never share your name or email address with anyone else. You won't be spammed!

Have fun raising your Travel I.Q. at
www.ricksteves.com

Rick Steves

More *Savvy*. More *Surprising*. More *Fun*.

COUNTRY GUIDES

Croatia & Slovenia
England
France
Germany & Austria
Great Britain
Ireland
Italy
Portugal
Scandinavia
Spain
Switzerland

CITY GUIDES

Amsterdam, Bruges & Brussels
Florence & Tuscany
Istanbul
London
Paris
Prague & The Czech Republic
Provence & The French Riviera
Rome
Venice

BEST OF GUIDES

Best of Eastern Europe
Best of Europe

As the #1 authority on European travel, Rick gives you inside information on what to visit, where to stay, and how to get there—economically and hassle-free.

www.ricksteves.com

PHRASE BOOKS & DICTIONARIES

French
French, Italian & German
German
Italian
Portuguese
Spanish

MORE EUROPE FROM RICK STEVES

Europe 101
Europe Through the Back Door
Postcards from Europe

RICK STEVES' EUROPE DVDs

All 70 Shows 2000–2007
Britain
Eastern Europe
France & Benelux
Germany, The Swiss Alps & Travel Skills
Ireland
Italy
Spain & Portugal

PLANNING MAPS

Britain & Ireland
Europe
France
Germany, Austria & Switzerland
Italy
Spain & Portugal

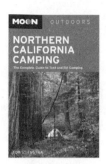

CREDITS

Researcher

To help update this book, Rick and Steve relied on the assistance of...

Daniela Williams

Born and educated in Munich, Daniela majored in Art History. She now makes her home in Avignon with her American husband. When not leading tours for Rick Steves, Daniela enjoys the Provençal life: bike-touring, playing basketball, and relaxing with family, friends, and a good glass of wine.

Contributor

Gene Openshaw

Gene is the co-author of seven Rick Steves books. For this book, he wrote material on Europe's art, history, and contemporary culture. When not traveling, Gene enjoys composing music, recovering from his 1973 trip to Europe with Rick, and living everyday life with his wife and daughter.

Rick Steves' Guidebook Series

Country Guides

Rick Steves' Best of Europe
Rick Steves' Croatia & Slovenia
Rick Steves' Eastern Europe
Rick Steves' England
Rick Steves' France
Rick Steves' Germany & Austria
Rick Steves' Great Britain
Rick Steves' Ireland
Rick Steves' Italy
Rick Steves' Portugal
Rick Steves' Scandinavia
Rick Steves' Spain
Rick Steves' Switzerland

City and Regional Guides

Rick Steves' Amsterdam, Bruges & Brussels
Rick Steves' Florence & Tuscany
Rick Steves' Istanbul
Rick Steves' London
Rick Steves' Paris
Rick Steves' Prague & the Czech Republic
Rick Steves' Provence & the French Riviera
Rick Steves' Rome
Rick Steves' Venice

Rick Steves' Phrase Books

French
German
Italian
Spanish
Portuguese
French/Italian/German

Other Books

Rick Steves' Europe Through the Back Door
Rick Steves' Europe 101: History and Art for the Traveler
Rick Steves' Postcards from Europe
Rick Steves' European Christmas

(Avalon Travel Publishing)

Avalon Travel Publishing
a member of the Perseus Books Group
1400 65th Street, Suite 250
Emeryville, CA 94608

ISBN (10) 1-56691-865-0
ISBN (13) 978-1-56691-865-7
ISSN 1546-2749

For the latest on Rick's lectures, guidebooks, tours, public radio show, and public-television series, contact Europe Through the Back Door, Box 2009, Edmonds, WA 98020, tel. 425/771-8303, fax 425/771-0833, www.ricksteves.com, rick@ricksteves.com.

Europe Through the Back Door Senior Editor: Jennifer Hauseman
ETBD Editors: Cathy McDonald, Jennifer Madison Davis, Gretchen Strauch
ETBD Managing Editor: Risa Laib
Avalon Travel Publishing Senior Editor and Series Manager: Madhu Prasher
Avalon Travel Publishing Project Editor: Kelly Lydick
Research Assistance: Daniela Williams
Production & Typesetting: McGuire Barber Design
Copy Editor: Matthew Reed Baker
Proofreader: Patrick Collins
Indexer: Laura Welcome
Cover Design: Kari Gim, Laura Mazer
Cover Art Manager: Laura VanDeventer
Interior Design: Jane Musser, Laura Mazer, Amber Pirker
Maps & Graphics: David C. Hoerlein, Lauren Mills, Laura VanDeventer, Barb Geisler, Mike Morgenfeld
Front cover photos: Front image, Nice © Carol Ries; Back image, Provence Road © David C. Hoerlein
Front matter color photos: page i © Europe Through the Back Door; page iv, Côtes du Rhône Wine Loop © Steve Smith
Photography: Steve Smith, Gene Openshaw, David C. Hoerlein, Rick Steves